OUR SOLARIAN LEGACY

For Ann
Mary

With appreciation
for your interest
and support

Paul Von Ward
1/01

Other Books by Paul Von Ward

Solarian Legacy: Metascience and a New Renaissance

Dismantling the Pyramid: Government by the People

OUR SOLARIAN LEGACY

LEGACY

MULTIDIMENSIONAL HUMANS
IN A SELF-LEARNING UNIVERSE

PAUL VON WARD

HAMPTON ROADS
PUBLISHING COMPANY, INC.

Cover design by Steve Amarillo
Cover art by PhotoDisc

For information write:

Hampton Roads Publishing Company, Inc.
1125 Stoney Ridge Road
Charlottesville, VA 22902

434-296-2772
fax: 434-296-5096
e-mail: hrpc@hrpub.com
www.hrpub.com

If you are unable to order this book from your local
bookseller, you may order directly from the publisher.
Call 1-800-766-8009, toll-free.

Library of Congress Catalog Card Number: 2001091198
ISBN 1-57174-214-X
10 9 8 7 6 5 4 3 2 1
Printed on acid-free paper in the United States

For

My Mother

and

*All mothers whose yin receptivity make possible
transmission of the human legacy
and whose yang nurturing contributes to
achievement of our potential.*

Contents

Acknowledgments

This book, like all human creations, is a product of the species and the universe of which we are parts. As I cannot claim credit for all of it, neither can I give credit to all who have made contributions. The initial inspiration for it came from my own seeking of answers to the questions with which we all grapple when faced with awareness of our apparent mortality. But the energy and thoughts necessary to bring such disparate pieces of human knowledge together have flowed from an all-sustaining life force and the unseen fields of our collective consciousness.

Most of the information used in this book has come from the research and analysis of friends and colleagues on whose shoulders I stand. Many of their works are referenced in the notes and suggested reading list. I have only added my unique perspective on how all the pieces fit together, drawing new inferences from the material. Thus, I must take responsibility for the decisions on what to include in the final version of what was truly a community effort.

Earlier versions of significant sections of the material in this book were originally published in *Solarian Legacy: Metascience and a New Renaissance*. I express my appreciation to the people of Oughten House for its publication and to those at Medicine Bear Publishing for its distribution. All those who participated in the preparation of that volume have my eternal gratitude. If you have read *Solarian Legacy*, I trust that you will find many of the ideas expressed in it to be much more fully developed in this book, and that you will appreciate the new research and concepts incorporated here.

While it is impossible to satisfactorily attribute credit to the many individuals who have made significant and direct contributions to this book, I would like to name a few. All know how they helped make a theoretical concept into a palpable reality: Brenda Sanchez, Tonette Long, Judith Cope, Nancy Parker, Rosemary McMullen, Celeste White, Michael Brein, Brian O'Leary, Elliott Dacher, Rosemary Whitford, Jim Schuette, Kelesyn Winter, Tony Stubbs, John White, and Joyce Shafer.

Finally, I wish to thank Frank DeMarco for believing in the merit of the work, and making support and resources available for its publication, and Richard Leviton for his constructive critiques and editorial finesse. The quality and beauty of the final product are due to their commitment and the excellent work of all the good staff at Hampton Roads Publishing Company.

Preface

Are you ready, in the company of frontier scientists and metaphysicians, to engage in an assessment of many of society's most cherished assumptions about the history of the Earth and its human inhabitants? Are you ready to look at published research, material developed by independent scholars, and to personally test their insights with your own experience? If you are, I promise a dramatically reshaped perspective on the human legacy and, consequently, on your approach to daily life, by the time you complete this book.

As humanity faces some of the most profound challenges in our history, I believe we are simultaneously provided with the internal resources to meet them. In expanding our view of this universe, we will also enhance our grasp of the inner resources available to us. Though our telescopes cannot yet see beyond the curve of space-time, we can open our inner eyes to the full spectrum of a multidimensional reality.

The book that follows is not intended to cover all the evidence for our Solarian legacy. (You'll learn the full meaning of that term in the following chapters.) Over a hundred and fifty books and articles are referenced, and many more contribute to this new view of the cosmos. I attempt to articulate a provisional, but realistic, picture of the human legacy by synthesizing the ideas of countless others who willingly test alternative perceptions of reality. I examine material that has been either dismissed as unscientific by the intellectual establishment or ignored because of its unconventional sources.

Included are studies on improperly labeled "paranormal" phenomena, reports of intelligent nonhuman beings, intriguing evidence of forgotten advanced civilizations, compelling findings of frontier science, and wisdom germinated in some cosmic seedbed that springs up in unexpected ways.

Though the material and its implications can be disturbing at first, I believe they ground us in a more stable field of conscious awareness. I try to balance openness with a healthy skepticism in this effort to move beyond a period of self-imposed blinders, into an era of our being self-conscious and self-directing cosmic beings.

Although I am passionate about the ideas set forth here, my fervor should be tempered by your own experience. As this book reflects my ongoing testing, I invite you to put its explicit and implicit assumptions to critical review. They should be found credible only if the following conditions are met:

• the integration of my ideas makes intellectual sense to you,
• the interpretations resonate with the your own observations, and
• your own experiences validate the hypotheses.

You will take them seriously for your own reasons. These ideas do not come from a "chosen person" with a "special message" from "a divine or higher source of knowledge or power." I hope you find it valuable to engage in a joint exploration with a committed fellow human seriously trying to be as self-aware as possible in order to learn how to realize his full potential.

A Time of Reckoning?

Much ado has been made of the current era, but does it have any particular inherent significance in human history? Should we really believe something profoundly new is under way? Did the start of a new Christian-calendar millennium have any intrinsic meaning? As you will learn in this book, I believe in taking a hard look at the evidence and drawing the most simple and direct conclusion possible from it.

For example, different traditions have different calendars: Christian, Chinese, Muslim, Jewish, Mayan. Each represents artificial reference points to position us in relation to particular historical events. Consequently, there is no universal validity to any one of them. So, a millennium date provides only a social consensus for reflection, like using a birthday for reviewing the past year or making resolutions at the start of a new year.

Many prophetic and esoteric traditions describe the period from now to 2030 as a human transition from one age to another. In her book *Children of the New Millennium*, P.M.H. Atwater[1] places several of these traditions in the context of her work with children's near-death experiences (NDEs). She believes the aftereffects of their NDEs will "jump-start" the evolution of a new human in the Age of Aquarius beginning around 2020. Similar predictions she and others highlight include the Edgar Cayce (the famous twentieth-century psychic) prediction of a new human race appearing between 1998 and 2010, the coming of a "blue race," the Christian Second Coming of Christ, the prophecy by early Americans of the coming of the White Buffalo, and the Mayan calendar indicating a new era that starts in 2012. We must wait for events to confirm or deny such theories.

Self-Starting a New Epoch

I do not think we have to resort to such esoteric and subjective messages to entertain the probability of a significant shift in human development. The pieces for a new model of reality have already been discovered by frontier historians and frontier scientists. We now only have to put them together. And look at their ramifications. The effort, as I suggest in this book, gives us a wholly new way of thinking about the nature of the universe and our place in it. The newly synthesized material has many external implications, but the most dramatic change will be in the inner realms of consciousness and subtle senses. While the potential for a new epoch is there, its manifestation will depend on humanity's collective choice. We can accept the challenge of self-actualization or defer it for a later generation.

Profound advancements in human knowledge over the past several decades beg for a beyond-the-millennium review of what I call our Solarian legacy. I use the term "Solarian" because the evidence is now clear that we are more than mere byproducts of the planet Earth. Humans are not the accidental result of a random Big Bang universe that created life "by chance." Neither are they unique creatures born in a Garden of Eden subject to the absentee parenting of an anthropomorphic (made in the image of man) god. Humans are local manifestations of a universal consciousness that informs all life. If not yet cosmic beings, we are at least Solarians, with a heritage from the stars. In our Solarian microcosm, I believe, humans mirror all the characteristics of a powerful self-learning organism. This book develops the concept that that organism is the universe itself.

The universe can be assumed to be alive because we are alive. On Earth there is a glorious proliferation of life-forms and behaviors. All this running, eating, sleeping, rutting, birthing, growing, learning, and dying involve the most ordinary of materials—the same particles that constitute the lowest forms of dirt and mud and pollution. The very same particles, and their quanta of energy, fill the universe.

The basic question likely asked by any self-aware species is: What consciousness animates this whole thing? I believe the evidence covered in this book points in the direction of a self-manifesting, conscious universe that continues to develop through a process of self-learning. I hope by the end of this book, you will take seriously two notions: that the universe arose from a conscious force that manifests matter and energy to experience itself in as many ways as possible; and that conscious beings, including humans, are local manifestations of that original consciousness, designed to actively participate in the experimentation, adaptation, and survival of a living organism—our universe.

If such a role is our Solarian destiny, getting there means full use of all human capacities. It requires an epoch that accepts the challenge to experience life to its fullest, using all senses and powers to understand the reality of which we are parts, and taking responsibility for our impact on the entire organism.

If we accept this challenge, we must reassess all areas of human assumptions and experience. We can no longer focus research in narrow professions and ignore many aspects of human experience that do not fit our particular profession's vision of reality. It is time to identify our complete and true heritage and potential. As this book will demonstrate, humanity has a much longer and more complex history, and potential, than currently portrayed in academic texts.

In the 1980s, the discussion of the idea of a paradigm shift in the physical sciences and other intellectual disciplines became popular, promoted by the books of people like Fritjof Capra and Gary Zukav. Marilyn Ferguson's book *Aquarian Conspiracy: Personal and Social Transformation in the 1980s*[2] helped give mainstream credibility to the idea of a new age of societal thought and behavior. In the 1990s, writers and workshop leaders with channeled material prophesied the advent of a new era. Many philosophers and scientists promoted in books and conferences a merger or synthesis of science and religion. At the end of the millennium, science touted breakthroughs that would revolutionize our interactions with the physical world and our own bodies. So the stage is set for the initiation of a new epoch in human history.

Transcending Science and Religion

In my view, the popularly envisaged new epoch requires more fundamental change in thinking and practice than the merger of traditional religion and conventional science. We must *transcend* both to reach a new level of human consciousness, one that goes beyond such limited ways of knowing. I believe we need a metascience that combines all channels to knowledge (physical, emotional, and mental) and uses a multidimensional approach to reassess even the basic tenets of science and religion.

Given the breadth and depth of the multileveled insights emerging from the frontiers of research, it is impossible for one or even a few to see the whole emerging pattern. Therefore, it is no surprise that we perceive only fragments of potentially the most significant human material, psychological, and intellectual breakthrough in 6,000 years. In this context, the most I can offer is a new framework for seeking answers to the perennial questions that call out for new understandings. In the Introduction, I try to make explicit my implicit assumptions and identify my suggested hypotheses for what they are: one person's effort to see through the glass less darkly.

The mosaic of new insights from metascience has revealed a whole much greater than the sum of individual discoveries. The cutting edge sciences of quantum mechanics, consciousness studies, and prehistory, combined with widespread intellectual and psychological receptivity, are triggering a shift in consciousness more profound than a new intellectual paradigm. Current increases in human knowledge *and* awareness of what's unknown, with the sense of a concomitant increase in human potential, are unprecedented in recorded history. The scope of incipient fundamental change dwarfs the Industrial Revolution of 200 years ago, the European Renaissance of five centuries ago, the Roman Empire's co-optation of Christianity 1,600 years ago, and the establishment of kingship and priesthood in Sumeria and Egypt more than 5,500 years ago.

The most important parameters of this new metascientific perspective on humanity and our universe, the evidence for which is reviewed in this book, may be summarized as follows:

- Our self-manifesting universe is self-learning and consciously self-directing. This singular organism has three facets: physical matter and energy, subtle energies, and universal consciousness.

- Consciousness is the primary field whence all else arises. Local manifestations of universal consciousness inform and sustain all life-forms, including humans.

- Intelligent human life has existed on Earth much longer than we have believed. Humans are consciously, emotionally, and physically interdependent with all species.

- Beings similar to *Homo sapiens* live in other solar systems, and some have had a long history of interaction with humans.

- Science and technologies at least as advanced as that of the twentieth century were used on Earth millennia ago. Technology ahead of the current human level exists beyond Earth.

- The history of Earth and its inhabitants have been dramatically affected by cataclysmic events that left gaps in the geological and archaeological record.

- Human beings are more mentally, psychologically, and physically interactive with each other and the rest of the universe than we normally imagine. There are no separations, and human consciousness mirrors that of the universe's creators.

- Our conscious awareness is not limited by the world of five senses. We have subtle and noumenal senses parallel to our physical ones to function in our multidimensional reality.

- Human beings have much more inner power to influence internal and external events among themselves, and in the universe at large, than most now understand.

- Humanity is on the threshold of understanding its true identity as co-designers of our self-learning universe.

As these understandings become widely known, I believe humans will embark on a new phase of human participation in the ongoing development of the universe that can exceed all the predictions of a new era mentioned earlier.

A New Cosmogony

Elaboration of most of the above new concepts is best left to the appropriate chapters, but one central idea needs explanation from the beginning: the self-manifesting and self-learning nature of the universe. My decades-long study of the material covered by or referred to in this book has led me to a modification of currently accepted cosmogonies (theories of the origin of the universe).

Modern science has replaced the long-standing concept of a "clockwork universe" with labels such as "unfolding," "holographic," "reflexive," "recursive," "conscious," "self-organizing," "living energy," and "self-aware." But I believe that when we incorporate evidence of intentionality, feedback, and conscious change into our model of the universe, a degree of purposefulness emerges. When individual aspects of nature exhibit the capacity for learning from experience, as evidence indicates, we can reasonably infer that the whole organism is engaged in a process of self-learning.

Many physicists and metaphysicians now agree that the evidence suggests that the primary substrata of all matter and energy is the element we call consciousness. This is all documented in chapters 1, 2, and 4, but the relevant point here is that if consciousness is the origin, then the way it manifests itself has some meaning. If that meaning is reflected in the way consciousness operates in humans and other beings, then we should be able to infer something of the ultimate from the specific. Both physics and biology, and ordinary human experience, reveal that life (consciousness at any level) initiates, senses, reacts, and changes to start the cycle over again. That simple process is self-starting, self-learning, and self-directing.

(English, unfortunately, does not have the common use of reflexive verbs that we find in Romance languages, so we must get accustomed to attaching "self" to a number of verbs to describe the circular processes at work in the universe. For example, using the logic of reflexive verbs, "self-learning" implies "I myself learn, including learning about myself." So bear with me in the next few paragraphs.)

"Autogenesis" is the best word available to characterize the origin, from consciousness, of the universe as we now understand it. That means consciousness is self-creating or outwardly manifesting its inner essence. (I choose not to speculate on how that original consciousness got started. For the moment, until we know more about our own universe, I prefer to accept it as autonomous and self-sufficient.)

In an autogenerating universe, the most appropriate term to describe its ongoing development is "autodidactic," meaning teaching-of-self, or self-learning. Both terms "autogenesis" and "autodidactic" imply conscious awareness of self and one's ongoing processes. So, if the universe is self-learning, then what humans learn, about themselves and everything else, contributes to the learning of the whole universe. It follows then that conscious beings in a fully conscious, self-learning universe must be at least somewhat self-directing. As microcosms of the macrocosm, we have its same characteristics, only on a local scale. (We are not co-equal directors, but we are limited partners in the process.)

Recognition of such a role for humans in the universe can lead to a transformation, transmutation, or metamorphosis of thought and behavior. With this new awareness comes a new sense of power *and* responsibility. In this context we may describe the coming human epoch as the maturation from a self-aware species[3] into a self-learning species.

Contrary to some New Age beliefs, in an autodidactic universe, no conscious entity in the universe decides to hit humans on the head to get our attention. Earth is no school for beings who must be taught particular lessons; they learn what they teach themselves. All parts of the universe respond to the actions of other parts, whether humans or other forms of consciousness. Part of our process is to figure out the connections. There are no a priori lessons to be taught to us, only lessons to be learned from our own style of engagement with the other aspects of our own host organism, the consciously alive universe. We are both the students and the teachers.

Individual Choice

My experience has been that most of us find it difficult to wrestle with our long-established assumptions about reality. However, individuals and societies are sometimes given reason to pause, assess performance, and decide if they are living up to their potential. Circumstances—economic, political, natural, or personal disasters—may lead us to conclude that course corrections are necessary. In such times we dare to question long-held, life-shaping shibboleths. I believe we now find ourselves in such circumstances.

Despite an apparently booming materialistic society, and perhaps because of it, large numbers of us perceive the discrepancy between the external status quo and the internal potential for greater fullness in life. Untold numbers now seem ready to question the veracity of some inherited myths that underlie modern society. This book is meant to provide support for those already on or about to make the choice to start this personal journey.

Notes

1. P.M.H. Atwater, *Children of the Millennium: Children's Near-Death Experiences and the Evolution of Mankind* (New York: Three Rivers Press of Random House, 1999).

2. Marilyn Ferguson, *The Aquarian Conspiracy: Personal and Social Transformation in the 1980s* (Los Angeles: J.P. Tarcher, 1980).

3. Amit Goswami, *The Self-Aware Universe: How Consciousness Creates the Material World* (San Francisco: J.P. Tarcher, 1998).

Introduction

People are intolerant of others with differing viewpoints, because . . . deep down they are uncertain of the . . . validity of their own beliefs, and . . . do not want to face the possibility . . . that they may not know the truth after all.

—Yasuhiko Kimura[1]

In the preface, I described humans, with physical roots in the Earth and consciousness from the stars, as ready for the next big step in conscious development. Such a leap requires a rethinking of our identity. Thus, I have offered the Solarian concept to elicit a larger vision of our human legacy and destiny. That is why this book deals with fundamental questions. We will reexamine conventional ideas about the origin and nature of the universe. We will reconsider traditional concepts of humanity's place in the scheme of things. We will start by recognizing how little we really know, and begin a fresh review of the central aspects of human knowledge and history. Even so, remember that much more work is still required before we can be confident that we have in hand the basic elements of the true human story.

A review of all conventional assumptions is necessary for two reasons. First, if we are to proceed in the new millennium fully conscious, we have to be aware of our true legacy and heritage. As will be demonstrated later, many recent rediscoveries of historical architecture and knowledge undermine traditional accounts of human and planetary history. Second, we actually know very little about anything. Indisputable facts in every intellectual discipline are very limited. Very appropriately, my frontier science colleague Lloyd Pye[2] titled his 1997 book on human origins *Everything You Know Is Wrong*. That phrase applies in almost every important area of human beliefs. This situation makes it essential that we start with what we don't know.

At the beginning of a trial, defense and prosecution attorneys can stipulate that a piece of evidence be accepted as "true," not to be disputed by either side. This is usually done when both believe objective observers (the jury, in this case) would agree to its veracity. Then the litigation can deal with items that one side or the other considers "not true."

However, in the physical and social sciences, psychology, metaphysics, and religion, I believe consideration of each fundamental question should begin with the opposite approach, with stipulation by believers and nonbelievers of the "unknown." If a "jury" representing different disciplines and ways of knowing cannot agree that the evidence demonstrates they have a true answer, all parties, in good conscience, should label it as belief, assumption, or hypothesis. Applying this standard, most of what we label "truth" would actually have to be considered "unknown."

What We Don't Know

When one conscientiously takes this approach, it quickly becomes clear that the list of what we don't know far exceeds that which we do know. The following examples illustrate the many important questions to which we do not yet know the answers. Add your own examples as you read.

Anthropology/Archaeology. What and where was the first civilization? How did human language arise? Who discovered higher mathematics? Who invented the first alphabet? Was it related to the mathematical frequencies of sound? How did languages and mathematics appear to arise simultaneously in different parts of the globe? Who domesticated cats and perfected crops for human consumption? Who discovered the medicinal values of herbs?

Biology/Chemistry. What started life on Earth, or anywhere in the universe? (In other words, how do we link physics and biochemistry?) From where do full-blown new species come? How and when did different races within the human species develop? What is the smallest life-form? What causes sleep? What is the origin of the patterns for DNA instructions in cell differentiation? Is there natural death in contrast to externally caused death? What survives it, if anything?

Cosmology. What is the origin of the universe, and are there others? How and when did consciousness arise? Do conscious beings similar to humans exist? How does a human mind observe its body or other objects while physically separated from them? What is the nature of energetic interactions between galaxies? What is the nature of reality beyond this universe? Have we discovered all the Sun's satellites?

Physics. Where does the universe's matter come from? What is dark matter? What is the smallest particle? What is the nature of antiparticles and antimatter? Are there unmeasured energy spectra beyond the electromagnetic spectrum? How does consciousness act upon matter? What is the subtle form seen by many entering the body at birth and departing it at death? Is there universal time that contrasts or correlates with local time? What causes geographic and magnetic pole shifts?

Psychology. Where does the personality reside? What are dreams? Why do placebos heal? How do we perceive objects and events at a distance? What is the nature of nonhuman consciousness? Where are memories stored? Do changes in the brain's neural pathways precede changes in consciousness, or vice versa? What are the relationships of environment and genes to intelligence? How do we communicate with each other outside of space-time? How can we see things before they actually happen?

Much human experience and accumulated evidence points towards possible answers to all these questions, but the definitive "truth" still eludes us.[3] For each of the above unanswered questions, many hypotheses and assumptions have been suggested, but few would be accepted as truth by a "planetary jury" of serious researchers. A planetary jury does not require a unanimous vote to declare a universal truth. After all, some people are simply unwilling to accept any evidence that contravenes their prejudgments. But consensus among several competing epistemologies (ways of knowing) is necessary for a planetary label of truth.

What practical difference does it make if our labels are misleading? I believe the practice of misusing the "truth label" is a serious matter. Asserting "truth" when honesty demands something be labeled "unknown" divides people. It results in prejudices, antagonisms, social conflicts, and even wars. Also, blindly clinging to assumptions that do not warrant the label "truth" hinders our seeing contradictory evidence that is in plain sight. If we were honest about "what we don't know," it would be much easier to have a dialogue that identifies commonly accepted facts.

After reaching agreement on "what we don't know" in a particular area, the discussion can quickly identify "what we do know," that is, that upon which there is already general agreement. In most areas of life that is actually very little. As we have seen, the "unknown" pervades nearly all fields that we consider human knowledge.

In our search for truth or common ground, we should not dismiss any well-thought-out hypothesis before we test it. Some apparently far-out idea may be as good as any other as a starting point. As we learn more of the complexity of our universe, what is likely to be ultimate truth is beyond our wildest current imaginings anyway. Let's identify a few of the current incompatible, far-out ideas that different groups call "truth."

There are several mutually exclusive ideas about the origin of the universe, such as random Big Bang plus 15 billion years, God's one-week creation, offshoot of another universe, and the conscious conception of primal forces. There are several different explanations on how life started: lightning striking the primal sea, panspermia, activation by a creator's voice, seeding at birth of universe. At least three contradictory perspectives on how *Homo sapiens* came to exist are also proffered: direct creation; chance mutation; and manipulation by more advanced beings.

Comparable divergences of belief exist regarding all the questions listed above. Obviously such different answers cannot all be correct. Yet proponents for each of these varying theories speak, write, and act as if they already possess an exclusive truth. If the proof for one or the other is so self-evident, why are these contradictory interpretations still held by intelligent and conscientious people?

Why are we loath to admit we possess only best estimates or inspirations? Why are we hostile to the hypotheses offered by others? Does the fear of not having enough certainty, as described by Yasuhiko Kimura in the opening quotation, make people more adamant than they know the facts permit? Or do some of us simply overstate our evidence because it gives us attention and power over others? The answers to these questions also fall into the category of "what we don't know." We know people stretch the truth, but we don't know all the reasons they do it.

Whatever the reasons for such unwarranted claims to truth, the next epochal leap in human progress requires more honesty about "what we don't know." Only by such honesty can we be open to discovering a closer approximation of universal truth. Open-minded scientists and metaphysicians have always been willing to admit fallibility. But when dogma reigns, as it does in most of our laboratories, pulpits, classrooms, and media, in our millennial review we must take no "truth" for granted.

Before attempting a fresh start on new research, we must go back and make corrections to our narrations of history. The assumptions we begin the third millennium with have been warped by significant distortions in conventional history. Unless we correct major misunderstandings of our past we cannot be on sure footing for future initiatives.

Revised Historical Perspective

Official history never truly represents reality. Institutions publish a mixture of historians' selected facts and further selective interpretations of them. In human power struggles, those who come out on top write the story, whether it is religious or politico-military. With their ensuing economic dominance, winners try to control the rate at which new knowledge can be introduced to the stories on which our power is based.

As mentioned earlier, various thoughtful people have called for an updated human story. They include a great mythologist, the late Joseph Campbell, renowned journalist Bill Moyers, psychologist Stanley Krippner,[4] cosmologist Brian Swimme,[5] and futurist Barbara Marx Hubbard.[6] Although approaching the current human myth from differing perspectives, each has recognized the need to bring it up to date and make it more accurate.

Any action "to set the story straight" is worthwhile just for the sake of truth, but there are also more urgent reasons. It will expose arbitrary sources of political and religious power. It will democratize esoteric knowledge not yet available to all. It will empower individuals to take more responsibility for our own actions and the future of the planet. And it will facilitate progressive social change.

The conventional history of modern civilization, more fully revised in chapter 3, misleads people by false assumptions that underpin at least three crucial areas:

- many current values and institutions in society
- theories of nature and human development
- views of individual and group potential

Three core discoveries (or rediscoveries) of frontier science reveal why it is so important to set the record straight and revise our conventional assumptions:

- Twentieth-century civilization had widespread roots beyond the last 5,000 years. Current society is not built on all the lessons available from the human planetary experience.

- *Homo sapiens* are just one self-aware species among many levels of consciousness. We are not necessarily the most advanced, and other beings influence our development.

• We possess inner powers that have atrophied due to the physical-sense focus of industrial society. Humans have subtle senses parallel to the physical and are more interconnected with each other and all of nature than we imagine.

It is amusing to note that the United States government requires a revision, based on the latest developments in scientific research, of official dietary guidelines every five years. Yet no major institution has accepted the role of periodically revising the commonly agreed on human story on the basis of new evidence. In fact, most institutions, including the officially supported scientific community, resist as much as possible changing our established versions of reality. Therefore, the task is left to individuals outside the establishment who are willing to take on the challenge.

So first, let's take the way our traditional scholarship has provided the public with a rather limited sense of planetary history and humanity's place in it. Anything more than 10,000 years ago has been considered prehistory. Simple views of civilization held by most Westerners[7] have encompassed less than the last 5,000 years, assuming it started in the Middle East and Egypt and spread through Greece and the Roman Empire to the rest of the world. Scholars have not been able to reveal why civilization flourished so quickly in the Fertile Crescent less than 6,000 years ago. We have no theory to explain how preliterate tribes developed sophisticated agricultural techniques and complex cities without obvious antecedents. We have no good rationale for the evidence of high civilizations in the ancient Americas and Asia.

When fossil research revealed that 65,000 years ago, Cro-Magnons in Europe had a brain capacity equal to twentieth-century humans, conventional scholars still kept to their theory that sixty millennia were spent in primitive hunting and gathering activities. We are afraid to guess the nature of a "missing link" that would explain the appearance of high civilizations from nowhere 6,000 years ago. We fail to explain how within 2,000 or 3,000 years, the "hunter/gatherer intellect," allegedly resulting from gradual evolution over millions of years, could reach the Moon and send space probes to the stars. Alternatives to this illogical view of history are not officially taken seriously. Nevertheless, *Our Solarian Legacy* offers a very different but *plausible* perspective on this whole matter, grounded in artifacts, historical events, physical research, human experience, and human reason.

The oversimplification of history described above omits mounds of evidence pointing to more ancient civilizations, including prehistoric evidence of advanced intelligence in the remains of vast cities and sophisticated artifacts. Serious scholars cannot ignore physical ruins and archaeological finds just because they are left out of history books. Neither can objective researchers pretend that anomalous human experiences—meaningful dreams, telepathy, precognition, out-of-body experiences, communications with other dimensions, and so on—do not exist simply because they are not part of the current scientific paradigm.

For these reasons, which will be more fully documented in the chapters that follow, this book dramatically modifies traditional notions of the *Homo sapiens* legacy on planet Earth. It reveals a largely unrecognized part of the history of our ancestors, expands the scope of human knowledge, and increases our understanding of human capacities. It revises mainstream beliefs about the origin of life and the development of the human species. It enlarges conventional science's concepts of the nature of the universe and the place of conscious beings within it. It offers a radically more powerful vision of the human potential than either science or religion. Using innovative historical research and cutting-edge developments in science, it seeks to validate the story we tell about ourselves and to set the stage for a more truthfully lived future.

The following chapters also challenge basic assumptions about the nature of current reality held by most of us in religious and scientific positions of leadership. The challenges are not simple rhetorical argument, positing one opinion against another; nor do they resort to some unverifiable supernatural explanation for legitimacy. I have tried to ground my interpretations in documented research and data that can be tested by others. My extrapolations from reported human experience can be subjected to validation by third parties. Because I consciously attempt to avoid established dogma, I believe my reasoning provides a less biased interpretation of history and anomalous research data.

My intent has been to subject every conclusion to the test of internal congruency and every new hypothesis to the test of rational extrapolation from verifiable human experience. Every statement is offered to the reader as a tentative assumption to be validated by personal and group experience.

My Personal Bias

I do not pretend I am an objective being. None of us can totally escape the perception- and thought-shaping influence of the socialization process that establishes our values and world view. So I want to explain how I have tried to avoid many of the unspoken biases that inform the writing of most of us who are from academe and other intellectual professions. How could a conventional person like me come to have such iconoclastic views?

Three decades of my adult life were spent in a diplomatic and educational, cross-cultural environment that required me to be continually aware of how individuals' languages and beliefs influenced their communications and behavior. To be successful in those circumstances, I had to try to understand my own underlying worldview as well as that of the people on the opposite side of the table. This required the development of what I call the "observer perspective," which enabled me to grasp the assumptions behind the obvious statement.

I now employ this "observer" to ask why writers and speakers interpret a given piece of evidence a certain way. If it appears that their conclusions do not agree with relevant evidence, I look for the implicit assumption. Usually, an *a priori* overlay of philosophical, religious, or professional school of thought shapes their thinking. The assumption accepted by the writer or speaker is not explicit in his or her comments. This approach reveals a large amount of unspoken bias. Here are some examples:

- An evangelist shouted at the youth, "If you don't stop that kind of behavior you are going to Hell instead of Heaven." (He did not know the youth had no fear because she did not share his belief system.)

- Scientists took Hubble space telescope data indicating an accelerating speed in star systems 7 billion light-years from Earth to be definitive proof of the Big-Bang/Open-Ended Universe theory. (They did not consider that the existence of rhythmic patterns in the universe—predicted by the early Hindus—would equally account for the same data.)

- The woman yelled at her lover, "You would not have done that if you really loved me." (She did not realize that they did not share the same definition of the word "love.")

- A friend wrote, "Extraterrestrial advanced beings (ABs) could not have a genome compatible with humans because they didn't evolve from the same DNA tree we did." (He seemed oblivious to his implicit unproven assumption that our species uniquely evolved by chance from Earth's primordial ocean.) I favor the use of the term "advanced being," or "AB," to the use of "ET" or "alien," both of which imply origins or pejorative differences that may prove to be incorrect.

Faced with such unspoken assumptions or interpretations, I take recourse to the principle known as Occam's razor—choose the most simple, natural, logical, and verifiable explanation, and slice away other assumptions. This way I can see when the writer or speaker resorts to some illusory truth that we cannot test. In taking this "observer" approach, it is important to have no vested interest in any particular religion or profession.

As I have no formal status in an intellectual discipline that I must protect, I can make the calls as I see them without fear of peer ridicule or censure. Telling the truth as I see it does not jeopardize my career or livelihood. I feel I must add that I have had academic and intellectual training comparable to most. My undergraduate degree program from Florida State

University, where I earned a Phi Beta Kappa key, gave me a solid grounding in the liberal arts and sciences. My graduate degrees from Florida State and Harvard University provided me with a deep understanding of research and analysis in the social sciences. While they honed my intellectual skills, they also made me aware of how such university experiences condition a person's thinking. (I have also had postgraduate training in one French and two other U.S. institutions.)

I also know about the influence of "group-think" that produces illusions inside competitive and closed professions. My time as an officer in the U.S. Navy and as a Foreign Service Officer in the U.S. Department of State demonstrated the limitations successful careers in such institutions place on one's intellectual and emotional freedom. In the Navy I received two very rapid promotions before leaving for the Foreign Service, and in the diplomatic service I was the youngest of my cohorts to reach the grade at which I resigned. So I think there is no doubt that I understood the expectations that shape the culture in such professional institutions. Early in my career as an ordained Baptist minister, I learned how difficult it was to question established dogma in a religious profession. Thus, having seen how quite a range of self-selecting and self-maintaining groups influence one's thoughts and actions, I am sensitive to evidence of group mind-sets. (My early 1980s book *Dismantling the Pyramid: Government by the People* dealt with these issues for bureaucracies in general.[8])

I am also aware that a person's IQ score does not preclude the blinders of implicit unproven assumptions. In many discussions among colleagues in Mensa (top 2 percent of IQs) and in the Foreign Service (only one or two applicants out of several hundred pass all the examinations), we engaged in very skilled intellectual reasoning based on fallacious assumptions. These finely crafted arguments were frequently totally unrelated to available self-evident facts. Thus, we cannot assume that one's high intelligence, education, or professional standing exempts our views from the cross-examination of humans who have a different experience with reality than we have.

Testing Our Assumptions

Even with my effort to challenge unsubstantiated claims, I would never presume that the elements I ascribe to our Solarian legacy constitute the totality of any truth. I only suggest them as reasonable working hypotheses to fill the gaps in "official knowledge" and present a framework that does some justice to the full range of human experience. These hypotheses suggest an alternative perspective on large chunks of our intellectual heritage, including academic disciplines that underpin popular concepts of human development, social institutions, political and economic systems, and the biological and physical sciences. They call into question core tenets of religions, psychological theories, beliefs about instincts and motives, concepts of male and female, and the nature of intelligence; in effect, the current definition of human selfhood. They require reexamination of ethical and value systems based on obedience to "official" or "divine" authority.

Consideration of this book's new hypotheses requires a willingness to question all assertions by those who claim a historical right to truth. This includes all current officeholders appointed or elected to official positions in any institution. If a current claim to authority cannot stand the test of the most rigorous public scrutiny of its historical justification, then the knowledge it claims must be placed in our list of things to be reassessed. Such a review should result in a redefinition of our heritage, one that recovers a more complete and accurate history. It should also incorporate the role of universal and locally incarnated consciousness into the realm of science. These steps will lay a foundation of principles that I believe can lead to a new global consensus and planetary harmony.

Widespread engagement with recently discovered historical reality would, I suggest, correct our myopia about our past and future. Expanding explorations in the realms of extraordinary or inner reality would give us an entirely new sense of who we are. The growing acceptance of evidence of other conscious beings in our space-time would provide the sense of a larger community of consciousness. We would see humanity and its potential as a part of multidimensional reality with many facets embedded in and superimposed on each other.

Society-Shaping Influences

To see how humans reached the state of readiness for such a potentially dramatic shift in world view, let's sketch modern-era developments that shaped human progress in the twentieth century.

We harvested fruit from the intellectual seeds of natural science planted by the Descartes-Newton-Locke revolution of the seventeenth century. These seeds were fertilized by the later Enlightenment of the eighteenth century, but selectively cultivated by the Industrial Revolution that gained power in the nineteenth and beyond. The blindered thinking required by the industrial age emphasized the external, physical, and mechanical areas of science. The ephemeral, but ultimately more powerful, aspects of science were ignored or suppressed. Thus, the following reality-shaping scientific insights and technological breakthroughs of the twentieth century were only a selective part of the seventeenth-century heritage.

- Guglielmo Marconi moved transmissions of the human voice from wires to the airwaves.

- Albert Einstein's theory of relativity completely revised our appreciation of how the physical universe works. His famous formula $E=mc^2$ and the work of Ernest Rutherford led to the discoveries of atomic structure and fission that ushered in the nuclear age.

- The Wright brothers learned how to defy Newton's gravity, to be followed by Wernher von Braun and others who would help mankind escape Earth.

- William Shockley and colleagues introduced the transistor.

- James Watson and Francis Crick helped unravel the DNA blueprints of living matter.

- Steve Wozniak and Steve Jobs, followed by Bill Gates, led the democratic computer revolution that set the stage for the information age of the late twentieth and early twenty-first centuries.

But all of these were based only in the purely rational and physical concepts of the seventeenth century.

In the 1600s, the trinity of René Descartes, Isaac Newton, and John Locke, joined by Thomas Hobbes, is generally considered responsible for reintroducing (last seen in classical Greece) the rationalistic path to knowledge that had been suppressed by the Catholic Church. Although each had broader interests, they became known for a mechanistic view of the universe governed by inflexible laws and the notion that five physical senses were the only route to truth. (For example, Newton spent two-thirds of his life exploring the esoteric and inner nature of reality, but official history has ignored or impugned that work.) Economic powers chose to emphasize rationality, concrete experience, and individuality. The idea that a human was born a tabula rasa (blank slate), to be shaped by the experience of his environment, was music to the ears of manufacturing and commercial leaders who wanted to develop workers and consumers.

The Industrial Revolution, beginning in the late 1700s, gained momentum in the nineteenth century. Then it reached what is likely to be its apogee in the late twentieth. Industrial corporations built upon the power accumulated by wealthy capitalists in the commercial revolution from 1400 to the 1700s, largely as a result of New World exploration and colonization. Their strategy had several tactics: application of mechanical power to agriculture and industry, harnessing of new fuel sources, development of factory and bureaucratic structures, speeding up of transportation and communications, and capitalistic control over most sectors of society.

Material satisfaction was provided to the masses by the Industrial Revolution, but its long-term external effects have been devastating. Examples are the negative impacts on our natural ecosystems and social institutions of internal combustion engines, oil drilling rigs, refineries, urban sprawl, highways, box-like buildings, belching factories, boilers, power grids, strip mines, dumps, and noisy jet planes.

The same mechanistic mentality in medicine gave us the cut, poison, and burn approach to treating the cancers caused by our trashing of psychological and physical environments and of our foods. Medicine's external approach has resulted in drugs to suppress symptoms instead of remedies that deal with the root causes. It has also substituted police tactics to control problem children instead of providing them with love and community support that fully incorporates them into society.

What led us to this point? Academics and scholars among us divided reality into smaller and smaller bits, writing and teaching more and more about less and less. We who were scientists studied ever thinner slices of life and forgot what a person, plant, or planet looks and feels like. Religious leaders among us expended enormous time and energy distinguishing our version of reality from that of other religions and defaming those we feared would steal our flocks. We who were politicians let partisan concerns distract us from the overall good. The result was interpersonal and emotional chaos at the end of the twentieth century that called for a new sense of direction.

Taking New Directions

Despite the materialistic focus of a large majority at the end of the twentieth century, a rising number of individuals were rediscovering the perennial wisdom suggesting a multi-dimensional reality. Support for its existence came, to the surprise of many, from the unintended discoveries of industrial science. We who were physicists attempting to manipulate smaller and smaller subatomic particles came face-to-face with the effect of human consciousness on our experiments. Those of us who were medical researchers trying to prove the efficacy of one drug over another could not escape the evidence of the power of mind in healing. Geneticists among us searching for the keys to human differences found a 200,000-year-old gene pool independent of other species previously assumed to be our ancestors. This parentage of modern humans (so-called Adam and Eve) was dated to a period identified by some historians as the time frame for possible genetic manipulation of humans by ABs. These and other discoveries ripped holes in both mechanistic seventeenth-century science and supernatural dualism.

Without our fully recognizing it, by the early twenty-first century, the vision we had in 1901 of ourselves and the universe had been profoundly undermined by work on the frontiers of science. Focusing attention on space-age technologies, including the global electronic communications revolution, had kept most people from perceiving the gaps in human knowledge. But human experience had revealed that many things were not as taught in school and church. The universe was not solely mechanical. The origin of humans and our history had been very distorted.

We now recognize that we have lost sight of our interdependence with each other, nature, and the stars. We have been so busy dividing the territory among ourselves that we have lost sight of our interconnectedness and failed to treat each person as part of the whole. Desiring to stake out areas of specialized knowledge and control, we have lost sight of the cosmos from which every being arises.

Rapidly accumulating evidence now leads to new hypotheses. The universe is conscious and self-learning. Humans, while indigenous to Earth, have become hybrids due to interbreeding and conscious communication with ABs. The universe has at least three facets; and these are consciousness, subtle energies, and the polarities of physical matter and energy. The universe is a singular organism with all parts interconnected through these three facets. Humans have a set of parallel senses in each facet. These subtle senses and their related inner powers make humans partial co-creators of reality in the self-learning universe.

Some of us have recognized that these developments may be the basis for a global renaissance, one that could catapult humanity into increasing exploration of both inner and outer space. They make it possible to envision our species and the planet at large in the context of a larger, galactic community of conscious beings. They push us beyond superficial experience, forcing us to seek the inner dimensions of life and selfhood. They offer rites of passage that unite us within and among generations, calling for more passionate group experiences of celebration and despair; of birth, life, and death. They link seemingly disparate events, giving cohesion to group consciousness and individual meaning.

One of the reasons for so much alienation from authentic living is that during the last four centuries, the two great intellectual forces in life, science and religion, left their common roots and branched into separate paths. Each in its own way became severed from the inner emotion and knowing that continually shape the individual's life experience. Yet each person retains an inherent impulse to return to a unified state of being, a oneness with the whole. We sense ourselves to be part of something inexplicably vast when holding the hands of dying loved ones who slip in and out of other realms. Farmers and botanists among us witness an inner order in dry seeds that, in answer to some secret bidding, spring from the soil and grow into the plants that serve our needs for food and beauty. Sensing the pull of the stars, we intuitively seek to understand the influences of forces beyond our planet.

A New Human Story

This brings us back to Joseph Campbell and the movement to rediscover our mythological past and interpret it in terms of twentieth-century experience. In a PBS interview with Bill Moyers, he stated, "Myths are clues to the spiritual potentialities of the human life." Moyers rejoined, "Myths are stories of our search through the ages for truth, for meaning, for significance." Both were correct. If the myths of the past do not accommodate new knowledge about ourselves and the natural world, they lose credibility. As we proceed into the twenty-first century, no credible universal myth bonds the fragmented human species.

In this context, myths are the stories we tell ourselves to give coherence and meaning to life's experiences. They may be composed of combinations of fact, fiction, and fictionalized fact, but they make sense to those for whom the stories are told. Such myths can be used to describe historical events in a manner that serves to explain certain beliefs, practices, and institutions in a society, as in the myth of Moses and the Children of Israel in Egypt and their escape across the Red Sea. A myth may embody a more fundamental idea, such as a Native American creation myth, or a set of cultural values, such as the hero myth of Paul Bunyan. A myth may include a veiled explanation of an enduring truth, as in Plato's allegory of the cave or Jesus's parable of faith as a mustard seed. Many myths are the residual memories of human experience with beings we now call gods.

Humanity needs a new *humans-in-the-cosmos* myth, a new description of our Solarian legacy, one that is powerful enough to encompass believable descriptions of our membership in a larger community of beings. It must include theories for things unseen and lead to significant behavioral choices. It must deal with such profound issues as the creation of the universe and its creatures, evolution of social institutions, and human relationships with nature and other beings. Its recitation must connect seemingly disconnected events to reveal their inner meanings. Such a myth for the twenty-first century must recall the perennial wisdom of the past, consolidate and integrate the lessons of many cultures, and take advantage of the insights of science that can be validated through human experience.

Despite the anomie of the current age, a limited new myth has already begun to emerge. Religions or spiritual alternatives to fundamentalism have increased in popularity, even as fundamentalism's adherents increase among those who are most threatened by change. Growing numbers seek new insights in Eastern mysticism. Traditional beliefs in goddesses and shamans now offer contrasts to patriarchal icons. Native American teachings and esoteric mystery schools introduce the public to perennial wisdom. New Age beliefs in higher consciousness and more refined frequencies appeal to still others. While limited and frequently divisive in nature, many of these belief systems will evolve in a common direction through incorporation of nonideological frontier science and nondogmatic metaphysics. From among such human searches for new answers will come support for a twenty-first-century vision.

Leaders in the above trends have generally supported greater openness and sensitivity in persons seeking new answers. But even with these developments and constructive insights published by creative writers, no new humans-in-the-cosmos myth has yet appeared to draw the global community together. No contemporary intellectual or religious vision has been able to unite the human race around a few valid natural principles that will facilitate global peace, health, social progress, and ecological well-being.

I believe that metascience, the synthesis of validated knowledge gained from frontier science and traditional wisdom, can form the basis of such a vision. This would be a cosmic myth to resonate with the inner experience of most and become a powerful guide for the behavior of all. I call this nascent myth our Solarian legacy, and if it rings true for you, maybe other people also will be inspired to test it.

Although a definitive intellectual consensus on which to build this new cosmic myth has not yet emerged, enough evidence from new and ancient sources does exist to provide a plausible framework for a starring *human* role in the galactic story. This book presents solid analytical and research underpinnings for such a provisional new story.

This comprehensive new picture lies within the intellectual grasp of all conscious beings. The fundamentals of the universe require no professional elite for interpretations. No true and perennial wisdom is arcane; only those who wish to exercise power over others would disagree. Each of us has the capacity to grapple with the three existential questions: From where do I come? What is my purpose here? Where do I go after this? If we use all states of conscious awareness, life gives us enough data to test our tentative answers to these questions. As a multidimensional cosmic being, each individual touches the farthest, innermost reaches of the universe and feels its breath on our lives.

This new unifying picture includes a more complex sense of reality, portraying the fullness of physical, emotional, and conscious experience. It directs the light of ordinary intellectual awareness onto the inner reality of life in a universal consciousness. It allows us to be both the subject and the "observer" in scientific research on ourselves. It reveals the connection among all things, showing emphatically that our place is *everywhere*. The Solarian legacy gives new meaning to seventeenth-century John Donne's, "No man is an Island, entire of itself." Recognition of the legacy's validity brings about a reunion between the scientist and the mystic, the rationalist and the intuitive, and the followers of narrow tenets and those with no tenets at all.

Let's now look at some of the implications of such a new perspective on the human species.

Political Ramifications

In all ages when the basis of power held by any particular group is called into question by discoveries or the development of new social ideas, those benefiting from the perks of power resist the revolution in thought. They discredit the new ideas and dispose of those proposing them; in whatever form, the attempted new order is rejected as long as possible. Does the new version of human history suggested by the Solarian legacy threaten those currently in positions of power? I believe certain aspects do.

Let's assume the human experience on the planet includes other civilizations and maybe the influence of more advanced beings. Let's consider the documentation of ancient cultures demonstrates that our species has already realized more peace and harmony than current institutions consider feasible.[9] Let's accept that the new story discredits the idea that our present religious and political institutions proceeded from a divine origin or by a neutral process of selection of the fittest. What is likely to happen if such conclusions are supported by the evidence? History is filled with the persecution of heretics and the stamping out of revolutionary thinking. Modern versions of censorship and suppression are not unknown.

In earlier eras now suppressed or ignored by official historians,[10] significant historical knowledge about the natural origins of religion and kingship was erased. For example: the Roman, Christian, and Muslim burning of ageless documents and killing of archivists in the libraries of Alexandria and Carthage; the Christian Church's destruction of the leaders, records, and artifacts of pre-Columbian America; Emperor Qi's burning of ancient Chinese books; and many others. Current leaders, from bishops to kings to ministers, presidents, generals, judges, professors, and all other members of bureaucracies who claim special rights of "officialdom," benefit from the current amnesia of the human race. Many of us in these positions would not welcome the revelation that the only lasting power that can be vested in us is that freely given by others who have the right to take it away.

When political institutions are based on untestable and mutually exclusive assertions about "divine selection" or histories of "manifest destiny" (as they are in all major nations), military and social conflicts are inevitable, and they benefit only the elites among us who beguile groups of followers. The result is the same as if an explicit agreement existed between scientific and other elites (religious, political, and economic) to prevent objective research dealing with key social assumptions. Thus, we in these positions have a vested interest in the censorship of compelling evidence like that presented here. We don't like it because it suggests that twenty-first-century institutions were not inevitable and that all our systems are artificial and could be changed by popular will.

The self-evident power of the false premises of "divine ordination" and "natural selection of the fittest" illustrates why powerful institutions use such dogma to justify their practices (which result in social divisions and materialistic consumerism). Even though we as followers may question specific practices, we let the authoritarian basis for such decisions go unchallenged. And the exercise of arbitrary powers by some of us over others goes on.

The authority of the official scientist is equally threatened by evidence that casts doubt on the underpinnings of our alleged truths. For example, to argue that conscious mind happened by chance (as publicly paid scientists now declare) requires that the phenomenon occurs only in one place. Therefore, proof of the existence of comparable minds earlier than our present stage of "evolution," or elsewhere in the universe, would nullify the core tenets of modern science. That is why most who are scientists fear a more honest story of what we know (about other beings) and what we do not know (about the origins of life).

Implications for Science

There are other paradigmatic ramifications of emerging discoveries for twenty-first-century science. Here are a few. The "catastrophist" view (cataclysmic events have dramatically affected Earth and human history), which was discarded for the "uniformitarian" perspective (closely linked to the gradual theory of evolution) in the nineteenth century, finds vindication in new research.[11]

Evidence is mounting that dramatic shifts have already occurred, and can occur again, in climate, tectonic plates, electromagnetic grids, and sea levels. Evidence suggests civilizations were sundered by some of these events, which may have been caused by human actions. These rediscoveries add credibility to ancient texts and oral traditions; we can no longer dismiss information that points to civilizations over 10,000 years ago. The evidence calls for reinterpretation of the archaeological and fossil records by interdisciplinary and intermodal (all ways of knowing) studies.

What are the implications of the probability that ABs have directly influenced the development of human society?[12] History suggests there may have been various possible forms of AB knowledge transfer to humans: exposure to advanced technologies, revelations through altered states, and direct training by aliens. Three mythical examples of AB teachers are

Prometheus to primitives, Thoth to Egyptians, and YHVH to Enoch. Acceptance of even one of these possibilities that advanced knowledge has come from beings with more experience and access to higher wisdom upsets our notion that humans are the most advanced life-forms.

Accumulating evidence of other levels of consciousness and ABs may relegate humans to the role of provincial cousins, and adolescents at that, in the family of cosmic beings. Evidence of extraterrestrial life-forms will suggest a new research approach to the possibility of "seeds of life" and whether they are transported across galaxies and among star systems. The new field of exobiology (study of non-Earth life-forms) will be greatly expanded.

To assume that ABs (whether they were colonists or native to Earth) left a significant imprint on earlier human civilizations means some current social practices may be more malleable by conscious choice than we have thought. The enigma of racial hatred and strife may be neither inherited genetically (as some think) nor a product of social environment (as others think). Perhaps our ancestors learned these patterns through their forced servitude to ABs who treated them as vassals in their own conflicts. As one effect of child abuse is an individual acting out in adulthood what happened to him as a child, could some violence in the human species be explained by our ancestors being abused by ABs? Dealing with the influence of universal consciousness and other conscious beings on human behavior will require a new psychology.

If we suspect that prehistoric ABs possessed knowledge that was only partially understood by early humans, our assumptions about their reported practices deserve a new look. Three possible areas generally ignored by modern science seem self-evident: (1) ways to identify the influences of subtle energies on human behavior (e.g., astrology, numerology, Feng Shui); (2) ways to discern the potential for positive interaction with external events or forces (e.g., *I Ching*, runes, Tarot); (3) metaphysical perspectives that are more comprehensive than modern science (e.g., Hermetic texts, Kabbalistic analyses, Rig Vedas). The following are some specific illustrations.

Our understanding of slight genetic variations that seem to occur spontaneously could perhaps be enhanced by integrating the insights of astrology into research designed to identify the relevant variables. The vibrational basis of both astrology and numerology could be useful in developing a greater understanding of all energetic influences, including electromagnetic and gravitational ones, on the activation of DNA and RNA. Numerology (based in the assumption that letters and numbers represent the vibrational frequency of sounds) could provide insight into the energetic aspect of thoughts and emotions.

Our understanding of subtle energies and morphic fields (emotionally charged ideas) could be deepened through work with various traditional methods of divination like the *I Ching*. All of these areas can help increase understanding of many of the so-called anomalous human experiences that involve the use of inner senses and subtle energies. The effect will be to expand the scope of solid scientific research.

Individual Impacts

Where the material in this book weakens or destroys views held by some in positions of power, it has the obverse impact on several beliefs strongly held by most. Some old ideas will no longer have the same repressive psychological power over our thoughts and behavior. When the concept of divine ordination of kingship, priesthood, and other inherited roles is weakened, a sense of the power in individuals is restored. The awe in which most citizens hold those who claim special connections to the gods (or secret societies and esoteric knowledge) will be diminished. As we understand that special position does not result in some inherent special status, we will demand to have equal access to all knowledge. This new view already manifests itself in calls by citizen groups for the end to government secrecy regarding ABs and UFOs and its secret actions regarding both.

When people understand that traditional acts of sacrifice and subservience to authorities may derive from coercive practices of ABs and their representatives in ages past, not from our species' inherent nature, we will claim our individual rights to equality. The follower-leader covenant will break when the followers among us discover that we have been kept from the whole truth about our collective history, including links to other races or species. Blind obedience to authoritarian rules or assumptions will not continue. So-called divine rituals will no longer hold the same allure. Artificial rites of initiation to inner circles (ordination, licensing, etc.) will be recognized for what they are: devices used by one group of humans to shape the thinking of others, and therefore exercise power over them.

This means that initially anyone who has vested interests in restricting information about the truth of our multitrack history and how the universe works will resist the dissemination of ideas like the ones contained here. This will include those who are religious and political public figures who fan the fires of sectarian and partisan differences around the world (even in North America and Europe). Resistance will also come from those who are less obvious elites in churches, universities, associations, and businesses whose power derives from followers who unquestioningly accept that we as officials, experts, and scholars have some unique access to truth.

I believe the holding on to such advantages will be temporary. When the resistance to new truth becomes egregious and too dogmatic to allow self-correction, it also makes prisoners of those who depend on the dogma. We limit our own freedom of creative thought and personal growth. We will recognize that as we hold others back, we do the same to ourselves. Thinking people everywhere will recognize that when the old myth is publicly replaced, the greater human potential of everyone will be liberated and energized.

Positive Outcomes of Adopting the Solarian Legacy

Thus, the rejection of outmoded beliefs will produce many positive benefits for all humans. Fundamentalist scientists and students will be freed to explore multiple modes of research, opening the way to new fields of study and social progress. Religious believers in denominational and sectarian tenets will be liberated from divisiveness and judgments enabling them to intellectually and emotionally enjoy the beautiful complexity of all religious traditions. New celebrations honoring the universal elements of life will be co-created by diverse groups.

When exclusive religions are revealed to be reflections of AB-based ideas distorted by subsequent generations of humans, efforts to forge a new concept of human interaction with the universe will be generally embraced. When we recognize that various religious practices result from historical influences rather than supernatural gods, we will become more tolerant of different belief systems. They will be treated for what they are: cultural creations that are part of a global folk-life festival to be enjoyed by all. A new Solarian consciousness will emerge.

The mother lode of traditional knowledge (that which is known by shamans, healers, sages) can be mined by researchers and practitioners in the fields of health maintenance, ecological stewardship, and psychological growth. Old principles will be dusted off to complement or replace current technologies in energy generation, communications, and transportation. A widespread understanding of the intrinsic equality and power of individuals will empower people and give them encouragement to manifest their greater potential.

The combining of rediscovery with new discovery will result in an intellectual and, subsequently, a societal transformation that empowers everyone and raises all groups to levels of development beyond those now expected by anyone.

Notes

1. Yasuhiko G. Kimura, "A Letter to the History Makers," *Cosmic Light* (Spring 1999).

2. I suggest the book *Everything You Know Is Wrong (Book One: Human Origins)* by Lloyd Pye (Madeira Beach, FL: Adamu Press, 1997).

3. For some other examples, see *Why Aren't Black Holes Black?* by Robert M. Hazen and Maxine Singer (New York: Anchor Books, 1997).

4. S. Krippner, "New Myths for the New Millennium," *The Futurist* (March 1998); 30–34.

5. Brian Swimme, *The Universe is a Green Dragon: A Cosmic Creation Story* (Santa Fe: Bear & Company, 1988).

6. B.M. Hubbard, *Conscious Evolution* (Novato, CA: New World Library, 1998).

7. See *Newsweek*'s March 24, 1997 discussion of human society at the time of the previous passage of the Hale-Bopp comet of 4,000 years ago.

8. Paul Von Ward, *Dismantling the Pyramid: Government by the People* (Washington, D.C.: Delphi Press, 1981).

9. S. Andrews, *Atlantis: Insights from a Lost Civilization* (St. Paul, MN: Llewellyn Publications, 1997).

10. C. Knight and R. Lomas, *The Hiram Key: Pharoahs, Freemasons, and the Discovery of the Secret Scrolls of Jesus* (Rockport, MA: Element Books, 1997).

11. D. S. Allan and J. B. Delair, *Cataclysm: Compelling Evidence of a Cosmic Catastrophe in 9500 B.C.* (Santa Fe, NM: Bear & Company, 1997).

12. Zecharia Sitchin, *Divine Encounters: A Guide to Visions, Angels, and Other Emissaries* (New York: Avon Books, 1995).

PART 1

Three Perspectives on Reality

Modern science, through Hubble space telescope photographs and the popular media, has supplied us with data about and images of the vast and strange universe we inhabit. Traditional myths have filled the unseen cosmos with wondrous and powerful beings. Internal human experience has revealed intriguing dimensions and levels of consciousness. Our Solarian legacy encompasses all this knowledge and experience; and to live authentically, humans must incorporate it into their daily lives.

Applying the metascientific approach presented in the introduction to understanding all of human experience, part 1 of this book looks at the universe and human history from three vantage points. The first is the macrocosmic scale used by physicists and philosophers alike. It deals with the origin and development of the nascent universe to the point where conscious life appears on the scene. The second considers the microcosmic level, the smallest segments into which we can divide reality and how they come into being. The third takes a nonconventional historical perspective of Earth and human history.

For each chapter we use metascience to illustrate the cost of limiting our analysis to only one epistemology (way of knowing). Each incorporates into the scientific model insights from traditional wisdom and possibly from advanced beings or other dimensions of consciousness. This approach expands our thinking about the place and role of humans in the cosmos.

Physical science has given humans a rich appreciation for the complexity and detail of our tangible universe. It captures a palpable model of the vastness and richness of galactic systems and the stew of particles and waves of which they are made. Spiritual traditions have given us a feeling for inner realms and forces that hold together the almost unimaginable magnitude of a universe that is 99.9999999 percent space. Recent writers attempting to synthesize the two perspectives have given us either physical models that lead to an anthropomorphic God or metaphysical models that incorporate the human-centered material realm.

Until the sixteenth-century advent of Copernicus, most European scientists and philosophers held to the Ptolemaic geocentric view that the Earth occupied a stationary position, around which the rest of the universe revolved. Even though scientists since Copernicus have known the Earth revolves around the Sun and our solar system spins within a galaxy, there is still a strong tendency to act as if the Earth and humans are unique and alone in the vast universe. A few scientists still argue that the life-filled Earth is a rare if not unique event.[1] But even some of the most thoughtful among us who accept the probability that life and conscious beings may exist throughout the universe hold on to implicit assumptions that place humans on a uniquely local evolutionary path in the center of a Great Chain of Being.[2]

In the twenty-first century, as we have given up the "geocentric model" of the universe, we must move beyond our current "homocentric concept" of life and consciousness. We cannot hold fundamentalist religion solely accountable for the idea that all the universe was created especially in support of human purposes. Science and philosophy, too, share responsibility for the prevailing human-centered view of the universe.

I believe the concept of a Solarian legacy, transcending the current models of both science and religion, will help us take a "nonhomocentric" view of reality. It will help us understand humanity's place in a universe where we are neither the center of attention nor the most advanced consciousness around.

The first three chapters make the assumption that humans are part of a universal phenomenon of life/consciousness manifesting in local space-time, parallel with similar events in other parts of the universe, and that events are controlled by the same embedded principles throughout the universe, with some at more advanced stages than others.

Notes

1. Peter D. Ward and Donald C. Brownlee, *Rare Earth* (Tokyo: Springer-Verlag, 2000).

2. Ken Wilber, *A Brief History of Everything* (Boston: Shambhala, 1996); Duane Elgin, *Awakening Earth* (New York: William Morrow, 1993); Peter Russell, *Waking Up in Time: Finding Inner Peace in Times of Accelerating Change* (Novato, CA: Origin Press, 1998).

1

A Self-Conscious Universe

Physicists and astronomers have used mathematical formulae to infer the material history of today's universe. From its birth billions of years ago through periods that can only be imagined, these professionals have created a marvelous portrayal of phenomenal forces, of bits of matter swirling through space that slowly settle into stars and planets, eventually producing human beings.

However, this unidimensional story has significant weaknesses. First, it assumes that a unique consciousness arose only recently on Earth as an epiphenomenon (the accidental result of material developments). Second, it assumes a straight, relatively uniform line of development. Third, it deals with only one dimension: the electromagnetic spectrum of energy waves and particles subject to testing with our five physical senses. These assumptions neither hold up under rigorous scrutiny by frontier scientists nor offer plausible explanations for much of the experience humans have living in the universe.

Thus, the modern scientific model leaves us with many questions. Where did the original design come from? How did principles that govern such complexity find their expression in inert matter? When and how did consciousness enter the picture? Does human self-awareness suggest a self-conscious universe? While conventional science doesn't have verifiable answers to these questions, an ancient system of thought summarized as the Hermetic Principles might offer new leads for research.

A Living System

This chapter presents the unquestioningly appealing picture of our universe's birth and development as painted by brilliant materialists. It also identifies the blanks or gaps in their representation of known reality, and it offers suggestions for filling them in.

The myths of supernatural religions, assuming divine beings independent of nature, offer parallel explanations of the origin and development of the universe. However, many features of these myths have been shown to be inconsistent with the verifiable data identified by science. Therefore, in order to account for both the scientifically derived data and the less tangible aspects of human experience, we need a more comprehensive and more nuanced conceptual framework. I believe the metascientific approach presented in this book, combining all ways of knowing, successfully incorporates both the *observed* reality of the material realm and the *experienced* reality of the internal realm. It rationally accounts for the fact that humans generally sense the entire universe as a living organism.

Modern humans now find themselves somewhere between the natural, seamless view of early humans and the wholistic understanding achieved by more advanced beings. Twentieth-century society, with its focus on physical science and technology, almost totally ignored the inner and more subtle aspects of human experience. Humanity's next level of development requires recognition of insights from both traditional and modern perspectives and their incorporation into a new synthesis.

Perhaps recalling the personal memories of childhood and accessing thinking of traditional peoples can aid in overcoming the limitations of modern science. Taking advantage of systems of thought apparently given to humans by ABs in prehistory can also help us expand current science's conceptual boundaries. This chapter suggests ways in which those paths to insights into nature can enhance our metascientific quest.

The next few pages remind us of the value of traditional wholistic thinking, and highlight how science has limited that vision. They illustrate how the Hermetic perspective, drawn from an allegedly advanced civilization, may offer a more satisfactory set of explanatory principles for the actions of matter, energy, and life than do the mechanistic laws of modern science.

Let's first sample some prescientific perceptions of reality, from the experience of childhood and contemporary traditional cultures, to grasp the challenge before us. If the reasoning in this book succeeds, in the last chapter each of us should be able to reclaim our childhood sense of being connected to the whole, without giving up our hard-won scientific gains in knowledge. That is why I start now and end the book with some personal reflections.

The sky darkened as clouds moved across plowed fields. I saw lightning and heard thunder just before rain began to pelt the tin roof. I felt spirits lurking around us and souls of ancestors lounging higher up. As a small country boy, I experienced this seamless reality in which animals, sky, Earth, Heaven and Hell, family, and ancestors were all integral to the universe created by God for His purposes.

We knew when neighbors were coming to visit long before the sound of their wagon or truck. The fact that we communicated nonverbally with our pets and livestock was understood. We knew that the farmers and gardeners who talked with their plants had a better harvest. With no money for doctors and medicine, we experienced the power of prayer circles. Dreams were not just imagination; they included information that we could use in steering our daily lives.

Growing up in the 1940s in a primitive section of northwest Florida, I felt the cycles of my life as parts of a larger whole, sensed myself inextricably linked to the daily rising and setting of the Sun. It lit the morning sky even before the blazing ball itself appeared on the horizon, marking the hour to feed the animals. Its warmth thawed the ground in preparation for planting as its movement north made the days grow longer. The waxing and waning Moon determined planting schedules; its magnetism affected the response of seeds to the Earth just as it affected the fertility of the women and the female animals.

Sitting on the porch after supper, we would start our night watch with Venus in the evening sky, anticipating the calls of the whippoorwill and the hoot owl as we talked of all the beings touched by the same God. We could sense their presence, just as we felt the breezes evaporating the sweat remaining on us from last-minute chores. As the Big Dipper and Orion's Belt became discernible in the darkening sky, we were confident of our understanding of it all.

Except for the Christian God, my childhood worldview had many similarities with that of shepherds on pre-Christian Middle Eastern slopes, or Australian Aboriginals on a walkabout following their "dreaming tracks" in the outback, or Native Americans planting and harvesting with seasonal rites keyed to the movement of the constellations. For all prescientific peoples, including my family, the living Earth was subject to the living sky. We knew we were children of a living universe. Nothing was dead, nothing was separate. Our lives, except for a limited ability to maneuver among daily events, were shaped by forces beyond our control.

This basically naive but comprehensive view of the interactive nature of the cosmos has for millennia dominated the perceptions of traditional peoples in the world. Incidentally, throughout the book the terms "cosmos" or "cosmic" imply something larger or beyond the material universe as we know it with our five senses. However, since the time of Aristotle

(*On the Heavens* written in 340 B.C.)—the Greek philosopher from whom we have many modern intellectual concepts—a more restricted view has become dominant among so-called developed peoples. A rational, materialistic perspective, spreading from ancient Greece westward to Rome and up through Europe and over to the Americas, has shed light on many parts of reality, but has reduced our understanding of the whole. Propagated by the Anglo-Saxon and Latin-centered worlds of thought and technology, Western civilization's mechanistic view of the universe has been a two-edged sword: As scientists dissected the universe, they excised sectors of human experience from their scrutiny.

Aristotle's theory of solid spheres containing various heavenly bodies rotating in fixed circles around a stationary Earth was followed by the discoveries of Ptolemy, Copernicus, and Galileo. Galileo's observations in 1609, made with the help of his newly developed telescope, proved that not all heavenly bodies were orbiting the Earth or the Sun. People began to perceive that moons orbited planets that in turn orbited the Sun, and that suns and stars had their own tracks within galaxies. Isaac Newton's theory of gravity, published three-quarters of a century after Galileo's observations, provided an explanation for the spinning, elliptical movements of heavenly bodies. (Johannes Kepler realized the orbits were elliptical, not perfect circles, in the early seventeenth century.)

As telescopes became more powerful, people saw more stars. But they continued to assume they were looking at a largely static universe, set in place by a supernatural being with the human observer at its focal point. No one knew how the world and universe got started. (Aristotle had earlier postulated the theory of an undefined "Prime Mover.") The supernatural religions of the West—Judaism, Islam, and Christianity—believed the universe started with a creative act of their personal god.

From the seventeenth to the twentieth century, many philosophical arguments surfaced about the nature of creation, the limits of the universe, and the issue of time. Yet the basic perception of the macrocosm remained essentially the same, whether people believed that it had evolved from a natural event or that it had been divinely and fully created at the beginning of historical time. Both groups considered the universe something whose laws could be discovered and whose elements could be manipulated by humans. Whether the laws were mechanical or divine, they were all seen as focused on humans—the homocentric view of reality.

The perception of a static universe with fixed boundaries was shattered in 1929 when Edwin Hubble (after whom the orbiting Hubble space telescope is named) saw that other parts of the universe were moving rapidly away from us. (Five years earlier he had discovered galaxies beyond ours.) Hubble interpreted such movement to mean the universe was expanding; and if it was expanding, it had to have a history of accumulating events. These events could result from either a single creative event such as the Big Bang or a continuing process of external influence. Since the latter opens difficult questions about the nature of unknown forces outside our universe, most scientists have settled on the simplistic Big Bang theory. As a result, modern humans are still locked into very limited assumptions about themselves and the inner nature of cosmic reality.

Science mostly follows its fragmented search for knowledge, separating it into isolated disciplines. That makes it easier to categorize some human experiences as natural and normal and dismiss others as anomalous, accidents, or artifacts of overactive imaginations. For example, most aspects of the ancient discipline of astrology are ignored by official institutions, although the experiences of untold millions indicate strong correlations between actions of celestial bodies and human behavior. Likewise, the link between thought and the microcosmic activity of cells is still largely ignored by mainstream science, as is the whole area of extrasensory communications. Science's focus on four forces of physics, assuming we have discovered all of them, precludes the study of other likely forces, ones that could explain the many so-called anomalous phenomena.

Despite institutional fragmentation, a renewed sense of wholeness is now emerging. Forward-thinking professionals in physical science, archaeology, anthropology, psychology, and consciousness research now take a systems approach, treating humans as parts of a larger organism. (Ken Wilber's use of the concept of "holons," parts within parts of a larger whole.) The new scientists are joined across institutional barriers by nonsectarian mystics to expand the time frame of assumptions about human history and definitions of matter and consciousness. Each intuitively is rediscovering the singular, living universe of traditional peoples, the same seamless reality I experienced in childhood.

I hold that science's understanding of the living universe can be enhanced by gleaning insights from our legacy of knowledge from earlier civilizations. A reassessment of some traditional beliefs may reveal they have much to contribute to a new metascience model. For example, the ancients appear to have known that matter arises from different vibrational patterns in a field of invisible energy, an insight rediscovered by quantum mechanics in the twentieth century. Remember Fritjof Capra's 1970s book *The Tao of Physics*.

The Judeo-Christian tradition proclaims, "In the beginning was the Word." The Australian Aboriginals believe the ancients sang the world into being.[1] "Word" and "song" imply that the use of sound or vibrations lead to the formation of the material universe. They also imply that the energetic vibrations that shape energy quanta into particles are not just random patterns. They have inherent meaning, not unlike Plato's view that ultimate reality was form or idea. This suggests that consciousness must preexist matter to conceive of the ideas or forms of different vibrations that underlie various configurations of matter.

Most mythic traditions—whether from Central America, North America, India, China, Egypt, Greece, or the Middle East—include allusions to a conscious being or force that formed something out of nothing. The fact is that neither the traditionalist nor the scientist knows how it all started. Later in this chapter I have chosen to use British physicist David Darling's poetic story of the beginning of material time[2] to illustrate conventional science's current assumptions about

11

how our present universe came to be. To fill some of the gaps in this conventional view, I introduce in this chapter what I believe to be some useful advanced scientific principles from antiquity.

Several esoteric traditions developed their own explanatory (scientific) principles for the workings of the universe. One such system, the Hermetic, which has come down to us from prehistory, I find comprehensive enough to have used its framework for many analyses in this book. I believe its relevance will become self-evident in this and following chapters.

Hermetic Principles

The Hermetic Principles, named after a legendary personality known to ancient Greeks as Hermes Trismegistus (meaning "thrice great"), have been known and articulated by intellectual elites for more than 5,000 years. Recorded history identifies a being who transferred several fields of advanced knowledge to humans differently in different cultures. Thoth, or Seth, was his Egyptian name; in India he was Manu; and in the Judeo-Christian tradition he has been called Lucifer or the Serpent.

Despite the lack of clear information about its origins, Roman-influenced scholars knew the collection of knowledge by its Latin name *Corpus Hermeticus*. Many consider it to be the source of basic natural teachings that infused all the intellectual, scientific traditions of Egypt, Greece, the Near East, and Europe for several millennia.[3] A few learned initiates guarded the insights and passed them on discerningly over the centuries to those deemed ready for the teachings.[4] During the Inquisition and other periods of religious persecution by Christians and Muslims alike, it has been dangerous for independent scholars to reveal their belief in a natural reality that does not assume divine intervention. Consequently, most of the Hermetic insights were lost to the masses, as well as to most scholars and students, before the advent of the modern era.

The term "hermeticism" has been primarily associated by many with alchemy, or the alleged transmutation of metals into gold. However, it involves a broad and integrated approach to the understanding of matter, energy, and more subtle forces. It provided the intellectual precursors to Western mystery traditions that seeded the European Renaissance. The term "hermetic" has come to mean secret or sealed for that reason.[5] From information that fills volumes, I have taken a classic distillation known as the Hermetic Principles. The seven are Mentalism, Polarity, Correspondence, Vibration, Rhythm, Gender, and Cause and Effect.[6] (See table 1 below.) Although they can appear to be so simple and mundane that the casual reader is wont to lightly skim them, they may actually be more far-reaching than the basic assumptions of Newtonian mechanics or quantum physics. The current work of a number of researchers included in this book tends to confirm the validity of these concepts. Readers can judge for themselves whether they add to one's understanding of each of the following chapters and make it possible to relate seemingly different phenomena to a unifying set of principles.

Table 1. Hermetic Principles

1. Mentalism:	Everything exists first as an idea.
2. Polarity:	There are two aspects to every phenomenon.
3. Correspondence:	The same fundamental rules apply at all levels.
4. Vibration:	All elements of the cosmos are in constant motion.
5. Rhythm:	Each entity, energy, and idea has its own cycles/patterns.
6. Gender:	Yin and Yang, receptivity and expressiveness, exist at all levels.
7. Cause and Effect:	All aspects of the cosmos are in a singular interactive system.

Mentalism

The Principle of Mentalism is reflected in the Biblical quotation, "In the beginning was the Word/Logos." Ultimately all external reality is based on idea or concept. In the context of quantum physics, Mentalism means the physical world can be reduced to patterns of potential connections among potential concentrations of matter/energy that might or might not come into form, depending upon the introduction of some level of conscious intent.[7]

Twentieth-century physicists and consciousness researchers were on the edge of unraveling the implications of Mentalism that Hermetic initiates have known all along. Now anyone can grasp its meaning: the basic force in the universe is mental, the realm of universal and local consciousness.

Polarity

The Principle of Polarity embodies the observation that two seeming opposites are in truth different aspects of the same thing—two sides of the same coin. This principle applies in all realms of human behavior, as in the complementarity of expressiveness and receptivity. Photon particles are inextricably linked in pairs, with each as either the positive or negative aspect of the other. Hot and cold are but different aspects of the same temperature gradient.

Any aspect of nature or cosmic experience has its own gradient—large and small, high and low, black and white, sharp and dull, male and female. There is no absolute in anything, even in behavior, where there are only shades of good and evil. The crucial point here is that all such polarities are only different vibrations on the same continuum. As we will see later, with the Principle of Polarity, one extreme can be easily transmuted into the other.

Correspondence

The Principle of Correspondence, "as above, so below," means that one can infer the nature of smaller-scale entities from the characteristics of larger, more distant realms, and vice versa. The dynamics of cells parallel those of galaxies. Just as a small laboratory or computer program can simulate the behavior of stars billions of light-years away, the local consciousness of an individual being can confer with the universal ultimate consciousness that existed when there was only the "Word." This principle implies, for example, that humans need not be in awe of exposure to the ideas of, say, extraterrestrials; they are derived from the same universal consciousness.

Vibration

The Principle of Vibration, which asserts that everything flickers in and out of existence in a continual state of motion, is now a basic tenet of science. Subatomic particles continually oscillate and move in relation to each other in every concentration of energy and mass in the universe. The patterns of vibration occur in all manifestations—from dense stone, to gaseous molecules, to the thoughts and emotions of human beings.

We intuitively grasp the validity of this principle when we sense "good vibes" or "bad vibes" about one thing or the other. When we are on different frequencies with someone, we can "wind down" or "ratchet up" the tension to become congruent with their level of vibration.

Rhythm

The Principle of Rhythm means that everything manifests itself in a pattern of to and fro, up and down, in and out. The movement in one direction is always compensated for by a return. This is manifested in the wave sign of any force. For every action there is a reaction and for every advance there is a retreat. The principle applies in all the affairs of the cosmos—stars, beings, minds, energy, and matter. It works in the interactions within a plane, and in communications between dimensions. Over time, the rhythms result in spiraling shapes that characterize much of the universe.

Understanding the dynamics of this principle makes it possible to mitigate some of its more extreme effects. We can recognize that fatigue, followed by rest, leads to renewed energy. Anger gives way to remorse and pain succumbs to release. By being aware of the rhythms, one is less likely to resist their flow, thereby reducing the buildup of extremes.

Gender

Gender remains the most obscure principle, because we tend to equate gender with primary physical sex characteristics.[8] However, every being and every realm in the cosmos contains the dual elements of yin and yang, feminine and masculine. Senses (feminine receptivity) require expressions (masculine) to have something to sense, and expressions of anything require a receiver. The term "gender" recognizes this complementariness within all organisms of the universe. Even in apparent single-sexed entities, one aspect is the receptive nurturer, while another is the expressing creator.

Each principle honors all others. The Principle of Gender itself obeys the Principles of Polarity and Rhythm, in one circumstance manifesting the masculine aspect and in another the feminine. Neither is ever totally absent: in space-time, balance is assured. Fully aware beings seek harmony in living their dual nature (Gender), honoring the ebb and flow (Rhythm) of organic development in self, society, solar system, and universe.

Cause and Effect

The Principle of Cause and Effect is too simplistically known in the West by formulas like "x acting on y causes z." From the Hermetic perspective, the principle means each effect has many causes. Carl Jung suggested this multilevel reality by use of the word "synchronicity" to describe events that, though outwardly appearing to occur by chance, result from the working of inner connections. Indeed, all events are at some level the workings of various seen and unseen relationships. What we attribute to chance is usually an event whose governing law is not self-evident. True chance or randomness probably occurs solely at the level of quantum gaps, where the only true break between past and future can occur.

The Hindu concept of karma illustrates the Principle of Cause and Effect, as does the Christian reminder "as you sow, so shall you reap." Human societies have recently learned the dramatic effect of this principle in ecological systems. Now humankind must become more aware of this cosmic law in the realm of consciousness. It is this principle that makes humans conscious co-creators of the universe.

These seven principles are simple keys to the mysteries of consciousness, subtle energies, and matter/energy (itself two polarities reflected in Einstein's formula E=mc^2). (See table 2 below.) I believe they can open gateways through which a profound transformation of human perception becomes possible. This book is an argument for undertaking such a journey, postulating that transformation on the mental and energy planes will have immediate consequences in the material realm. Not one principle stands alone. All affect each other in a mode of reciprocity, thereby assuring the cohesion and unity of the multifaceted universe.

Table 2. Application of Principles

Hermetic Principle	Physical Events
1. Mentalism:	Superstrings Periodic Table
2. Polarity:	Positive/Negative Charges Matter/Antimatter
3. Correspondence:	Atoms and Star Systems Cells and Families
4. Vibration:	Electromagnetic Spectrum Other Spectra
5. Rhythm:	Birth, Life, Death Creation, Elaboration, Decline
6. Gender:	Male/Female Expressing/Sensing
7. Cause and Effect:	Warmth to Sprouting Love to Creativity

For example, jazz, as experienced by both the musician and the listener, illustrates the interplay of all Hermetic principles. Vibration and Rhythm are communicated through sound and sight. Gender is evident in the artistic expression and the receptive audience. The continual creative act of Mentalism finds its way into the Polarity of sound and silence where the Correspondence of scales manifests in several instruments. Music that is universal taps into the vibrational signature of a species, causing effects in emotions, health, communications, and a sense of community.

Contrasting Views of the Universe's Origin

Now let's return to a physicist's description of that first burst of ordinary matter and its consequences. Here we can see how the Hermetic Principles function both sequentially and simultaneously in the development of the physical universe. To facilitate understanding the difference, I have put the conventional materialist view of the universe's history in italics. In many places where one or more of the Hermetic Principles apply, the relevant names are shown in parentheses in the contiguous text. In using such juxtapositions, I do not intend to denigrate the efforts of my physical science colleagues, but to demonstrate the value of complementing a modern perspective with the insights of some ancient, but obviously useful, wisdom.

Scientists feel confident that somewhere between 13 and 20 billion years ago there was an explosion (Vibration) into form, a Big Bang, when out of no-place, no-time, and no-thing the universe appeared. At that moment, from a seedlike but invisible point, came streams of protons, electrons, and neutrons. The electron is almost nothing; the protons and neutrons are 1,800 times heavier. But there are many electrons swirling around, vibrating in emerging space. Each electron has an antiparticle (Polarity) called a positron.

Each electron or positron is equal in mass to its respective twin, but the twin's electric charge is reversed. (Manifesting the Polarity Principle), the positron's charge is just as positive as the electron's is negative. The two are in reality only halves (Polarity) of a pair, but one that also represents the poles of gender. Male and female, they jump about forming the stuff of ordinary matter, engaged in the cosmic dance of creation. As long as they keep the right distance, held in position by their opposing electric charges, they function as matter. While the appropriate distance in this attraction of polar opposites is maintained, they are stable. But when they breach an invisible boundary, they destroy each other.

Given this destructive potential, why didn't all the electrons dissipate billions of years ago? In destroying each other, electrons and positrons create (Cause and Effect) a pair of different particles—new photons. Thus, death leads to birth, and that which disappears returns in another form, manifesting the Principle of Rhythm.[9] These new photons are different from the old particles; they are particles of light, pure energy with zero mass or charge. The Rhythmic Principle insures an ongoing equilibrium. When two of these new photons collide they give birth to two new particles, replenishing the reservoir of matter.

It is worth noting that Genesis 1:1-3, reflecting advanced knowledge in antiquity, has the correct order for this ongoing process of creation. First the void, chaotic darkness without form. Then, "God said, 'Let there be light,' and there was light." Photons followed the chaotic swirling of electrons, neutrons, and protons. The creation and destruction of subatomic particles involved a repatterning of pure energy, governed by inherent principles of unknown origin. Whatever the origin, this implicit design illustrates the Principle of Mentalism.

Theoretical physicists believe they can calculate back to the point when the universe was 10^{-43} second old. One ten-thousandth of a second equals 10^{-4} on an exponential scale. So 10^{-43} is only 100 million, trillion, trillion trillionths of a second. At this "Planck time" (named after Max Planck, a founder of quantum mechanics) all forces and matter acted as one unified force. Because their mathematical calculations do not work beyond the moment of Planck time, physicists assume gravity had split off from the singular force that hypothetically existed in the beginning (The Principle of Cause and Effect does not support such inferences).

At 10^{-35} second old, physicists postulate the existence of two forces: gravity, and another that combined the currently understood electromagnetic force (Vibration and Rhythm) and the weak and strong forces (Gender). The universe was pure energy, with point-like particles of quarks and leptons. (See chapter 2.) Matter and antimatter were equally balanced (Polarity). Physicist Blas Cabrera at Stanford University has hypothesized the existence of monopoles or free magnetic poles that formed another kind of matter (Gender).

At 10^{-32} *second, the universe was only about the size of a grapefruit; gravity and the strong force now stand with the electro/weak force (electromagnetic and weak forces still combined). At 10^{-20} second, black holes may have formed (Polarity). At 10^{-12} second, the temperature of the universe was 1,000 trillion °C. At 10^{-10} second, according to a "hot" bang theory, the universe was about the size of our own solar system. At this point the four forces labeled by modern physics were distinguishable from each other. (The Principle of Gender comes more fully into play in this array of weak/strong, restraining/liberating forces.) Between 10^{-6} and 10^{-4} the stew of quarks began to coalesce into triads and form neutrons and protons, elementary particles that coexisted with leptons.*

At *one-hundredth of a second, the universe had cooled to 200 billion °C. Hundreds of types of particles were engaged in the cycle of birth and death and re-creation (the Principles of Rhythm and Gender).*

At *the end of one second, the universe was a bubble of space only 200,000 miles across, according to a "cool" bang theory. Its temperature was 10 billion °C. The antiprotons and the antineutrons had gone. On another track, some electrons had merged with protons to yield neutrons and neutrinos. The latter are so infinitesimal in mass, if they have mass at all, that they can achieve almost the speed of light and pass through the most dense matter unimpeded.*

The Hermetic Principles pose intriguing questions about the preceding conventional description of the process. What if antimatter (feminine gender) forms the black holes we find scattered around the visible universe? Do current assumptions adequately take into account the role of a balanced polarity in matter/antimatter ratios? Is a new cycle of creation (Rhythm) started when antiparticles rejoin and destroy their twins in the world of ordinary matter? Could this be the basis for hypotheses regarding the origin of multiple universes?

Stephen Hawking[10] has attempted to better understand the dark counterpart (Polarity) of visible matter. He postulated the existence of billions of tiny black holes (necessarily formed in the early fractional second when pressure and temperature were high enough). This theory marked a shift from his and others' earlier view that black holes were caused only by collapsing stars. Hawking broke with another earlier assumption and now believes such holes may emit energy and explode. These attributes are predictable from the Hermetic Principles of Polarity and Rhythm.

During the early nanoseconds (one-billionth of a second) of the universe, time as we know it did not exist. With such concentrations of mass and energy, developments occurred at an exponential rate. As much could happen in the first one-tenth of a second as happened in a second, and the first ten seconds, and then the first one hundred seconds, and so on (a scaling function of the Principle of Correspondence).

The initial explosion produced unimaginable heat, but as the seconds turned into minutes, actions slowed down and things cooled off. The subatomic particles coalesced into elements—ordinary hydrogen, heavy hydrogen (deuterium), and the heaviest hydrogen (tritium). Next, the various densities of helium came into being. On and on through the periodic chart, elements formed as particles bonded according to some a priori set of inherent ratios and relationships (Mentalism). (The orderly pattern of reality reflected in the periodic table of elements indicates that even at this early stage a conscious order was at work.)

Three to four minutes after its birth, the universe was filled with radiation, caused by electrons destroying almost all the positrons (Cause and Effect). The strong force started forming the nuclei of the above-mentioned heavy atoms. At about this time, a hydrogen/helium ratio of 3:1 is believed to have developed (Rhythm).

At the end of thirty minutes, the temperature was 300 million °C (only fifteen times hotter than our present sun). The average density of everything was less than one-tenth that of water.

As the hours turned to days and years, space expanded, but the quantity of matter stayed approximately the same. For thousands of years there was only a mist, charged and swirling in a huge electromagnetic field, before strings (long, thin, wriggling tubes of energy) began to appear.

Emerging Patterns

While the collective theories of modern physicists, italicized in this chapter, may be descriptive of the universe's physical development, they cannot be considered explanatory. The

existence of emergent patterns (strings) from the very beginning of the universe implies that something other than chance
was at work in the mist (Principle of Mentalism). Scientists
have not assumed an a priori set of patterns or inherent design
in the Big Bang point from which the rest of phenomenal matter burst forth. Had humans been around, they could have
seen the patterns emerge, but now we can only attempt to
reconstruct them from the traces that remain. Research in
physics has explicated some of those patterns, but as this book
demonstrates, important parts of phenomenal reality (and
most of nonphenomenal reality) remain unexplained.

Physicists and astronomers in NASA's COBE program
(Cosmic Background Explorer) have measured the apparently
ubiquitous background radiation (long wavelength
microwaves) spread throughout the universe. It is assumed to
be at the edge of the universe, revealing its age and expanse. In
early 2000, a team (led by Andrew Lang of the California
Institute of Technology and Paolo de Bernardis of the
University of Rome) reported the best defined yet minuscule
temperature differences (less than one hundred-millionth of a
degree) in this radiation. The differences are analogous to ripples on an otherwise smooth pond surface, but in this case they
are ripples (referred to as strings, earlier) in the fabric of space-
time. Thus, 10 to 15 billion years ago, shapes (termed "fossils of
creation" by astrophysicist George Smoot) began to differentiate themselves in the primeval fog of the universe. What caused
those ripples and how they led to the complex organisms in
today's universe (superstring theory) are still unknown.

Even with great scientists, mind-sets sometimes get in the
way of increasing knowledge. Einstein believed so fervently
that the universe was stable—not expanding or collapsing—
that he initially adjusted his own perfectly working equations
for his theory of general relativity in order to support his bias.
When a highly reputed contemporary theoretical physicist
like Stephen Hawking, without looking at the facts, dismisses
solid evidence from the field of psi research, it discourages
other scientists. What some science writers labeled the "most
important" discovery of 1998, measurement that the speed of

separation was accelerating among some parts of the universe, illustrated how new data are forced into preexisting models. People committed to the Big Bang/Open-Ended theory were unwilling to consider the possibility of rhythmic expansion *and* contraction as being as integral an aspect of the macrocosm as it is in the microcosm.

These examples illustrate the danger of self-limiting assumptions. Physicists' deliberate exclusion of the role of other principles, including conscious intent in the coherence of energy and matter, calls into question their Big Bang theory and related hypotheses. Increasing recognition of the way mind influences the behavior of subatomic particles—at the core of quantum physics—requires that consciousness now be considered an element in the building of such theories.

A complex universe could not have *randomly* evolved from the protomaterial and nonmaterial elements, were they merely floating around in absolute chaos. Certain preexisting, unseen forces or dynamics were essential in bringing form from the primordial stew (Mentalism, and Cause and Effect). Modern scientists have discovered four such forces—gravity, weak nuclear force, electromagnetism, and strong nuclear force—which they now hope to reduce to a single principle called GUT, or Grand Unifying Theory. But why assume that all operative forces have been discovered? How can one believe in a single force that excludes consciousness?

Science, asserting that matter creates mind, still appears caught in the Cartesian trap of dividing mind from matter. While matter is coextensive with mind and cannot exist without it, the consciousness-manifests-matter postulate (Principle of Mentalism) can be validated in human experience (healing with imagery) and in formal experiments (the creation of neuropeptides through positive thought). Other examples are discussed in later chapters.

In the rush to reduce four physical principles to one GUT, some conclude that all forces except gravity may be a single force operating within the atom. In 1979, scientists Steven Weinberg, Sheldon Glashow, and Abdus Salarn received the Nobel Prize for experimentally demonstrating that electromagnetism and the weak nuclear force (that which controls radioactive decay) were two aspects of the same force. Subsequently, others have tried to demonstrate that the strong nuclear force (which holds the nucleus of atoms together) is another dimension of that singular force.

To the extent that these conclusions are not congruent with the Principles of Polarity and Correspondence, they will likely prove to be only partial explanations for observed phenomena. (See chapter 4 for further analysis of the gaps in reality not covered by the four forces.) Until our models can explain all observed phenomena and human experience, we must continue our analysis of the developing universe before we presume to have an all-encompassing theory. But for the moment, let's continue with the physicist's story.

Within the seething mist, differentiation began to occur; localities seemed to assert themselves. While much of it continued to expand in all directions, small areas began to coalesce. Something seemed to be luring bits of matter together. Only within certain frequencies could the electro/weak/ strong force triad come into play. Something controlled the frequency shifts. Possibly a function of random temperature changes. (Or were they the result of patterns implanted in the embryonic universe before its birth, something like the patterns that shape the DNA sequences that imprint the fetus in a mammalian birth?)

While we do not know the origins of these inherent patterns, we do know that throughout this mist of primeval matter they could be discerned as shapes began to manifest. The Hermetic Principles of Vibration and Rhythm seemed to be operating as the frequencies of ordinary matter changed (most slowing down) and masses became more dense.

Some scientists say the coalescing resulted from the strong force splitting away from the remaining electro/weak pair. They postulate the existence of cosmic strings—great loops of tension composed of energy moving at nearly the speed of light—that broke up the uniform mists. Initially small strings combined in ever increasing sizes until they became powerful enough to draw large collections of particles together.

The above descriptive theory regarding the early condensation of matter still falls short of an explanatory theory. At what point and how were the cosmic string patterns ingrained in the event? As the strings became larger and longer and put ripples in the smooth surface of space-time, they gradually disappeared. None exist for us to see today at the cosmic level, but their analog—the DNA helix now so familiar to us—still works its way (Principle of Correspondence) in the creation of plant and animal life.

Thirty thousand years after its birth, the infant universe was composed of matter and light clouds kept intact with light energy.

At 300,000 years (keep in mind the exponential timeline), the universe was bigger and cooler, the temperature dropping below 8,000°C and the color moving from hot colors toward the green and blue side of the electromagnetic spectrum.

At 500,000 years, electrons and nuclei from the primordial stew began to form permanent attachments in the shapes of atoms. As matter coalesced, it increased in complexity, including the separation of a still-hypothesized dark matter from ordinary visible matter.

Attracting Forces

Does this separation of matter into two qualities or properties reflect the Hermetic Principles? The dark cannot be seen, but it appears to exert a powerful influence on the behavior of the universe. The Principle of Gender works to juxtapose the receptive/nurturer aspect with the expressive/creator aspect. The black-and-white yin/yang symbol aptly illustrates this dynamic gender polarity.

Yin-Yang Symbol

As the twenty-first century began, physicists in Italy, China, and the United States reported surrogate evidence (traces of their hypothesized impact) of the existence of dark matter particles.[11] They needed to demonstrate that a certain quantity of these particles is present in order to balance out their calculations of visible matter and the overall mass of the universe. They assumed that some form of overall balance characterizes the universe. The question is which factors balance which? The Principle of Polarity would insure that factors in one area are absorbed (birth and death) or matched (coexistent with) by the opposite pole in a contiguous part of the universe.

One hundred million years into its existence, the universe begins to seed protogalaxies. Connections appear as the unseen pattern (Logos) weaves matter and antimatter, strings and mist, mass and energy, light and darkness into the components of a vibrant universe. From a protogalaxy will come one galaxy—to be called the Milky Way—which is centered in the direction of a constellation to become known as Sagittarius.

But we're getting ahead of the story. Something like the Principle of Correspondence ensures the similarity of patterns in atoms and planets, in molecular and star systems, and later in various species of conscious beings. New stars pop into view, glowing in a field of thinning dust, but they are not alone. A dark twin or energetic force (Gender) is always nearby.[12]

Each galaxy, including our own, has a black hole. NASA's Chandra X-ray has now (2000) observed 33 of them. Black holes both suck up and expel matter (both genders in one). The power of this reciprocation may play a role in the rhythm of universal time. Some speculate that black holes are interdimensional channels through which time travel could occur. General relativity theory says mass affects time and space. So black holes with such mass could pull light toward itself, speeding the light up to fade into the future. This could happen if the so-termed worm hole—a black hole linked to a white hole, in a yin/yang polarity—expels in the reverse plane all that it swallows from this plane. A few scientists speculate that such a worm hole would permit intergalactic travel.

The phenomena of black and white holes are cosmic-scale demonstrations of the Principles of Polarity and Gender.

Emissions in infrared wavelengths through the galactic dust indicate great bursts of energy as matter is drawn into the maw of a black hole. A black hole is so powerful that it can swallow a star that comes too close and hold in the light, resulting in high winds that create a million-degree black bubble.

Now, a billion years after the universe's grand rebirth (explained in the next section), different types of galaxies are evident. A few appear to have quasars[13] at their center, many have ordinary stars, and some have black holes. Others have spirals at their core. All are different, but clearly are of the same species.

Our galaxy, the Milky Way, is approximately one hundred thousand light-years across, only one of an estimated hundred thousand million galaxies—more or less—each in turn containing about one hundred thousand million stars. All the other galaxies appear to be rapidly running from us. We believe this because, in a manifestation of the Principle of Vibration,[14] their colors become more red (as the wavelengths become longer).

After 5 billion years, many of the stars in most galaxies have consumed all contiguous matter. Some of them became so heavy with this ingested matter that they imploded, and then exploded into supernovas (Rhythm). These explosions resulted in the creation of dozens of new elements, which later became the building blocks of ever more complex life-forms.

The countervailing influence exerted by black holes, quasars, and other less powerful concentrations of energy (poles) on adjacent star fields reflects the dynamic tension of balance suggested by the Principle of Polarity. Following the Principle of Rhythm, these galactic-scale poles shift positions over time, not unlike the shifting of Earth's magnetic poles.

Ten billion years pass. More stars are born; many die. Much matter is pulled together into the various shapes of galaxies, but intergalactic space is still filled with a flurry of tiny specks—the material from which worlds are created.

The Hermetic Principle of Gender is at work from the cellular to the galactic level. In the latter, a dark fertile (feminine) force dances with a light mercurial (masculine) force in the rhythm of destruction and creation. With the appropriate degree of engagement, the possibility of offspring exists.

Due to the Principle of Cause and Effect, we see the products of this cosmic dance of stars and dark holes: their "children" are born as new planetary systems, just as in Greek myths.

Although other planets may have formed earlier, our Earth was born about 5 billion years ago to an average-sized yellow star on the fringes (28,000 light-years from the center) of the Milky Way. At the edge of that galaxy, in a backwater eddy of this gigantic maelstrom, cosmic forces drew scores of stars larger than our sun to the brink of a black hole. These same cosmic forces spawned a chain of events that eventually gave birth to conscious beings.

Starting from Zero

While most scientists accept the idea of an explosive birth for the universe, heated debate still continues as to whether the universe will perpetually expand, or some eons from now, reverse direction and collapse back on itself. It is assumed to be currently expanding about 8 to 10 percent every billion years. Given estimates of forces at work and the amount of matter (star systems and dark holes), some scientists postulate that the universe will continue to expand forever.

The Big Bang theory is supported by some evidence of a uniform presence of background microwave radiation throughout the universe (although that is incompatible with some current assumptions of quantum mechanics and recently discovered evidence pointing to minute variations in the radiation). The 3:1 ratio of hydrogen to helium, assumed to have been developed in the first few minutes of the universe, can be observed as far as we can measure. The universe appears from Earth to be the same in all directions (predicted by the Principle of Correspondence), even though we are not in the center of it.

Jonathan J. Halliwell identified some of the problems with the Big Bang model of the universe.[15] For example, a number of vast regions are moving away from each other at a rate that appears to indicate they could never have been in contact with other parts of the universe in their entire history. He asks: Why are these unconnected parts so similar? Why did the universe remain flat rather than spherical if there was a uniform explosion from a single point? How did small-scale fluctuations in the near-zero moment lead to the later large and varying structures?

In this situation, an explicit assumption of "cause and effect" relationships based on predesigned principles makes more sense than belief in a random explosion. The Big Bang theory does not offer an explanation for either the source of the single point that exploded or the origin of the space into which it exploded.

A relatively new theory posits that at a fraction of a second after point zero, something called "inflation" by physicists acted on the expanding explosion that set patterns in place that resulted in the star systems, planets, and human beings we observe today. This "superstring" theory holds that infinitesimally small loops, 100 billion times smaller than a proton, could lead to such complex organisms evolving in the undifferentiated space. Once again, it stretches credulity to make the leap from a "random bang," through chance "strings," to "complex conscious beings." This is the corner physicists have painted themselves into.

One escape for them is a theoretical combining of general relativity (Einstein) and "singular theorems" from quantum assumptions (Hawking and Penrose) that makes it possible to postulate a point close to the universe's birth when "external" influences could have impinged on the universe's development trajectory.

In effect, these scientists now recognize the likelihood of preexisting forces, or "parents," who influenced the birth and/or infancy of the universe. If the conception and birth of the universe observed the same principle of male and female input as its parts (Principles of Gender and Correspondence), then its parentage might most appropriately be considered a Grand Couple (if we wish to use anthropomorphic terms).

Some scientists postulate a flat, uniform universe, while others predict a contraction or a "Big Crunch." Whether the expansion is indefinite or time-bound seems to depend on there being a certain threshold of density to matter. Many cosmologists believe the universe to have exceeded that critical mass and therefore believe it will cease expanding. Lange and de Bernardis (mentioned above) believe the hot spots at the edge of the galaxy will warp the universe enough to preclude further expansion. The light distortions seen by the Hubble space telescope in group NGC 2300 at 150 million light-years from Earth, indicating a gravitational force thirty times that which we experience, add credence to the contraction view. This kind of "dark matter" could keep the visible matter from expanding indefinitely, and even cause it to collapse back on itself.

The Hermetic Principles, if they are in fact relevant to the macrocosm, could shed some light on these questions. The Principle of Correspondence would predict that an entire universe experiences cycles like those of its components: birth, growth, decline, decay, and rebirth. If the universe is governed by the same principles as all levels of life, once its growth phase ceases, it should enter the aging part of the cycle, to end up back at a point to be recycled. In such a context, the event now considered a Big Bang would be more accurately described as a Grand Rebirth (see table 3 below).

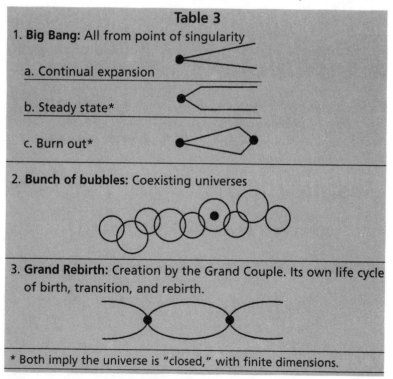

Table 3

1. **Big Bang:** All from point of singularity

    a. Continual expansion

    b. Steady state*

    c. Burn out*

2. **Bunch of bubbles:** Coexisting universes

3. **Grand Rebirth:** Creation by the Grand Couple. Its own life cycle of birth, transition, and rebirth.

* Both imply the universe is "closed," with finite dimensions.

Parallel to the Hermetic view of a universe life cycle, the ancient Hindus had a similar understanding. The Year of Brahma was believed to be 311 trillion years long—a period that represents the expansion and contraction of the universe. Both of these esoteric views may yet be validated by Western science.

Although theories about origins and endings of the universe may not seem relevant to our current lives, at least one theoretical question may directly affect our experience: Are there parallel universes? Some scientists accept the possibility of multiple or "bubble" universes. (See table 3.) If they exist, conscious beings may be able to experience them through worm holes that serve as gateways from one part of our universe to another or between separate universes. If multiple universes exist and humans can experience them, we must be multiverse beings.

Some scientists argue that, even if other universes exist, we cannot "know" them because of the boundary of our own (termed an "event horizon"). In what may be only a question of semantics, others hypothesize that our universe is really a branch, located somewhere as only part of a larger system. If consciousness is cosmic (transcending the "event horizon" of one universe), then conscious beings may not be bound to one universe. Some people, including a few physicists such as Fred Alan Wolf, speculate that such universe hopping could account for some of the so-called paranormal and psychic phenomena (discussed in later chapters of this book).

Whether the multiverse theory can stand depends, according to some, on the existence of a GUT that explains everything for our universe. Right now the apparent indestructibility of the proton is one factor holding up the proof of a GUT. If the decay of this particle can be proved, some scientists believe they can be assured that all four forces collapse into one. On the other hand, the proton's indestructibility might prove that the universe is inherently unstable, and therefore subject to manipulation by external forces.

The Hubble space telescope (HST) has now revealed that stars apparently are being created from the clusters of energy formed from colliding galaxies, energy that is equal to 500 billion suns. The HST has revealed that the blue star *Eta Carrae,* previously thought to be fading into oblivion, is in fact erupting.[16] It appears that stars, like other organisms, are born and then die, but before they die they join violently with other stars to produce offspring that perpetuates the stellar family. The same may be true, if the Principle of Correspondence is operative on a larger scale, of entire universes. If universes die and are born again, is a process of conscious reincarnation at work?

Animating Consciousness

With the mention of consciousness, this discussion of our universe takes a dramatic turn. We know consciousness exists because we have it. Consciousness is more than thinking: in consciousness we are aware of our thinking. Yet few physicists attempt to confront the everyday reality of human self-awareness because it cannot be perceived directly and measured by the five ordinary senses. The physical world clearly manifests the effect of consciousness, but not how consciousness influences it. Thus, many of us subsequently ignore evidence of so-called paranormal abilities, including the anomalous results of telepathy and psychokinesis that show specific characteristics of a fifth and/or sixth force.

As human beings, we elaborate our individual experience of consciousness through the physical senses, but we are keenly aware that we are more than they reveal. In this book, as we review the ways in which individual and group consciousness affect matter and energy through forces focused by human intent, it will become evident that a larger consciousness is at work around us. Even though most scientists personally recognize the inconceivability of a universe such as ours occurring by chance, the profession's norms discourage formal inquiry into external consciousness as causation. (See the suggested reading list at the end of chapter 9 for examples of expanding the frontiers of science.)

Some scientists who admit the impact of consciousness on the behavior of matter, but have no theory about it, conclude with a concept Brandon Carter has called the "anthropic principle." Carter's theory, drawn from quantum physics, holds that we as human beings create the universe by the way we look at it, just as an experimenter who wants to measure light finds a wave of light where another could observe a particle. Unfortunately, the circular logic of this concept permits one to escape without fully addressing the issues of primary consciousness. From where did consciousness originally arise? How does it work? Must it always be connected to matter?

Any comprehensive theory of the universe must take into account the role of mind and consciousness. One theory, that of hyperspace, which posits up to six dimensions beyond our four-dimensional version of the universe, leaves room for a "scientific incorporation" of consciousness into a descriptive model. But most scientists still believe our everyday world can be accounted for by a limited number of basic physical laws. Thus far their formulation of laws is not as comprehensive as the Hermetic Principles, which do provide for conscious intent in the patterns of creation.

This chapter has, up to this point, focused on the objective universe, from the outside looking in, with a selective interweaving of the Hermetic Principles that combines physics and metaphysics. Before we leave the macrocosmic scale, we introduce an expanded schema that integrates consciousness and as yet unnamed subtle forces with the material universe. This schema assumes that at least three facets (consciousness, subtle energy, and matter/energy) are necessary to account for the full range of human experience (to satisfy a condition of metascience discussed earlier). Those facets must function at all levels in a singular, integrated model of the universe, and together create space-time from a void some call the "ground of being." (Paul Tillich used the term in theology for the state before creation, and physicists use the term "ground state" to mean the lowest possible level of energetic activity.)

The graphic on page 34 identifies all these components. How they interact in nature and among conscious beings will be the subject of the rest of this book.

For the time being, I assume the ground of being is beyond our knowing, the source from which our universe in all its knowable facts and dimensions arises. In a living universe the elements interact with each other in a reciprocal fashion (described in the next two chapters), but the basic flow of the model is simple. The focus of intent (ideas or patterns) by a certain level of consciousness appears to cohere forms of subtle energy (chi, zero-point energy, etc.) that have the effect of concentrating electromagnetic charges into waves or particles. This ongoing process of sequential formation of quantum events (from the subatomic to the galactic level) results in the basic four dimensions[17] of our space-time universe.

The important point here, to be further developed in the subsequent chapters, is that the same processes involved in the initial formation of the universe shape all interactions of life as we now know it. The principles that led from zero point

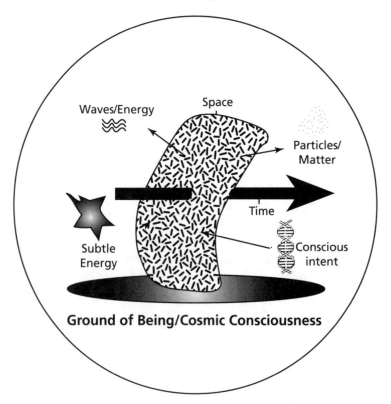

to particles and waves also led to stellar and galactic systems. As these principles shaped stellar families, they informed families of organic beings, now in untold numbers of species throughout the universe. The result is beings who have become self-aware, not only of their own behavior, but of some of the principles that underlie it.

The central thesis of this book is that self-conscious humans and other beings have natures that reflect, even if only dimly, the self-learning and self-directing nature of the conscious forces that gave birth to the universe in the first place. While I think it premature to undertake the search for the why of that ultimate consciousness, I believe we are capable of and compelled to address the question of how self-aware beings, such as ourselves, came to be. To be successful, I believe that conscious quest must be broader than any contemporary institutional effort of science or religion. That is why I call for a metascience, involving all paths to and all sources of knowledge. *Our Solarian Legacy* is an attempt to demonstrate the efficacy of that approach.

This chapter has illustrated the approach by focusing on the macrocosm. We can see how the Principles of Mentalism, Gender, and Polarity may complement the four forces of physics in explaining the universal birth process, whether it results in galaxies or humans. Any entity born of that process is first only a gleam in some eye of consciousness (Mentalism). The impulse to actualize the ideal (a yang or masculine expression) must find an energetic field with the potential (a yin or feminine receptivity) before it can manifest in concrete form. Thus, the Principle of Gender also requires the Principle of Polarity, where polar entities of equal force (represented by the following examples) can join to create a new one.

In the portrayal of the early moments of the universe, we saw that the energetic joining of the electron and positron (Polarity) resulted in the creation of photons. Some aspect of their design (Mentalism) resulted in the exchange of information between the two that created the new energy form. The explosive joining (*pas de deux*) of the two particles in a fertile energy field (Gender) resulted in the appearance of something new. The same thing happens in the mating dance of human lovers and other life-forms. The merging of polar energies results in the creation of offspring ("spring" is an appropriate term, given the energetics involved). This process is repeated among the stars.

Astronomers believe our Sun has a mate (Gender), a "brown dwarf" named Nemesis located about 25,000 times the distance of the Earth from the Sun. The mating of their energetic centers (Polarity) has produced our family of planets, moons, and asteroids. Early in the twenty-first century astronomers had discovered more than fifty such stellar pairs, apparently producing planets in a manner similar to the "lovers" Sun and Nemesis.

Now we have discovered a similar birthing process at the galactic level. Our galaxy has at its center two huge force fields that emit several times as much radiation as our sun and are a strong source of radio waves. These two energetic centers (Polarity) may include a dense, fiery group of young stars and/or a black hole. Thus, they appear to fill the role of "parents" (origin and maintenance of stellar offspring) in our galaxy.

Given this symmetry, I believe it is not too farfetched to postulate an analogous pair of energy centers engaged in a mating dance of creation at the level of the universe itself. I have somewhat humorously labeled it the "Grand Couple." But this book goes deeper than descriptions of interesting physical analogies. Key to its central thesis of a self-conscious universe is the hypothesis that a certain form of consciousness has manifested itself at each of these levels, from the microcosmic to the macrocosmic.

If that hypothesis is correct, then all forms of manifestation in the physical universe involve an expression of conscious intent, as in the schema presented above. The following chapters present evidence suggesting that the expression of conscious intent coheres some form of subtle energy into morphic fields.[18] These fields possess the ability to concentrate ordinary energy into physical form. The result is that consciousness informs and transcends all organisms. In this manner nontemporal awareness benefits from conscious experience in transitory phenomena, in what I have labeled a "self-learning universe."

Gary Schwartz and Linda Russek, in their book *The Living Energy Universe*,[19] clearly illustrate how memory is retained in all aspects of the universe. Their research shows how memory lives on in so-called inert matter, living cells, and larger systems. With memory access to past experience, each new moment enables a conscious entity to assess the difference between past and present, and experiment against its perception of still unrealized potential. This is the learning process: projecting an outcome, attempting to realize it, and accessing the degree of success. Awareness of the resulting degrees of congruence or incongruence between the actual experience and the original intent leads to self-learning.

I have chosen to speculate that the conscious intention to fully experiment with itself impregnated the subtle-energy womb of the Grand Couple. From that desire came the physical universe with its polarities of energy and matter—or "matenergy," as I prefer to label the two poles. The power of the original expression of intent was strong enough to cause a part of the original force to concentrate itself as the medium of subtle energy. The further coherence of the subtle energies transmuted them into the world of spirits, atoms, molecules, and organisms. The next chapter explores how our universe still vibrates at the microcosmic level from the kinetic energy generated by that initial desire to self-actualize.

Notes

1. Bruce Chatwin, *The Songlines* (New York: Penguin Books, 1988).

2. David Darling, *Deep Time* (New York: Delta, 1989). Most current estimates of the age of the universe range from 15 to 20 billion years.

3. Some believe the same or a comparable being was a source of knowledge for the Toltecs, Mayans, and Incas of the Western Hemisphere. For example, the Mayan calendrical system has several principles similar to the Hermetic ones presented here.

4. This tradition is the basis for the plot of James Redfield's popular book *The Celestine Prophecy*.

5. Three Initiates, *The Kybalion: A Study of the Hermetic Philosophy of Ancient Egypt and Greece* (Chicago: The Yogi Publication Society, 1912).

6. In Hindu metaphysics we find similar principles: The primordial sound of AUM demonstrates the Principle of Vibration, while the concept of Brahman coincides with the Principle of Mentalism.

7. Fritjof Capra, *The Tao of Physics* (Berkeley, CA: Shambhala, 1975).

8. See Ivan Illich's book *Gender* for an excellent portrayal of the distinction between gender and sexual characteristics.

9. The concept of reincarnation of souls (local manifestations of consciousness) mirrors the same principle on a higher level of complexity.

10. Stephen Hawking, *Black Holes and Baby Universes* (New York: Bantam Books, 1993).

11. James Glanz, "Stanford Experiment Shakes Dark Matter Claim," *New York Times News Service* (Feb. 25, 2000).

12. Science has gathered evidence on the nature of this balance at a cosmic scale. Black holes are no longer viewed as an isolated phenomenon created only where an old star collapses on itself. They cannot disappear, for they cannot become smaller than the original primordial universe. Some are quiescent. They come in all sizes, like light-bulbs. One, 3 million times the mass of the Sun, may be only 2.3 million light-years from the Earth. Some now believe certain black holes could be spread so thinly that we could pass through them without knowing it.

13. Quasars (from quasi-stellar) are bright, starlike entities that convert matter to energy and emit gamma rays, the highest frequency on the electromagnetic spectrum. The quasar's energy output could be a thousand times stronger than that of our entire galaxy and ten trillion times more potent than our sun.

14. The modern term used to describe the principle is the "Doppler effect": as the source of light moves away from us its frequencies appear to slow down, like the sound of a horn moving away in the distance.

15. Jonathan J. Halliwell, "Quantum Cosmology and the Creation of the Universe," *Scientific American* (December 1991); 76–85.

16. "Stellar Vision," *The Sciences* (March-April 1994).

17. P. D. Ouspensky, *Tertium Organum* (New York: Vintage Books, 1982). The arrow of time used here is neither the subjectivist (perceived by us) nor the absolutist (eternally apart from us) view of

time, but a statement of entropy or other organic progressions inherent in the phenomenal realm.

18. Rupert Sheldrake, *The Presence of the Past: Morphic Resonance and the Habits of Nature* (London: Collins, 1988).

19. Gary Schwartz and Linda Russek, *The Living Energy Universe* (Charlottesville, VA: Hampton Roads Publishing, 1999).

2

From the Void

Chapter 1 sketched an expanding and, I think, a more reasonable view of how our universe could have come into being and reached its current stage of development. While that theoretical approach is more complex than either the conventional scientific or religious models, is it congruent with the details of our current research findings? I believe the proof of such a macrocosmic model lies in the microcosm.

From where do the complex but elegant subatomic particles come that make up all the beautiful life-forms, including humans, who inhabit the universe? Physical science takes us on a microscopic journey from cells through molecules and atoms to a shimmering world of subatomic particles. Each refinement of our instruments reveals smaller and smaller bits of matter, jostled about by unseen, but measurable forces.

Great progress was made in the twentieth century in our ability to describe parts of this realm. However, we still seek explanatory theories that satisfactorily deal with the how and why. Here are some of the questions that remain. Why are particles and subparticles here one nanosecond and gone the next? Where is home when they're not here? What creative power brings them into being? Why do humans seem to share that power? How does consciousness, which seems nonmaterial, master energy and matter?

This chapter reviews recent concepts in particle physics—the study of the appearance of matter at the subatomic level—and suggests ways the Hermetic Principles can help explain observed and experienced phenomena in the microcosm. This material is important for everyone who wants to comprehend the basis for the power and scope of human consciousness. We cannot fully appreciate the power of prayer, mind-body healing, psychokinesis, and other inner human capacities without understanding how mind interacts with matter and energy.

Dealing with quantum mechanics and space-time in the microcosm requires us to grasp the concept of creative activity devoid of energy and matter as we know it. At this point we have come full circle in the Einsteinian concept of relativity: the infinite nature of the macrocosmic universe is not different from the infinitesimal nature of the subatomic one. Both levels arise from "something" that has been described as "nothing." But as we saw in chapter 1, the concept of a Big Bang (something from absolutely nothing) defies reason. The ground of being from which the universe and its microcosmic parts arise can only be considered "nothing" through five-sense reasoning. I believe we need concepts that bridge the gap between the physically tangible universe and that unknowable ground of being. That gap appears to be filled with some as yet unknown forces with which local concentrations of consciousness, as in humans, can interact.

Therefore, to understand the nature of microcosmic particles and waves that seem to appear from nowhere and disappear at will requires a mental leap. We must picture a source of patterns (the design of those particles and their various combinations) that has the power to shape apparent nothingness into tiny quanta of something. We cannot use the term "void" or synonyms such as "space" or "vacuum." We now know the vacuum of space is not really void of everything. When we remove matter from space to create a vacuum, we leave the energy of wave fluctuations.

Therefore, for this realm of nonform and nonmateriality beyond space-time, I have chosen the term "noumena," which means the realm of only concepts or ideas. It is the realm of consciousness that the Greeks also sometimes labeled Logos. How does this realm relate to physical reality?

Space-time is composed of three dimensions or directions, plus time. In space-time any event can be located, if only approximately, at a given point for a given instant. Even though some scientists speculate that there may be as many as ten or more such defining dimensions, they are all extrapolations from the physicist's perspective. (Michio Kaku and others have popularized the idea of ten or more dimensions that allow time travel and parallel universes.[1]) The noumena, on the other hand, appears to work with principles and through a medium of forces not subject to the currently known rules of the physical universe (phenomena in my model).

In seeking a metaphor to help illumine the nature of this noumenal realm and its relationship to ordinary reality, I have chosen the familiar "looking glass," or mirror, from Lewis Carroll's *Alice's Adventures in Wonderland*. The mirror is a useful device (also used by physicists John Briggs and David Peat) because it helps us visualize reality as having tangible and intangible aspects. It represents a simultaneous existence that can be viewed but not permanently inhabited from this one. It also allows for the fleeting appearance of objects with a translucent quality, an attribute of virtual reality. Additionally, the mirror metaphor captures another aspect of the microcosm: we cannot be sure from which side the initiative comes.

Before mentally jumping through the glass to the noumena, let's approach it from our current knowledge of the microcosm. Popular science writers like Peter Russell[2] have begun to use scientific terms indicating the ephemeral character of the primary strata of the universe. He describes photons of light as quanta without mass or charge, so near to nothing that they easily wink in and out of existence. Other scientists postulate a force that shapes amorphous vibrations and waves into neutrino quanta that manifest no matter, yet may comprise ninety percent of the mass in the universe. These and the following concepts move us closer to understanding the link between nothing (noumena) and something (phenomena).

Building Blocks

Matter has successively been revealed to be broken down into smaller, more elusive bits. For a long time people thought of distinct elements as the irreducible constituents of matter. Then philosophers hypothesized and scientists proved they were made of atoms. Students learned an atom was the smallest indestructible piece of reality (a trillion million of them fit on the head of a pin). But atoms in turn were revealed to be made up of electrons, protons, and neutrons. Theorists thought the building blocks had been figured out, and they categorized elements by the ratios of protons to neutrons and grouped them according to the number of electrons in the outermost shell of the atom (as in the periodic table of elements). Then several combinations of even smaller particles were discovered within each atom. But the breakdown did not stop there.

Physicists now have taken us into the world of even smaller bits of what many consider the frontier of the physical realm.[3] To converse about phenomena at the bottom edge of the barely visible world, we use the concept of quantum, which means "how much" in Latin. In the physical universe everything appears to happen in quanta—the progressions, or leaps, from one level or state to another with nothing in between. This smallest unit of measurement signifies that matter or energy cannot be broken down into another unit: the application of additional force would transform it into nothing. The following review shows how far the search at this level has taken scientists.

The smallest quanta to have been perceived through mechanically enhanced senses fall into four families: leptons (with six particles), quarks (with six particles), clasons that include photons and gravitons, and weakons that include "W" and "Z" particles. Since all particles seem to exist in complementary pairs (Principle of Polarity), the number in any family is always equal. Therefore, as only five quarks have been found, it is assumed that for the "down" quark, a sixth or "up" quark must exist. The latter is a most tenuous bit of matter, believed to exist for a mere fraction of a millionth of a second. Researchers theorize it exists, but during the last decade of the twentieth century they were only able to report *traces* of what they inferred was the "up" quark. Other hypothetical subatomic particles, although as yet unproved, have been given names like "neutralinos," "subquarks," "selectrons," and "axions."

Given our dependence on mechanical devices to perceive these tiny bits, some believe such subatomic particles may be only artifacts of the technology. Therefore, it is difficult to determine if we are measuring something as it exists or if it appears in that form because of the way we measure it. This is an important issue when one introduces the factor of human conscious intent and the conversion of subtle energies to ordinary phenomena. Mastery of the process of materialization of matter and energy from the noumena requires identification of the level or levels at which it occurs. If that conversion process operates at the atomic level for humans, it makes the subatomic level irrelevant for purposes of conscious creation. However, if our intent works at levels smaller than the atom, the current subatomic taxonomy may be helpful in learning the scope of influence inherent in human consciousness.

Quarks, making up the neutrons and protons that form the nucleus of an atom, always act in triads. (According to the Principle of Correspondence, the triangular shape provides strength to structures at many levels of life. Note the use of the trinity in several religious traditions.) Leptons counterbalance the quarks, making up the subatomic particles that revolve around the nucleus. These two categories of matter (quarks and leptons) are counterbalanced by two families of energy (clasons and weakons), with two members each. (Is this the Principle of Gender at work here?)

Analysis of these four members (gravitons, gluons, photons, and "W" and "Z") provide the underpinnings for the four basic forces of the universe introduced in chapter 1. Conventional thinking considers that of the four, all except the graviton have their effect inside the atom. Some physicists have adopted a new view holding that gravity is an electromagnetic-like charge, placing it alongside the other three forces.

These four represent the reciprocal forces of cohesion and disintegration that characterize the two tendencies of all matter and energy. All manifestations in space-time of matter and energy in any form occur when the two tendencies are momentarily in balance (Principles of Polarity and Rhythm).

Scientists postulate another category of matter—"virtual" particles or fields—but as of yet we have no instrument to reliably measure them. We see only traces of where we think they have been. At this very microcosmic level, the dividing line between a particle and its unmanifested pattern is very fuzzy, hence the term "virtual." Nevertheless, this conceptual plank begins to bridge our material existence and the noumena. It introduces the possibility of a medium of interaction between the two. For example, Gabor Belovari, a Hungarian physicist,[4] believes discord in a body's "virtual photon field" could wreak havoc on the physical organism. In the human context, this corresponds to the idea that damage to the auric field results in ill health.

The Hermetic Principle of Polarity would suggest that this so-called virtual state is different from antimatter (the opposites of all particles) and dark (invisible) matter. These two are complementary polarities of all matter and visible matter, respectively, all of which are in the phenomenal realm. All matter and energy in the phenomenal realm can be converted from one form to the other. But all these forms initially come into being out of the virtual state. I believe this area of virtual reality may be an aspect of the intermediate, subtle-energy state I label "energeia."

Such an intermediate state could help explain the power of conscious intent and morphic fields (charged ideas) in various forms of complementary medicine. For example, Candace Pert, in research at the National Institutes of Health, found that consciously induced emotional shifts (thinking positive thoughts) could give rise to the creation of neuropeptides (molecules that help enhance the immune system).[5] Homeopathy can work on the basis of dilutions of substances in water to the point that no particles remain. It is hypothesized that the remaining "energetic patterns" alone affect the body.

These and other examples suggest that some intermediate force field can be activated by a pure thought or pattern to affect the world of matter and energy, particles and waves. I use the label "energeia" (meaning all subtle energies) to combine ancient concepts such a *chi* and *prana* with modern concepts like zero-point energy and orgone. While many terms have been used to describe these subtle forces, they all point to this energeial link between the subatomic world of physics and the world of mind or consciousness I call the noumena.

Looking Glass Metaphor

Returning to our metaphor, what is the nature of the noumena beyond the glass? We have used huge telescopes to push our sight toward the edges of the macrocosm. We have used powerful microscopes to peer into the depths of the microcosm. Whether we look at outer or inner space, we end up with the same intangible nothing. It becomes clear that the boundaries of the universe are like the personality of a human being: both have no matter. This noumenal level is Logos, only ideas, tendencies, and potential patterns. It appears to be a field no more substantial than cosmic memories, yet it appears to be more powerful than galactic-scale lightning converting energy to particles, or black holes swallowing star systems. The logos reportedly preexisted our multibillion-year-old universe and may still exist if it collapses back into itself, gestating for another cycle.

Unfortunately, our language is not conducive to a discussion of how something can exist before it exists. Perhaps the Muslim belief in an "uncreated Koran" and the Buddhist tenet "Form is emptiness and emptiness is form" can help us. They imply the reality of a potential before it becomes manifest. In what might be called a Zen paradox, we have to use our mind to clear our mind of all previous concepts of reality in order to make this imaginary leap. Will we discover William Blake's poetic truth? Looking through the glass at our invisible soul, we find that our material self is the perfect reflection of it.

The Buddhist concept of *shunyata* may help us understand how one particular manifestation could arise from infinite potential. A *shunyata* universe holds the seeds of infinite possibilities, where those that flower are determined by accident or conscious action. Similarly, on the other side of our glass, potential is unlimited, but what is actually created depends on behavior or decisions on this side. As illustrated below, the looking glass frame (the event boundary of our universe) does establish limits to the freedom of choice enjoyed by conscious beings. We do have some limits to our powers of conscious design, but we have not yet fully identified them.

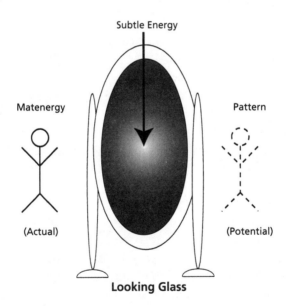

Looking Glass

It is important to remember later in the book that limits (Polarity) determine our freedom to consciously create. The scope of freedom for human self-directed development increases as we move from phenomena through energeia to the noumena. It is easier to change an idea than an emotion, which in turn is easier to change than a physical condition. Therefore, this model suggests that the noumenal force of conscious intent is the most potent power we have to shape future events. Charge up a new idea, and the physical shift will follow.

As we will see later, humans are not confined to this side of the mirror. Through meditation, dreams, and other beyond-the-body states of consciousness, we can "see" this side from the noumenal side of the mirror. Keep in mind that all three (pattern, subtle energy, and matenergy) are just different aspects of one whole (the object, the mirror, and the reflection as an ensemble), but understanding the three facets is essential for the next level of human development.

In his book *The Holographic Universe*, Michael Talbot[6] suggested that—at a level beyond the current concepts of physics—matter, energy, and consciousness blend into a single field. But simply combining that triad obscures a range of unexplained influences and communications experienced by human beings. To explain the ability of the individual's mind to interact with and influence ordinary matter and energy in its body and externally at a distance, another medium must be invoked—the energeial realm of subtle energies. More comprehensive treatment of how the three facets interact comes in chapter 4, but for this chapter, we need to focus on the indirect impact of human consciousness on matter at the microcosmic level.

Mind and Creation

Humans, like all organic beings, possess a level of consciousness-incarnate that we call mind. (The word "mind" throughout this book represents consciousness in an active state.) Considerable evidence demonstrates the power of a human mind to influence the behavior of matter. Here are some examples:

• Deepak Chopra has popularized the earlier-referenced research by Candace Pert that demonstrated the human ability to think neuropeptides into existence.[7] He has illustrated its role in self-healing.

- Microbiologist Celeste White has summarized significant evidence to indicate that individual human mental effort can have a minute, though vital, impact on the creation and/or manipulation of crucial bits of matter, including DNA sequences. Her review includes methods to reduce the electrical excitability that triggers epileptic seizures; guided imagery to affect the immune system, blood flow, and heart rate; and use of hypnosis to cure genetic illness (warts).[8]

- Robert Becker, in *The Body Electric*,[9] shows how the expression of feelings or thoughts causes direct current (DC) to flow along the body's nerve sheaths (perineurals). In this instance, the mind shapes waves of energy parallel to its previously described influences on particles of mass.

These examples of physiological and biochemical reactions to conscious intent show that the two basic categories (matter and energy) of physical building blocks are susceptible to the power of one being's mind.

Applying the Principle of Correspondence, one can assume that scaling up the mental/emotional effort (by many individuals concentrating together) likewise scales up the physical effect. Research at Princeton University's PEAR (Princeton Engineering Anomalies Research) Laboratory has demonstrated that effect with physical objects and computer software.[10] The larger the number of people who share and focus the same intention on an object, the greater the effect; but we cannot yet be certain of the ratio of increase. Perhaps five people acting together have as much impact as ten or twenty-five acting separately. (This principle explains why group prayer or community rituals are more powerful than isolated and independent individual efforts to promote healing from a distance.) These experiments demonstrate the interconnectedness of all beings and all dimensions.

One difficulty with the looking glass, or any other physical analogy, is that it still perpetuates the idea of a dichotomy, like that of spirit/matter, brain/mind, or heaven/earth. We must somehow be able to see ourselves, the mirror and frame, *and* the reflection as a whole within an even larger whole.

For example, a colleague was rapidly deteriorating from an alleged HIV-induced decimation of her immune system, fading in and out of consciousness. One day I gave her a black-and-white photograph I had taken and carefully developed. Seeing it, she sighed and asked how I knew to offer it to her. "That's exactly how I have been feeling," she remarked. The next day she passed from this incarnation. The photo was of a basket of kittens looking at themselves in a mirror. It was impossible to distinguish between the furry, playful animals and their reflections. We need metaphors, like the Zen moon-in-the-water concept: the image in the water is the subject and the moon in the sky is the object, and "moon-in-the-water" is a field jointly created by the apparently separate subject and object. But the metaphor, too, is part of a larger field encompassed by our mind.

Even the process of selecting a metaphor reveals the requirement for some overarching element, like conscious intent. Such an element is necessary to account for a particular choice from among many available options. The simplest answer to the question of how creation works is that conscious intent has the power to collapse infinite possibilities into manifestation.

Conscious Intentions

The ongoing flow of conscious intentions continually shaping matter and energy in our universe never ceases. Making individual choices is like paddling one's canoe in it, taking advantage of eddies and whirlpools, but unable to stop the stream whose origin lies in some unfathomable spring. So the issue for individual conscious beings is how to express intent while in the continuous flow. The answer lies in the moment-to-moment choices people make, at the finite level where there is freedom to choose. To pose no resistance to the current is as much a choice as direct action. The Principle of Cause and Effect works in the act of nondecision as it does in deliberate choice.

Even with a small choice, one can manifest a different emotion (a form of subtle energy) than would occur from habit (past choices). For example, as mentioned earlier, the simple intention to be happy creates a neuropeptide out of the available stock of the hydrogen, carbon, oxygen, and other atoms in our brain cells. Thus, a single thought, while not redirecting the river, initiates a reaction that affects the human body's "canoe route." We need more research to identify the points where the "paddle" of individual intent can be most effectively inserted in the flow of life.

French scientist Jacques Benveniste and his colleagues, researching homeopathic medicine, found evidence to indicate that a treated liquid continues to have the same effect even after the liquid has been diluted to a point where no physical trace of the antiserum can be found. Their research suggests that something like an energetic trace or residue exists independent of the original material. (Schwarz and Russek in their book give many other examples of memories stored in seemingly inert matter.) If the patterns can be assumed to exist by their continuing effect (like the traces left by virtual particles), there must be a mechanism that communicates their instructions to the material involved.

While we do not yet understand the operating mechanism, such noumenal pattern traces can be projected by computer-generated light waves or by human thought. Rupert Sheldrake's description of morphic fields may explain how these non-matter-bound patterns can have such power. These fields, described as "thought bundles" by Nancy Parker in her fine novel *Omega Transmissions,* contain the invisible, but energized, constructs or patterns necessary for manifestation in the physical realm. Whether it is in the movement of material objects, the creation of a molecule, or the repatterning of genes, the above studies clearly suggest that some type of energy or force transmits the conscious intent to the matter involved.

Through the joint action of trace patterns and morphic fields, matter is influenced by ideas—whether latent memories or newly created ones. A latent memory trace may exist from a creative source outside our space-time or be the result from a long-ago conscious thought developed within our space-time.

(It could also be a residual from a previous life or shared memories.) A newly created field can come from almost any contemporaneous source.

Given the power of the ongoing river of consciousness, if parents-to-be do not consciously energize their intentions to shape DNA patterning at the time of conception, does the memory of an earlier creative act—embedded in the parents' genes—determine all the zygote's inheritance? The two possibilities appear to be either that all genetic instructions passed from parents to the newborn preexist conception, or that some new patterns are introduced. Thus far, we have only anecdotal accounts of correlations between parental images at conception with subsequent experiences of the child. However, may this be one way that microevolution (caused by conscious intent) occurs within a species?

It is interesting to speculate whether since the original appearance of the human species, whose genetic structure represented some "first" intention, there has been deliberate, external intervention (physical or mental). In other words, has some intermediate creative force subsequent to the initial unfolding of the species acted on the human gene pool? The next chapter suggests that the answer is yes. Regardless of the final answer to that question, I think it is reasonable to assume that every current genetic pattern, in any species, is the trace of a bygone creative thought.

Patterns Reflect Intent

The following graphic summarizes my inferences about the interplay of three aspects of our integral universe: the noumenal void (1) where infinite patterns exist; a subtle-energy field (2) where the intentions—expression of pattern—can cohere morphic fields; and matenergy (3) from which the morphic fields concentrate physical forms.[11] Only after one potential pattern is selected (by consciousness acting within itself), energized into a subtle form (in the intermediate realm), and manifested (balanced between cohesion and disintegration in the realm of matter and energy) do we have a space-time event.

Creative Event
Results in Space-Time

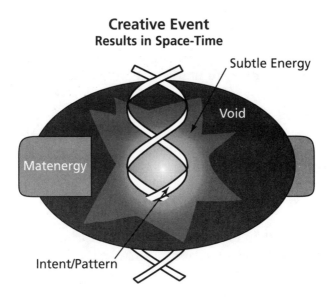

It would appear that we can draw on a preexisting repertory of the universe's patterns that can be rearranged by human will. (Perhaps they are the precursors of the mythical superstrings of modern physics.) In other words, at least at this point, the universe carries a set of inherent patterns that, when used in varying combinations and with appropriate energy, cause matenergy to manifest. Lynnclaire Dennis, during a near-death experience, perceived a series of intricate shapes and flow patterns that seemed to represent what we know about the inner relationships of the building blocks of life.[12] For several years now a group of scientists have been exploring the implications of using these patterns to understand the fundamental wave structure of the universe.

At this point it might be helpful to clarify possible confusion about the term "energy." In the context of space-time, electrical engineer Thomas Bearden helps us to understand that we use the word "energy" to describe both the capacity for activity and activity itself.[13] He and others see the capacity as the source. But as both the capacity and its active state are in space-time, as two aspects of a polarity, many agree there is another form of energy—sometimes called subtle energy. This is what I have described as the nonmaterial force activated by conscious intent that serves as the transforming medium. The concept of a subtle energy linking the two other aspects (physical and imaginal) of our universe implies consciousness is the highest-level "organizer." Prior to either an intentional or accidental joining of matter and energy comes the truly creative event, when the idea or pattern is first conceived. This purposeful thought or conscious intent that designs the initial pattern must come from the realm of either a local mind or general consciousness.

The experience of a three-faceted universe, where all facets coexist to the point of singularity, and are wholly interdependent, is difficult to model graphically. Michael Talbot and Itzhak Bentov (scientist and mechanical engineer, respectively) believed the holographic model moved closer to explaining the totality of such a multidimensional universe.[14] (Edgar Mitchell, *Apollo 14* astronaut and founder of the Institute for Noetic Sciences, is a current proponent of a hologram concept based on quantum mechanics.) In a hologram, you can literally know the whole from the part, a modern demonstration of the Principle of Correspondence. The smallest fragment of a holographic record can be broken off and still reflect the entire image when subjected to laser light. The hologram itself is a record of "interference patterns," that is, the way an object breaks up the waves of light from two directions. To make the image visible, the film is illuminated by a laser beam like that used in producing the hologram. The interference patterns then redistribute the laser waves (all the same frequency), revealing the photographed object suspended in a field of space.

The holographic principle is reflected in every human cell (except red blood), where all the DNA instructions for the entire complex of organs lie quiescent, yet capable of giving birth to whatever is ordered—a brain, a kidney, a toe. At the same time, each cell knows its own place, its own purpose. Geneticists involved in genome research believe the 95 percent of DNA formerly known as "junk" may include these instructions. The inescapable conclusion is that the patterns for any part exist in every part of the universe. Though invisible and unmeasurable, like the holographic laser beam, conscious intent converts their potentiality into actuality.

In the omnipresent noumena, decisions to manifest one part or the other are communicated instantaneously throughout the whole, unlimited by matter, energy, or the speed of light. Physicists demonstrate scientific proof of this capability by separating paired subatomic particles and registering that they react in tandem when either one is individually acted upon. Researchers also have caused one cluster of photons to disappear, only to find a cluster with identical information appear in a new location (the popularly known "Beam me up, Scotty" experiment[15]). Similarly, biologists prove the same point when they separate human white cells at great distances from the body and track the cells' reactions to changes in the donor body's state.[16] We see the result of the communications; we do not yet understand how it occurs.

Current theories positing explanations of this holographic communications phenomenon include Irish physicist John Bell's 1964 assertion that the primary substance of the universe is nonlocal (exists everywhere), and British physicist David Bohm's belief that an invisible field connects all matter and events in the universe.[17] This field is assumed to exist outside the domain of ordinary reality, clearly part of the other side of the glass in the mirror. It acts—like the Christian Holy Spirit and the Hindu Brahman—as the breath of life for cosmic beings.

The holographic construct, to some extent, raises a question about the Big Bang theory with which we must grapple (and for which quantum mechanics offers no easy explanation). Recall this book's opening chapter's descriptions of that "incomprehensible first second." How could the potential for everything that is now contained in the universe have survived in unconnected fragments blown apart 15 billion years ago? Yet its present entirety is still wholly represented within each infinitesimal part. This fact illustrates the Principle of Correspondence, where microcosm reflects macrocosm and vice versa.

Now to the next question. At what point does organic, self-reproducing life (in contrast to general innate consciousness) enter the picture? How does the generic breath of life become focused in a pattern that informs a living entity?

Life from Matenergy

We can gain some insight into the dynamic of conscious creation by examining the building blocks (larger than the subatomic ones discussed earlier) of organic systems. Atoms make up organic submolecules such as sugars and aminos. Combinations of these submolecules result in molecules that in turn combine to create the nucleic acids (DNA and RNA), proteins, carbohydrates, and lipids that make up living cells. The cells then link together to form tissues. Tissues make up organs, which in turn make up fully functioning systems such as the human body. All such local acts of creation must take existing elements and build with and upon them: nothing totally new is manifested in what is essentially an act of reorganization.

Human knowledge today encompasses the capacity for gene information (DNA) manipulation that reorganizes and duplicates life-forms. But we do not yet know how to create a totally new species. It is possible that some level of conscious beings exists, between humans and the ultimate yin/yang Grand Couple, with the capability to co-design and activate new species. However, we are currently unaware of beings with this power.

We humans have a keen interest in learning whether we can achieve that level of knowledge and skill. The central question is whether the technology involves physical or mental manipulations. Or both. If consciousness is the primary force in creation, do humans individually or collectively possess enough of it to manifest new life-forms through conscious intent? Or are we limited to reorganizing that which is already here? Let's review what we know about life arising in the universe.

Louis Pasteur, who discovered how to use heat to kill microbes in food, "proved" to the French Academy in 1864 that life on Earth could not have arisen spontaneously. Earlier experimenters had mistakenly supported the idea that life could arise on its own because organisms had begun to grow in solutions they had prepared. The problem was that they had not excluded airborne microbes. Pasteur proved that the organisms in those test tubes came from airborne microbes. By insuring no airborne microbes could get into his solutions, Pasteur dealt a mortal blow with his experiment to Aristotle's idea that a particular mixture of inorganic particles could by chance spring into life. Nineteenth-century scientists were left with the obvious: seeds of new life anywhere in the universe must come from somewhere else.

Still unconvinced, twentieth-century science continued to seek the creating link between inert chemicals and life-forms. Remember that the *italicized* conventional story in chapter 1, recounting the development of elements and celestial bodies in the universe, does not include the development of life-forms. Biologists have assumed a chance formulation of life, and focused on trying to understand the process of mutation and evolution among single-cell and higher life-forms. No one has yet shown how to bridge the gap from inert matter to a single-cell organism.

Cyril Ponnamperuma at the University of Maryland and many other chemists have tried to fill the breach. One theory he examined is that extreme heat, such as that found in volcanoes at the bottom of the ocean, may serve as the catalyst for the spontaneous production of bacteria. An earlier hypothesis held that lightning bolts struck the rich ocean soup and catalyzed chemical bonding, resulting in a cell that could move and regenerate itself. The applications of huge amounts of energy in various forms (heat and electrical) in many experiments have failed to prove such a hypothesis.

In fact, science has not revealed how the first cell of any particular life-form got started. However, once initiated, cells reproduce their own kind according to patterns of DNA and RNA. The DNA form nucleotides, or letters of the genetic code. This code, or message, is contained in the way the molecules are bound together and aligned in a long, ladder-like chain. The RNA molecules play a role in transferring and interpreting genetic messages.[18] The central point here is that the DNA, assisted by "messenger" and "transfer" RNA, dictates all activity in the body—chemical manufacture, transfer, modification, and usage. DNA is the blueprint that shapes life-forms and the operating manual that sustains them. But we are left with the question: What architect designed the DNA and the "editor" genes that rearrange it?

Were all potential DNA blueprints present in the noumena at the universe's creation, awaiting activation according to a built-in schedule or changes in environmental conditions? If so, how do they become activated? Social scientist Jean Houston teaches that human potential is encoded, waiting to be released by experience and conscious efforts. She draws on the Greek concept of entelechy (promoted by German embryologist Hans Driesch in the early part of the last century) that implies an innate, nonphysical drive to self-fulfillment. This view means that all beings, in effect, are programmed to activate and develop within an inherent range of potential. It may be characterized as the "seedbed" theory. In a self-learning universe, once activated, organisms would possess some ability to physically adapt from one generation to another on the basis of experience. We call this microevolution.

Whatever the source, all life on Earth—from the simplest virus to the human being—has a common base. The human genome has approximately 3 billion individual links or base pairs that provide the blueprint for the multibillion-celled human body. The Human Genome Project, funded by the U.S. National Institutes of Health and Britain's Wellcome Trust, finished mapping the coded sequence of all these fragments on each gene in 2000. The common earthworm, by contrast, has only 959 cells (including 302 nerve cells). Although the two bodies exist on vastly different scales, the same genetic principles apply.

Does the Earthly genome contain the basis for all life in the universe? The presence of comparable forms in meteorites reportedly from Mars indicates there may be a common base, at least in our solar system. Examination of alien beings may reveal that Earth residents possess the same key as life anywhere in the universe. But until we are certain we have definite samples of off-planet AB or AB-human hybrids, geneticists are limited to the manipulation of Earth species. (A number of reports allege the U.S. government already has access to this information.)

Have humans finally eaten of the mythical tree of knowledge by achieving the skill of genetic engineering? Tomatoes, celery, carrots, peppers, potatoes, corn, coffee, and other crops have been "improved" through genetic manipulation to increase durability and corporate profits. With recombinant DNA, genetic engineers can take genes from one species (either plant or animal) and splice them to others. For example, chicken protein makes potatoes more resistant to microbial infections, and Arctic fish protein prevents frozen vegetables from turning soggy. More recent developments involve altering genes in fish and animals to make them grow larger and produce more edible meat. (Many people have grave concerns about the negative unintended side effects of such genetic engineering.)

Other initiatives are under way to use genetic manipulation to cure human diseases. Retrovirus-based technology is now used to treat some illnesses by inserting new DNA between the tail and head of the diseased cell. Several researchers have attempted similar processes to cure certain forms of cancer and AIDS.

Could retroviruses—they invade and modify the cell's genetic code—be vehicles for significant redesigning of the human gene pool? The 1997 announcements of successful mammalian cloning with adult DNA led some to believe that the long-run limits of genetic manipulation may be constrained only by the human imagination.

Reports of the side effects from genetically modified foods and experimental gene therapy have revealed the Pandora's box nature of such work. After the first successful cloning of animals (Dolly the sheep) and reproduction of replacement organs for human transplants, the ethical as well as the practical issues of genetic manipulation have become a public priority. Many are concerned that we may have unleashed a monster without knowing the implications of such alterations to the rest of the natural system.

While scientists can manipulate the genetic content, they do not yet understand the genetic off/on switch that results in cell differentiation, or how different tissues derive from what started as a single cell. While humans have identified the keys to the reorganization of life-forms, they know neither how to duplicate the keys nor how the original set was made.

Power of Thought

The use of conscious intent may turn out to be a more effective route to human participation in the life-creation process, including health maintenance, than purely mechanical manipulation. Examples given earlier in this chapter demonstrate how the mind calls into existence simple matter (neuropeptides) and influences energy (the flow of current). It remains for us to explore the possibilities for human use of general consciousness in more direct creation. To add to the earlier discussion of Pert's, Becker's, and White's work, let's review more examples of what we know about the ability of the human mind to influence the behavior of matter. Then perhaps we can reasonably hypothesize a role for the human mind as a catalyst to life.

Long before Cleve Backster, whose research stimulated the best-selling *Secret Life of Plants,* hooked his interspecies-communication-testing polygraph equipment to the leaves of a *Dracaena massangeana* (a common house plant),[19] the Kahunas (traditional shamans) of Hawaii taught people to ask the desired food for its permission before harvesting it to eat. Traditional Hawaiians believe plants and animals have feelings about their purpose and function in the food chain, and appreciate being asked and honored before being eaten. Generations of experience have taught them that plants taken home after a sincere request live and flourish, while those unceremoniously ripped out do not. Believing an omniscient consciousness extends to rocks as well, they do not haul them from their place, knowing the spirits of the rocks can make trouble. The local Hawaii post offices reportedly receive rocks returned by tourists with plaintive notes asking that they be taken back to the mountain from which they came.

Similarly, the Native American tradition of asking permission of the game before hunting it and of vegetation before its gathering, then thanking them before eating, is rooted in an appreciation of both the physical connections and the conscious channels that link all living species. These people, too, believe the foods we consume have feelings that deserve expressions of our respect.

Backster's research on the communication link between human and other species has confirmed that the response of living cells to the prospect of being eaten is muted when humans tell them in advance what is to happen. He has found that unplanned acts by the researcher to boil an egg or eat yogurt result in intracellular agitation, measurable by electronic sensors. Conversely, he has found that the researcher's expressing the intention in advance has a "calming" effect on the food cells. Such examples of the impact of thoughts or intentions on matter illustrate the flow of some level of communications between the human mind and organic materials.

Assuming there is an ongoing, reciprocal flow of such behavior-influencing communications among local concentrations of consciousness (animals, plants, and individual cells), how does the conscious being deliberately intervene in the natural flow to bring about a desired end? The answer—at this point, it's an intuitive one—involves a clarity of focus grounded in strong emotional energy.

The process appears to work in a manner analogous to the progression from gas through liquids to solids. Within three phases (conceptualization, energization, and actualization) there are three incremental steps, like moving from amorphous through evolving to clear. Look at table 4 as you read the next sentences. A vague new idea falls into the amorphous step. Once this idea evolves into a clear concept, its patterns are defined enough to create a morphic field in the realm of subtle energy. There the potential image enters a state of becoming, like virtual reality. As the pattern, now turned into amorphous form, becomes definite, it actualizes in the material realm. One can observe the three progressive small steps in each of the phases: idea (to conceptualize), motion (to energize), and form (to actualize). Ayurvedic philosophy divides all existence into three analogous *doshas* (categories): *vata* (thought), *pitta* (initiative), and *kapha* (endurance). These three phases will be central to the further development of the three-faceted model in chapter 4. The sequential process applies to agriculture, food preparation, health, psychokinesis, sports, politics, or economics.

Table 4. Three Steps in Creation		
Conceptualize	Energize	Actualize
Idea	Motion	Form
Amorphous	Potential	Space
Evolving	Becoming	Energy
Clear	Definite	Matter

The idea of democracy first starts with clarity about a few basic assumptions. Only when a number of individuals attach emotional support to the idea does democracy have real potential. That emotional energy translated to action results in the practice of democracy. Similarly, a vision of health must be underpinned by emotional commitment in order for the cells to get the message to do their part and for the individual to eat appropriately. To facilitate the bending of a spoon through conscious intent, one focuses the intention on the metal. The metal's atoms become agitated. When the concentration of matter softens, only a slight pressure can bend the spoon. (I have experimented with this process several times and have a pile of oddly twisted spoons and forks on my desk to show the results.)

Can this process apply to direct manifestation of new objects, with a sufficient level of conscious intent? The Principle of Correspondence predicts that the operation of this three-step process in the more tangible realm means an analogous one works within and between the other realms. If this is true, currently perceived constraints on the role of mind in the interaction of matter and energy may actually be due to false or limited interpretations of universal laws. If a thought is more than a fleeting fantasy of potential, emotionally energized to a level of probability, will it be realized? Or are there certain categories of thoughts that cannot be actualized in space-time? When we learn the answers to these questions, will we command the power to affect or even create new matter, or even life, through conscious intent?

The literature of yogis and saints describes manifestations of such powers. Their experiences suggest fertile areas for independent research efforts. Unraveling the generic principles would help us to consciously manage them.

Nature Limits Us

Let's review some currently available evidence to see if it suggests natural limits to our powers as conscious creators of life. By examining selected experiments, I believe we can begin to develop a sense of the limits of the creative powers of human consciousness.

A previously mentioned experiment at the subatomic level may help us better understand this as yet undefined medium—variously referred to as *chi, prana,* ether, or some other subtle force—that affects matter. In 1775, Franz Anton Mesmer labeled the unknown force "animal magnetism" or universal life force; hence, our current use of the term "mesmerized" to indicate the use of an unexplained force. When physicists split a pair of photons and project one to the opposite end of an accelerator, their manipulation of one photon is accompanied by an instantaneous counteraction in the other; that is, when one manipulates the negatively charged particle, the positively charged particle reacts in a complementary fashion. It is as if both exist in some form of hyperspace where distance is immaterial, a phenomenon currently unexplained by established science.

The separated, but obvious, action-reaction link suggests that the subtle force field, perhaps parallel with the electromagnetic spectrum, is not bound by ordinary space-time. Something like the principle involved in this physics experiment could account for many so-called paranormal experiences. Humans appear to actively manipulate that subtle (connective) force in many situations: using hands to massage a person's aura field, manipulating objects with psychokinesis, telepathic communications.

Recent research by Cleve Backster (reported by Robert B. Stone) shows the same magic (i.e., something still unexplained) at work between matter separated from human beings and their subsequent thoughts. Backster has conducted experiments in which white cells taken from a person and transported miles away react to changes in the mental state of the donor. By simultaneously monitoring the activities and emotions of the donor and the electromagnetic activity of the stored cells, Backster has been able to chart significant correlations of the latter with the former.

Remote "senders" at the Institute for Resonance Therapy in Cappenberg, Germany, help to improve the health of forests, gardens, and lakes by mentally focusing positive images on plants and marine life. As in Backster's work, the institute staff's emotional charge connected with specific images seems to activate organic cells at a distance. The plant and animal cells absorb food and resist pollutants more vigorously.[20]

The energy or communication flow is instantaneous, with no apparent attenuation of speed over distance. From this work, we know we can act through the subtle-energy field at a distance, but the question of limits remains unanswered. Such thoughts may travel faster than the speed of light, which for decades has been assumed to be absolute. That hypothesis could, using Backster's research protocol, be adequately tested on interplanetary trips like NASA Mars missions.

Given the research highlighted here, it is now justifiable for a prudent person to accept that mind does communicate with and influence matter at the subatomic and cellular levels.

Through the mechanism of thinking, consciousness or mind shapes reality in more ways than we can currently conceive. It is important to remember, however, that human consciousness—individually and collectively—can shape microcosmic reality only within limits, due to certain characteristics of the organism of which we are parts. One of these limits appears to be the direction of the arrow of time.

Some assume that if there is a "prime mover" there must also be a "prime motion" characteristic to the universe. In our space-time universe, the direction in which microscopic particles move (flow of time) determines an important aspect of their nature. For example, a particle can be either a positron or an electron, depending on the direction it is traveling. A positron becomes an electron when it is forced to move in the opposite direction. This seems to indicate that we cannot simultaneously change the nature of a phenomenon and maintain its directionality.

To change a vector (velocity combined with magnitude and direction) of anything requires the application of a greater force. For example, light travels in a straight line unless it is bent by a great star—or other powerful center of gravity—that warps the light of local space-time. If humans were able to apply enough force, perhaps they could affect the flow of time, but not without counterbalancing consequences (Principles of Polarity and Correspondence).

Physicists have speculated that worm holes or super-strings may make it possible for some types of matter to travel faster than others, thereby having the effect of going backwards, but these theories do not dispose of the argumentation set forth here. The only way we have to conceive of and measure time is from our observation of the sequential accumulation of concrete events. It seems that only a power beyond our universe can mitigate the influence of its inherent arrow of time.

Another constraint on the power of mind appears to be the innate mortality of ordinary matter. Each entity in the universe, as a function of its specific design, has a built-in time to expire. Even at the most elementary level, each particle, atom, and element has its own cycle, after which a rebirth is necessary for a new cycle to commence (Principle of Rhythm). These life cycles range from a nanosecond for subatomic particles to eons for star systems.

For example, the human life span appears to be related to the duration of the Earth's rotation around the Sun. The implication of biorhythms and other patterns is that the power of any level of consciousness less than the ultimate must operate within inherent constraints. Discovery of the constraints operative in this stellar neighborhood would make it possible to infer the degree of power its beings have for conscious co-creation.

If this principle affects the process of gene therapy, we may have a challenge to our current methodology. Experimentation is now under way to extend life by direct insertion of new DNA fragments. Can renewal of time-degraded DNA be accomplished by a conscious act?

If the momentary expression of an individual's intent to be joyful can create molecules, what could thousands of united minds (group mind) accomplish in one powerful expression of emotional energy sent coursing through animals, plants, and ecosystems alike? As the mental/energetic effort is scaled up, the physical effect is likely to move up proportionately.

Since the 1987 Harmonic Convergence ritual involving thousands of synchronized meditators, groups have attempted to affect world events. By judicious extrapolation from such experiments, it may be possible to calculate just how much prayer is necessary to heal a malignant tumor, or how many meditators are required to bring peace to squabbling factions, or how to reverse trends in local ecosystems and microclimates.

Another constraint is the reverse flow of influence that matter has on consciousness. The ingestion of certain substances by the body's cells can influence the person's state of consciousness, as can the removal of substances on which the body has come to depend. For example, a deficiency in serotonin (an important brain chemical, or neurotransmitter) has been related to an increase in depression or anxiety, and the ingestion of melatonin (another chemical, secreted by the pineal gland) appears to induce sleep. The conscious being has to continually deal with such material influences on its mind and energy.

All activity in the universe, then, appears to be subject to certain inherent constraints, yet some of those constraints may be more malleable than we have thought. For example, some physicists now question the immutability of Newton's Law of Gravity, positing that its effect may be a function of charge rather than mass.[21] Meditators who levitate point to a possible answer. Humans should test and retest each perceived barrier to our use of mind. We are likely to learn that many barriers fall by the wayside as the scope of conscious awareness expands.

From Cells to Systems

The universe has a built-in impulse toward increasing complexity, balanced by another impulse toward consolidation. The combination of constructive and destructive principles informs the growth and differentiation of organic systems from cells. Assuming the Principle of Correspondence, better understanding of the dynamics of biological systems will likely lead to more effective approaches to behavioral issues. Both involve the science of information and are more fully discussed in part 3.

The most elementary form of organic life appears to be at the cellular level. (Science currently dates the first microorganism on Earth to around 3.85 billion years ago.) A living cell is a chemical factory of life, becoming so through the ordering power of DNA instructions. The pattern of the widely recognized double helix determines what kind of cell the molecules will organize themselves into. Depending on the instructions, the cell either becomes a self-sustaining organism or fulfills a specialized role as part of a larger system.

Following its internal DNA guidance, a cell—comprising nucleus, cytoplasm, and other organelles—takes its place as part of a whole tissue in plants and animals. The tissue in turn is but a subsystem of the organs for which it serves as building material. These organs join to make possible living organisms, including humans—the most complex organism of which we are now directly aware. The DNA principles appear to be conducive to more and more complex beings, suggesting it is likely there are beings more complex than humans elsewhere in the universe. Since the material building blocks can be rearranged by infinite DNA patterns, the degree of complexity is likely to be a function more of consciousness than of physical constraints.

Spectroscopic and other measures of light, radio waves, and particulate radiation show the Earth's elements and compounds are not unlike those elsewhere in the cosmos. Physics and chemistry that appear universal lead to the tentative conclusion that the same building blocks of life may exist throughout the whole (Principle of Correspondence).

The living cell is a microcosmic manifestation of all the Hermetic Principles. Each cell has a definite rhythm to its life cycle. Its maintenance of boundaries, the internal dynamics of its components, the intake of new matter, and its reproductive mechanism have a striking correspondence to the lives of other living systems, including star systems. The responsiveness of cells in their service as building blocks for organs and larger living systems demonstrates the working of Cause and Effect. Cell behavior illustrates the omnipresence of Vibration. Its subparts clearly show the working of Polarity, and Gender is operative throughout cell regeneration. Thus, we can learn much about the whole organism as we focus on the cells.

If my reflections on the interconnections among all levels of life and the influence of transcendent principles throughout our universe are correct, we can extrapolate from the subparts to build new hypotheses. For example, study of an anomalous interaction in particle physics (the above-mentioned separated photons reacting simultaneously) leads to insights about the execution of psychokinesis (thoughts affecting matter at a distance). Both involve instantaneous communication through subtle channels. Discoveries in either area could also help increase knowledge of the dynamics of successful prayer.

Humanity has its own particular place of power. The unique impact of human consciousness on the phenomenal realm is made feasible by our "in-between" character. We are more than biologically determined extrapolations from a lower animal order, yet we are not total masters of our own fate. Better understanding of the microcosm should result in a more accurate sense of our limitations and freedoms.

Microcosm Reflects the Whole

From the perspective of the Hermetic Principle of Correspondence, we can apply insights from the microcosm to other aspects of life in our universe. An example of the correspondence between levels is the behavior of atoms roughly simulating the actions of heavenly bodies. In an experiment with the "Rydberg atom" in which electrons are artificially placed far away from the nucleus, the orbiting electrons behave like planets. Such examples do not definitively prove the Principle of Correspondence, but they do provide the basis for such a hypothesis.

Attention to the quantum, molecular, and cellular levels has provided sufficient evidence to reveal the connections among the realms of matenergy, subtle force, and consciousness. Having split the atom in the era of fission, humans can now focus on extrapolating micro-insights to larger individual and societal issues (see chapter 9), taking the path of integration of knowledge and experience to an era of gentle fusion. This is not to be confused with the misguided government-funded effort to harness useful and safe energy from "hot" fusion.

The modern scientific focus on breaking down the microcosmic level—identifying the "trees" in the "forest"—has resulted in great advances in physics, chemistry, and biology. With a shift to focus on finding the connections among microcosmic fundamentals, we should begin to perceive patterns that we did not know existed—Gregory Bateson's "patterns that connect." The holographic nature of the universe insures that patterns in the microcosm will lead us to patterns of the whole.

An unfailing impulse toward wholeness within each person animates the movement toward a new sense of the whole. A friend of mine, who at age fourteen realized her oneness with all of creation, has spent her adult life trying to explain it and elaborate it through literature. William Blake had his experience of unity at age four and sought to communicate it through poetry and engraving.

Philosopher Renee Weber[22] has identified this search for transcendent principles as a common trait among mystics and scientists who forge new paths in history. For example, Plato thought perfect forms were the inner fabric of reality. Newton believed his Law of Gravitation unified all masses in the universe. Maxwell identified the unity of magnetism and electricity. Einstein experienced his transcendent awareness through an intuitive encounter with the reality of relativity. He elaborated on its implications for several decades and spent the last thirty years of his life seeking to unify matter and energy and space-time into a singular force.

An entire generation of physicists has followed in Einstein's footsteps, seeking to integrate their abstract concepts into the Grand Unified Theory. Although the search for that single integrative principle before all mutually exclusive but complementary principles have been sorted out may be premature, their impulse to do so is a natural human trait. We perpetually seek our individual and collective answers to the puzzle of Humpty-Dumpty: how do we put the pieces together again?

A recent example of such impatience is Steven Weinberg's *Dreams of a Final Theory*.[23] A Nobel prize winner for showing (with two other physicists) how two forces of nature (weak force and electromagnetism) could have been unified in an early phase of the universe, Weinberg believes that the current scientific paradigm will soon reveal all the fundamental laws of nature, included in some beautiful yet fixed "theory of everything." Unfortunately, as is clear from mind-over-matter, telepathy, and other so-called paranormal experiences of ordinary life, the materialistic and deterministic theories of

Weinberg and his colleagues still omit a large part of our universe's reality. Any effort to formulate a unifying theory must account for the role of consciousness at the microcosmic level, described in this chapter, and the as yet poorly understood subtle-energy medium through which it works its way in matter and energy.

Practical Implications

The admonition of Alexander Pope, "The proper study of mankind is man," now assumes even greater relevance. Within ourselves and in our conscious interaction with the universe, we employ all the elements necessary for exploring the connections among consciousness, the subtle energies and matenergy within the context of space-time. We are the most obvious subjects at the present time for testing hypotheses explaining the effects of consciousness on matter and vice versa. Our challenge is to study ourselves in an integrated way, beyond the current divisions of scientific and academic disciplines. The purely physical scientist leaves out consideration of consciousness and therefore the vital base of a triangular reality. The mystic or spiritualist eschews a powerful medium of communication with nonbelievers when he or she refuses to subject personal hypotheses to scientific scrutiny.

Although most physicists today attempt to dissect the moment of the Big Bang, they hesitate to theorize about the nature of that which existed prior to the explosion of the single point. Metaphysicians usually do not hesitate to hypothesize that matter is controlled by consciousness. Ancient wisdom, such as the Hermetic Principles and other esoteric concepts, assumes that the reconciliation of these different facets of experience lies in a broader vision of reality. *Our Solarian Legacy* suggests the unity may best be conceptualized via a comprehensive metascience that transcends current science and metaphysics.

Subsuming the outer testing of physics (a mystical endeavor itself) and the inner questing of metaphysics under a metascience of human self-exploration and experimentation could lead to unparalleled insights into the nature of this universe. Gaining an understanding of the human capacity to think thoughts that create matter will begin to reveal the dynamics of the Old Testament, Logos-based theory of creation of the material universe. Experiments using inputs of individual and group consciousness in hypothesis-testing interplay with natural events and with other beings will identify the extent to which humanity is truly a co-creative force in the evolution of the universe.

Some examples of this possibility are had in the disparate experiments at Princeton's PEAR Lab (mentioned earlier, they are led by Robert Jahn and Brenda Dunne) and the Fortean Research Center in Lincoln, Nebraska,[24] that demonstrate the impact of intent on the behavior of material objects. The Princeton work provides mainstream scientific evidence of the ability of humans to have an impact on the behavior of plastic balls and computer-controlled experiments in affecting random patterns. By the expression of intent, individuals and small groups can cause statistically significant deviations from the normal distributions of balls in a mechanical apparatus and of numbers in a computer-software-controlled random-numbers generator. In the Fortean experiments, the ability of subjects to manipulate small objects at a distance (psychokinesis) is measured by the standards of traditional science. Widespread application of these findings to other fields will contribute greatly to expanding the frontiers of knowledge of consciousness-matter interactions.

When basic principles are discovered at the microcosmic level, practical insights easily follow. The field of health is a good illustration. Instead of misdirecting billions of dollars in public resources into inappropriate, externally based chemical and mechanistic medical research, we would be wiser to study the internal cellular changes wrought by the human mind in the dynamics of the self-healing process.

Cancer is a good example. Almost three decades and untold billions of dollars after the passage of the National Cancer Act—an official declaration of a "war on cancer"—we still do not know what causes cancer or how to stop it. New types develop and spread. One out of three Americans now alive will develop a malignancy. Melanoma, a skin cancer, is becoming the fastest-growing cancer in the world.

In search of explanations, some hypothesize that ultraviolet rays, unfiltered due to ozone depletion, shrivel DNA.[25] Others see the roots of growing cancer rates in oxygen deprivation or electromagnetic field anomalies. Many now point to possible genetic causes. Yet in a healthy human body, the immune system routinely kills cancer cells as they develop. Problems arise only when the immune system goes awry. Since we do not know how the immune system works, we do not know why it fails.

The matter-to-matter approach of allopathic (conventional) medicine includes antibody research (attaching killer cells to cancer cells) and toxin delivery systems (matching toxins to the cancer cell receptors). Yet metastasis—the spread of cancer to other parts of the body—more often than not outwits these localized cancer "fighting" efforts. (Perhaps if we had begun by calling it something other than war, we would have conjured up less resistance, less of an enemy.)

Chemo-prevention, finding anticancer chemicals in food that naturally feed the cells, is receiving increased attention. It has more success because natural systems spread the effects of food more efficiently than do drugs alien to body processes. While there is some progress in identifying natural substances that activate natural healing systems,[26] too little attention is given to exploring the microcosmic-level interactions among the three fields whose reciprocal play determines the health of organic life: mind, body, and emotions.

The seminal work now being done on the power of an individual's positive attitudes and conscious intent to heal oneself deserves to be society's top priority, as does the healing effect of the conscious intent of others expressed through prayer, touch, and other forms of explicit conscious support. Such practices involve the whole-body communication systems and the mind-body-energy nexus at the atomic and cellular levels described in this chapter, and avoid the attack-oriented approach of conventional treatments.

Deliberate patterns of thought energize the cells in the body to return to a state of wholeness that effectively eliminates the virulent symptoms. The mental message communicated to the cells is that they can and should reject this or that as an outsider. Such natural responses avoid the side effects of typical allopathic blockbuster doses that frequently do more harm than good. Conscious intent, by precipitating the response of the *whole* system, enables the body to reject the disease patterns.

This chapter exemplifies the metascientific approach by integrating cutting edge research from the physical sciences with innovative studies of the interactions of consciousness and subtle energies with the material realm. It demonstrates ways in which conscious intent influences the microcosm of particles and cells and suggests how subtle energies facilitate that interaction. The result is an expanded vision of the potential humans have to consciously participate in the natural system and their ongoing development.

Notes

1. Michio Kaku, *Hyperspace: A Scientific Odyssey Through Parallel Universes, Time Warps and the Tenth Dimension* (New York: Anchor Books/Doubleday, 1998).

2. Peter Russell, "Mysterious Light," *Noetic Sciences Review* (December 1999-March 2000).

3. Richard Morris, *The Edge of Science* (New York: Simon & Schuster, 1990).

4. Gabor Belovari, "IANS Updates," *New Science News* (Spring 1993).

5. Candace Pert, *Molecules of Emotion: Why You Feel the Way You Do* (New York: Charles Scribner, 1997).

6. Michael Talbot, *The Holographic Universe* (New York: HarperCollins, 1991).

7. Deepak Chopra, *Quantum Healing: Exploring the Frontiers of Mind/Body Medicine* (New York: Bantam Books, 1989).

8. Celeste White, "Consciousness and Gene Regulation." Proceedings, Conference of International Association for New Science, Denver, CO, October 1996.

9. Robert O. Becker and Gary Selden, *The Body Electric* (New York: William Morrow, 1985).

10. Information on the scientific study of consciousness related to physical phenomena by the PEAR Laboratory at Princeton University can be found at Web site www. princeton.edu/~pear/.

11. Paul Von Ward with Harold Puthoff and Paramahamsa Tewari, *Free Energy* (Video, vols. 2 and 3) (Ashland, OR: New Renaissance Communications, 1994). Note the discussions of advanced physics.

12. Lynnclaire Dennis, *The Pattern* (Mendocino, CA: Entagram Productions, Inc., 1997).

13. T. E. Bearden, *The Final Secret of Free Energy* (Huntsville, AL: Association of Distinguished American Scientists, 1993).

14. Itzhak Bentov, *A Cosmic Book* (Rochester, NY: Destiny Books, 1988).

15. "Teleportation" experiment by University of Innsbruck in Austria reported in *Nature*, December 1999. Anton Zeiling and colleagues wanted to see if they could teleport quantum information. They destroyed photons in one space and had them simultaneously show up at another location.

16. Robert B. Stone, *The Secret Life of Your Cells* (Westchester, PA: Whitford Press, 1989). This book deals with Cleve Backster's research.

17. Ilya Prigogine and Isabelle Stenger, *Order Out of Chaos* (London: Heineman, 1984); James Gleick, *Chaos* (New York: Penguin Books, 1987); David Bohm, *The Undivided Universe: An Ontological Interpretation of Quantum Theory* (London: Routledge, 1992), and *Wholeness and the Implicate Order* (London: Routledge and Kegan Paul, 1980).

18. James D. Watson, *Double Helix* (New York: Atheneum, 1985).

19. Peter Tompkins and Christopher Bird, *The Secret Life of Plants* (New York: Harper & Row, 1973).

20. Institute for Resonance Therapy, Am Struckmannsberg 32, D-44534 Lunen, Germany (e-mail: IRT-Cappenberg@T-Online.de).

21. B. Haisch, A. Rueda, and H.E. Puthoff, "Beyond E= Mc^2," *The Sciences* (November-December 1994); 26–31.

22. Renee Weber, *Dialogues with Scientists and Sages: The Search for Unity* (London: Routledge and Kegan Paul, 1986).

23. Steven Weinberg, *Dreams of a Final Theory* (New York: Pantheon, 1993).

24. Martin Caidin, "Telekinesis Demonstration," *Fate* (January 1994).

25. Linda Murray, "The Cancer War: Stories from the Front," *Omni* (February-March 1993); 50–56.

26. Meecie Moore, *The Miracle of Aloe Vera: The Facts About Polymannan* (Dallas, TX: Charis Publishing, 1995).

3

The Earth Perspective

Most people who have calculated the odds now believe in the likelihood of many species of conscious beings in the vast expanse of our universe. We cannot be certain that Earth-like conditions are necessary for highly developed life-forms. Given the range of conditions that support life on Earth, it is reasonable to assume that many natural habitats would support various species. Obviously, a viable location must have physical conditions that support a system of mutually supporting life-forms. Advanced beings in other solar systems would be embedded in their respective local "webs of life" with complementary flora and fauna. Local energetics, subtle as well as ordinary, would have to be conducive to organic life.

But the essential ingredient may be the presence of concentrations of conscious intent. In other words, sufficient numbers of nonphysical entities may have to be desirous of physical incarnation.

With humans embedded in our planetary matrix of life-forms, physical and energetic, the Principle of Correspondence would predict that stellar-based systems are nested in an extended galactic family, and that the galactic is nested in the universal. As yet undiscovered symbioses undoubtedly smoothly link all these levels of organic life and consciousness.

Much available evidence already points to the existence of an extended society of cosmic beings, with whom many of us have already reported contact. I believe we possess something of our extended family's cosmic heritage. To prove it, we need to review documented legends, ancient artifacts, historical records, existing science and technology, and current social institutions. To get the most accurate fix on who we are, many scholars must cooperatively study the blanks in the official story; all human experiences not explained by conventional wisdom must be analyzed. Only then will we have a more valid picture of humanity's history and destiny, what I call our Solarian legacy.

Human beings are poised between the microcosm and the macrocosm, somewhere in the vibrating totality of the living universe. What is our place in this marvel? Unique creatures in a divine garden, especially created by a personal god for a religious purpose? A cosmic accident, the unlikely coincidence of random mechanical and chemical forces that somehow evolved into beings capable of pondering the nature of their own existence? Figments of a divine imagination entertaining itself? A more satisfactory answer than any of these must draw on a broad range of available evidence from the past and present. In my view, we are both less and more than we think we are.

We are less than the sole progeny of a personal godlike entity totally devoted to our quotidian and mundane concerns. The current deification of human beings (Jesus, Mohammed, Buddha, Krishna, and others) does not appropriately honor the nature of our cosmic parentage. We are more than the mutations of a process of random biological evolution. I believe we are full members of a large and diverse community of conscious beings situated throughout the space-time of an alive universe. We are inextricably connected with all of them and all facets of our universe. Unfortunately, the current limitations of our habitual assumptions and our intellectual blinders may restrict us to a diminished role in the cosmos. The following pages empower us by suggesting an expanded concept of who we are.

Self-Learning Beings

We are more Solarians than just planetary beings. There are sixty-six moons in our solar system, and sixteen have water, one basic ingredient necessary for organic life. (Five have both water and an atmosphere, and one has only an atmosphere.) Mars appears to have been capable of supporting life before it lost most of its atmosphere (for reasons not yet known). A number of esoteric traditions and some scientists suggest that humans may have originated on Mars. Other sources of information, primarily channeled, attribute earlier life-forms to other planets. This and the following facts seem to me to warrant our thinking of ourselves as Solarians.

Our Sun's nurturing warmth facilitates life in our planetary system, through the process of photosynthesis and heat-generated chemosynthesis. Photosynthesis has produced the primary deposits of coal, gas, and oil that have made possible the rise of modern petroleum-based, techno-mechanical society. Photosynthesis in plants provides for the conversion of inorganic substances into food that sustains animal and human life that could not otherwise exist. So, even as potential space-voyaging beings, humans, as a function of their incarnation, are ultimately linked to this solar system.

Beyond providing life support, our solar system seems to shape the inner design of planetary organisms. For example, the irreducible dimension of sunlight is about the size of the surface of a cell. Sunlight's resolution—the shortest distance a visible photon can travel before colliding with a higher-energy photon—corresponds to the distance between base pairs along the double helix structure of DNA. Thus, the essential underpinnings of life (the cell and its blueprints) seem to be correlated with characteristics of our supporting Sun, the defining host of our stellar neighborhood. Consequently, we may infer that life inhabiting other planets and moons of our Sun would likely have comparable organic parameters, although not necessarily the same physical appearance. (Recently life-forms not dependent on light have been discovered on Earth. This may expand the parameters of our image of consciously aware beings. For example, it is conceivable that matter-based beings without physical sight could operate in different environments with the aid of only subtle senses, not unlike blind or deaf humans. See chapter 4 for discussion of the inner senses.)

Our solar history may or may not parallel that of similar stellar neighborhoods throughout the universe. As we entered the twenty-first century, NASA had counted over forty identified planets outside our solar system, and more are being discovered every few weeks. Astronomers have recently discovered, in hundreds of locations, disks that appear to be about the size and mass of our solar system. These disks are composed of dust grains and gas, suggesting that sun-like stars have the raw material of planets. Observations of activity around the star 51 Pegasus (reported at a 1995 conference in Florence, Italy) suggested that these specks of matter coalesce into asteroids that then collide and meld into planets. Some theorists think it probable that our stellar neighborhood originally came into being the same way, implying systems conducive to life may be widespread. If that is correct, we have many galactic cousins populating other neighborhoods.

Our solar family is likely a recent generation compared to those from other parts of the universe. We can imagine that only five billion years ago, a sun and its dark mate—like Sirius the "dog star" and its unlighted twin—danced at the edge of our galaxy. Forces of gravity drew matter from the galaxy in a celestial mating dance of yin and yang polarities that pirouetted across a portion of the Milky Way. Hunks of coalesced ordinary matter fed the appetites of the dark and the light. Those closer to the dark hole were gradually sucked away through the spatial expanse and into its hungry maw. Delicately balanced in between were nine to twelve bodies gently suspended in orbits around our self-lighted Sun. The process was not unlike the seeding, coalescing, and refining of human families. Was a stellar or galactic level of consciousness involved? If so, how?

How could these globes of matter maintain their orbits and not collapse upon their own mass? Are there naturally occurring rhythmic sizes and distances from the parent sun

(Principle of Rhythm)? One such principle was hypothesized by Johann Titius (1766) and popularized by Johan Bode (1772). Bode's Law held that planets should fall into proportional distances from the Sun in a series of 0, 3, 6, 12, 24, 48, and 96. Using his theory, Bode saw that all the planets were close to these ratios, and he postulated that a planet was missing between Mars and Jupiter, where the asteroid belt is now located.

The positioning of our planet in a particular orbit, with implications for sustaining life, is contingent on the reciprocal gravitational pulls of the Sun, Moon, and our sibling planets. As humans, our lives are also affected by this interdependent family of celestial bodies. Humanity's planetary home base lies in the vortex of multiple levels of gravitational, magnetic, and other forces,[1] some of which manifest in physical ways such as regulation of the timing of female menses. Others are less obvious. Astrologers believe the conjunctions of countervailing planetary forces are powerful energetic locations that influence personalities and behavior.

Since Pluto's discovery in 1930, conventional astronomy has considered nine bodies to be the planetary "children" of the Sun—Mercury, Venus, Earth, Mars, Jupiter, Saturn, Uranus, Neptune, and Pluto. From the time of Bode's calculations in the eighteenth century, researchers have speculated about the existence of another body—Planet X. Recently, scientists have identified perturbations in the orbits of several planets, including Pluto, that could be indirect evidence of such a wandering body.

In 1976, Zecharia Sitchin published the first volume of a remarkable series of books—*The Earth Chronicles*—that not only documented the existence of the mystery Planet X, but also posited its role in the origins of Earth and its human inhabitants. Sitchin's eight-book series, including *Genesis Revisited* and *Divine Encounters,* is based on an in-depth study of the thousands of clay tablet fragments produced over 6,000 years ago by the Sumerians of Mesopotamia. Predecessors to the Assyrians and Babylonians, the Sumerians had a highly developed civilization that influenced all Middle Eastern cultures, and in turn much of the rest of the world. Nineteenth-century European archaeologists "rediscovered" them when they uncovered these "olden texts" on clay tablets.[2] Even if Sitchin's interpretations are only partially correct, they call into question conventional contemporary assumptions about the origins of human beings and their uniqueness in the universe. Greek scholars have discovered the physical basis for the mythical tale of Troy and Spartacus, with its story of the seduction of the lovely Helen whose face launched a thousand ships and the clever ruse of the Trojan Horse. What was myth has now become history. Why would the myths of the gods of Olympus be any different?

These tablets bore the Sumerian recordings of the teachings of advanced beings—ABs[3] who claimed to have been from a twelfth planet. The Nibiru home body—a planet way beyond Pluto, like the Planet X of modern astronomers—was labeled the "twelfth planet" because the Sumerians considered the Sun and the Earth's moon, in addition to the nine planets, to be full-fledged members of the stellar family. The tablets contain descriptions of star movements in antiquity that could have come only from an off-planet perspective, not from sky-watching shepherds. The Sumerian record makes a persuasive argument that a large planet with an orbital period of 3,600 years (and with an apogee six times farther from Earth than that of Pluto) collided with a former planet in orbit between Mars and Jupiter (where Bode predicted) billions of years ago.

Roughly half of the satellite remained intact, becoming our Earth, a planet with a single dry continent surrounded by a monolithic sea. It settled into a new orbit, our current one. The other half became the asteroid belt—the "bracelet of heaven" composed of asteroids, ice balls, and millions of hunks of rock—that still fills that space and orbits the Sun.[4] (See the graphic.) Our Moon could have been near the current path of what is now the Earth and been captured by its gravity, or it could have been a piece remaining from the smashed planet.

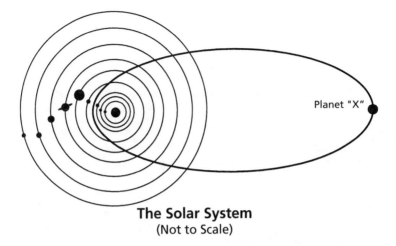

The Solar System
(Not to Scale)

According to Sitchin's interpretation, Planet X, coming from the far reaches of our solar system, not only reshaped the Earth, but brought seeds of life picked up on its long voyage. Whether that life was in the form of simple spores (postulated in the theory of panspermia) or conscious beings, our stellar neighborhood seems not to be as sparsely populated as we have believed.

Cataclysmic Past

Our search for answers about external reality must start with our home base. The currently postulated and generally accepted geological ages of Earth are shown in table 5. But we do not yet have the whole story. The fact is that we know very little about our past. For example, legends of the Great Flood and the sinking of Atlantis—both recorded in Western historical documents—hint at relatively recent cataclysmic events. How many more are there?

When we survey our planet's past, we confront tremendous gaps in knowledge about many cataclysmic events: the rise and fall of continents; widespread ice ages and floods; the disappearance of dominant life-forms; and unexplained shattering of large areas by comets, asteroids, and radioactive explosions (like the low-altitude Tunguska River-area explosion in Siberia that leveled hundreds of square miles of forest in 1908).

Age in Millions of Years	Geological Eras	Developments
5,000-4,000	Earth's Birth	Oldest date of rock.
4,500-2,500	Archean Era	Reverse RNA sequencing indicates life 3.8 billion years ago.
2,500-570	Proterozoic Era	Very simple life-forms.
570-245	Paleozoic Era	Movement of animal life from sea to land. First land plants. First amphibians. First reptiles.
245-65	Mesozoic Era	First mammals. Called Age of Dinosaurs; extinction.
65-present	Cenozoic Era	Current life-forms. Follows extinction of dinosaurs and 2/3 of all species.

Table 5. Earth's Geologic/Fossil Record

What are the forces that have subjected our home to such trauma? What is the likelihood of similar occurrences within our civilization's time horizon? Are conscious beings able to predict and do anything about them? Have our ancestors in some way been responsible for any of these events? Is humanity currently engaged in activities that have the potential to precipitate a new Armageddon?

There is evidence, for example, to indicate that humankind suffered as not only the result of geological, atmospheric, or other "natural" cataclysms, but also at the hands of more advanced beings. For example, the story of the Tower of Babel in Genesis 11:9 records that survivors from the flood—warned and instructed in the means to escape by one of multiple "gods"—were then scattered over the face of the Earth.

The ongoing debate between "stabilists" and "dynamists," with their opposing ideas of the degree of upheaval caused by cataclysmic events, has divided the scientific community. The former are also called "uniformitarians" and the latter "catastrophists." Up until the early nineteenth century, scholars of the "catastrophist" school were in the majority. But during the era of Darwin, the idea that everything (the Earth as well as life-forms) evolved gradually over long periods of time gained the ascendancy. That incrementalist view of history has now been challenged by the accumulating evidence.

The best summary of much of this evidence can be found in the book *Cataclysm* by D. S. Allan and J. B. Delair. They focus on the period around 11,500 B.P., which is believed by many to be the period of the last flood of Biblical and other legendary fame. The following brief examples from their book illustrate the indefensibility of pat assertions about the Earth's past and justify the posing of questions like those above.

Archaeological and geological records show several periods of instantaneous reversals of the Earth's magnetic poles, with attendant shifts in its polar axis. This means a wandering of climatic zones over the Earth. Remains of much flora in current climates that are wrong for them prove the shifting of zones. Sunken continental connections and dislocated faunas attest to cataclysmic breakups of prior land arrangements. Evidence of fierce hurricanes, firestorms, precipitous freezes and thaws, prehistoric "nuclear winters" (when the atmosphere is so filled with particulate matter that temperatures drop dramatically), widespread volcanoes and earthquakes, and floods show that these have destroyed the status quo many times in the Earth's history. An eaten buttercup flower found in the stomach of a frozen woolly mammoth presents an interesting piece of evidence of the near-instantaneous nature of some of these events.

Allan and Delair collected evidence suggesting that almost all these events occurred simultaneously about 11,500 years ago. They attribute them to the near miss of a rogue heavenly body that passed between the Earth and Moon. The evidence is congruent with legends from the dawn of the current era, collected in all areas of the globe.

The Earth's fossil record has provided paleontologists with evidence of two other mass extinctions—one around 245 million years ago, when more than 90 percent of existing species became extinct; another 11 million years ago, when 30 percent were eliminated. Other abrupt shifts on the planet have been documented, such as the much discussed extinction of dinosaurs and two-thirds of all species around 65 million years ago.

Most scientists now agree that a huge object (containing large amounts of the rare metal iridium) from outer space slammed into Earth about 65 million years ago, leaving a crater 110 miles wide on Mexico's Yucatan Peninsula and causing a dust cloud that could have killed off dinosaurs and other life. (The Earth has about 140 known craters of similar size. The world watched an analogous event as the 1994 Shoemaker-Levy-9 comet string smashed into Jupiter.) Some dismiss the impact and dust cloud theory and attribute the extinction of dinosaurs to shifts in the Earth's magnetic field or changes in the ratio of oxygen in its atmosphere. The record is by no means definitive, but theorists attributing this and other dramatic life changes to atmospheric fluctuations have some evidence on their side.

Dramatic declines in the ozone layer have affected plant life and the weather system, which in turn has affected the depth of the polar ice caps. The atmosphere at the end of the last Ice Age had much less carbon dioxide than today. Pankaj Sharma, a scientist at the University of Rochester in New York State, has concluded that cosmic-ray bombardment was 41 percent more intense 21,000 years ago than it is at present. This suggests that the Earth's magnetic field was then much weaker.

The atmosphere is not the only fluctuating aspect of Earth. For a long time, geologists believed the Earth's mantle (varying from 40 to 2,000 miles of thickness) was a solid piece of dead rock. But recent research has shown it to be composed of many types of rock and zones of varying temperature and density—a finding that indicates a more volatile planet than many previously thought. An innovative theory—"crustal displacement"—implies the entire crust of the Earth shifts, at a rate faster than its heavier core. Such movements could account for the alternative freezing and thawing of ice layers on various parts of the globe.

Sitchin stated that the Earth originally—when propelled into its current orbit by Planet X—consisted of a single land mass. In the 1920s, Alfred Wegener, a German scientist, postulated the theory of a single land mass. The breakup of that continent over the eons through geological, and possibly humanoid-initiated, events dramatically affected surface life. (Some posit that a single land mass originally inhabited by one civilization, later divided by continental breakups, could account for the universality of various art forms and common primordial, multicultural myths that now span the globe. But, as we will see, another explanation of almost universal cultural forms makes more sense.)

Ordinary forces of gravity and heat transfer, as well as changes in both mass and vibration, may have led to periodic shifting and breaking of the continental mass. Jason Morgan's tectonic plate theory, put forth in 1968 and now universally accepted, suggests the Earth's crust, including dry land and sea, is divided into ten to twenty plates (which are subdivided into platelets). The plates "float" on a layer of liquid and jostle against each other, both horizontally and vertically, at fault lines. The friction at fault lines results in earthquakes, volcanic eruptions, and the violent lifting or sinking of huge areas. An example is the rising of the great mountain ranges of the Andes, Himalayas, Rockies, and Alps through volcanic eruptions, earthquakes, and continental drift that may have occurred near the end of the Cretaceous period, 70 million years ago. Over the eons the configuration of land surface and water surface has probably changed several times, including episodes during an earlier ice age (600,000 years ago) and the most recent glacial period that ended around 10,000 years ago. It is also possible that civilization's influence on surface temperatures may have been important in such volatility as the movements of liquids below.

Evidence documented by Allan and Delair and others indicates that relatively recent tectonic activity (10,000 to

12,000 years ago) submerged large parts of land connected to what is now Florida and Central America, Morocco, and the Iberian Peninsula of Spain. Perhaps the whole area now known as the Mid-Atlantic Ridge—considered to be the site of the lost continent of Atlantis—underwent just such an upheaval and subsidence around the end of the last Ice Age. There is evidence that a now lost civilization existed at the time of this cataclysm, and may have played a precipitative role in its happening. See Shirley Andrews and Charles Berlitz's books on Atlantis for cogent and plausible presentations on this theme.[5]

Some of the evidence Andrews and Berlitz describe includes core samples, dating between 10 and 50 thousand years ago, taken from the ocean floors in this area that reveal animals and plants from surface life-forms. Stone structures have also been photographed at great depths in this area. Similar structures were found on the Atlantic shelf of the Canary and Azore Islands by sixteenth-century European explorers. Other structures and roadways found leading off the shorelines of Florida, Mexico, and Belize demonstrate the sinking of land on which apparently highly developed settlements once existed. (Similar evidence of structures have been found in Japan's offshore waters.)

During that same time period, with the end of the last Ice Age and the start of warm ocean currents in the North Atlantic and North Sea, three major civilizations (Egyptian, Babylonian, and Hindu) developed their historical calendars. The Mayan and Olmec calendars also have a beginning date during that period (10,570 or 10,500 BP). Were the calendars "reset" for a new cycle after the global cataclysm by survivors—now scattered over disparate areas—from a lost continent?

A few scholars believe there is evidence that some of these Earth changes may have involved the actions of other intelligent beings. Javier Cabrera has published an analysis of millennia-old pictographs found on at least 11,000 stones in Peru in the 1960s. They were allegedly discovered when an earthquake and/or floods shifted the terrain of the immense

Ocucaje Desert.[6] According to Cabrera's interpretation, these ancient engraved "Stones of Ica" portray a global warming—occurring perhaps a million or more years ago—caused by a buildup of heat that could not escape an atmosphere saturated with gases, primarily carbon dioxide. The stones depict humanoid activity contributing to this vapor shield. Resulting temperatures were so scorching that rock-like surfaces were softened and new continental configurations were fused. He also posits that some dramatic climate shifts, tilting of Earth's axes, and biosystem changes can be attributed to the effects of such ancient technologies.

Cabrera believes the Stones of Ica document the existence of highly developed beings during a period when eight continents spanned the planet, including land masses which could account for the fabled continents of Atlantis and Lemuria. (Providing support for Cabrera's thesis, the book *Forbidden Archaeology* includes evidence of the influence of conscious activity 55 million years ago in the area that is now California and elsewhere on the globe.[7]) The stones indicate that the current areas of North Africa and Europe were at one time connected and that today's Asian continent comprises three land masses that were previously widely separated. Current geological analysis of the respective rock strata support these interpretations.

We still have no clear idea of how the forces of nature (gravitational, electromagnetic, biological, and others) combine to act on the Earth's mantle, literally the foundation of our continental home. Many believe that as a result of global warming (repeating Cabrera's reading of the Stones of Ica) the twenty-first century may bring another reconstitution of our habitat, that could include the melting of polar ice caps, higher temperatures and higher water levels in the short term, and magnetic pole shifts in the long term. But we are getting ahead of the story.

When we return to the investigations of Cabrera, we find reports of prehistoric beings who appear to have been akin to modern humans. In 1984, when researching the stones, Cabrera discovered part of the backbone (lumbar vertebra) of a hominid similar to *Homo sapiens* in the sedimentary geological strata that included fauna and flora of the Mesozoic Era. Discoveries near the Biloxi River in Texas have revealed humanoid footprints alongside those of dinosaurs in rocks over 100 million years old. These footprints and a fossil of an index finger match those of contemporary humans. The planet's turbulent history and the discoveries of Sitchin, Cabrera, Allan and Delair, and many others call into question the "uniformitarianism" of Darwin and the theory of a recent creation.

Beyond Creationism and Darwinism

Most in mainstream institutions still assume an essentially Darwinist theory of evolution, and much of the general public doesn't question it. In this view natural selection accounts for all current complex life-forms. This process allegedly involves random mutations in DNA, which are genetically transmitted to successor generations by the most procreative individuals of a species. Although the Earth's fossil record demonstrates an evolution of details contained in the forms of a given species, no evidence exists to prove that a different species has evolved from another by natural selection.[8] The facts of increasing diversity and complexity in fossil strata do not prove the Darwinist explanation of cause.

Evolutionists cite evidence of intraspecies mutations during Earth's long history to support the theory of the origins of radically new life-forms. But thus far geneticists have not been able to demonstrate with the necessary robust results a mechanism for speciation (the development of a new species from another). They theorize a gradual chain of development—from inert chemicals to simple life-forms to highly developed ones. Yet there are holes in their postulated schema—and lack of evidence to fill them—that call for more reasonable hypotheses. In reviewing this issue, we should be honest about what has been proven and what has not.

Scientists have no definitive evidence—despite over forty years of chemical experimentation by scores of labs around the world—that proves biological life sprang randomly from chemical molecules. Existing simple life-forms do not reveal their origins, nor do they contain attributes that demonstrate they are precursors to other forms. Laboratories have artificially produced molecules of amino acids—the building blocks of proteins—but the molecules remain inert. Until self-reproducing life-forms spring forth from organic molecules treated with ordinary catalysts (heat, radiation, or lightning) or from chemical formulas, the random spark hypothesis cannot be considered credible.

Nevertheless, evolutionists start with this unproved hypothesis of how the first spark of life occurred, and then argue that the similar chemical and physical structure of cells in all Earth life points to their common development from an original singular live cell. But, as we see from the continuing and parallel groups of even the most simple life-forms, this hypothesis remains unvalidated.

Albert Engel of the Scripps Institute of Oceanography in La Jolla, California, discovered fossil evidence—the oldest to date—showing that heat-loving, sulfur-eating bacteria existed 3.5 billion years ago in South Africa. James A. Lake of UCLA found that the same type of bacteria still exists in isolated pockets, such as hot water vents in the ocean floor and geysers in Yellowstone National Park. According to the theory of natural selection, all other life evolved from these (or similar) first bacteria, where the weaker ones would have died out as the stronger mutants took over. But Lake argues that these three categories of one-celled organisms (prokaryotes, with no nucleus; eukaryotes and archaebacteria, both with nuclei) have remained independent of each other for billions of years.

Scientists disagree as to how these bacteria types could have evolved into more complex plant and animal cells. Some biologists, including Lynn Margulis, well known for her association with the "Gaia" concept, promote the idea that more complex organisms could be the results of symbiosis between two distinct but mutually beneficial partners. Perhaps the mitochondria (a respiratory organelle) and chloroplasts (site of photosynthesis) of one-celled eukaryotes (one of the earliest life-forms on Earth) merged to establish new levels of organisms. However, plants have fungi on their roots to help them get nutrients, and herbivores have microorganisms in their guts to help digest food. The nature of these interactions counters the notion of random evolution.

Darwinism depends on an extended period of stability for modern complex life to have evolved. The fact that an extremely long-term process would be necessary for macroevolution (with a 2 percent DNA change in a million years) weakens the theory when confronted with the evidence of a cataclysmic past. To deal with this contradiction, some scientists now postulate that cataclysmic events like those described earlier may have resulted in "punctuated development," where some steps are compressed into very short periods of time (creation of coal, fossils, rock strata, and even new species).

It may be that our accepted time frames for history are not accurate. Currently we say reptiles and dinosaurs were exclusive to the Mesozoic Era because we have dated some fossil remains to that era. Any evidence that does not fit that assumption about the time frame is ignored; we automatically assume our conventional theory is correct. For example, the discovery of fossils from extinct animals believed to be millions of years old mixed with humanoid imprints in the Western Hemisphere (Utah, Texas, and elsewhere) has been interpreted to mean there must be problems with the animal dating, not that intelligent beings could have lived a long time ago. Such assumptions can easily lead to underestimating the antiquity of intelligent ancestors to modern humans.

Analysis of trace radioactive elements in contiguous rock deposits has dated a primitive "Lucy-being" back 3.4 million years. The "Lucy" theory postulates a single female being (or at least a small homogenous group of females) from whom all subsequent hominids (the primate family of which *Homo sapiens* are considered the most recent) are descended. This coincides with Sitchin's theory that ABs used indigenous beings found in Africa for their genetic experimentation.

Those who tout a single gradation of development have ignored the discovery of contiguous footprints—much like those of modern humans—in ancient ash deposits in East Africa and Texas (noted earlier). They dismiss the idea that a being, supposedly at least 2 million years younger, could have left footprints at the same time as its supposed "ancestor." But the current physical evidence, indicating the two generations lived at the same time, calls for reassessment of our human story.

The review thus far of the physical evidence has not included inferences about the evolution of consciousness, which will be discussed in chapter 5. Consciousness cannot be proved by the physical remains available for modern laboratory analysis. Our limited means of dating fossils—potassium/argon decay rates in rocks; fission-track dating in damage to mineral crystals; and electron spin resonance counting of free electrons in solids—make it impossible for science writers to speculate about anything other than physical developments.

Table 6. Dating Ranges for Hominids and Genus Homo

Group	From	To
First Hominids	15-4.5 million	1.2 million
Homo habilis	2.5-1.6 million	1.6 million
Homo erectus	1.8-1 million	300,000
Homo sapiens	750-270,000	100,000
Neanderthal	300-200,000	30,000
Homo sapiens sapiens	270-100,000	Present
Cro-Magnon	120-30,000	15,000
Historical Peoples	15,000	—

Ranges derived from archaeology, anthropology, and DNA studies

Table 6, depicting current academic thinking on human evolution, shows there are too many unexplained overlaps of dates and groups to get a clear sense of the actual history of the hominid family (the primate category that includes humans) and the genus *Homo* (the category that includes modern humans and extinct species). The concurrent existence of so many groups does not provide for enough time for the assumed process of macroevolution (one species slowly leads to another by genetic mutation and drift). And conversely, no evidence has been found, in the fossil record or in genetic experiments, to prove the hypothesis that new, more complex species can mutate from lesser ones. The evidence does demonstrate a process of microevolution, or adaptation, within a species. Some examples are increased height in successor generations, the spread of antimalaria genes, and the addition of lactose tolerant genes.

Extraplanetary Intervention

If macroevolution falls in the face of facts, so does creationism. While the creationists' "sacred" texts, used to support their interpretation of the origin of modern humans, cannot withstand the scrutiny of historians, they may point to some facts of prehistory. Believers read the texts and avow that the Earth and its inhabitants were miraculously given their present form by a supernatural creator in the very recent past. Yet this interpretation is contrary to the scientifically dated fossil and archaeological evidence, including ancient artifacts that predate the Biblical timetable. Fortunately, many of the religious texts themselves include references that suggest humanity's nondivine origins, involving the intervention of flesh-and-blood advanced beings in human development. Adding to the picture, contemporary evidence also points toward AB involvement in the development of modern humans.

We must now give serious attention to the likelihood that advanced civilizations predated our historical era. It is plausible that some arose naturally on Earth, then fell, with only threads of their knowledge preserved in the surviving populations. Artifacts or ruins that fall outside the recognized history of civilization are not necessarily evidence of extraterrestrial visitations. Some of these remains (the Great Pyramids in Egypt, Machu Picchu in Peru, the Easter Island monuments, fallen structures beneath the Atlantic) could be explained by the existence of early, solely human civilizations destroyed through cataclysmic earthly events like those described earlier.

However, traditional sources, in addition to the Biblical and Sumerian texts, describe ABs in various stages of human experimentation using a combination of earthly materials and etheric elements.[9] According to legends of the Bushmen of Southern Africa, Cagn, a powerful being, gave orders that caused human beings to appear. In the cosmology of Heliopolis, men and women were formed from the tears of the Egyptian AB Atum. In Old Babylonian myths, Nintu, the female AB ruler, molded mankind (Lullu, the savage) out of clay and animated him with the blood of a slain male AB. The Zuni believed all beings of Earth came from the lying together of *Awitelin Tsita* (an Earth AB) and *Apoyan Ta'chu* (an AB from the sky). For the Quiche Maya, mankind resulted from several phases of trial and error by a Creator AB and a Maker AB. The Aborigines of Australia believe their ancestors were created by wandering ABs from other stars.

Obviously these legendary stories should not be accepted literally, but neither should they be dismissed out of hand. When they are added to the kind of evidence included in this book and prehistoric discoveries by more and more scholars, no thoughtful person can ignore the possibility of external intervention in human history. The emerging story requires a re-framing of our historical assumptions.

The case for revising our conventional history is further strengthened by current indications of galactic beings more technologically advanced than modern humans. Worldwide UFO and AB sighting reports lend support to the hypothesis of AB intervention in human affairs. During the last few decades alone, thousands of cases[10] of interventions by non-human beings in the lives of people have been reported. They suggest the possibility that ABs are presently involved in some manner with earthly life, intervening covertly in its development. Current abduction reports and new assessments of the origins and purposes of various historical artifacts give credence to many of the primitive creation legends. It is quite plausible that creationists confuse the work of ABs (any conscious entities more advanced than humans in certain areas) with the notion of divinity.

I believe a more accurate history of human life on planet Earth very likely involves some combination of natural development and externally conscious intervention or technical assistance. To get a better understanding of this possibility requires a synthesis of creation myths, Sumerian cuneiform writings and pre-Incan pictoglyphs, the gap-filled record of the evolutionists, reports of genetic engineering by people abducted by aliens, and analyses of various unexplained artifacts. Much of the groundbreaking research has already been done and is referenced in this book.

My own interpretation of this material leads me to believe that early humans who were indigenous to Earth, a part of this planet's "unfolding seedbed," had their natural development interrupted and redirected by ABs who were several thousand years ahead of us. These early humans were generally peaceful, egalitarian naturalists who knew how to coexist effectively with their environments and also develop their creative capacities. However, modern humans, we *Homo sapiens sapiens* who appeared about 100,000 years ago, resulted from genetic manipulations and some form of technology transfer by our technological superiors. The stocks from which we came—apparently *Homo erectus* (pre-Neanderthals) or Early Aboriginals (perhaps *Homo sapiens*)—have largely disappeared, overwhelmed by their AB-colonized cousins who learned to expand their own spheres of influence.

Homo erectus (known by several labels) is believed by some to have lived from about 2 million B.P. and overlapped for a time with Neanderthals who may have appeared before 300,000 B.P. The latter allegedly disappeared around 30,000 B.P., but currently credible reports of strange beast-like creatures around the globe may belie those assumptions. Americans call them "Bigfoot," the Asians know them as "Yeti," Siberians call them "Alma," and the name "Abominable Snowman" is used in the Himalayas. Some early aboriginals may have survived amalgamation by escaping from AB influence to the edges of Africa and migrating to other sparsely populated areas.

In the early 1970s, Erich von Daniken gained notoriety with the publication of *Chariots of the Gods* and *Return to the Stars* (later published as *Gods From Outer Space*, which sold millions of copies). Free of the constraints of institutional censorship, Daniken surveyed the evidence for the existence of extraterrestrial beings and advanced technology on the Earth from more than 100,000 years ago. He speculated that these beings intervened in the evolution of hominoids (the family of primates) through genetic manipulation. Since then, many other serious books and papers—some described in this book—have offered supporting evidence and fresh analyses.

Some writers—including Zecharia Sitchin and Javier Cabrera—stand out with very convincing interventionist arguments. Sitchin has amassed considerable archaeological, linguistic, cultural, and scientific evidence that supports the idea that Earth was colonized 450,000 years ago by the Annunaki, a race of beings from a distant planet. Even the name of our planet adds credibility to Sitchin's intervention theory: a word linguistically similar to "Earth" is used in many languages: Erds (German), Erthe (Middle English), Ereds (Arabic), Erd (Kurdish), Eretz (Hebrew), and Ordu (Persian). These all appear to derive from the Sumerian or Akkadian term "E.RI.DU.," which means "house in faraway built"—very appropriate if given to our planet by visitors from far away. Of equal interest is the Sumerian name "E. DIN," meaning the "gods' home." This seems to be the basis for the Biblical Eden.

Sitchin's multivolume series of interpretation and analysis of the literally thousands of six-millennia-old Sumerian clay tablets makes a compelling case, supported by many other scholars, that human history was dramatically changed by these colonists. The Anunnaki brought their technology to Earth, exposed humans to it, involved them in its maintenance, and taught humans a higher level of civilization. On the other hand, the Anunnaki took advantage of humans for labor, military service in their wars with each other and, to some extent, sexual relationships. Humans inherited many of their institutions from the Anunnaki, including the ideas of kingship and priesthood. After the cataclysm known commonly as the Biblical Flood, the human survivors were helped to restart civilization.

According to Sitchin's translations of the Sumerian texts, the Annunaki bioengineered the species *Homo sapiens* from indigenous hominids in the period 250,000 to 300,000 years ago. The Anunnaki settlements are purported to have existed around three great river systems (the Nile, the Indus, and the Tigris-Euphrates) and in southern Africa. Supporting this interpretation is archaeological evidence that early human civilizations arose without antecedents in these areas.

Other support for this AB-intervention hypothesis comes from DNA research. Studies of mitochondrial DNA (found outside the cell's nucleus), transmitted only through the mother, point to a common female gene pool in Africa about 275,000 years ago for all current *Homo sapiens sapiens*. (That is within Sitchin's time frame and coincides with the geographical location where the Anunnaki first used humans as laborers in gold mines.) Other DNA studies indicate the movement of Caucasian genes from Africa to the Middle East about 100,000 years ago. Again, this is consistent with the tablet's time frame for the Anunnaki movement of members of its African worker colony to Mesopotamia. Other studies of the dispersion of genes, languages, crops, and social institutions are not incompatible with the AB-intervention hypothesis.[11] Much additional research needs to be done, but thus far no direct evidence has disproved the AB-intervention theory.

Recent DNA analyses of a 900-year-old, oddly formed child's skull from Mexico—in an area known for stories of sky beings who interbred with human females—have uncovered unknown DNA sequences, along with evidence of the human male Y chromosome. While we can't state that it has AB parentage, it has characteristics unexplained by current medical categories. (Research findings can be found at www.starchild.com.)

William Bramley[12] and Arthur Horn[13] present systematic and comprehensive reviews of currently available evidence to support the view that extraterrestrials (ABs), acting as "custodials," have manipulated human events in order to perpetuate social and political conflicts for their own ends. Their historical arguments are compelling, even though particular interpretations of linkages among specific events cannot be proven today. Lloyd Pye's book *Everything You Know Is Wrong: Book One—Human Origins* is a cogent argument for the AB-interventionist theory.[14] He draws heavily on Sitchin's work, but elaborates on it in a very persuasive manner. Many other researchers are expanding the evidence for the revisionist approach to the human story.

Folk traditions often include visits by ABs from elsewhere in the cosmos. The oral traditions of the Dogon tribe in Mali describe visitors (amphibious space travelers) from the Sirius star system who taught them the knowledge of civilization. They informed the Dogon ancestors of a dark star (maybe the black hole of modern physics) companion to Sirius. This information was published in Europe and America fifty years before the dark star was discovered by modern astronomers.

Early American traditions portray "sky maidens" who marry humans, have children, and disappear into the sky. The Hindu Vedas describe avatars (gods incarnate) like Vishnu as being half-fish/half-human (perhaps arising from their spacecraft after splashdown). Genesis 6:2 and 6:4 speak of "gods" who consorted with the daughters of men. Greek legends portray ABs consorting with humans and producing hybrid beings. In the Hindu *Puranas* (stories), a physical Krishna had intercourse with milkmaids.

I believe these stories refer to the time reported in Sumerian tablets of widespread social and sexual intercourse between the "gods" and the men and women of Earth. Modern cases, reported in large numbers, include various levels of such interactions between ABs and humans. Highly credible scientists like Harvard's John Mack and many others now take such reports seriously.

Most evolutionary scientists have operated on the assumption of "gradualism"—the theory that evolutionary changes occur gradually over eons, but some scientists recognize the evidence for "fast-forward" periods in history. American paleontologists such as Stephen Jay Gould and

Niles Eldredge have promoted the concept of "punctuated equilibrium" where, aperiodically, dramatic shifts occur very quickly. Although they attribute such short periods of rapid change to natural phenomena, it is possible that such bursts of evolution could instead be the result of conscious, external intervention.

For example, no proof exists that our reputed three-level (reptilian, mammalian, and neocortex) human brain is the result of gradual evolutionary phases. Scientists observe the brain's structure and then assume it was due to progressive human mutation through several species, but that is only a hypothesis. Genetic manipulation or other forms of "grafting" could produce the same result in a time frame that is consistent with the historical record. Our own twenty-first-century genetic engineering technologies demonstrate that the possibility of advanced outside influence on human development is not unthinkable.

In the last decade, scientists have discovered the mechanism through which such deliberate intervention could have been accomplished: recombinant DNA—the result of splicing a strand of DNA into a different DNA molecule of a particular cell. This is not unlike the farmer cutting a limb from one fruit tree and splicing a similar section from another fruit tree onto the first. Scientists are now aware of the existence in humans of deactivated retroviruses that are available for DNA experimentation. It is conceivable such retroviruses were used in the redesign work of the Sumerian-era ABs. Civilizations with a few thousand years head start would likely be far ahead of us in this and other gene-manipulation technologies.

The Mars Factor

People have long suspected our sister planet Mars of having supported earlier life-forms. The numerous valleys and channels on its surface appear to have been carved by running water in a manner similar to that which occurs on Earth (Principle of Correspondence). Although Mars today appears to have no liquid water, its polar ice caps consist of frozen water and carbon dioxide. Large areas of permafrost may also exist. Whether

Mars at one time supported fully conscious life has been hotly debated. Given the previously mentioned evidence of historical and current space travel, the notion of conscious inhabitants on Mars—an idea embraced by several esoteric traditions—does not seem farfetched. (NASA engineers have developed a device for use by humans on Mars to produce their own oxygen from Mars's thin, mostly carbon dioxide atmosphere.)

Some believe humans or human ancestors lived on Mars before it became uninhabitable. Rudolf Steiner's cosmology,[15] for example, holds that human predecessors lived on Mars and other planets in earlier phases of spiritual, physical, and intellectual development.

Mars is currently the source of considerable interest and controversy, due to speculation about life-forms in a Martian meteorite and photographs taken by NASA's 1976 Mars *Viking* orbiter. The pictures revealed formations that resemble a human face, pyramids, and a fortress.[16] Scores of reputable independent scientists extensively analyzed the Mars photographs. These analyses, reviewed by Stanley McDaniel,[17] make a persuasive case for additional investigation of the hypothesis that the photographed objects are consciously designed artifacts. NASA in 1999 rephotographed the area, but subsequent interpretations still have not settled the issue. Mark Carlotto, one of the capable specialists studying the 1976 data, has concluded the latest photographs reveal that the so-called fortress appears to be natural rock formation.

Some who believe Mars may still have hidden inhabitants find intriguing several mysterious mishaps with human probes of Mars. During the planned 1993 orbits of the Mars *Observer* vehicle, NASA scientists could have rephotographed, with forty times greater resolution, the Cydonia region containing the alleged artifacts. But NASA reported that the *Observer*'s computer malfunctioned just as it was entering a Mars orbit, and was therefore incapable of obtaining pictures. The failure of the earlier Russian photo mission described below suggests the possibility of a more sinister explanation.

The Russian photographic vehicle *Phobos*, in a 1989 mission similar to that of 1993 Mars *Observer*, also failed to obtain photographs. The final frames captured by the *Phobos* before it ceased transmission reveal images that appear to indicate it was under attack. In 1999, NASA lost contact with two more vehicles as they attempted to enter the Martian airspace. Could it be that Mars is still an active base of operation for some beings? (See Courtney Brown's very speculative book *Cosmic Voyage*[18] and the movies *Total Recall* and *Mission to Mars* for just such a hypothesis.) If so, how do they fit into our history? These questions make a human exploratory mission a high priority.

Ignored Artifacts

The "official version of history" over the past two or three centuries holds that significant human civilizations only came into being about 6,000 B.P. along the Nile, Tigris, and Euphrates Rivers. Archaeologist Anna C. Roosevelt has amassed evidence, including very sophisticated pottery, that indicates the Amazon River valley was the site of a rich civilization similar to the great river valleys of the Nile and Ganges. It is not totally inconceivable that the rich diversity of the rain forest was the result of ancient human (or, at least, conscious) management that bred useful species for food, drugs, and other social and economic needs. In the "official" view, not until about 10,000 B.P. did humans begin domesticating animals and living in villages, and not until much later did they begin extensive farming, widespread ocean exploration, and development of mechanical power. A number of pioneering researchers have pointed out serious misunderstandings resulting from this limited assumption.[19] Discoveries, like those below, could validate the existence of extended civilizations.

The Great Pyramids of Egypt have been seen as products of the period of the pharaohs, dating from about 5,000 B.P. The Great Sphinx was believed to have been created during the Fourth Dynasty, making it about 4,500 years old. Now Robert M. Schoch, a Boston University geologist and anthropologist, estimates it to be at least 8,000 years old. Using sound waves to analyze the weathering of the statue's base below the current surface, Schoch theorizes that the Sphinx may have been carved from a single piece of limestone remaining in place as rock was quarried from around it. This adds credence to claims that link the pyramids and Sphinx to the ending of Atlantis, around 12,000 B.P. Sitchin's study of the earlier-mentioned Sumerian tablets suggests the Great Pyramids were part of the Anunnaki preflood spaceport. (See his volume *The Wars of Gods and Men.*)

Examples like these erode the claims of those who maintain the conventional view. We have perhaps too quickly dismissed the possibility of civilizations more than a few thousand years old. In these and other monuments we have the problem of dating stone. Dates cannot currently be fixed in increments smaller than about 50,000 years, which means many ancient monuments could be much older than we have speculated.

An intriguing mystery surrounds the extraordinary work of Javier Cabrera, who discovered the juxtaposition of humanoid figures with long-extinct plants and animals on the earlier-mentioned prehistoric pictographs carved in the Stones of Ica. The ancient stones suggest varied and sophisticated levels (even beyond some of today's frontiers) of science, technology, and social development. They also contain parallels with the most ancient finds in other parts of the globe, notably Egypt and Sumeria. According to Cabrera, the stone carvings also portray maps of the universe, a zodiac, a calendar, planetary maps, continental maps, instruments for study of the heavens and the microscopic world, machines for launching flights, advanced surgical techniques (organ transplants) and implements, animal and human embryology, parasitology, ritual dances, and musical instruments.

Ranging from 15 to 20 grams to 500 kilograms (1,100 pounds), the stones appear to have representations from the Cenozoic Era (beginning 65 million years ago), the Mesozoic Era (over 180 million years ago), and the Paleozoic Era (over 400 million years ago). The carvers appear to have been familiar with the internal organs of the animals depicted as well as their external appearances. If they are authentic, the carvers would have had to coexist (or possess geological records only recently rediscovered) with flora and fauna of those eras. This would mean conscious beings, in some form, would have studied Earth 400 million years ago. (The oldest known genus *Homo* fossil is now estimated to be less than 4 million years old.)

Composed of andesite, the stones, including the etchings, are covered by an oxide patina that may indicate they are ancient. Determining the age of the stones would require stratigraphy and paleontology, permission for which has been denied Cabrera by Peru's Patronato Nacional de Arqueologia since July 1970. The threat such revelations would pose to that nation's Catholic theology and political institutions (not unlike the situation portrayed in James Redfield's best-selling book *The Celestine Prophecy*) may be a deterrent to scientific investigation. Although his secretive nature about the location of the ancient stones' repository and the keys to his deciphering may make Cabrera himself the biggest obstacle to third-party validation. My efforts in 1998 to elicit cooperation from Cabrera in a process of third-party validation were politely turned away due to his alleged fear of having such valuable artifacts misused by others.

There are numerous additional reports of advanced technology in antiquity. In 1973, Indian anthropologists reportedly found "human-like fossils" in Mesozoic rocks dating back 230 million years. A 1997 television show narrated by Charlton Heston, *Mysterious Origins of Man,* revealed the discovery of small, symmetrical stone balls containing a machine tool groove that date back 2.8 billion years.[19]

In his book *Atlantis,* Charles Berlitz reports several examples of evidence of technology more than a million years old:

- a silver chalice found in 1851 near Dorchester, Massachusetts, in granite rock that could have taken millions of years to form

- a gold screw found in similar granite near Treasure City, Nevada, in 1869

- a gold thread product and a gold animal figure with gears inside found near Cocle, Panama, in rock over a million years old

- a godlike figurine with a metal core of wire and ceramic parts, discovered in the ancient rocks of the Coso Mountains of California

- seven hundred and sixteen stone-like (cobalt) disks, carbon-dated as 12,000 years old, discovered in ancient graves in the Bayanb-Kara-Ula mountains of Tibet by Russian Vyacheslav Zaitsov. The disks had hieroglyphic symbols and grooves spiraling from a center hole. When cleaned, they vibrated as if charged with an unknown energy.

By now the list of alleged prehistoric artifacts by various researchers is quite large. Cabrera's book *The Stones of Ica* lists reports of additional astounding artifacts:

- an atomic battery found in Gabon that stopped working 100 million years ago

- electric batteries dating from prehistoric Iraq

- synthetic fibers in ancient Chinese burial grounds

- magnifying glasses found in prehistoric sites in Egypt, Iraq, and Australia (That the glasses were ground with cerium oxide—produced through a process of electrolysis requiring powerful generators—points to a technologically advanced civilization.)

Such devices could only have come from earlier advanced civilizations, either off-planet or home-grown. Either explanation threatens the conventional tenets of our science and theology. Imagine what would happen if Sitchin's idea that ancient Israelite communication with alien "gods" sometimes came through a radio were validated by the discovery of a receiver in the Ark of the Covenant? A Catholic scholar recently told me the Vatican has the same view of the Ark, based on Biblical descriptions of its dimensions and components. The psychological blow to the Judeo-Christian believer of such a revelation would be tremendous.

To accept such intriguing individual artifacts and the presence of the ruins of large cities as evidence of advanced civilization, predating the current historical era, requires a new mindset. But there is some reason to think such a widespread shift may be close. In the 1990s, movies, television, and other media programs reviewing the discoveries described in this chapter and others like them found a receptive audience. By the year 2000, according to popular polls, two-thirds of the American public believed we would make contact with extraterrestrial life in this century.

In addition to small artifacts, there are monumental structures of unexplained origins scattered around the globe. Beyond the Middle East areas discussed earlier, South America has many such treasures. (Many people circulate accounts of underground cities and tunnels, some inhabited by humans and others by ABs, but I have not seen any public evidence that could be considered credible.)

Sacsahuaman—a prehistoric center of wisdom and knowledge in Peru—is the site of hundreds of stone blocks, many weighing over 200 tons and placed more than two miles above sea level. How did they get there? Legend holds that Sacsahuaman was constructed untold thousands of years ago, along with the Nazca Lines, the Pyramid of the Sun of Pachacamac, Lake Titicaca, the City of Ollantaytambo, the Sun Temple of Cuzco, and of course the renowned city of Machu Picchu. Thor Heyerdahl, Ivar Zapp and George Erikson (authors of *Atlantis in America: Navigators of the Ancient World*), and others have theorized that links existed between these sites and those of Egypt, Mesopotamia, and the Indus Valley.

In 1966, Robert J. Menzies discovered the remains of an ancient city off the coast of Peru where myriad unidentified ruins dot the shore and the adjacent arid desert. The ruins lie in the Milne Edward Deep several thousand feet below the surface. Yet another example is the more than 20,000-year-old Bolivian city, Tiahuanaco (pre-Incan "City of the Dead"), with artifacts of a highly developed civilization and portrayals of people very different in height and features from modern inhabitants.

These monuments to conscious achievement challenge our traditional recording of history. Supplementing the lore of legend, they provide much potential evidence of our forgotten history. The famous psychic Edgar Cayce reported visions of a civilization on Atlantis that existed for a period of 200,000 years, lasting until the last island sank beneath the waves around 12,000 years ago. Shirley Andrews' book, *Atlantis: Insight From a Lost Civilization,* provides an excellent overview of the evidence that supports the material Cayce accessed in the noumena.

We have always assumed that artifacts found in surface or near-surface sites were habitations from the first humans. For example, after discovering the remains of beer in 5,000-year-old sites in Iran and Iraq, researchers concluded that the Sumerians were the first brewers. But maybe they weren't the first; perhaps they were continuing an industry that was already many millennia old, or even practiced in other worlds.

The questions still remain: Did our human ancestors rise to heights of civilization yet unknown to us, destroy it, and then survive in remnants to start over again, and perhaps again? Or did other beings independent of the human family tree come and go, leaving their traces behind?

Both possibilities are worthy of further investigation. Human beings may have existed throughout various ages, with a rhythmic rise and fall of scientific and social achievements. Cultures could have been destroyed or died from within, but small groups could have started again from nearly zero and then surged ahead. ABs could have introduced science and technology in places such as Sumeria, Egypt, the Andean region, and Central America. For the time being, on the basis of currently available evidence, we must remain open to either possibility, or a combination of both.

Forgotten Knowledge

As you do your own research, I believe that you will find the fact of the unexplained artifacts and mysterious cities builds a strong case for the existence of intelligent life that predates conventional anthropological estimates. So why has knowledge from these eras been lost? It seems almost as though at times it was wiped out and we had to start over again. Nevertheless, threads of knowledge appear to have survived in various ways.

Many believe advanced knowledge has been covertly held by a few in esoteric circles down through the ages. Some question the origin of scientific discoveries that do not appear to result from trial-and-error experimentation, but which spring fully blown from some unknown source. Such information could latently reside in our collective memory. It is possible, within the concept of a general field of consciousness (noumena) presented here, for humans to rediscover the memories of concepts and techniques practiced on the planet long ago.[20] Of course, it is equally plausible that ABs provide us the information, directly or through inner communications.

Genetic engineering may be one of those areas of knowledge that was lost and then rediscovered in the noumenal memory field. This possibility is underscored by the report that James Watson "intuited" the DNA double helix structure while daydreaming. The assumption of prior existence of such genetic information is reinforced by Sitchin's interpretation that the Anunnaki manipulated the genes of hominids and by Cabrera's 1970s conclusion from the Stones of Ica, mentioned earlier in this chapter, that genetic brain surgery had been conducted on humanoids in prehistoric time.

Interestingly, in early 1993 American physicians and researchers began seeking approval from the National Institutes of Health to administer such treatment to patients with brain tumors. The process involved removal of brain tumor cells that were then genetically altered and reinjected into the patient. The theory was that these injections stimulated the person's immune system to fight the cancer. Was Cabrera prescient or did he have historical evidence?

Early AB genetic experiments may have involved amphibians and reptiles before mammals. Experiments with the last, in one view, led to modern humans. One bit of speculation is that the notharctus (a bear-like hunter of insects and fruits), possibly the most intelligent of prehistoric animals (given its brain/body ratio), benefited from the insertion of cognitive codes more than 50 million years ago. Molecular compounds of nucleic acids and proteins could have been implanted at the embryo genetic phase by ABs.

Modern genetic manipulations and cloning projects seem like eerie parallels to the alleged ancient acts. It seems fitting that through genetic engineering, our ancestors may have given us the potential to learn to do gene manipulations on ourselves. With time and experience, we may go beyond it to "boost" other species, improving on a practice used by the "gods" on us thousands or millions of years ago.

Both Sitchin and Cabrera have mounted highly credible arguments that ABs were to a large extent "designers" of modern humans, undermining literalistic creation myths involving divine beings. Yet neither has been able to accept the full implications of his work. Both still project a supernatural being between humans and this book's view of a self-manifesting consciousness as the origin of our universe. Cabrera told me in 1998 that he keeps hidden part of his trove of artifacts because they confirm his Catholic cosmology and he wants that to be the ultimate conclusion, not one that prematurely turns researchers off.

Sitchin, in a private communication circulated to some of his followers in 2000, reports that he reached agreement with Vatican scholar Corrado Balducci on several points. The existence of flesh-and-blood ABs is consistent with Catholic cosmology. AB intervention in human physical development does not preclude God's spiritual contribution. Balducci reportedly said ABs could have dealt with man's physical body while God dealt with his soul. Sitchin said he thought of the Anunnaki as only emissaries of the divine, Almighty God, carrying out His wishes and plans.

Maurice Chatelain[21] and others have suggested that much significant prehistoric knowledge is not actually missing, only unrecognized. Here Chatelain exemplified the Biblical admonition, "Seek and ye shall find." By taking into account the deceleration of Earth's rotation at the rate of 0.000016 of a second each year, he calculated that the Nineveh constant (the

109

number 2,268 million, which is a factor in many calculations of the solar system) was first identified 64,800 years ago. This makes a strong case for prehistoric intelligent activity. With additional mathematical analysis, he traced parallels between Egyptian and Mayan calendars, dating their origins to almost 50,000 years ago. Having found compatible instruments of measurement and similar bases of counting systems[22] in widely disparate ancient cultures, he became convinced of the existence of one or more unknown prehistoric civilizations.

Visitors or Immigrants

In addition to the presence of physical artifacts and intriguing theories of knowledge transmission, our collective cultural stories point to a multidimensional history. Indeed, religious and folk historical accounts (not to mention oral, unrecorded history) have recorded so much interaction with other intelligent beings that it may be a misnomer to think of them as "extraterrestrial." If they were commuters, we do not know if they were commuting to or from the Earth.[23]

Even if they originally came from elsewhere, such a long history of presence here places them more in the category of immigrants than of visitors. Assuming that UFOs and similarly anomalous phenomena originate externally to our world may have led us down a scientific blind alley. These beings may be other Solarians, cohabiting with us in this planetary system, but with access to advanced knowledge and other dimensions of reality. It would help us better understand how we fit into the universe if we understood how they fit in.

Since the flurry of UFO reports in the years immediately following World War II, thousands of credible sources have reported witnessing maneuvers by alien craft. The first sighting covered in the national media was by Kenneth Arnold on June 24, 1947. In July 1947, occupied alien crafts allegedly crashed near Roswell, New Mexico, offering tangible evidence of extraterrestrial visits. In attempting to assess the level of Earth technology, the visitors may have pushed the limits of their technology too far. (Other crashes reportedly occurred shortly thereafter.)[24]

Since 1947, hundreds of sightings have been solidly documented by authentic photographs, traces left on the ground, and multiple witness descriptions. In the first third of 1992 alone, in Gulf Breeze, Florida (near my childhood hometown), scores of appearances by anomalous craft (which continued into 1994) were photographed. On November 29, 1989, 125 detailed sightings of three-dimensional craft were recorded in a period of a few hours around a small town in Belgium. The national police and Belgian air force authenticated photographs and radar recordings of these craft and shared the information with the public.

In the United States, well-publicized alien contact began with the abduction of Betty and Barney Hill in 1961, was highlighted later by the six-day abduction in 1975 of Travis Walton of Snow Flake, Arizona,[25] and continues today. The Mutual UFO Network (MUFON) has several thousand members who do serious research on UFO sightings and alien contacts. Online reports of sightings and contacts from around the world are published weekly at Jeff Rense's Web site (www.sightings.com). The material is varied in quality, but keeps one apprised of nonconventional perspectives in this area. According to several Roper and Gallup polls, as many as 2 to 5 percent of the U.S. population believe they have experienced some sort of UFO contact.

If all this goes on daily,[26] why has the SETI program (Search for Extraterrestrial Intelligence) failed to locate them? One answer is that we have been searching in the wrong place with the wrong instruments. ABs have already been here, and likely still operate in various folds of reality that we have arbitrarily excluded from scientific and academic research.[27] Using a farm metaphor from my youth, plowing a limited furrow, programs like SETI are blind to the possibility of parallel rows to cultivate. Despite waves of documented appearances in most regions of the world at some time over the last forty-five years,[28] the U.S. government has kept such information highly classified, denying public access to what government officials think of the phenomenon. Government files are believed to include information about, and possible physical evidence of, crashes or debris from as far away as Norway and Brazil, and as near as a farmer's field close to Washington, D.C.[29] (In my limited role in foreign intelligence work in the 1960s and 1970s, I was aware of the U.S. government's global search for eyewitness reports and artifacts, but I had little access to specific cases.) Government secrecy means that established scientists fear undertaking public research on such matters.

Given so much secrecy and gaps in our knowledge, all reasonable approaches to discovery and contact have something to contribute to a more accurate understanding of these beings, their origins, and the nature of our relationship to them. Some groups have attempted to manipulate UFO behavior by simplistic signals, in hopes of precipitating a landing of an AB treaty delegation. Since history is already replete with many AB contacts, I think such efforts are largely futile except for the effect of psychologically opening participants to acceptance of other advanced species. From the AB perspective, beings who have been operating in our airspace, mindspace, and homespace for so long, the initiative rests with them. Given their superior mobility, technology, and scope of awareness, it is naive to think we can set the agenda, so let's try to learn what we can from historical accounts of their interactions with our ancestors as well as more current ones.

An ancient Chinese tale describes small, gaunt men who descended from the clouds. For 40,000 years, Australian Aborigines have passed from generation to generation a "dream" of space beings landing in their territory. (An Aboriginal painting of that dream was hanging in the World Bank in Washington, D.C., at the time I was drafting this chapter.) The sacred lore of Native Americans details the visits of ancient gods over thousands of years. The Mogollon culture in Arizona (located near the site of Travis Walton's abduction), along with that of the Navajo, Hopi, Pueblo, and Zuni, includes a very strong tradition of such visits. Similarly, in New Mexico, the Mescalero Apache Indians of Sierra Blanca tell of creatures from another world who came from the stars to interact with the ancestors of modern humankind.

Reports of AB contacts have had a degree of consistency over the centuries, even millennia, when superficial differences in cultural content are taken into account. For example, the abduction phenomenon of the late twentieth century resembled the "incubus" legends of the fifteenth and sixteenth centuries. During those earlier periods, people in numerous small villages reported being visited by strange beings at night who sucked vital energies from them. Similar waves of historical experiences include vampires, ghosts, poltergeists, and so on.

Instead of dismissing all such folk history as fantasy, we who would be serious scientists must bring our analytic minds to the study of past and current interactions with the apparent extraterrestrials. Some of society's present problems may conceivably stem from negative influences in such external visitations.[30] Could our violence toward one another derive from the example set by warring "gods" (as in Greek mythology)? Could human violence have been predisposed by physical or intellectual abuse? Would public confirmation of these experiences free humans from such long-forgotten influences, as the recovery of childhood trauma releases the dead hand of the past adults who were abused children?

The ABs alluded to above so impressed our ancestors that they called them "gods." As they returned to the skies, some of the "gods" may have given instructions pertaining to the care of the Earth and its beings, instructions that we took as holy writ. (An example of this possibly occurred when Yahweh [an AB in the Sumerian accounts] dictated laws, rituals, dietary guidelines, and constructive societal rules to Moses.) For some humans, the threat of the alien return was enough to stimulate dread and anxiety, which demagogues used to gain control over them. The aliens' lessons about inner powers could have been turned into worshipful rituals by less knowledgeable humans, to be performed as rote without delving into their value. (Some believe Freemasons and similar groups have strayed from original knowledge in this manner.) Failing to take seriously their own access to inner powers, most humans see no need to go more deeply than the surface ritual, as the Jewish people were explicitly exhorted to do by the Old Testament books of Leviticus, Numbers, and Deuteronomy.

If one thesis of this book is correct, that the oral traditions and historical accounts of advanced-being involvement with humans refer to actual events, then the notion falls that divine gods (which have been based on those same legends) ordained our religions. If humans and all other beings are the products of a progressive natural process arising from the interaction of universal consciousness (noumena) with its two other aspects (energeia and phenomena), then there is no room for supernatural beings. I believe metascience points to such a self-generating and self-learning universe in which all levels of consciousness takes responsibility for its destiny within the whole.

In this context, I often wonder just how much our religious tendency to place the responsibility for our fates in the hands of imagined divine beings weakened our own resolve to tackle social and psychological problems head-on? How much have we inappropriately used worship of advanced beings as a scapegoat for our own weaknesses?

A new unabridged history, dealing with all the artifacts and legends from "the ages of the gods," would deflate our egotistical vision of ourselves as the first and most advanced sentient beings. I believe a more accurate picture of Earth's past would include a history of cyclical rising and falling of civilizations, some with planet-wide impact. It would cover cataclysmic events—resulting from conscious actions or natural forces—that have destroyed civilizations and technologies. Influences of intermittent engagements with extraplanetary groups, involving very high levels of consciousness, would be credited. With a more accurate historical foundation, humans would be better able to understand our current institutions and future potential. By recognizing that our history is not totally our own creation, we would empower ourselves to declare our independence and separate ourselves from any undesired influence of our AB colonizers.

World War II marked a threshold of technological development that may have stimulated renewed extraterrestrial interest in Earth. Humans harnessed the conversion of mass to energy in a tremendously powerful nuclear weapon, perfected jet propulsion technology that presaged travel to the stars, and mounted a powerful radar system to reveal aerial surveillance. All these developments occurred in the late 1940s at U.S. government installations in an area of New Mexico proximate to the locations where alien aircraft reportedly crashed in 1947. The last fifty-plus years have seen a continuing escalation of UFO/AB activity, and only a small fraction of it is described in this book.

The moment may be approaching when, having completed their current reconnaissance or research objectives on humans and animals,[31] ABs desire formal contact. For the first time in modern history, humans may be in a position for effective, two-way, mutually beneficial engagement. Citizens are now taking the initiative, including referenda on state proclamations urging the national government to grant a waiver of its security agreements to permit present and former military and intelligence officials to testify before Congress on what they know.

All this will require the demise of the unilateral government cover-up of knowledge and contacts that has involved every president since Harry Truman, but excludes senators and congressmen alike. Politicians who have publicly admitted UFO/AB experiences or interest, such as Presidents Carter and Reagan, and presidential candidate Barry Goldwater, have suffered the censorship of the covert system. In the 1990s, the late New Mexico Congressman Schiff's attempts to review government knowledge of the Roswell incident were totally rebuffed. He died from cancer a short time later.

A Stellar Home Base

By now I hope you will agree with me that we need to rediscover our true legacy. Our recorded social history is just as spotty as our knowledge of the planet's geological and physical chronology. Every day we learn how much more we do not understand or how our "facts" are wrong. Even from this abbreviated review of the evidence, it should be obvious that the human story is much more complex than the one described in our formal history. We need only to weave together forgotten or ignored strands of knowledge gathered from science, cultural anthropology, and interdisciplinary analyses of historical artifacts to discover we are fascinating beings with a very colorful past. Fundamental correction to history on such a broad scale will be a monumental task.

Scientists and educators will be challenged to update and expand every discipline in order to incorporate knowledge of the extended human past and its multilevel cosmic influences. *Homo sapiens* have only a dim memory of wisdom from that past, but a core of understanding about our true cosmic nature remains in accounts of perennial wisdom. Combining ancient wisdom with truly new discoveries would result in a much richer understanding of our planetary organism.

What some religious traditions consider "the fall of man" may have been only expulsion into "the world of adulthood," when humans were forced to learn to be self-sufficient, without the oversight of more advanced beings. Perhaps, as Plato hinted, the gods left us to our own devices with a few insights or scientific secrets that would provide keys to later understanding. Tales abound of great teachers appearing under different guises around the planet. Stories of a Jesus-like being appearing in India, Central America, and even Glastonbury in England, may be examples of historical AB intervention in the natural order. Humans now acknowledge our own role as interventionists in natural developments on Earth, so perhaps in the future we will venture out from home base to be "advanced beings" elsewhere.

Enough pieces of ignored knowledge now exist for an entirely new story of our origins and purpose, a new living myth for humanity—our Solarian legacy. With such a legacy, where do we go from here in terms of outer space exploration?

Arthur C. Clarke (the science fiction writer whose work inspired the film *2001: A Space Odyssey*) and others have proposed that *Homo sapiens* should garden (terraform) the planet Mars. Drawing on research (by David A. Paige, et al., of UCLA) that showed water deposits frozen just under the Martian surface, Clarke postulated that we could cultivate grains and forests that would serve as catalysts for the formation of lakes and oceans. Clarke—who in 1946 predicted our current network of space satellite communications systems—saw our agro-development of Mars as a matter-of-fact extension of human development on Earth. Many others now agree.

Responsible extraterrestrial exploration and stewardship are more than an extension of humanity's scientific and technological quest. They are a natural consequence of our cosmic consciousness. As we come to understand that our inner essence is not earthbound, we realize that neither is our physical presence. Our heritage and our future are not confined to this planet. As we have been seeded and/or nurtured by beings from elsewhere in the cosmos, our birthright includes a comparable mission. This planet is only home base. The material frontier for expansion of our civilization is almost as unlimited as the boundaries of our consciousness.

Our home base Earth is a stellar one in two senses of the word. Like "seedbed" planets in any galaxy, it is perfect for the birthing and maturation of a potentially high-performance species. And it provides a launch pad for our exploration and travel to other solar systems. As NASA's sixty-plus-year space exploration plan proposes, we should work our way in stages beyond Pluto's orbit; and I agree. Those stages include going through the area filled with comets (Kuiper Comet Belt) just outside our planetary orbits and crossing the Sun's energetic boundary (the Heliopause). The NASA-proposed TAU Mission would then take us into the interstellar winds and beyond the Oort Cloud of 200 billion comets. After that we would head for Alpha Centauri, 250,000 times the distance from Earth to the Sun.

My two modifications to the NASA plan would be: an effort to actively engage any ABs in sharing their knowledge with us, and to incorporate the use of the inner senses for communications with other-dimensional beings. In both cases, it would make sense to seek their assistance and company on this long journey. For me, there is sufficient evidence to actively seek such cooperation. Combining inner space exploration with physical space research, as suggested in the following chapter, could mean reaching our target in less than half the time, with the additional effect of psychological and social progress.

Notes

1. "Science and the Citizen," *Scientific American* (November 1995).

2. Zecharia Sitchin, *The Twelfth Planet: Book I of The Earth Chronicles* (New York: Stein and Day, 1976).

3. I use the term "AB" instead of ET, with its "alien" and "different origin" connotations. "AB" can mean "advanced being," "alternative being," or "another being."

4. Such fragments sporadically break free and traverse Earth's orbit in erratic routes. According to a scientist with the U.S. Geological Survey, about 110 such asteroids, ranging from just over one-half mile to twenty-five miles in diameter, pose a potential threat to the Earth, just as the Shoemaker-Levy 9 comet did to Jupiter in July 1994. Perhaps up to 4,000 other large asteroids and small comets (ice balls) also pose danger to the Earth. NASA and the Air Force now track these objects, and many scientists (members of the International Astronomical Union) want the U.S. and other nations to develop ways to disable any that approach the globe. They suggest using lasers, small asteroids, or nuclear explosions to divert or destroy them.

5. Shirley Andrews, *Atlantis: Insights from a Lost Civilization* (St. Paul, MN: Lllewellyn Publications, 1997); Charles Berlitz, *Atlantis: The Eighth Continent* (New York: Ballantine Books, 1985).

6. Javier Cabrera Darquea, *The Message of the Engraved Stones of Ica* (Lima, Peru: Servicio Grafico "2000," 1989).

7. Richard Thompson and Michael Cremo, *Forbidden Archaelogy: Hidden History of the Human Race* (Badger, CA: Torchlight Publishing, 1996).

8. Richard Milton, *The Facts of Life: Shattering the Myth of Darwinism* (London: Corgi Books, Transworld Publishers, 1995).

9. Barbara C. Sproul, *Primal Myths* (San Francisco: Harper San Francisco, 1991).

10. Jerome Clark, *The Emergence of a Phenomenon: UFOs from the Beginning Through 1959*; *High Strangeness: UFOs from 1960 through 1979*; and *UFOs in the 1980s* (Chicago: Center for UFO Studies, 1990–96).

11. Steve Jones, *The Language of Genes* (New York: Anchor Books, 1993); Luigi Luca Cavalli-Sforza *The Great Human Diaspora: The History of Diversity and Evolution* (Reading, MA: Addison-Wesley, 1995); Graham Hancock, *Fingerprints of the Gods* (New York: Crown Publishers, 1995).

12. William Bramley, *Gods of Eden* (New York: Avon Books, 1993).

13. Arthur D. Horn, *Humanity's Extraterrestrial Origins* (Mt. Shasta, CA: A & L Horn, 1994).

14. Lloyd Pye, *Everything You Know Is Wrong (Book One: Human Origins)* (Madeira Beach, FL: ADAMU Press, 1997).

15. Rudolf Steiner, *Cosmic Memory* (New York: Harper & Row, 1959).

16. Richard C. Hoagland, *The Monuments of Mars: A City on the Edge of Forever* (Berkeley, CA: North Atlantic Books, 1987).

17. Stanley McDaniel, *The McDaniel Report: On the Failure of Executive, Congressional, and Scientific Responsibility in Investigating Possible Evidence of Artificial Structures on the Surface of Mars and in Setting Mission Priorities for NASA's Mars Exploration Program* (Berkeley, CA: North Atlantic Books, 1994).

18. Courtney Brown, *Cosmic Voyage* (New York: Dutton, 1996).

19. Immanuel Velikovsky, *Worlds in Collision* (Garden City, NY: Doubleday and Company, 1950); Louis Pauwels and Jacques Bergier, *Eternal Man* (Frogmore, St. Albens, UK: Mayflower Books Ltd., 1973); *Mysterious Origins of Man* (Video) (B.C. Video, Inc., P.O. Box 97, Shelbourne, VT 05482).

20. See my article "Whence Human Knowledge?" published in the May 1999 issue of *Aspectarian* and available at www.vonward.com.

21. Maurice Chatelain, *Our Cosmic Ancestors* (Sedona, AZ: Temple Golden Publications, 1988).

22. The number 60 (squared at 3,600 and used as 360 for Earth-bound geometry) encompasses the counting systems used by the Sumerians (60), Mayans (20), Egyptians (10), and Gauls (12).

23. An interesting twist on this question comes from an alleged group of future humans who came back to Earth about 1,200 years

ago and left a complex of twenty-three chambers inside a mountain in northern New Mexico. According to www.wingmakers.com, this group of future humans became adept at time travel and decided to set up the information chambers so current humans could learn to make use of time travel to save the Earth from an external takeover in our near future. (Please recall this when you read the discussion of the limits of time travel in chapter 5.) The information was allegedly furnished by a defector from an inner National Security Agency group charged with interpreting the information in the chambers. The originally posted site provided no additional material over a two-year period, so it is impossible to validate the claims made by the anonymous Web site producer.

24. Kevin D. Randle and Donald R. Schmitt, *UFO Crash at Roswell* (New York: Avon Books, 1991).

25. The film *Fire in the Sky*, released in March 1993, details Walton's abduction in November 1975, when six friends saw him knocked down by a beam of light from a spacecraft. His book with the same title published in 1996 gives additional facts.

26. A recent review of the historical record shows that in each year of the twentieth century, one can read about credible reports of UFO/AB contacts somewhere in the world. The Center for UFO Studies in Chicago now has on CD-ROM over 100,000 sightings incorporated from the databases of several researchers.

27. Jacques Vallee, *Confrontations* (New York: Random House, 1990).

28. Bruce Maccabee, *The UFO-FBI Connection.* (St. Paul, MN: Llewellyn Publications, 2000).

29. Richard Hall, *Uninvited Guests* (Santa Fe, NM: Aurora Press, 1992).

30. Depictions of priests (Mayan and others) drinking blood in various rituals may be modeled after AB blood transfusions and organ transplants, or other medical practices. It is possible that naive humans—in an attempt to align themselves with the so-called gods—later emulated the form without understanding the substance of AB practices.

31. Linda M. Howe, *Alien Harvest: Further Evidence Linking Animal Mutilations and Human Abduction to Alien Life Forms* (Philadelphia: L.M. Howe Productions, 1989). With regard to animals, the aliens

have taken the same callous approach as humans have—if indeed they are responsible for dissecting and removing organs from live-stock in many areas of the world. Carcasses left behind contain the marks of advanced surgical procedures performed without regard to the consciousness of the animals.

PART 2

Consciousness Manifests Itself

By now I hope you agree with me that our universe and our history are much more complex than we ever imagined. This section explores the nuanced multidimensionality of humans in the context of a conscious, self-directing universe. It takes a nonhomocentric view of reality, where humans are only one group of actors in a cosmic drama, minors aspiring to the big league of self-learners.

The implications of recent discoveries in frontier science, when integrated with insights into nature from ancient but highly advanced sources, suggest that the universe as a whole arises from the state we call consciousness. Many experiments like those covered in part 1 point to consciousness as both the origin and arbiter of developments in physical reality. *Homo sapiens'* study of nature, including their own experience of it, intimates that all levels of reality have some degree of awareness of what happens to them and something of the cause. On the basis of this awareness of cause and effect, all conscious entities (even viruses) can engage in adaptive behavior. This makes it possible for any level of consciousness to assess the results of its intention (or purpose, even if only to survive) against the reactions of all other levels. In other words, an individual conscious entity (or a collective of entities, such as a species) can learn whether a specific intention can work in the context of the whole universe, and if not, what will work.

If such learning can result from the interaction of local consciousness with energetic and material existence, then it is not unreasonable to infer that universal consciousness learns from the synthesis of the self-learning from all the parts. Further, if all those self-learning parts derive from one singular consciousness, then the conscious universe in its entirety must be self-learning.

With increasing awareness of self and environment, it is normal for *Homo sapiens* as conscious beings to seek the code that will reveal how they fit into the whole. Part 1 gave us a sense of the universe from the microcosm to the macroscosm. It also reviewed what we have discovered of an extended human history in our solar system. Now let's attempt to understand how humans as conscious, organic beings function as a part of the larger system. Part 2 attempts to fit the human piece of the puzzle into the model of a self-learning universe.

To do that, in chapter 4 we first look at the three facets of reality in relation to organic beings. Remember, the three facets introduced in part 1 are the noumena (consciousness), the energeia (subtle energies), and phenomena (physical). We review how physical beings are both composed of those facets and interact with the three external to themselves. We develop an understanding of the powers of sensing and creation at all levels, and how beings use the subtle senses to expand their grasp of the universe. In chapter 5 we look at the realm of universal mind, and how individuals are embedded in and relate to the whole, at how general consciousness connects all beings in a mutually supportive system. Chapter 6 deals with how universal consciousness concentrates part of itself into a local form (the process of incarnation) and how the resulting individual maintains its integrity in space-time and beyond. The implication of the predominance of consciousness among the three facets is highlighted for human learning and development.

4

A Three-Faceted Reality

The universe, from the conventional scientific perspective, is unidimensional: everything is part of and limited to the material realm. Even most multidimensional-physics models are limited to matenergy and various concepts of space-time. Many philosophers think of the universe in dualistic terms: mind and matter. Some religions see three parts: body, mind, and spirit. Metascience offers another concept: a multifaceted universe with all elements interactive and conterminous. In this idea of an integral universe, all facets are dependent on one another—one part cannot exist as it is without all the others.

In a three-faceted universe where consciousness is supreme, conscious beings, by definition, include all three facets (noumena, energeia, and phenomena). This means *Homo sapiens* and all other life-forms comprise and interact with consciousness, subtle energies, and ordinary matter and energy to varying degrees. In my view, the subtle-energy facet is the realm of emotional charges.

Activities of the universe involving matenergy can be perceived by the physical senses, but other levels of reality require more subtle senses. The next leap in human knowledge needs an integration of all ways of knowing. A review of the full range of human experiences, including those now often called anomalous, reveals the need for a more expansive intellectual framework to understand interactions between individual beings and the whole. The framework offered here (three facets and multiple senses) can help us make sense of all types of human experience and interpret our contacts with as yet unexplained realms.

Having selectively explored the macrocosmic and microcosmic dimensions of the universe and our human legacy, we now turn to the question of how we know what we think we know. For classical Greek philosophers, the concept "phenomena" included all concrete things in objective reality. But they also believed in a nonphenomenal realm, the permanent essence of things that could be known through intuition. What I call the "noumena" was the subjective domain of ideas and abstract forms. The two are bound together by a third realm of subtle energy or forces that I labeled "energeia" in chapter 2. We know the universe comprises at least these three interdependent realms or facets of one whole because, as this chapter demonstrates, it takes these three to adequately categorize human experience.

The noumenal and energeial, or inner, ways of knowing have been devalued over the last four centuries by the increasing global acceptance of the Newtonian view of physical science. The result is that currently all formal human institutions of significance—those defining our "official truth"—are dominated by phenomena-based thinking.[1] Most of us believe that being "objective" in any aspect of life, and particularly when undertaking scientific research, means limiting ourselves to the five sense channels: smell, touch, taste, hearing, and sight. But not everyone limits themselves to these five.

The Bushmen of southern Africa, sensitively described in the books of Laurens van der Post, have their sense of "tapping," a sensation deep in the chest that indicates they are on the track to food or that they are relating properly to their habitat or community. The water-well or lost-object dowser continues to develop a feel for a presence that cannot be seen or touched. Serious scientists, like an Einstein or a Tesla, do not reject solutions that come in visions or dreams. The clairvoyant does not stop using an inner eye. The successful businessperson does not ignore hunches. Millions in all walks of life believe in basing important decisions on their intuition or inner sources of information. Fully conscious beings in any species seek to combine all feasible ways of knowing.

Design—Forces—Matter

To take advantage of different ways of knowing requires that we develop an understanding of how humans operate internally, beyond their biological systems. Then we can understand how all these internal (to us) elements interact with other entities and fields of consciousness and subtle energies.

Modern science has limited itself to the empirical process of physical verification. By using refined instrumentation that extends the reach of scientists' sight and touch, we manipulate the subatomic realm of ordinary matter. But this success has its price. Stuck on the tactic of trying to understand the inner workings of materiality by crashing through its outer walls, researchers use physical hooks to open the doors to atoms, molecules, cells, organs, and bodies of all kinds. We observe events like chemical reactions, tumors, comets, storms, or flowers, and immediately start looking for the physical causes. This approach only leads to other material connections which, as we have seen in the microcosm, become more and more difficult to pin down.

To understand mind and emotion, still mysteries to materialistic science, we must conceptually reach beyond the phenomena to infer the dynamics of various forces at play (energeia) and to infer the patterns and principles behind those dynamics (noumena). The implications of hypothesizing these two additional facets can be tested in the mundane world. Experiments can be made in areas of human experience now outside the explanatory power of traditional science. Mind-body healing and telepathic communications are examples.

This three-faceted model is reflected in many other perspectives. What Gregory Bateson might have labeled "substance" (phenomena), "energy" (energeia), and "no thing" (noumena), Michael Talbot would have labeled, respectively, "mass," "energy," and "information."[2] Parallel Christian concepts (Father, Son, and Holy Spirit) and teachings of the

Jewish Kabbalah point to the same insights in esoteric knowledge. As seen in chapter 2, the discipline of particle physics has identified the basic triadic nature of the subparticle level.

That is why I contend that a combination of these metaphysical and scientific concepts helps create a broader science: a metascience with a more comprehensive approach to knowing. Metascience points to theories that postulate an intermediate or subtle-energy field with its own set of forces responsive to permutations of thought or ideas. It can enhance our understanding of the processes that, to use the concepts of quantum mechanics, collapse a potential pattern of reality into experienced or observed reality.[3]

As we saw in chapter 2, the phenomena and energeia first exist in potential form, to be activated by conscious intent. This means subtle energy and ordinary energy and matter exist in inchoate states until consciousness imprints them with its patterns. These patterns then manifest themselves from unformed energeia and phenomena as perceptible entities, shaped by the subtle and physical senses. (This is consistent with the anthropic concept in physics that material reality does not exist until conscious beings perceive it.) This is why human emotions (energeial-level events) are determined by preexisting beliefs (noumenal-level intentions). Our metascientific challenge is to understand the dynamics of transformation of subtle and ordinary energy from its potential (state of rest) to its kinetic (action) state.

Scientific knowledge of all energy spectra is still fragmentary, with our understanding becoming more diffuse as we move from top to bottom on the continuum shown below. We think we understand gravity in the mechanical arena[4] and chemical energy expressed as heat in the conversion of matter, but the other areas seem less certain as one moves down. For example, Robert Jahn of Princeton University hypothesizes that consciousness interacts with the material realm through a quantum wave function, but it is unclear where that interaction fits on such a spectrum in terms we can verify.

Energy Continuum

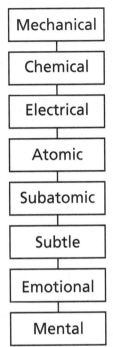

| Mechanical |
| Chemical |
| Electrical |
| Atomic |
| Subatomic |
| Subtle |
| Emotional |
| Mental |

The common forms of energy all occupy the phenomenal realm (electrical, nuclear, solar, muscular, etc.). But new concepts of energy beyond the electromagnetic spectrum have become necessary to understand various phenomena. Research with scalars—waves that continue to reverberate whenever matter is removed from space—now leads to progress in the development of so-called free energy technology. Scalars have been considered cosmic waves by some, because they are believed to be faster than the speed of light, leaving no trace in the material realm. The term "tachyon" has been used to designate them, and the term "zero-point energy" (ZPE) is also used by some to refer to this mysterious energy.

Waves like the above, but not part of the electromagnetic spectrum, may be the subtle energies of the energeia. I employ the term "subtle energy" when referring to any energy assumed to be in the energeial realm, because it avoids confusion with the ordinary energy of the electromagnetic spectrum (which can be either wave or particle).

In the model offered here, subtle energy or energeia arises from consciousness, as matenergy appears to rise from energeia. But new experiment designs are needed to test how an idea (from the noumena) acts on subtle energy (from the energeia) that in turn shapes matenergy. Recall that matenergy denotes a polarity of matter and energy, two ends of the same dimension in the phenomenal realm.

Metescience research projects should begin with the assumption that energies in the energeial and the noumenal realms, like the phenomenal, possess both potential and kinetic states. Therefore, the research design must incorporate the possibility of spontaneous, nonlinear conscious response. Perhaps the ancient Tao philosophy (expressed in the Tai Chi Chuan school of Chinese martial arts) which says Wu-Chi, the state of nothingness that holds the potential for both static and dynamic states,[5] requires mindfulness in its use.

In its potential form, physical energy is force waiting to be released, whether a precariously balanced rock, a piece of wood or food, or an atom. In my three-faceted model, embodied (incarnated) emotions are derived from potential subtle energy, and local mind derives its potential from general consciousness. In our four-dimensional world, kinetic energy involves vibration in space-time, be it in the rebounding billiard ball or a surge of electrons. The pulsing of prayers and telepathic transmissions, like the movement of air molecules and the flitting of electrons, are manifestations of kinetic energy.

The important point here is that all levels of energy transformation from potential to kinetic involve the expressive aspect of some form of communication. Each is ultimately caused by an expression of intent.

When humans understand that various forms of energy and matter come from conscious events, we open the doors—using the receptivity of all our senses—to greater expression of our inner power. The making of imaginal choices creates thought patterns (morphic fields, as in the popular hundredth monkey theory) that energize physical reality. Between ideas and their manifestation lies the interface where the subtle energies of the emotional realm (energeia) await activation by mental patterns. (As we'll see later, this interface has an expressive—yang—and a receptive—yin—side.) These concentrated emotions, in turn, activate the media of electromagnetic, mechanical, and chemical energies to affect the phenomenal realm.

The earlier discussion of the role of ideas and emotions in the creation of neuropeptides offers an illustration of this sequence. The fully conscious being in a multidimensional, feedback-using universe requires multilevel senses to act as gateways between the realms. The following review of different categories of senses illuminates how the three realms interact, providing feedback to one another. This feedback loop, revealing the effects of initial intentions and adaptations, is essential in a self-learning universe.

A conscious entity demonstrates its self-learning nature when its mind (noumena) receives subtle-energy messages (energeial emotions) of an impending deterioration in cell functions (phenomena) and changes its mental polarity from negative to positive. This shift of attitude (noumena) gives rise to positive emotions that stimulate molecular change in cells. And the circular learning process continues as long as one remains fully aware of the interactive levels of sensing.

Five Physical Senses

In her book *A Natural History of the Senses*,[6] Diane Ackerman uses the written word in a sensual exploration of a world teeming with physical stimuli that define the limits of our material world. Humans luxuriate in a flood of wonders that, while sharpening their focus, actually limits their experience. Given the quality of interaction available within the rich material environment, it is no wonder that many of us end up stopping there.

The five ordinary senses are the entry points through which data from the relatively dense material plane connect with our physical bodies. At the outer perimeter of the physical body, these specialized cells receive input from the external environment and send it to the brain for analysis. Some of these stimuli serve as catalysts for involuntary, physical reactions. Others require conscious input to decipher their meanings for the individual. It is helpful to think of the sensory receptors as corporeal extensions of the central nervous system, analogous to mechanical extensions like the telephone, the telescope, the smoke detector, and the stethoscope.

In each category, a sense organ does not make sense of anything; it only takes in bits of data. The mind, working through the brain and the nervous system, makes sense of what is perceived. The most appropriate term for the five senses, therefore, is "receptors." The eyes *see* rather than look. The skin sensors *feel* rather than touch. These examples make it clear we need to be careful with our terminology. Although receptive, the five ordinary senses are not passive. For this reason, the gerund (noun) form of verbs—seeing, hearing, smelling, feeling, and tasting—is used here.

Seeing. Seeing is our outer perimeter guard post for understanding what is going on in the world around us. Its range is the longest of the five ordinary senses, literally to stars deep in the universe. Seventy percent of our body's receptors are devoted to it. The retina takes in the light waves and focuses them on photosensitive rod- and cone-shaped cells. Different cells, perceiving different colors on the electromagnetic spectrum, send electrochemical signals to the brain's visual cortex. The visual cortex—used by the mind in making sense of these signals—does the actual looking. (This is important to remember later when we discuss televiewing.)

The visible light our eyes perceive constitutes a very limited range of the electromagnetic spectrum. The old saying "what you see is what you get" is misleading. We get much more than we see: the richness of all light helps us survive and thrive in our habitat. The light not seen by our eyes affects biological as well as psychological rhythms. Our development and health are bound up in the cycles of light and dark.

Hearing. Hearing is the registering of sound, of waves of air molecules that dissipate over relatively short distances. These moving molecules (like the circles caused by dropping a stone in a pond) can come from the vibrations of any object. Like waves on the beach, the sound waves crash on our eardrums, making them vibrate, tripping the tiny hammer-, anvil-, and stirrup-shaped bones. These bones push fluid in the inner ear against membranes that jostle tiny hairs, which in turn cause nerve cells to send electrical impulses to the brain.

Sound waves, like all other waves of energy, have various frequencies. High-pitched sounds have high frequencies. We can generally hear frequencies between 16,000 to 20,000 cycles per second, a range of about ten octaves. Vibration over 20,000 cycles per second is considered ultrasound. (Although ultrasound cannot be heard, its force can be harnessed for a variety of tasks in healing, heating, lifting, etc.) And though the ear is particularly fine-tuned, our entire body registers sound waves—acting as a huge acoustical receiver.

Smelling. In our noses are olfactory sites—the neurons in 5 million receptor cells—that are sensitive to odorous molecules drawn into our system. This drawing-in is a receptive process, an integral part of our inhaling. Upon exhaling we send the molecules back out, our brain's limbic system having interpreted their electrical messages about the state of the contiguous world. Once again we have the yin and yang: a person both smells (senses) and gives off smells.

Smelling is one of the body's main-line defense systems. Through smell the hypothalamus senses nearby danger, mating potential, food sources, and other factors related to survival (like toxic air). Odorous changes in the Earth and in people, through the medium of pheromones, stimulate biological reactions—adrenaline rushes, salivating reflexes, and sexual changes (including modified menstrual cycles). Artificial pheromones can be used to stimulate affectionate or rejecting response patterns.

Feeling. The functions of the skin—a two-layered membrane less than two millimeters thick—are to feel and to serve as our physical boundary. (Remember our sense feels, while our touching—yang expression—of others is felt by them.) The largest organ in the body (six to ten pounds), the skin keeps more in than it lets out, but is by no means impermeable. Its cells breathe and excrete as all cells do. The skin blocks out some of the sun's rays, fends off microbes, serves as an insulator, and metabolizes vitamin D. The outer layer, the epidermis, constantly renews itself.

The inner layer of skin—the dermis—has several kinds of sense receptors that respond to pressure (touching). More receptors are concentrated in hairy areas of the skin, hair itself being a receptor. These receptor cells, depending on the quality of contact (heat, pressure, or vibration), respond with a repertoire of electrical signals to the brain. Crucial for psychological as well as physical well-being, feeling is the first sense that becomes operative for the newborn.

Tasting. Tasting, like smelling, involves ingestion, but it is a much grosser screen. Our taste buds require thousands of times the number of molecules required for smell. But, like smelling, tasting also requires that geometric molecules fit the sense receptors in order for electrical impulses to be sent to the brain.

Tasting is our ultimate line of defense against threatening substances that might otherwise be taken into the body. It also helps us know what is good for us. Taste is a measure of likes and dislikes. To have a taste for something is to need it or to desire it. There is a direct relationship between our physical tastes and our subjective states.

Multiple Senses in Tandem

All five physical senses are interrelated, working in tandem to keep us informed of our situation relative to other beings and our environment. For some people, like my daughter, who says colors have smells, one sense stimulates another. In the extreme, this condition is called synesthesia. Although no single sense is absolutely essential for life, as a team they make navigating our physical environment easier and more pleasurable.

The five physical senses seem to deal with such different kinds of information that we unthinkingly consider them separate and distinct. When viewed in the context of the electromagnetic spectrum that shows their essential similarities, the perceived "gaps" between these senses disappear. Whether light waves, sound waves, or pressure waves, each and all are perceived by specialized organs of one integral human body that uses them to orient itself in the pool of universal matenergy in which it thrives. Whether the chemical fit is sensed by the nose or the tongue, whether the pressure is sensed by the skin or the ear, the result is the same: a sample of the immediately contiguous physical environment.

Each of the five physical senses perceives only a part of the range of stimuli for which it is designed. We see only certain light waves, hear only limited frequencies, and smell only certain scents, and so on. Table 7 reveals how much on the electromagnetic spectrum our senses miss. The range of stimuli we perceive with each sense seems to be related to our immediate survival needs. Consider how dull cosmic existence

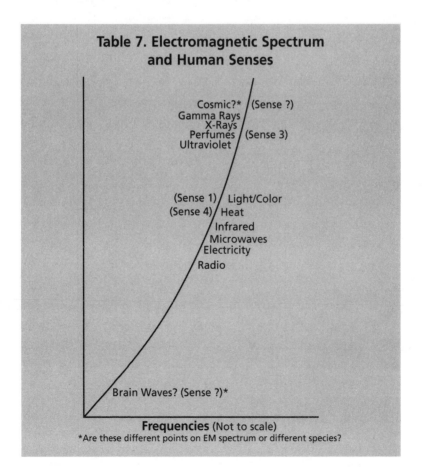

Table 7. Electromagnetic Spectrum and Human Senses

Cosmic?* (Sense ?)
Gamma Rays
X-Rays
Perfumes (Sense 3)
Ultraviolet

(Sense 1) Light/Color
(Sense 4) Heat
Infrared
Microwaves
Electricity
Radio

Brain Waves? (Sense ?)*

Frequencies (Not to scale)
*Are these different points on EM spectrum or different species?

would be if we were limited to just five senses. Fortunately, we have a larger set of capacities at our disposal.

All senses require the expression of something else's output (masculine) which they then perceive (feminine)—respectively the yang and the yin functions. There must first be an expression toward us that we then sense. Without an ear to hear, the falling tree makes no noise. The two arms of the matrix in table 8 indicate the interplay between expressing and sensing, the output/input process necessary for self-learning organisms.

We frequently confuse sensing with expressing by using the same word for both the yin and yang acts. We often say we are touching something external to us when we actually are feeling the touch of someone or something else. When something has an odor, it has a "scent" and we "smell" it.[7] When we hear, we are detecting the vibrations of something else. The ear cannot hear its own vibrations. Thus, if all physical senses are receptive functions, the same must be true for any subtle senses that exist in the energeial and noumenal realms.

The Principle of Correspondence would predict that all physical senses have analogous subtle senses in both the emotional and mental planes.[8] Therefore, I suggest that humans have at least five subtle senses that parallel the five primary physical ones. (See table 8.) All specialized channels through which we engage in self-learning with each other and for the universe encompass the polarity of sensing/expressing. That means we likely have fifteen or more identifiable senses. If the seven main chakras[9] involve energeial or subtle-energy senses—as I believe they do—then the number of identifiable human senses is even greater. These subtle senses are our natural gifts. They develop spontaneously, but can be enhanced through conscious effort.

Examples of animal senses outside the ordinary five can help us grasp the idea of the subtle senses. Some animals are extremely sensitive to one or more physical stimuli: magnetism,[10] electrical fields, ultraviolet light, polarized light, barometric pressure changes, and infrasounds. Animals can pick up these perturbations from great distances, sometimes hundreds or thousands of miles away. Some birds may guide themselves on long flights by matching imprinted patterns with sun angles and constellations. Bees, too, use polarized light from the heavens to navigate. Bats fly sensing sonic reverberations much as jet planes use radar. Fish respond to changes in the salinity gradient and "hear" through the vibrations of small stones (otoliths) nestled in a bed of nerve hairs on each side of the brain. Sharks are attracted by small increases (just a few

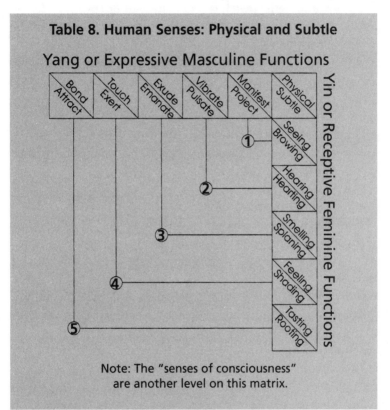

Table 8. Human Senses: Physical and Subtle

Note: The "senses of consciousness" are another level on this matrix.

parts per billion) in the blood gradient in water.

Humans may have residual forms of some of the animal senses mentioned above. Some of our seemingly disoriented behavior may be caused by perturbations in senses we do not recognize we have. We also appear to share more subtle senses with animals and/or more evolved beings.

If the five senses based in the phenomenal realm reflect the characteristics of that realm, the subtle senses help distinguish the differences between the realms. For example, since the subtle senses are not of the physical realm (not dependent on matenergy) they are not limited by time and space. In effect, we can infer the realm or dimension in which any sense communicates by its characteristics. For example, the "tapping" of the Bushmen works through the energeia, while precognition of images operates in the noumena.

Looking at this another way, the evidence of senses at work beyond the phenomenal realm confirms the existence of the subtle realms. Instantaneous transfer of information validates the hypothesis that a noumenal realm exists outside the boundaries of space-time. Ruptures in a heart-energy connection felt across great distances confirm that individual energy fields are not limited to a few feet around the body. This means that research with subtle or inner senses, gathering proof of such specific communications among beings, can provide validation of multidimensional principles.

Five Subtle Senses

As the physical senses are all characterized by their electrochemical nature, the senses of the energeia involve the subtle energies of the being's emotional field, and those of the noumena convey the power of pure thought. I suggest labels for five senses of the energeia, recognizing that it is only a beginning and that further conceptual development and research are required. My taking the liberty of creating new terms is an effort to bring a fresh perspective to the senses that are often indistinguishable under catch-all labels like "intuition," or "sixth sense."

The five senses described below are, like the physical senses, receptive and interrelated. They are reciprocals of complementary expressions of subtle energies in currently unknown spectra (see table 10 later) parallel to the electromagnetic spectrum.

Given the experiences of Western healers, martial arts practitioners, and psi researchers with the ancient knowledge of chakra centers as vortices of human subtle-energy fields, I believe major chakra points serve as subtle senses/gateways between individuals and the external environment. No widespread consensus exists on the existence and character of such a schema. However, there is a significant degree of congruence among the ancient Tantric tradition, the current work of light-energy healing specialist Barbara Brennan, and my own research. (See Table 9 on page 140 for a comparison of the three perspectives.)

The following schema, according to pilot studies I have conducted over the last several years, offers promise for increased understanding of energetic/emotional communication between conscious beings. I propose it as a catalyst for further research.

Browing. "Browing" corresponds to the ordinary sense of seeing. A form of televiewing, it is not limited to line of sight or the speed of light. It is our channel for sensing coherent forms of subtle energy. People who can "see" auras understand this sense without difficulty. But all of us can perceive amorphous images within the energeia without regard to physical location, both in local time (remote viewing) and beyond time (precognition of subtle forms and retrovision).

With "browing" we can access the energized forms that derive from strong conscious activity as well as the ongoing energy fields of phenomenal events or artifacts. Such forms may also include energized group reactions to events. The events themselves are only transitory and are not stored; only the memory fields are, as so-called archetypes. In the Hindu chakra system, "browing" relates to the third eye or sixth chakra. "Browing" is not the same as seeing clear images or precise patterns in the noumenal field. That receptivity exists in the noumenal senses.

Hearting. "Hearting" monitors shifts in frequency that result from changes in the love/hate (connection/rejection) polarity of another being or group. Relating to the fourth or heart chakra, the vibrations of this subtle force and those of sound are analogous. "Hearting" and hearing have the same root syllable. In both realms, these parallel forms of energy can be either highly strung and defensive or serene and malleable, depending on their frequency. Making behavioral waves is therefore a visible manifestation of negative subtle-energy vibrations.

Table 9. Subtle Senses and the Chakras

Chakra	Tantric Yoga	B.A. Brennan*	Von Ward
1. Root	Smell (Desire/Anger)	Touch (Movement)	Tasting
2. Sexual	Taste (Astral Plane)	Emotional	Smelling
3. Solar Plexus	Penetrate/Fire	Intuition	Feeling
4. Heart	Hearing/Touch	Loving	Hearing
5. Throat	Hearing/Breathing	Hearing/Speaking	Empathizing
6. Third Eye	Divine Consciousness	Seeing/Visualizing	Seeing
7. Crown	Union/Polarities	Knowing	Integrating

* Barbara Ann Brennan, *Hands of Light* (Bantam, New York, 1987)

With this sense, our interpersonal disposition can be perceived by those attuned to us, even over vast distances. Through this sense one "hears" the cry of one seeking connection or "knows" of another's remote pushing away. When we tell another, "I not only heard you, but I really hear what you're saying," we attempt to reflect both the physical and subtle dimensions of our multilevel capacity to communicate.

Splaning. Through our ability to "splan" we sense another's particular emotional state. One's general degree of openness versus defensiveness is communicated through the site of the second chakra (near the spleen or sexual organs). This subtle sense also measures the expression of the fight/flight polarity: we "splan" subtle confrontations by others or, obversely, their potential withdrawals from the potential engagement. This does not necessarily imply a physical struggle. It also deals with the issue of introversion versus extroversion.

On a subtle level, it is almost as if we can smell the intentions of another being, not unlike an olfactory engagement with a skunk in bad humor or the hormonal signals exchanged between potential sexual partners. Through the sense of "splaning," one is aware of the unspoken desire of the other for mutual engagement or avoidance.

Shading. A lion signals its impulse to dominate territory or exert control in a manner that is obvious to the physical senses; humans send out similar signals, but there are others not necessarily so obvious. The "shading" sense helps us register the state of another's aggression index, through the degree of expressed nonphysical pressure. (Some expressions of telekinesis can be perceived through this sense.) Beyond overt behavior and the field of chemical and electrical exchanges, such proactive impulses are communicated through the medium of energetic patterns at the prematerial level, perceptible through "shading."

Received at a distance beyond the range of the physical senses, through the third chakra (in the navel or umbilical area), this sense registers the umbra, or shadow, of another. When attempting to describe our reactions to data received through this sense, we often say we have a gut feeling, as if an invisible shadow casts perceptible force in our direction. (Above-normal defensive or aggressive subtle-energy projection—expressed as emotion—in this chakra adds physical weight to the abdomen. Large girths may reflect more than consumption habits.)

Rooting. Our "rooting" ability serves the same role for individuals as the court taster does for the king: it keeps us alive. Energetic communications warn us of an impending noxious encounter or seduce us into agreeable interaction with other cosmic beings. The other's basic inclination to cooperation or competition is perceived through our first chakra, even without our being face-to-face.

Messages transmitted through this sense of energetic compatibility (mistakenly called "chemistry") are much more reliable indicators of interpersonal harmony than common physical characteristics. The survival of individuals, families, and races depends on the reliability of this channel of communication. In such important matters, the messages exchanged through the root must take precedence over those of the heart or the spleen. The energetic "taste" of this long-wave signal is a truer indicator of sustainable relationships than the phenomenal frequencies of vibration received by the ear and the heart.

Senses and Consciousness

In the subtle-energy realm, as in the physical one, when we receive the vibration of another, consciousness is necessary to make sense of (and validate) the communication. The meanings we attach to energetic signals determine the ultimate nature of our reactions, as in the tasting of food.

Etymology, the study of language development, indicates that the sense of color differentiation has become more complex in humans over the past few centuries. We now label more differences in the wavelengths and amplitudes (shades of color) on the light spectrum than we could previously. We do not know if that is a result of evolution in the physical eye or in the mind that interprets its input. Regardless, the same process undoubtedly will refine the capabilities of our subtle senses. The first step is to become more consciously aware of them.

Neural networks that send and receive expressions operate in all the physical senses. (Humans now simulate some of them in the mechanical world of computers.) Since subtle senses can be categorized as remote sensing—there are no neural (physical) connections—some other medium appears to be involved in this so-called paranormal transmission of subtle signals. I contend that the energeial or subtle-energy realm provides the medium. It is analogous to the role of water or air for the transmission of sound waves.

Cleve Backster, whose work was first popularized in the book *Secret Life of Plants,* calls this level of awareness "primary perception." He has found that cellular reactions in the receiving organism to distant expressions of emotional intent precede transmission of chemical or energetic stimuli in the central nervous system. Contrary to common belief, the physical neural network may simply *demonstrate* the flow of this primary (consciousness) communication, rather than cause it. This sequence is indicated by the evidence that the subtle-energy transmissions travel instantaneously.

According to the three-faceted model I use, there also exists a set of noumenal senses that parallel the five (or more) physical senses and the five (or more) energeial senses. They would receive levels of noumenal information. Some examples include musical notes (not sounds), numerical patterns, geometric shapes, operating principles (like the Hermetic Principles), and abstract concepts.

I have done only preliminary experimentation in workshops with these reputed senses, but I believe they could account for precognition, remote viewing, certain forms of channeling, and some telepathy dealing with symbols and ideas. These senses would be the source of visual impressions received while in an out-of-body (OBE) state, which, of course, involves both the energeial and noumenal bodies. Much further theory development and experiential research must be done before we understand the dynamics involved.

All levels or species of beings are composed of various manifestations of the three facets; in effect, they have three overlapping bodies. The emotional body is subtle energy infused with consciousness. The physical body is materiality infused with emotions. The mental body is a local manifestation of the universal mind. In three-faceted beings like humans and other animals on Earth, the so-called bodies exist together as different aspects of the same being perceived from distinct but interrelated perspectives.

Senses and Manifestation

The corresponding nature of sensing between the phenomenal and energeial bodies may imply that the senses are the channels of reciprocity between realms. The sense nodes of our being may be where the overlaps between realms occur, and, therefore, may be the channels of creation. For example, the subtle senses may be fundamental to incarnation, perhaps to the point of serving as channels for transmitting the energeial precursors to DNA patterns in the process of cell formation. Thus, preexisting conscious intent could work through the subtle medium to manifest itself in matter.

The subtle senses stand as sentries at the perimeters of the subtle energy (emotional or auric) body, as the physical senses do for the physical body, thereby serving as the interface between materiality and emotionality. The analogous senses of consciousness are involved in conveying patterns or ideas from the noumena to the energeia, the field of subtle energy. Through these connections, consciousness has the ability to transform subtle energy.

For example, the overtly or internally expressed intention to open one's heart to connection with others first is sensed in the heart chakra, which then stimulates muscle relaxation. Cells in the heart and brain coordinate the physical relaxation, which corresponds to the chakra's expansion, which resulted from the expression of intent.

Human near-death experiences (NDEs), out-of-body experiences (OBEs), and other energeial travel (like shamanic and lucid dream journeys) reveal that all beings do not always manifest all three facets. The presence of other beings encountered in such experiences indicate they comprise only noumenal and energeial forces.

The following diagram attempts to illustrate the three aspects or bodies and the senses that facilitate their interrelationships. Although a two-dimensional illustration does not adequately portray the conterminous nature of the three bodies, it indicates something of the various interactions, internally and with the environment. While the graphic refers to an individual being, it also likely represents the manner in which the whole universe acts as a self-learning organism (Principle of Correspondence).

Cosmic Beings

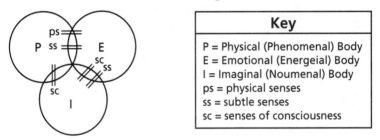

Key
P = Physical (Phenomenal) Body
E = Emotional (Energeial) Body
I = Imaginal (Noumenal) Body
ps = physical senses
ss = subtle senses
sc = senses of consciousness

According to this schema, when a physical event is perceived by the physical senses, the stimuli are converted to electrical impulses that trigger physical responses. Simultaneously, the event's subtle stimuli are perceived by the subtle senses, where they are channeled, via the as yet undefined senses of consciousness to the individual mind for interpretation.

Conversely, when consciousness creates an idea, it is conveyed via the subtle senses to the emotional body, where its intent and force are communicated via subtle energy to the brain/physical body, whereupon the body is activated. Thus, the singular and integral nature of the three-faceted being is maintained. The fact that data flow in both directions makes internal or individual organ learning possible.

The three levels of expression are normally consistent, but more advanced beings can partially dissimulate or feign differences between the physical and inner communications. This is why a physical act normally done with loving intent is perceived differently when it is undertaken with hidden distaste or anger. The actual conscious and emotional intention can be physically covered up, but the sensing person who pays attention to the energeial and noumenal messages is aware of the discrepancy and "knows the truth." (This is why attempts to deceive in communications in most relationships do not work; we generally perceive the correct subtle and mental messages.)

The electrical impulses from the physical senses that stimulate reactions in the brain and its nerve system have been mapped by neuroscientists. The subtle senses involve a similar or corresponding process of passing impulses through the emotional field, but we currently have no mechanical means to identify it directly. But anyone sensitive to these fields can perceive the impulses with the energetic receptors in our hands. The work done by chakra and acupuncture specialists may be way ahead of Western scientists in this regard.[11]

Even more elusive is the process through which thoughts energize the emotional body. Although the local mind can observe directly the physical result of its idea, it can only reshape it through the medium of subtle energy. Directions of flow in the above diagram provide for this hypothesis.

If the emotional body (coherent subtle energies) and noumenal body (focused images/memories) are the intermediary stages between the material dimension and the universal noumena, then many previously unexplained "paranormal" events become fathomable and testable within this model. Any subtle event (remote viewing, psychokinesis, healing touch, prayer influence, etc.) should parallel a physical one and be connected through the subtle senses. With these basic insights, one can extrapolate descriptive and explanatory theories for the most out-of-the-ordinary, unexplained events—even teleportation.

In India, for example, thousands (including me) have witnessed Sai Baba and Baba Altamas (both known as avatars, or spiritual beings) teleport or materialize objects that can be seen and felt like any other phenomena. Some yogis believe the inner vibrations of such objects (see the expressive functions in Table 8) are the life force they call "prana" or "lifetrons." They believe the regulation of this pranic force by master practitioners permits them to rearrange the vibratory structure of the space plenum (filled with energetic waves) to materialize perfume, fruit, and other physical objects.

With a kind of reverse engineering, taking effects on the physical body as areas for research, we should be able to decipher this process whereby mind exerts primacy over matter. After all, our bodies may be excellent examples of the application of intentionality if they are the manifested desires of a higher level of consciousness.

Refocusing Conscious Awareness

Just as there are gaps in modern theories about the nature of inner reality, there are blank spots in our "official picture" of what we generally call "being realistic" about the reality outside ourselves. To advance with our "eyes wide open" in the new century requires that we attempt to rationally and scientifically account for every aspect of human experience. It is not logically acceptable for a civilization that considers itself advanced to ignore aspects of reality that do not fit its historically established assumptions.

Science philosopher David Hopes wrote, "Having discovered the wrong laws does not entitle us to declare that the universe is lawless."[12] Just because we cannot fit our experience into laws already accepted by academic circles does not mean other laws do not exist. What we have called "being realistic" may actually censor parts of reality we are less willing to examine, or are not yet intelligent enough to understand. Human fulfillment of its potential role requires understandings that go beyond conventional explanations of many phenomena.

The following four topics exemplify areas of well-documented human experience that are not accounted for in modern, materialistic thinking. Thus, established institutions pass them off as anomalous. Some call them delusions or figments of human imagination at worst, accidents at best.

- UFO/AB experiences
- healing arts
- psychic phenomena
- "free energy" sources

Data from these unexplained human experiences suggest realms of activity, energy, and knowledge that could enhance human performance. They offer potential solutions to some of civilization's most pressing problems if we were to tap them. They deserve scientific priority and the attention of all of us.

UFO-AB Experiences. That ufology is not regarded as an official field for investigation illustrates fearful, selective inattention by most of the scientific community. Because of the potentially unsettling impact that acceptance of an AB role in current affairs would have, we choose to suppress the evidence. The result is that ad hoc hypotheses addressing the origins and nature of UFOs are not well thought out, lacking repeatable and verifiable tests. Confusion also exists about which reported sightings and contacts are actually those of UFOs, in contrast to those that can be attributed to ordinary events. Nevertheless there are thousands of such reports that cannot be easily dismissed. Only people who are afraid (for personal or professional reasons), or totally given to prejudgment, can ignore the mounting evidence.

Although untold thousands of reported experiences with the occupants of UFOs (generally assumed to be ABs) have been persuasively documented, we still have no generally accepted explanations for such beings and our relationship to them.[13] Regardless of whether the occupants of UFOs intend to reveal themselves more dramatically anytime soon, the knowledge base of the general public would be considerably enhanced by serious, systematic study.

Since the 1940s, UFO fragments, beyond those of the widely researched Roswell, New Mexico case of 1947, have reportedly been recovered in several countries. For example, a piece of debris from a reported UFO explosion over the sea near Ubatuba, Brazil, was turned over to the Brazilian Mineral Products Laboratory. The fragment was subjected to neutron activation analysis and revealed to be almost pure magnesium, with only .001 percent impurities (barium, zinc, and strontium). This tiny degree of imperfection in the crystalline structure of magnesium is beyond any current state-of-the-art production capability. In the United States, pieces alleged to have been from the Roswell crash and others have been subjected to similar analyses with equally mysterious results. The U.S. government's Operation Moondust sought such items around the world for study. (In my U.S. State Department foreign service officer days, I was a minor participant in this exercise.)

Many cases of military aircraft contact with UFOs are widely documented, including the complete loss of planes and pilots. The electronic equipment of airplanes, police vans, and civilian cars has been affected by UFOs in their vicinity. Magnetic traces have been left on the vehicles. Gauss meters at UFO sites have shown unexplained variations in magnetic fields. Similar anomalies in gravity measures, as well as physical traces, have also been reported.[14] Many persons have had various physical reactions—rashes, bruise marks, and lesions—to UFO radiation. Widespread incidence of animal mutilations, frequently involving the reproductive organs, have been extensively documented by Linda Moulton Howe[15] and others. Humanity deserves expanded scientific studies of these unexplained mysteries in the physical sciences.

Healing Arts. Many areas in the healing arts await widespread scientific testing and validation. They include the use of frequency vibrations in Ayurvedic medicine, healing with music and magnetic fields, biofeedback, and various forms of mind-body healing.[16] Acupuncture is another modality—poorly understood in the West—that is used effectively by Chinese and American practitioners. While not a panacea, the technique of manipulating subtle-energy meridians is effective for certain symptoms (acute pain, nausea and vomiting, plus several chronic conditions).

Individuals can also channel an unknown healing energy, the most obvious manifestation being the laying-on-of-hands phenomenon. Marcel Vogel, reported in Brian O'Leary's *The Second Coming of Science*,[17] demonstrated that a coil filled with water and hand-charged with this energy can cleanse liquids placed near it of various impurities. In his workshops, O'Leary demonstrates how the passing of hands over and around an individual can enlarge the recipient's energy field, as manifested in the deflection of measuring rods, and increase health and vitality. Psychic surgery (well documented in the Philippines and elsewhere) is an analog to laser surgery. By focusing and directing subtle-energy forces as though they had a scalpel, healers can excise knots of misplaced energy that have resulted in diseased organs.

Medical doctors cite "spontaneous remission" of disease when their healing models cannot encompass the effects of attitude, prayer, or other acts of consciousness. But mainstream research findings on the effect of placebos demonstrates the healing power of belief, as does healing through prayer, which has recently received increasing publicity.[18] Research on the healing mind deserves public support instead of censure.

Psychic Phenomena. One of the most promising areas of underattended research is the field of parapsychology, or psychic phenomena. This area of study portends extensive understanding of the mind-energy-body interaction. New insights here could provide "quantum leaps" in understanding group behavior and fostering healthy social development. For example, U.S. government intelligence agencies have funded limited research on remote viewing (use of the subtle senses to obtain information about distant sites through the noumenal field). No longer restricted to defense and intelligence purposes, this effort is now being made public and expanded to other institutions.

Another subject for parapsychological research is the phenomenon of cell-to-cell communication, which indicates unexplained transmission of knowledge between species. In addition to an ability to communicate with living plants and animals, humans can exchange information with seemingly inert matter. One technique used almost worldwide is that of dowsing to locate water or other subterranean deposits. Dowsing is also used to locate lost persons or objects. Complementing the human ability to receive information in this way is the capacity to influence the behavior of material objects. Robert Jahn and Brenda Dunne's mind-impact-on-matter research at Princeton University solidly documents this human ability.

Research on ufology, ABs, and psychic phenomena overlaps to some extent. Some ABs reportedly excel in telepathic communications, hypnotic suggestion, precognition, out-of-body travel, levitation, and psychokinesis.[19] Ingo Swann, renown psychic, has noted that the very fact ABs communicate with humans telepathically proves we too have those capacities.

"Free Energy" Sources. Another area deserving open-minded exploration comprises alternative energy sources that hover at the edges of the phenomenal world. Bruce DePalma, Troy Reed, and others have developed one such alternative source—sometimes referred to as "free energy"—by working directly with the shape of magnetic fields. Instead of switching magnetic fields off and on as we do with conventional electric motors, Reed's "magnetic motor" produces mechanical energy (turning a driveshaft) by manipulating the shape of magnetic fields. DePalma's related work with zero-point energy is being further developed by researchers in India and Japan.[20]

Early claims about successful experiments with cold fusion, another "free energy" hypothesis, were initially dismissed by the scientific community and the popular media. Now scientists around the world are validating the 1989 findings of Martin Fleischman and Stanley Pons, whose work (in France) continues with support from Japan (whose lack of fossil fuel deposits gives it more reason to be open to this new science).[21]

A related development uses thermal gain that derives from collapsing the hydrogen atom below its ground state or by breaking up high density, charged clusters of molecules. According to Hal Fox, editor of the *Journal of New Energy,* the latter process can also produce direct electrical energy.

While the "free energy" concept appears to violate the second law of thermodynamics, it may imply that we must expand our understanding of the scope of physics. Harold Puthoff and other physicists have demonstrated in laboratories the existence of energy in a vacuum that is more powerful than a nuclear force and that can be tapped without destructive side effects. Even though the International Association of

New Science and its Institute for New Energy held five excellent conferences on free energy from 1993 to 1997 in Denver, Colorado, little mainstream media attention was given to these scientific breakthroughs.

Expanding Science's View

The preceding overview of some of the gaps in mainstream science reveals the need to expand our theoretical and research framework. In each of the above areas—ufology, healing arts, psychic phenomena, free energy—the biggest unanswered question is the role of conscious intent. That is why part 1 of this book focused on the case for taking general consciousness and its local manifestations of intent as the primary facet of a three-faceted reality.

The current state of a physical entity represents only one of several propensities to behave in a certain way. What actually makes one of those potentials become manifest is beyond the scope of known laws of physics. But a concept from quantum mechanics suggests a hypothesis. The term "quantum leap," used by some physicists, refers to either the shift of subatomic particles from one form to another or the jump from a virtual state to a tangible one. The quantum leap concept extrapolated to human behavior (Principle of Correspondence) connotes acting in a moment of uncertainty without being able to anticipate the outcome.[22]

In the model posited here, it is at this quantum level that conscious choice (free will) exerts its influence on the subtle and material realms. As a subparticle's leap in a particular direction collapses into form only one of many probabilities, a conscious intention shifts the energeial and phenomenal energies into a particular form. If a conscious choice is not made, habit prevails. (Remember that habits are the results of previous intentions.)

Humans can, under certain conditions, exercise the power of choice over habit, directing subtle energy toward the accomplishment of a desired effect. The scope of our co-creative power to make an "actual event" out of "multiple tendencies" is still unknown. To the extent we have free will, it exists at this level of quantum leaps when we choose one immediate potential direction from among myriad, if not infinite, possibilities.[23] Research in this area is not yet on the map.

Instead of seeking the challenge of leaping into this uncharted territory, most researchers are satisfied to incrementally expand their "maps" an inch at a time. But the twenty-first century calls for a new set of theoretical maps with lots of empty space, with a framework that points to potential relationships between present scientific knowledge and phenomena currently off the map. In building this framework, it is useful to extrapolate from our current *knowledge* base, but not from our current theoretical base. Theories not well validated, such as the theory of biological origins of consciousness and the deterministic model of behavior, should be suspended to permit a new look at the data we already possess.

Concepts and research principles that prove useful in predicting phenomenal outcomes, whether fitting traditional protocols or not, should be incorporated into a new methodology. For example, Cleve Backster's research on the interaction of human consciousness with plant and animal cells indicates that planned experimental replications (required by current scientific protocols) do not work because the cellular reaction occurs when the experiment is first conceived, not when it is executed. New research methods have to include the input of spontaneous expression of intent as well as planned ones.

Taking into account areas of human experience now labeled paranormal or anomalous requires a new framework that includes the functions of the phenomenal, noumenal, and energeial realms, and the principles of their interaction. The Hermetic Principles can contribute to an overarching framework that gives structure to new experimental maps. As a simple example, the Principle of Correspondence predicts that patterns of force and interaction that exist in one facet of the universe will also inform other facets. This thinking should be used in regard to the electromagnetic spectrum; a review of its known principles for their implications in theory building and research on subtle energies should be undertaken.

Scottish physicist James Clerk Maxwell (who in 1861 summarized equations on the behavior of the electromagnetic force) implicitly used the Principle of Correspondence when he predicted that electromagnetic waves should exist at all frequencies and wavelengths (illustrated in Table 7). Maxwell realized that his four equations pointed to something of a whole, so he tested them in the laboratory. He hypothesized that if there were waves at "x," "y," and "m" frequencies with the same speed of light, then there must be waves spread across all frequencies (and wavelengths). The result was the manipulation of previously unknown waves, including the development of the radio and X-ray machine. We have not yet identified all the frequencies that may exist on the electromagnetic continuum from zero to infinity, but Maxwell's theory has been confirmed by many examples of subsequent scientific, technological, and human experience.

Similarly, the Principle of Correspondence predicts that explanations of some psi phenomena (intuitive feelings, psychokenesis, psychic healing) may come by extrapolating from currently known physical principles. For example, the healer's passing of his or her hands through a person's emotional/auric energy field to realign it may be analogous to the passing of an iron magnet over the physical body. The work of physicist William Tiller exemplifies this kind of extrapolative hypothesis building and research.[24] With such innovative research, we should be able to understand the interplay of magnetic forces with the edge of the energeia where emotions affect the body. In the mid-1990s, the Japanese expanded the conceptual box when they launched a sea craft driven by "magnetohydrodynamic propulsion" (MHP).[25] This technology was based on an extension of current understanding of magnetic fields.

Why not use what we already know about magnetic fields to conduct analogous experiments with subtle energies? Magnetic fields are used to drive a solenoid, generate electricity, and turn motors, where these artificially created fields currently exceed the concentration of force of the Earth's magnetic field. The reported performance of some UFOs (high acceleration, hovering, right-angle turning, and noise-lessness) indicates that they may take advantage of magnetic fields. The U.S. government is secretly working on advanced concepts and engineering to tap this natural force for propulsion systems[26] and the use of psychokinetic energy to manipulate military equipment and weapons.

Discoveries in these areas, if we attempt to apply them to the energeia, could lead to insights in teleportation, environmental healing through conscious resonance (recall earlier discussion of the Institute for Resonance Therapy), and ways to transmute the emotional energy that often fuels social violence. Conversely, applying insights from subtle-energy studies could speed up the pace of discovery in the physical arena. The two following paragraphs contrast the conventional high-energy approach to production of useable power with a more gentle approach. The latter is only one step away from the use of consciousness to directly tap the energy of the physical universe.

Using the Principle of Polarity, Ronald A. Brightsen, a former official in the U.S. Nuclear Regulatory Commission, has claimed discovery of a heretofore unknown principle in the construction of atoms. The traditional view holds that all atoms are composed of individual neutrons and protons held together by the strong nuclear force. In that view, powerful infusions of heat—comparable to the dynamics of the Sun—are necessary to break the neutrons and protons apart and release the energy for controlled power. (This theory provided the rationale for the multibillion-dollar cyclotron project in Texas that was—wisely—defunded by the U.S. Congress in the early 1990s.)

Brightsen, one of the proponents of cold fusion, contends that atoms are really formed of gently bound groups of neutrons and protons. This means energy can be released by separating these clusters in a more gentle fashion. Thus, the claim that the flow of low voltage electricity through heavy water containing deuterium produces more energy than it consumes. More recently, other scientists (Shoulders, Gleeson, Ilyanok, Mesyats) have also discovered how to manipulate these high-density, "gently charged" clusters.

Since all sections of the electromagnetic spectrum, under most conditions, move at an average speed of 186,282 miles per second—the "c" in Einstein's formula $E=mc^2$—the Principle of Correspondence would predict that other spectra exist at other relatively constant speeds (see Table 10). Nikola Tesla[27] claimed to have detected another spectrum of waves— he called them "cosmic waves"—moving at fifty times the speed of light. Recent experiments by new energy scientist Tom Bearden are purported to have resulted in wave velocities of up to eight times the speed of light. At this point we can only speculate as to the inherent ratio, but undoubtedly another parallel spectrum (or more)—at an unknown factor of electromagnetic speed—exists. Experience with telepathy

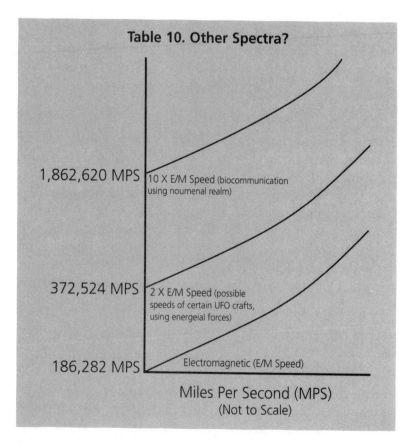

Table 10. Other Spectra?

1,862,620 MPS — 10 X E/M Speed (biocommunication using noumenal realm)

372,524 MPS — 2 X E/M Speed (possible speeds of certain UFO crafts, using energeial forces)

186,282 MPS — Electromagnetic (E/M Speed)

Miles Per Second (MPS)
(Not to Scale)

(Backster's primary perception) and psychokenesis indicate it affects our universe, and therefore our lives.

What tangible forces, susceptible to testing, could be involved in such yet to be identified spectra? The first candidate could be the force involved in cell-to-cell communication—the hypothesis being that, over distance, living cells exchange certain kinds of information faster than the speed of light. Although Cleve Backster's experiments seem to indicate instantaneous communication, the distances involved in his experiments are too short to allow accurate measurement of such speeds. In the three-aspect model presented here, the only theoretical limit to the speed of information transmission is the capacity for cognition.

Research involving cell-to-cell or biocommunication would require distances sufficient to measure speeds of perhaps more than one million miles per second. The hypothesis could be tested by sending human white cells on interplanetary vehicles and correlating, by use of time-synchronized instruments, the actions of the donor with respective cell reactions. This experiment would provide the necessary units for calculating the speed of information transfer. The findings could have implications for understanding subtle phenomena such as telepathy, clairvoyance, or remote viewing. The "Spindrift Experiments," conducted by Christian Science researchers, examined the mind's influence on seed germination, yeast, and healing.[28] Their research is deserving of replication.

The Hermetic Principles may offer theoretical insight here. Such a gentle binding force as Brightsen's is likely to exist only in a polarity where a strong force and a weak force operate in reciprocity. The subtle force that animates emotion is likely to have a spectrum of vibrations with lower frequencies of hate and anger and higher ones of altruism and joy. Will one end of the gradient manifest cellular damage, energy congestion, and ideational conflict, while the other provides healing, gentle flows of feeling, and harmony? How these unidentified forces and biocommunication relate is another gap in our knowledge.

We must reconceptualize such unknowns and integrate them into a larger hypothetical framework. Its gaps provide for testing, questioning what we now consider absolutes and seeing them in new relationships. One such path is the development of a metascience as described in the following section.

Defining the New Metascience

As suggested in the preface and introduction, multileveled human development requires a metascience, an intellectual and psychological approach to knowing that accesses all channels to knowledge, combining an openness to new ideas with a rigorous process of validation through collective human experience. Metascience consists of a synthesis of traditional wisdom with cutting edge discoveries in all disciplines. If suggested new insights don't fit the existing picture, then both the old picture and the new piece require scrutiny. Each new discovery, whether from prehistory or the frontier of science, has the effect of reconfiguring the "jigsaw puzzle" of consensus-based human knowledge. We start with the conventional physicist's four forces to illustrate metascience.

Given their limited scope, the four forces—gravity, electromagnetism, weak force, strong force—must exist in the context of a larger framework. Scientists have deduced these forces from our experience in and analysis of the phenomenal realm. We know apples fall from trees; therefore, gravity exists. We know iron filings gather around a charged iron bar; therefore, magnetism exists. We know stored current turns motors; therefore, electricity exists. When we sit in a chair without falling through it, we can believe some strong force is holding it together. When we hear a Geiger counter click and see our teeth in X-ray film, we can infer that some weak force permits atoms to separate.

Scientists tell us that everything that happens in the universe is due to the functioning of one or more of these forces. Formulae have been developed to demonstrate that all four have a common mathematical root. (See the Web site http://idt.net/~dglean19/dglhp22.html for an example.) Such a conclusion appears to be premature. These forces cannot account for the continuing process of reconstruction (creating and recreating) that counterbalances the phenomenon of entropy and characterizes the evolving universe.

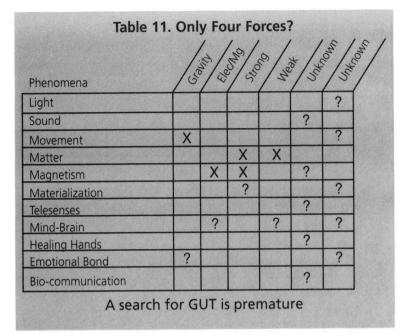

Table 11. Only Four Forces?

Phenomena	Gravity	Elec/Mg	Strong	Weak	Unknown	Unknown
Light						?
Sound					?	
Movement	X					?
Matter		X	X			
Magnetism		X	X		?	
Materialization			?			?
Telesenses					?	
Mind-Brain		?		?		?
Healing Hands				?		
Emotional Bond	?					?
Bio-communication					?	

A search for GUT is premature

The four offer no insight into the larger questions: What force caused the birth or rebirth of the universe? Why is there directionality within the system? Are the patterns that shape the ebb and flow of matter and conscious life inherent in creation? Are they subject to modification within the universe? Is the arrow of time really a spiral? Why do the four forces not explain many human experiences (as highlighted in Table 11)?

The reality seems to be that these four forces may be the least tractable in a universe that has at least two or more subtle realms. They are much less susceptible than those of the subtle energies to direct manipulation by the mind.

What we know about the four forces is limited by our current scientific tools. Each force affects the material realm through its own particulate matter. Gauge particles are exchanged between two objects, giving rise to mutual attraction, like heavy balls being hurled from person to person. Of course, the gauge particles are only mediators of the energy, not the energy itself. Could that energy be the energeia? And then, the elusive energy in turn is patterned by some designing force. Could it be consciousness?

Gravity is assumed to work through a hypothetical particle called the graviton, although scientists have not yet found one. Puthoff and others[29] instead argue that gravity is simply another aspect of the electromagnetic field. But photons, having neither mass nor charge, travel at the speed of light and seem to be the mediators for the electromagnetic force. We have the same problem with the other two forces. We identify particles, but we don't know what animates the particles. The strong force is mediated by eight types of gluons (appropriately named) and the weak force by two particles—a "W" and a "Z."

Metascience would posit other forces underlying these phenomena. It suggests a theoretical approach that is susceptible to empirical research. Its attempts to relate different levels and categories of unexplained human experience to the current scientific baseline makes them testable. Table 11 suggests two directions for new hypotheses that expand our analytical vision. One expands the search for influences of the four labeled forces that may not yet be understood. The other explores spectra beyond the electromagnetic spectrum that could account for some of the events now labeled paranormal.

For example, magnetic field effects seem to be much more extensive than was earlier imagined. On a mundane level, we have begun to learn of the impact of changes in the magnetic field (caused by cell phones, electric razors, and hair dryers) on cancerous cell growth. Slowly, recognition is being given to the relationship between cancer rates and high-voltage transmission lines. Do magnetic fields and mind-body organisms interact in a way that changes the functioning of the cells, causing them to react differently to external stimuli, including carcinogens?

What are the implications of forces in the realms of energeia and noumena that are parallel to the currently identified four phenomenal forces? Given Hermes' insights, the forces are likely to relate to the dynamics of attraction/repulsion, bonding/disintegration, two-way communication, and realm-to-realm transformation.

Table 11 is only a starting point. Unexplained experiences, including such mysteries as events that validate astrology and prayer, have to be fitted into this schema. Physics is now in a cul-de-sac of incoherent overelaboration, with a literal maze of particles and forces. A broader metascience could help to bring about needed order.

The placing of the four forces within the framework of a Hermetic-based metascience offers some intriguing areas for mind games and laboratory research. The Principle of Polarity can be applied to the forces of gravity and antigravity to incorporate explanations of matter and antimatter. The strong and weak nuclear forces appear to represent polarities of the same bonding principle, but what is the polarity of the electromagnetic force? Or is the magnetic force the polar partner of the electrical force? If so, where are the magnetic monopoles? (In anticipation, some scientists are actively looking for them.) We need to study the polarities that function between energy and mass and between thought and subtle energy.

All the physical forces—through the infusion of patterns that collapse them into vectors and form—seem to be susceptible to the influence of consciousness (Principle of Mentalism). They, like their obverse particles of matter, are imbued with vibrations subject to measurement (Principle of Vibration). The forces themselves, unseen by us, exhibit the masculine expressive gender; the mediating particles are the feminine receivers that embody and sustain the forces (Principle of Gender). Other Hermetic Principles are exemplified in the following two examples.

Scientist Eric Dollard, following up on some of Tesla's work, has identified naturally occurring patterns (termed the golden ratio spiral) in various kinds of energy release: a waterfall, a crack in glass, and water percolating through sand. The patterns seem to fit the wavelength and frequency of the energy discharged, bursting forth and then dissipating. Given this data, he has inferred a more general principle at work. Is this a function of the Hermetic Principle of Rhythm? Is that same principle relevant to the patterns of personal growth and social change (Principle of Correspondence)?

Russian scientists, not bound by the same academic conventions as their American counterparts, extrapolate more quickly from established thinking. Professor Alexis Zolotov,[30] for example, postulates three palpable energy fields parallel to the biological one that is generally accepted in the West: electromagnetic, "cinetic" motion, and information. Each of these, Zolotov believes, has carriers and vectors that affect all bodies, whether persons or planets. His ideas of the biological, energetic, and auric/information fields correspond roughly to the phenomena, energeia, and noumena posited in this book.

Although institutional science has not yet validated the existence of something like an information field, psychics and healers access it and use it. Rupert Sheldrake popularized the concept of a "morphic field" that can be developed over time by conscious intent and practice until it achieves a living force of its own.[31] The field's pattern of force can then affect the behavior of other beings as they come to resonate with its frequency.[32] Based on this concept of interfield communication, researchers can devise experiments to test Zolotov's and my ideas of how these fields interact with matter.

As the scope of a metascience broadens, we will find answers to many current questions that now require blind (usually misguided) faith for answers. We will develop a theoretical base for the obvious links between thought and the production of matter in the nervous system (Principle of Mentalism). We will identify a scale for measuring the bonding of individual and group thoughts to subtle energy, in turn creating emotional charges that affect matter—as in the physically empowering effect of distant prayer and the physically deleterious effect of existential fear.

John Horgan, in his book *The End of Science,*[33] concluded that science had reached its limits, but he accepted the current major scientific theories as a "modern creation myth" that will hold true for a thousand years. In fact, that myth is about to implode. That myth (in this case, unproved beliefs) includes the Big Bang, the four forces, the chance evolution of life, and the biological determinism of behavior—all of which have been shown to be inadequate explanations of experienced reality. Metascience points the way to a more comprehensive approach to scientific research, beyond the current levels of biology and physics, with practical implications for the full range of human experience in a multifaceted universe.

Notes

1. Gary Zukav, *The Seat of the Soul* (New York: Simon & Schuster, 1990).

2. Gregory Bateson, *Mind and Nature: A Necessary Unity* (New York: Dutton, 1979); Michael Talbot, *The Holographic Universe* (New York: HarperCollins, 1991).

3. Fritjof Capra, *The Tao of Physics* (Berkeley, CA: Shambhala, 1975).

4. Now some physicists believe gravity is a charge, perhaps inertial in nature, instead of an attracting force.

5. Tsung Hwa Jou, *The Tao of Tai-Chi Chuan* (Warwick, NY: Tai Chi Foundation, 1981).

6. Diane Ackerman, *A Natural History of the Senses* (New York: Vintage Books, 1991).

7. Illustrating the receptive nature of senses and clarifying some confusion in terms, Mark Twain allegedly remarked to a haughty lady, "Pardon me, madame, but I stink and you smell." She had reportedly said to him, "Sir, you smell!"

8. I tentatively label a third sensory level, beyond the subtle senses described here, as the senses of consciousness, but do not attempt to further develop an explanatory theory. Further exploration of this level is needed to move beyond the current tendency to lump several noumenal senses under terms like "clairvoyance" or "psychic vision."

9. "Chakra" means wheel in Sanskrit and comes from the wheel-like vortices that exist in the human subtle energy field. Chakras serve as channels for the flow of the life force (*chi* or energeia) into the physical body. Although there are many such channels for the passage of subtle energy into and through the body, convention labels seven as major. They are root (at the base of the spine), sexual (near the reproductive organs), solar plexus, heart, throat, third eye (in the center of the forehead), and crown (the top of the head). C. W. Leadbeater, *The Chakras* (Adyar, India: Theosophical Publishing House, 1927).

10. Several species have been shown to have a definite orientation to magnetic fields, but the impact of magnetic forces in human information processing is not yet clear. In *Human Navigation and the Sixth Sense* (1981), Robin Baker of the University of Manchester in England reported less directional certainty among blindfolded volunteers with magnets on their heads than those blindfolded and without external magnets.

11. The California Institute of Human Science in Encinitas, California, has developed considerable data on some of these subtle channels. The institute has done a particularly good job of identifying the subtle energy precursors to various states of disease. The institute's founder, Hiroshi Montoyama, has developed an apparatus for measuring the functioning of the meridians and their corresponding internal organs (known as AMI). It measures the electrical pathways he believes parallel the energeial pathways. Check their Web site at www.cihs.edu for additional information.

12. David Hopes, *Sun Magazine* (May 1992).

13. John E. Mack, *Abduction: Human Encounters with Aliens* (New York: Charles Scribner, 1994) and *Passport to the Cosmos* (New York: Crown Publishers, 1999). Mack, a well-known psychiatrist, honors abductees and takes their experiences seriously.

14. Richard Haines, "Fifty-Six Aircraft Pilot Sightings Involving Electromagnetic Effects." Proceedings, MUFON Symposium, Albuquerque, NM, July 1992.

15. Linda M. Howe, *Alien Harvest: Further Evidence Linking Animal Mutilations and Human Abduction to Alien Life Forms* (Philadelphia, PA: L.M. Howe Productions, 1989).

16. The National Center for Complementary and Alternative Medicine was established by Congress in 1999 (building on the Center for Alternative Medicine created in the early 1990s) to support basic, clinical, and applied research, research training, and dissemination of information regarding the nature, safety, and efficacy of frontier and traditional, indigenous medicine.

17. Also see Brian O'Leary's *Miracle in the Void* (Maui, Hawaii: Kamapua'a Press, 1995).

18. Larry Dossey, *Healing Words* (San Francisco: Harper & Row, 1993).

19. Raymond E. Fowler, *The Watchers* (New York: Bantam Books, 1991).

20. Proceedings, Institute for New Energy Conference, Denver, CO, May 1994.

21. *Infinite Energy,* published bi-monthly by Cold Fusion Technology, Inc, P.O. Box 2816, Concord, NH 03302.

22. Werner Heisenberg, *Physics and Philosophy* (New York: Harper & Row, 1958).

23. Fred Alan Wolf, *Taking the Quantum Leap* (San Francisco: Harper & Row, 1981).

24. William Tiller, *Science and Human Transformation: Subtle Energies, Intentionality, and Consciousness* (Walnut Creek, CA: Pavior Publishing, 1997).

25. MHP takes advantage of the Lorentz Force (named after its discoverer, Dutch physicist Hendrik Lorentz, a winner of the 1902 Nobel Prize). Used in motors and pumps, the Lorentz Force essentially involves harnessing the perpendicular force that results from two vectors of an electric current and a magnetic field positioned at right angles to each other. The movement of the electrically charged particles pushing against the magnetic field results in an opposing force that propels the seawater through a pipe. The result is thrust like that driving a jet plane. A similar technology, using gravity as a countervailing field, could be developed to achieve greater speed for airships than is possible with air as the medium for jet propulsion.

26. According to the British press, John Searl of England demonstrated such a propulsion system in a "flying disc" more than twenty-five years ago, but the technology allegedly was suppressed by the British government. Like the United States, the United Kingdom has a history of significant covert government research and corresponding cover-ups.

27. Nikola Tesla, the inventor of alternating current and wireless radio almost a century ago, developed a device now known as the Tesla Coil. This coil functions at the interface of form, energy, and thought (read "intention"). Derivatives of this pioneer's work include free energy motors, gravity field technology, and zero-point energy.

28. Robert Owen, *Qualitative Research: The Early Years* (Salem, OR: Grayhaven Books, 1988).

29. B. Haisch, A. Rueda, and H.E. Puthoff, "Beyond E= mc^2," *The Sciences* (November-December 1994); 26–31.

30. Jacques Vallee, *UFO Chronicles of the Soviet Union* (New York: Ballantine Books, 1992).

31. Rupert Sheldrake, *The Presence of the Past: Morphic Resonance and the Habits of Nature* (London: Collins, 1988).

32. The popular, though possibly apocryphal, hundredth monkey story illustrates an amazing phenomenon: the learning in one group of monkeys is somehow absorbed by a separate, distant group of monkeys.

33. John Horgan, *The End of Science* (Reading, MA: Helix Books/Addison-Wesley, 1996).

5

Mind as Universal Consciousness

From what we know of the experiences of primitive and aboriginal peoples, early humans sensed and interacted with realms outside of and beyond the five senses. As in nature-oriented societies today, they must have perceived inner communications from other species and the natural world around them. Records of art and rituals suggest they experienced a general realm of consciousness through dreams and communications with ancestors and other ethereal beings. In shaman-led rituals, their minds traveled outside the physical body. The most ancient myths indicate early humans understood the interconnectedness of all things, physical and spiritual. They, like traditional peoples today, acknowledged the power of this inner world of which they were only parts.

Throughout human history, including the period of pharaohs and Greek kings and up to modern times, people have sought to obtain counsel from the noumena. They used trances, dreams, prophets, runes, symbolic cards, the *I Ching*, and other forms of divination to sense the universal flow of energies and conscious trends that influence individual lives.

I believe that a new look at the role of ABs in human history will reveal that our ancestors' awe and misunderstanding of them brought about the advent of supernatural religions in the Near East. ABs arrived from interstellar space, communicating through the air with radios and telepathically with humans, performing feats of magic (advanced technologies), living life spans longer than humans, and disappearing into the skies. To the still naive humans, the ABs became the personifications of many of the natural phenomena they did not yet understand. The gap in knowledge was so great that the ABs were worshiped, assumed to have control of the powers that early humans thought were part of nature. This experience interrupted the natural progression of humans, during which they would have come to a working understanding of the three-faceted universe.

The Sumerian tablets describe how humans served the AB colonizers, becoming dependent on them for both their physical well-being and for scientific understanding. The inner circle of humans apparently understood the physical nature of the long life spans of the ABs and their journeys into the heavens. But the common folks easily confused such technical realities with their own simple insights about after-death and out-of-body travel. The stories humans told one another about the exploits of the ABs made them out to be immortal. (For Westerners the Hebrew, Egyptian, and Greek myths exemplify how fact became the legends of the gods.)

During the period we know as prehistory, some of the ABs (think of Thoth and Prometheus) apparently taught humans advanced concepts of the energeial and noumenal realms. But when the global cataclysm (known as the Biblical Flood) wiped out most of civilization around 11,500 B.P., much of that knowledge was lost. Human survivors became technically dependent on the ABs and also let their own inner powers fall into disuse.

When the ABs departed (for reasons still unknown) from their role as overt colonizers of Earth, humans developed forms of worship designed to entice them back. Many literally sacrificed themselves to induce favorable actions from the now invisible gods and to urge their return. Humans developed a psychological state of dependency, insecure in their own powers and holding the departed gods responsible for both the good and bad developments in their lives. Supernatural religions developed, based on the illusion that humans could be saved only by adherence to beliefs and rituals that called on divine (departed ABs') assistance.

Modern science in the European Renaissance originally grew out of the natural tradition of science and philosophy, based on human experience of all realms and the wholistic perspective of Greek and other mystery schools. But its focus on materialism, ceding the inner realms to supernaturalism, left behind any sense of an integral, three-faceted universe where consciousness and subtle energies are indispensable to the physical realm. Leaving theologians free to dominate human belief systems related to the inner realms, science chose to label as "anomalous" the human experiences of consciousness.

This development let fall into the crack an entire realm of natural human experience. No satisfactory answer was offered to many questions. How do we account for dreams and other alternate states of consciousness? What about evidence of communications from the dead and other beings outside our physical space? How do we explain the influences of thoughts on material objects? Where do memories reside? This chapter reviews evidence of a general field of consciousness and ways in which it defines the lives of conscious beings.

While scientific thinking holds that all action of importance takes place in the material realm (phenomena), the experience of conscious beings proves otherwise. Analysis of each phase in life (birth, struggle, joy, creation, growth, attraction, pain, death, etc.) reveals the functioning of emotions (energeia) and consciousness (noumena). For physically incarnated beings to perform at full potential, they must be aware of and open to the interaction of the phenomena with the energeia and noumena. Incongruence between or suppression of any one aspect dims the experienced fullness of life. Unfortunately, since the beginning of the current historical era on Earth, not much more than 5,000 years ago, humans, while elaborating various material technologies, have regressively reduced their awareness of and attention to the more subtle realms.

The spotlights of Western science and supernatural religion have drawn attention to the rational mind and physical senses, while ignoring the other aspects. Non-Western philosophy, whether Hindu or Muslim, also has a perspective as dualistic as the Cartesian view that differentiates between the physical universe and the hidden plane. They claim that the former is knowable and discoverable by science, but that the latter is separate and accessible only through, respectively, yogic meditation or the inspired Koran. But in reality there are no such impermeable barriers.

The evidence reviewed in this book indicates that the subtle realms usually thought of as beyond our natural reach are not really beyond after all. If all consciousness is a single spectrum, then even "heaven" and "hell" can only be different states of mind. If the Logos of ideas is a hologram, then any person can express or test any idea. While archetypes and collective emotions may affect us, we in turn can help change them. Regardless of the nature of the experiences—extraterrestrial, extradimensional, outside history, or beyond the waking state—they involve the same source and the same outcome in our seamless, conscious universe.

The discoveries of parapsychological research—including the antics of Tomaz Green-Morton in Brazil,[1] who performs materializations while drinking rum and blaspheming—demonstrate the singular and *neutral* nature of universal consciousness. Neither adherence to a specific scientific protocol nor a particular religious orientation is necessary for access to this realm. Metascience is a route to fully understanding the conscious universe because it combines *all* ways of knowing, eventually testing them in the phenomenal realm before claiming discovery of truth.

Metascience places access to knowledge in the hands not only of specialists, but also of independent individuals willing to test their hypotheses in all realms. The following discussion illustrates how consciousness permeates the realms of subtle energy and matenergy, and serves as the unifying force for every aspect of universal life.

Memory as Cause and Effect

Even though the noumena, from a conceptual perspective, is distinct from phenomenal reality, in existence and function it is not a realm beyond. As we have seen in chapter 3, the noumena and phenomena are synthesized through the energeia, which acts as the bonding and transforming force. As integrated parts of the whole, all three have mutually dependent functions, affecting the way beings live in the world of mundane affairs. The noumenal record of their ongoing interaction gives continuity to life-forms and their behaviors. Such continuity is sometimes labeled memory (cellular, muscular, energetic, mental, etc.). See the outstanding book *The Living Energy Universe* by Gary Schwartz and Linda Russek on the formation of memory at all levels.

Memory can be described as the glue that holds a particular set of patterns together. Thus, memories are the patterns of images and ideas that live on in the noumena. They remain in a coherent form as long as conscious beings have charged them with sufficient emotional energy, from the energeia, to keep them intact. The permanent Hall of Akashic Records, referred to in esoteric literature, would consist of such charged individual and collective memories. Passing thoughts or comments, unsupported by additional emotional investment, seem to dissipate quickly. When patterns or ideas have not been adequately charged (using subtle energy) even the most finely tuned brain cannot retrieve them (like computer images lost before we activate the Save key).

When reading this, think of your own experience trying to recall a fleeting thought to which you paid no real attention. When a thought has a subtle energy boost (emotional charge), it appears to be reflected in strengthened neurotransmitter connections. This involves the synergy of mind-emotion-body connection. I believe the Principle of Mentalism applies here.

If I am correct, the primal Logos or schema for the universe could have easily evaporated, had the Grand Couple not infused it with sufficient intentional energy to impel continuing manifestation in the phenomenal realm. On the human level, a single passing fantasy on a lazy summer afternoon never finds its form in the subsequent course of events, while a creative flash, powered by high motivation, can result in a new mechanical invention or social structure. In an interactive, multidimensional universe, strong ideas combined with emotion can even affect the performance of machinery, as we have seen in the PEAR Laboratory and personal experience with automobiles and computers.

When a being or group charges an idea with a strong emotional response, that idea becomes both a personal and noumenal memory, remaining available to open and receptive minds throughout the cosmos. Researchers who know nothing of each other's current work frequently discover later they were working on the same concept at the same time. This is another feature of a self-learning universe composed of self-learning entities. Shared dreams and other group beliefs are possible because of this noumenal field. For example, in the late 1980s, the idea of democracy remained vital while that of communism quickly waned. Communism's thought-forms in the energeia had a half-life (rate of decay) that was in inverse order to that of human freedom and self-determinism.

This relationship of the emotional charge to decay rate is why the great ideas of all time still resonate today and appear in dreams, meditation, or creative freethinking. They are not just stored in material data banks, but continue to have a long life in the noumena—parts of which were termed the "collective unconscious" by Carl Jung and the Akashic Records by Rudolf Steiner and others.[2] ("Akashic" is derived from the Sanskrit word "akasha," meaning all-pervasive space.) Enduring memories, contributed by all conscious beings from the Grand Couple forward, literally hold the universe together.

The decision to charge an idea with sufficient energy to make it survive can be either a deliberate or a quasi-autonomous response. When thousands of people deliberately spend one hour a day meditating for world peace, entire societies can feel the influence in the noumenal realm. In fact, some believe that the efforts of Western meditation groups contributed to the force of President Gorbachev's vision of perestroika in the former Soviet Union. When significant numbers in one generation systematically commit subtle emotional energy to any idea, it becomes an archetype that is strong enough to survive in the noumena and affect receptive members of a subsequent generation.

On the other hand, when millions respond spontaneously— but deeply—to the beauty of an image such as Earthrise as seen from the Moon, the thought (noumenal) form is charged with a force (energeial) that can also power decades of emotion and action. This example is the instantaneous formation of an archetype. Deliberate charging explains how imagery can be used over time to affect one's health and interactions with others, while the impact of one dramatic emotional experience demonstrates how a religious healing can work.

Given the Principle of Correspondence, in a holographic universe we should be able to infer the dynamics of the cosmic noumena from the workings of an individual's memory. In this context, the longevity and impact of an idea or symbol in either individual or noumenal memory would depend on the clarity of the symbol, the level of emotion bonded to it, and its subsequent recharging by one or more beings. An idea generated by a computer and never read by a person would not interact with the energeia and the noumena. Only symbols that have been *charged*, either positively or negatively, by the emotions of conscious beings can have a direct effect on the phenomenal world. The Kahunas of Hawaii understand these principles: they teach that a prayer will receive a response only when it is offered to the higher realm (noumena) with all the personal psychic force (energeial or subtle energy) one can muster.

How the brain assists in the acquisition, storage, and recall of specific images (whether words or pictures) is not clear; however, scientists have been able to follow the transmission of electrical and chemical impulses by neurons. Neuronal reactions to experience (internal or external) seem to be correlated with the quality and level of emotional excitation. Again, the sequence posited in this book is that a conscious idea coheres subtle energy into a morphic field that concentrates electromagnetic forces at the level of matenergy (and induces changes in the brain).

Personally experienced events, as the result of a stronger subtle-energy charge, affect more areas of the brain than do the acquisitions of secondhand memories. While a specific physical event is transitory (for example, an automobile accident happens and life moves on), specific memories of it seem to have their own relatively permanent existence. They can be transformed or modified, but do not disappear quickly. How long memories can last in the noumena is not known, but some memories from prehistoric periods can still be accessed through dreams or deliberate remote viewing. Psychometry is another technique for accessing information about a separate event or object. Inner senses can be used to "read" the information field associated with the target.

Humans can consciously access memories as physical events occur or after the fact. In a fateful example of the first category, the U.S. military had access to subtle-sense knowledge of Japanese ship positions as they moved toward Pearl Harbor (and later in the war as well). A lieutenant-commander who was a code specialist in the U.S. Navy gave this and similar information to his superiors, but it was discounted because he gained his information through "intuition," as opposed to deciphered radio codes. He knew how to decode memories of current events in the noumena.

Of a more permanent nature are the previously mentioned Akashic Records. Analogous to a video recording of an event in the five-sense realm, the Akashic Records retain the noumenal history for future learning. It serves as the memory bank of human experiences, including their interactions with other beings. The memories collectively making up the noumena may be as substantive and permanent as anything in the universe, yet they are only available to the inner senses.

Memory as Influence

Some of the more permanent, culturally based memories influencing behavior were first labeled "archetypes" (Greek for "original pattern") by Carl Jung. These patterns in the noumena, reinforced by conscious beings over generations, are bonded with enough subtle energy that they continue to exert subliminal influence over the ages. Archetypes like "hero," "victim," "journey," and "hunter" may indirectly shape individual lives until they are brought into awareness.

Large-scale morphic fields (described in chapter 4) are another illustration of how collective memories from the realms of noumena and the energeia shape matter and behavior.[3] In this process a specific idea becomes so energized by a critical mass of people holding it that it affects the thinking and behavior of countless others. Memory in archetypes or morphic fields plays the role of cause and not effect. For example, the impact of Cold War ideas on emotions and behavior, as far removed from the facts as the stereotypes were, can best be explained as the result of influence from energized thought-forms. (In a smaller scale indication of the power of thought-forms, individuals whose homes have been the site of intense emotional incidents have reported the ongoing influence of negative energies. They can be exorcised only by a more powerful expression of conscious intent. Dowsers, priests, and others who believe they have this power are successful in transmuting the negative energy.)

It is impossible to argue that telecommunications, since they did not exist, were responsible for similar values and emotions in the American and French revolutions of the eighteenth century. But the creations of a few writers, the noumenal constructs of "liberty, equality, and brotherhood," being fully charged in the energeia by masses of people on one continent, could motivate people energetically on the other side of the world. That energetic connection (not unlike the hundredth monkey theory mentioned earlier) could help account for the fervor of citizen armies.

Perhaps the patterns of political upheaval that traversed the globe in 1968 and 1989 were less influenced by television than the power of noumenal fields containing highly energized patterns of political thought. While telecommunications media and computer networks, by giving more people access to the same images and ideas, may help the thought-forms accrue more subtle energy, the fundamental force at work appears to be the noumena. For example, physically unconnected individuals wake up each day to "discover" through written materials that they share similar ideas and insights with previously unknown persons. Many such cases can be explained only by assuming individual parts of the whole social organism interact through the noumena.

Understanding such interactions millennia ago, Chinese scholars identified how certain fields of incipient noumenal patterns could affect individual events. Knowing it was possible for a person to divine living memory fields relevant to personal choices, they developed a process for obtaining this intelligence. The *I Ching*[4] process[5] connects a person's questions to the wisdom of accumulated memory. It is based on an appreciation of the resonance of ideas, subtle energy, and overt action. Ancient Chinese culture understood that a consciously lived life is an orchestrated nexus of all these realms. Living with the *I Ching,* runes, the Tarot, and other ways of tapping inner knowledge can help make one an active participant in synchronicity, where the desires and needs of the many are mediated through the invisible connections of the noumena.

Nonhomocentric Consciousness

The noumena and its interactions with physical life involves more than human ideas and communication. The communications of all beings involve and inform the noumena. There is growing recognition that all animals react to humans, and that the condition of plants and the Earth itself gives them feedback on their behavior. Many now know the interaction can be two-way and positive as well as negative. Some are coming to realize that the interspecies exchange of information and subtle energy is a feedback mechanism that could enhance the quality of all lives.

There are many examples of how consciousness works in interspecies communications. One example: In the fall of 1988 in Barrow, Alaska, three gray whales became trapped beneath an ice hole five miles from open sea. Although a series of new holes had been created by scientists and the local Inapt people, all efforts to entice the whales toward the new holes and the sea beyond failed. Finally, when Jim Nollman of Interspecies Communications arranged to send music through the hole the whales were currently using (which was about to freeze over) and also through one of the new holes, the whales moved to the new hole. The whales immediately started to migrate down the channel, surfacing to breathe at new holes along the way as music was played into each one.

The whales understood and acted in relation to human-generated music in a way that astonished onlookers who had no explanatory frame of reference. The indivisible noumena and energeia help explain the obvious multichannel nature of such intra- and interspecies communications.

Interspecies communication exists not only among humans, animals, and plants, but among conscious beings throughout the universe. Humans have experienced this through communications from ABs, angels, nonphysical channels, and many other forms. Many individuals who encounter another form of being automatically attribute to it godlike wisdom and/or demonic powers. The contactee frequently believes he or she has had a special encounter with a divine source. But the early Egyptians and Greeks had a clearer understanding: they saw the beings with all their foibles, as well as their insights or powers, as cohorts in the same field of consciousness. Their myths and legends imply these other categories of beings were involved in intellectual, emotional, and life cycles similar to those of humans. They all shared a common field of consciousness.

Just as perception of the electromagnetic spectrum is partial, knowledge of other realms is very limited. Being wedded to a mundane concept of space-time can interfere with understanding other aspects of the noumena and energeia. For example, the noumenal realm appears to involve an interspecies flow of information transcending the speed of light. (Recall the experiments with cell-to-cell communication presented in the last chapter.) Subtle-energy forms, while sometimes tied to a physical form (as in a person's auric field measured by Kirlian photography), appear not always to be constrained by space-time (as in OBEs).

The idea that noumenal and energeial forces exist outside the currently defined space-time universe is not farfetched. Newton explained there is no fixed space (everything is in constant movement), and Einstein's theory of relativity ended the notion that ordinary time is an absolute standard, uniform throughout the universe. These understandings make plausible the existence of reality outside the field of our typical five-sense perceptions. In the 1960s, Stephen Hawking and Roger Penrose proved mathematically that time as we know it had a beginning. If one accepts that proof, it becomes equally credible that other realms could have different beginning points. It is just as reasonable that an overarching cosmic consciousness should then be able to bridge the membranes that separate these parallel realms.

If people are to assimilate information from a wider spectrum of reality, they must reject not only a finite conception of space-time, but also the narrow view of consciousness promulgated by current science. As Robert J. Hannon aptly states, "science" can be seen as the domain of a group of professionals who sometimes decide what is "true" and what is "not true" before a hypothesis can be proved.[6] As an example, he challenges the assertion that the red shift (the earlier-mentioned fact that objects moving away from us appear to shift to the slower frequencies of the color spectrum) proves the continual expansion of the universe, calling it unsubstantiated. Similarly, when priests and gurus of any persuasion assert unproven dogmas that dismiss alternative interpretations, they too limit the search for wisdom.

Unified Yet Multifaceted

Experiments with mind travel, such as OBEs, remote viewing, and telepathy, appear to confirm the existence of a unified field of consciousness and lend credence to the view that humans are integral partners, not serendipitous bit players, in the cosmic drama set into motion by the Grand Couple.

Contrary to this, the sacred texts and legends of supernatural religions assert the existence of divisions among realms of consciousness. Simplistic Christian cosmology has three such realms: Heaven, Earth, and Hell. Catholicism posits two in-between realms: Purgatory, where the soul is purified before it is ultimately admitted to Heaven; and Limbo, where pure souls await assistance to ascend. In very general terms, the Nirvana of Buddhism is comparable to the Christian Heaven, while the Tibetan *bardo* parallels both Purgatory and Limbo as stages in the cycle of reincarnation. An afterlife, in the supernatural religion of Egypt, was believed to take place beyond the River of the Dead. Individual access to all such realms is believed to be controlled by independent, and usually divine, powers.

These and other religions were founded on the belief that a god personality from that divine realm either (1) bestowed divine status upon a chosen human on Earth, or (2) incarnated itself in human form to provide an exclusive channel between the different realms. These divine beings allegedly produced miracles and shared visions that followers took as evidence of their access to divinity. (With many examples of the so-called miracles being performed today by ordinary humans using their inner senses and powers, the assumption of divinity based on such events is questionable. Nor should advanced technological or psychic development in ABs be taken as proof of divinity.)

The presumed divine beings in early history were likely conscious entities whose "miracle"-producing skills were simply technologies beyond the human observers' experience. Some of the most comprehensive and best-researched evidence of this is from the previously mentioned *Earth Chronicles* (four volumes) and *Genesis Revisited* by Zecharia Sitchin.[7] His profound synthesis of many disciplines, with well-documented evidence involving numerous scholars over two centuries, supports the thesis of Earth's occupation by beings from elsewhere in the cosmos. Sitchin's analysis indicates that one group, the Annunaki, had mental powers compatible with humans, once again pointing to a singular pool of consciousness. The historically and currently reported ability of humans and such beings to communicate verbally and telepathically points to the unified field theory of consciousness.

This, too, calls into question supernatural claims of separate divine realms of consciousness.

Perhaps even more compelling evidence of a singular consciousness are the current activities of ABs on Earth (and possibly elsewhere in the solar system). In May 1992, the Rocky Mountain Research Institute and the International Association for New Science convened a forum in Colorado for the most comprehensive review ever of the evidence for extraterrestrial intelligence. Presenters at the conference demonstrated to the satisfaction of many skeptics gathered there that not only are other types of beings active in different parts of the universe, but that some of them evidently can transcend the familiar dimensions of our space-time. Evidence included photographs, artifacts, traces, human/AB contact case studies, and personal experiences.[8] Since that time, a review panel of largely skeptical scientists has concluded that such evidence merits serious and open-minded study. In recent years several governments, with the United States being notably absent, have established joint public/private commissions to assess the mounting evidence.

It is clear that a wider conception of reality is called for if we are to encompass the so-called alien experiences of a cross-section of humanity. In addition to humanoid ABs, who are the likely basis for the "gods of old" legends, many humans have encountered beings in disembodied form. Known as ascended masters, angels, spirit guides, and/or guardians, they speak to people directly, or are channeled through an individual in a trance who serves as their voice. There are reports of energeial beings channeling messages through computers and telephone answering machines, or other voice recorders. Seen as a source of wisdom and general insight, such "masters" also offer specific communications on departed relatives or stock market trends. The emergence of extensive channeling and the expression of "miraculous" powers (such as materialization, and psychic and healing powers) among the noninitiated has undermined the notion that communication with higher levels is restricted to a chosen few.[9]

Also providing additional evidence of human access to a unified consciousness are individuals who deliberately project their minds and energies into the nonphysical aspects of the universe. Instead of specific thoughts being sent into the noumena, the whole mind goes. Consciousness travel requires knowledge of the process and some practice, like that employed by the systematic researchers of the Monroe Institute in Virginia.[10] The late Robert Monroe assumed that individual consciousness is not bound by its corporeal home and discovered a gateway through which an individual consciousness can deliberately move between realms. The mind travelers at the Institute, in addition to breaching the physical wall, report they cross the boundaries between the energeia and the noumena. Sometimes their subtle senses become aware of other conscious beings in different energy-forms, while at others they perceive the beings as pure consciousness.

Participants at the Monroe Institute are placed in a Controlled Holistic Environmental Chamber that isolates them from light and some degree of electromagnetic radiation. In a process called "Hemi-Sync," headphones feed sound impulses of different hertz (cycles per second) into each ear. The right and left sides of the brain integrate the two into a new sound that results in hemispheric synchronization, which induces an "out-of-body" experience. The OBE travelers—in a state of "body asleep/mind awake"—report meetings with other entities, views of distant places, and awareness of a vast realm of consciousness other than self. However, the traveling self always sees itself as a part of that whole.

Acknowledgment and study of the above-described variety of communications would lead, one hopes, to serious mainstream study and scientific exploration. The following sections illustrate potentially fruitful areas for research, involving a number of ways in which the universe's unified field of consciousness is expressed: the role and function of dreams, the event we call death, parapsychology in the unbroken gradient of consciousness, communication with other beings, interdimensional shifts within a spectrum or among distinct spectra.

Dreaming. Alexander Borbely, in a comprehensive review of modern scientific research on sleep, concluded, "Not only are we investigating a process that usually occurs in the dark, but we are also almost completely in the dark about its function."[11] During sleep, dreaming—a natural and obviously important human function—is one of our most important channels to cosmic consciousness.

The physiological effects of sleep can be described. It can be artificially induced. Humans can manipulate its patterns, measure its electrical and muscular impact, label its different levels; but we cannot prevent it indefinitely. (Recent research indicates modern humans do not get enough of it. This finding appears congruent with the Principles of Polarity and Rhythm, which require balance on an ongoing basis.) Scientists have not detected all its specific benefits, nor do they understand why and from where the dream images come during sleep. In sleep, subtle input takes precedence over physical stimuli, as it does in meditation and other more porous states of local consciousness.

Dream images seem to be primarily caused by stimuli from the noumenal field of consciousness. (Of course some physical and emotional stimuli, internal and external, stimulate dreams as well.) Coming largely unfiltered by waking awareness during physical sleep, the input leaves the individual with greater latitude for various interpretations. In dreaming, an individual's energeial and noumenal senses receive signals like a radar. The blips give the direction, force, speed, and magnitude of the signals, but do not directly reveal the nature of their source. The patterns require a radar operator's mental act to interpret the data and decide on the reaction. The interpretation at the moment of stimulation is largely subconscious, unless one engages in lucid dreaming, and can therefore be affected by the preoccupations of the dreamer. Which is why it is so difficult to interpret memories of what was dreamt.

However, even though the personal membrane of consciousness is permeable, it always remains subject to at least the partial control of the aware being. Dream material, like all other sensory information, can pass through only with explicit or de facto permission. Some people have learned to partially monitor and intervene in their own dreams. All beings at some level are their own dream keepers, even those who have committed acts—such as the ingestion of chemical substances—that render them incapable of fully rational control. Like the gradations in the waking state, dreams in sleep are a composite of various degrees of awareness. Several hours of observing anyone's waking state reveal periods of concentrated mental focus, followed by moments of distraction when unbidden thoughts creep in. There is every reason to believe that similar variations in attention occur in the sleep state.

When one is awake but in a relaxed state, having suspended conscious effort at problem solving, breakthroughs frequently occur. Paradoxically, more overall conscious awareness is brought to bear on the problem than is possible in the midst of distractions created when the senses are narrowly focused. This dynamic is why dreaming, like controlled entry into meditative states where much sensory input is shut down, is so helpful for creative effort. It is often used by people who feel blocked; they articulate their questions and leave the mind free to search for the answers during sleep. Material can be perceived during such "conscious dreaming" from two almost unlimited sources, both of which are also accessible in the state of wakefulness: telepathic access (clairvoyant reception of current information) and Akashic Record access (tapping into the noumena for past memories).

Beyond Death. Near-death experiences (NDEs) and death itself provide further evidence of a realm where consciousness is not bound to a physical incarnation. As mentioned earlier, almost every culture believes in a realm where the personalities of recently deceased persons dwell, at least temporarily. Such beliefs are rooted in two planet-wide human experiences: perceptions reported in all ages of a continued nonphysical presence of those recently deceased, and specific and verifiable communications between individuals and their "dead" relatives.[12]

Since the time of early humans, people have had enough noumenal contact with relatives and friends after their deaths to develop various rituals and beliefs to assist the recently dead in transition to the next realm or to obtain guidance from them. Regarding early humans, modern scholars have mistakenly labeled such practices "ancestor worship" when in fact they only honored the reality of continuing communications. In the current era it is still common to find people reporting communications from relatives on the Other Side, even though modern scientific culture deprecates such stories. (Such communication does not seem to go on indefinitely in most cases, so there seems to be a principle of dissipation at work in maintenance of coherent contact.)

In the past several decades, thousands of reports from people having been resuscitated after "clinical" death (the cessation of respiratory and brain functions) reveal indisputable cases of conscious awareness in the energeial and noumenal realms. (See the NDE Web site at www.iands.org.) Surveys of many of these reports show attributes[13] similar to those of the nonphysical realm inhabited by those who have died, as in the table below.

Table 12. Attributes of the Nonphysical Realm
• Ability to hear conversations in the ordinary realm
• Feeling of peace and calm
• Various kinds of noise (from harsh to musical)
• Passage through a tunnel (usually dark)
• A sense of a nonmaterial body
• Meeting familiar others
• Encounter with beings of light
• Review of life's significant events
• A transition point (door, fence, fine mist)

NDEs and communications between the dead and living clearly demonstrate that a personal consciousness can range across realms and simultaneously perceive the phenomena and the energeia. They offer further validation of the three-faceted model of reality posited in chapter 4.

In the context of the assumptions in this book, the term "NDE," as popularized by Raymond Moody and Kenneth Ring,[14] appears to be a misnomer, because "death" may be the wrong term. The realm of the NDE experience, which involves beings we call dead, is not unlike that experienced in the "travels" of people at the Monroe Institute. Finding that consciousness transcends life and death again underscores its all-pervasive quality, even when specific perceptions of it may differ. Because the "other realm" sensory stimuli differ from those in physical reality, as in the dreaming experience, human OBE-ers and NDE-ers interpret them according to their personal life experiences. Thus, a Christian encountering a luminal being may label it Christ while a Muslim "sees" Mohammed.

The experience of an "ordinary death," then, may be only a particular form of OBE. During both OBEs and NDEs, one senses one's energeial body leaving the physical body and moving to another locale, yet one remains aware of what is going on in both realms. In contrast, a "final death" would be a return to the complete dormancy of the preorganic void, a state beyond current comprehension and apparently one that humans manage to escape through the universe's rhythm of conscious rebirths. Plato may have had it right when he described birth as going to sleep (and forgetting) and death as awakening (remembering). Death, or de-incarnation, with its greater access to the energeia and noumena and freedom from phenomenal boundaries, may give a personality greater liberty to roam the universe.

The Book of Revelation, The Tibetan Book of the Dead, and The Egyptian Book of the Dead, when read in the light of this new perspective, offer insight into the observed departure of consciousness from the physical body. In describing a phased process of disengagement, they refer to a period of life review and judgment. Free of the body's constraints on memory, the being can more easily recall the experience of many lifetimes, and assess how well it has lived this one. This possibility is compatible with the traditional concept of reincarnation. Perhaps greater study of NDEs and OBEs and their relationship to other so-called paranormal or energeial experiences can reveal how a being can consciously shift among different states during an ordinary lifetime.

The evidence for reincarnation suggests the ability of personalities to retain enough coherence of local memories to survive one or more transitions from life to death and back again. Whether this is a fully conscious and deliberate act, as some believe, cannot be asserted on the basis of current evidence, but the fact of humans alive today having verifiable memories of former personalities is beyond question. Ian Stevenson and others have accumulated innumerable stories of children who recall the experiences of people who have lived before, in some cases where there is no possible route for the information to have been gained since birth.

Some have suggested that such memories are carried in genetic transmissions, but this argument does not stand scrutiny. The cases mentioned above have no generation-to-generation genetic pathways connecting the two personalities involved. In many instances the two individuals involved are from different cultures, with genetic branching having occurred before the birth of the so-called previous life.

The only other explanation is that current beings somehow select the past personality's memory pool and tap into it through the noumenal web. Access to such memories is conceivable in a noumenal field, but such remote viewing connections do not account for the frequent similarities of physical characteristics (even specific birthmarks) between the two individuals separated by time and family trees.

Unbroken Gradient. The hypothesis associated with the three-faceted model of the universe posits that the noumena is a singular and integral force or field. In other words, consciousness is essentially the same everywhere, existing in various concentrations (called "local consciousness" by physicists and "personalities" by psychologists) in an analog to the electromagnetic spectrum. The unbroken nature of the field of general consciousness is demonstrated by the lack of definitive distinctions between an OBE and so-called parapsychological experiences. For example, what starts as a remote viewing experience, initiated in a deliberate manner, may end up as an involuntary OBE.

Where an individual's "paranormal" experience falls on the previously listed range of conscious states appears to be largely a function of intent. For example, the difference between remote viewing and flashes of telepathy is only a matter of degree. The former is a conscious act and the latter is more spontaneous, but they operate on the same basic principle, drawing on the collection of current images in the noumena. Precognition is also an exercise of the same subtle sense, except that it reaches forward into space-time and perceives the potential for events to come. Hypnotic regression reverses the same process, revisiting the past on the arrow of time.

All these communications are different ways to access aspects of the noumena. Each tunes the frequency of one's inner senses to an appropriate energetic range, somewhat analogous to physically accessing a radio frequency of the electromagnetic wave spectrum.

Let's summarize the many different ways in which a local point of self-awareness—that is, an incarnated being—has access to and takes part in the general consciousness that underlies and illuminates all existence. I assume that the perspective taken here reflects the view of any conscious physical entity. Whether all organic species share the same potential scope and flexibility in consciousness cannot be asserted on the basis of current evidence. From Earth-based experience, I believe we can reasonably assume the existence of different levels of maturation in consciousness elsewhere. (I have labeled these differences "CQ," to stand for "Conscious Awareness Quotient," to contrast it with IQ.)

Our ability to be consciously aware of all dimensions means we can, in effect, define boundaries in physical reality, from the microcosm to the macrocosm. Our local consciousness "makes sense" of all the input that comes through the physical senses. This same consciousness that surveys the physical domain also brings into itself information from and awareness of other domains accessible only through inner ways of knowing. The fact that a being's field of conscious wakefulness can access other sections of the conscious gradient and synthesize the data indicates that general consciousness has no internal barriers. Low magnitude of signal (the phenomenon of dissipation over time and distance) or efforts of other beings to concentrate defensive shields may hinder access, but in principle, all the noumena is accessible by a "local" personality.

Therefore, an incarnated being can utilize deliberate remote viewing, passive receptivity to telepathic signals, planned or spontaneous OBEs (and although not likely sought, NDEs), dreams, hypnosis or guided inner searches, and meditation or other techniques that relax the boundaries of local consciousness. The latter may include any number of techniques to induce an expanded state of awareness (drumming, dance, chants, hallucinogenic substances, or even fatigue). When physical beings approach death in phases, there is a tendency to shift back and forth between local and expanded areas of consciousness. Systematic exploration of all these approaches should enable a species to define the parameters of the energeial and noumenal realms as accurately as they define the physical universe.

Other Conscious Species. Another powerful category of evidence for a unified field of consciousness involves other beings with whom humans can communicate through both the physical and the inner senses. There are numerous historical and contemporary accounts of human contact with other groups of conscious entities.

Humans are not the only sentient beings on the Earth (and I don't mean other animals) and apparently have never been. As previously mentioned, since the late 1940s, thousands of sightings of "alien" spacecraft have been reported around the world, with many involving direct or telepathic communications with the occupants. Physical interactions (including medical procedures and sexual contacts) have been verified through material evidence, rigorous hypnotic techniques, and polygraph tests. The sources referenced in this book and many others provide credible descriptions of these activities.

Self-labeled galactic anthropologist Marcia Schafer's currently ongoing personal story is of particular interest in the context of consciousness.[15] Her descriptions of a wide range of species beyond our solar system and their various levels of conscious development and forms of communication are consistent with the three-faceted universe posited here. Her experience with flesh and blood entities and others who primarily inhabit the subtle realms supports the notion that consciousness can manifest itself in different degrees of subtle energy and material concentrations.

That many individuals have been involuntarily subjected to AB experimentation is now well documented. Ova have been taken from some women for fertilization elsewhere, while others have been impregnated and then had the fetus removed at a very early stage. Men have had sperm extracted or been forced to ejaculate into AB females. Some women have reported contact with their hybrid offspring.[16]

While shocking and outside the bounds of our concepts of civilized behavior (unless we commit the acts against animals or humans we consider beneath us), most of these encounters seem to involve no inherently hostile intent on the part of the AB abductors. They appear to have no desire to inflict unnecessary harm and frequently promise further contact and communication. Their potential for empathizing with the psychological terror felt by some of their human abductees may be blocked by the nature of their own situation. Some abductees have received the impression that the ABs need the abductees' genetic stock and something of their emotional force to strengthen their own weakening species. Humans and some ABs may be mutually dependent in some as yet unrecognized way.

Evidence also exists of more threatening types of AB presence. As among humans, these beings are clearly at different levels of moral and psychological development. Some appear to fall below the best of human ethical perspectives. (See earlier-referenced work by Robert Sprinkle on abduction experience.) As disheartening as it may seem (since we no longer need to take sides in the Cold War), many believe it may be necessary in the near future to seek alliances with some ABs in defense against others. Currently, covert operations involving opposing AB forces of potential threat to human society may be under way. A forthright public assessment of the various species of nonhuman beings and their compatibility with society's most progressive values is needed. But the relevant point here is that telepathic, trance, and dream communication channels exist between humans and such beings; we share a common field of consciousness.

A number of widely reported polls confirm that large numbers of American adults are prepared to accept the reality of other beings and the responsibility for dealing with them. Many claim to have had AB-related experiences themselves, and as these claims are taken more and more seriously, intelligent individuals will find ways to integrate the idea and reality of ABs into their own sphere of consciousness.

The three-faceted model of the universe postulated in this book will assist humans in developing plausible explanations for reported AB encounters and strategies for relating to them. We can no longer view consciousness in a homocentric manner; we are as likely on the periphery of consciousness in the universe as in its center. Let's review the three categories of interaction with other conscious beings.

The first type occurs when ABs are primarily operating in phenomenal reality. Interaction with them accounts for physical traces left by ABs and their vehicles and reported artifacts. It could also account for the wounds or other marks reported on numbers of contactees. Present in ordinary space-time, they are accessible through the five physical senses. Even though they may possess characteristics and abilities normally unknown to us, energeial and noumenal communications would occur simultaneously with the physical.

The second category involves experiences with primarily imaginal forms that become perceptible to people in the requisite open mental state. Jacques Vallee, for example, hypothesized that a significant element in the reporting of UFO and AB contacts could result from interdimensional perceptions or access to alternate realities.[17] This theory explains the number of passive memories of AB contacts (obtained through the subtle senses from another party) that may be exposed through dream recovery or hypnotic regression.

A third explanatory theory involves nonhuman beings inhabiting the subtle-energy realm, where they are encountered by people in altered states. Temporary shifts in subtle-energy vibratory pattern can explain why some individuals in a group can "see" an anomalous being while others cannot. Such a state of requisite "readiness" could also help explain the selective nature of contacts with beings that have been labeled "angels," "ghosts," "allies," or "nature spirits" by their human interlocutors.

It is not clear what mental or emotional states are involved in the last two categories of contacts. Research could start with the experience of dowsers who negotiate the departures of certain nonphysical beings caught in a local dimension. This theory, for which we have no direct evidence and which may be only a matter of semantics, provides for several dimensions within this space-time continuum. It may also be possible for humans to shift from dimension to dimension along this spectrum without completely moving to another realm. Information reportedly from ABs supports the idea that there may be such dimensions within each of the three facets.[18]

Several recent metaphysical books, such as *The Pleiadian Agenda* and *Bringers of the Dawn*, predict humanity is about to experience transition to higher dimensions or higher frequencies of vibration. Some of these allegedly involve types of consciousness different from those now experienced within the phenomena. However, such speculation can be treated neither scientifically, unless it can somehow be tested in this incarnation, nor reasonably, unless it is congruent with inner-experience testing by groups.

Arrow of Time. Despite popular time-travel fiction and reports of government research projects like the Philadelphia Experiment, from this internally congruent space-time, it would be illogical to believe incarnated consciousness can either go back and change past events, or directly manipulate the future from the present. The functioning of cause and effect means that a change in the past would change the present. Therefore, it is impossible to go from the status quo of the moment and change the past without modifying the present in a perceptible way. The resulting oscillating loop would become perpetual, breaking down the directionality of space-time.

Popular claims for simultaneous universes and parallel lifetimes for humans to manipulate past and future events are incompatible with the notion of a self-directing and self-learning universe; individual learning involves sequential experiences with directionality and a rule of cause and effect. Remember, just because something is mathematically feasible, using man-made rules, does not mean it is necessarily feasible within the universe we inhabit.

In *The Watchers*,[19] a nonfiction report of an abduction, alien beings remark, "We know what is likely to happen but we cannot intervene." That appears to be a statement of universal fact, at least as pertains to humans and similar conscious beings. A situation of which I was aware involved the forebodings of a prospective groom who just "knew" the carefully orchestrated wedding plans would not materialize. On the day prior to the scheduled wedding, the bride-to-be and four family members were all injured in an automobile accident. In such personal examples and those of professional psychics, what is seen of the future are projected potentialities that cannot be changed directly, psychically or otherwise. Whether or not they materialize depends on intermediate actions undertaken by conscious choice or through an accident. In either case the interim events influence which potential event actually materializes.

In a universe of freedom for each individual to choose among different potentialities at each quantum step, no form of remote viewing, even with powers of retrovision and precognition, could include the power to revise past or future decisions made by individual beings in ordinary reality. While the mind can travel along the arrow of time, but not directly change phenomenal reality, telekinesis can influence the behavior of matter at a distance, but is by its nature limited to this space-time where matter resides.

We may assume that universal consciousness has the power to change even itself, but its local manifestations (humans and other similar beings) are limited to taking advantage of infinitely small quantum leaps in concert with others. This now appears to be the only way we can play the role of redesigners of future reality. However, the uncertainty principle, the play of pure randomness, still introduces a degree of chance into the evolution of universal reality, thereby restricting the degree of individual and group control, even on a local level. One of the conditions under which individual conscious beings play in this universe must be the risk of such accidental occurrences. Conscious life carries with it the element of chance, which actually adds zest to existence. To remain in a conscious incarnation, beings must accept the challenge of riding the waves of creative uncertainty in search of learning opportunities.

Nonhuman Consciousness

Many current groups (fundamentalists, New Agers, frontier scientists—even mainstream analysts studying population, health, and resource trends) predict imminent, significant human mental and psychological shifts. Some see these shifts as natural cycles, involving periods of ideological revolution and overt conflict, when declines in political, social, and economic institutions are paralleled by a widespread deterioration in the quality of life. Others think in religious terms, hoping for some form of divine intervention to accompany the arrival of a bright new millennium.

If cosmic consciousness is a unified field, populated with a variety of beings in different realms or dimensions, humans in a period of exceptional chaos can potentially benefit from interdimensional communications. Some channeled material now being published, like Schafer's account described above, seems to be helpful advice from more experienced races. The messages some alien abductors give abductees have been seen by the latter as helpful. Whether such communications can benefit us in practical terms depends on our ability to validate them and apply them to present human needs.

Given the content of some communications, many believe ABs may be ready to assist humans in amending disastrous environmental practices or solving technology problems. Some see ABs as a catalyst to resolve conflict among different political and ethnic groups. Conversely, others fear the imposition of a new—not necessarily benevolent—world order by covert human groups in concert with AB forces. Those who anticipate dramatic Earth changes sometimes expect to be rescued by other-dimensional beings. The Apocalypse, followed by a new heavenly reign on Earth, predicted by fundamentalists in various religious sects, is interpreted by some as the advent of an alien occupation.

The number and complexity of thousands of unexplained crop circles in the last three decades have raised two intriguing possibilities about extrahuman consciousness. One may be that nonhumans are attempting to communicate with us through the symbolic nature of these artificial distortions of growing plants. The other is that humans may have a graphic impact on the consciousness of seemingly unrelated species in the plant kingdom. Some observers combine the two possibilities, believing that some unknown human behavior elicits reactions from more evolved beings, who respond by manipulating the crops into symbolic shapes. Giving credit to hoaxers for creation of a percentage of the formations, some researchers believe the authentic ones are interdimensional and interspecies channels of communication in need of scientific exploration. (I clearly fall in the category supporting such research.)

Even if nonhumans have no plans to mount an imminent public intervention in human affairs, humans still have access to the broader knowledge available in the noumenal field. Regardless of AB intentions for the future, humans have sufficient latent wisdom and skill to bring about their own transformation. With the will to try, humans are now capable of species-wide shifts in consciousness through increased use of the subtle senses. Acquisition of vast new knowledge on the phenomenal plane can be facilitated by expanded understanding of the energeia and the noumena.

Aided by current global communications networks, rapidly expanding human awareness could result in a radical transformation of basic assumptions about the nature and role of humans in the cosmos. A shift of this order of magnitude would be more than the acceptance of a new scientific paradigm. Willis Harman used the term "global mind change" to label the phenomenon of such a new perspective.[20]

While its full implication would take years to play out, as did the European Renaissance and it prehistoric analogs, this new perestroika (restructuring) of the mind would change the nature of all human institutions, and thereby the individual's relationship with others and the material universe. Such a revolution's ultimate pace and character will depend on the nature of leadership assumed by people who can transcend homocentrism. They will discern the potential of individual and group exploitation of the connection to universal consciousness. Let's review some of the characteristics of this connection.

Direct Access. In an integral, holographic universe each conscious being has direct access to the whole. This principle has been suppressed by leaders of supernatural religions in order to maintain the exclusivity of their channels to universal wisdom. There is a tendency among some now receiving communications from ABs to transfer their dependency on supernatural divinity to these entities. Some of the entities appear to pass themselves off as gods, but most portray themselves as fellow conscious beings sharing their experiences with humans. Considerable reeducation will be necessary for "followers" to accept that they have the same inner powers as their chosen "leaders."

The idea that certain men (rarely women) are gods-incarnate has been perpetuated through recorded history. All the major Middle East–based religions have founders and current leaders reputed to have unique channels of communication with their god. Eastern religions also claim to have avatars and divine incarnations with special access to universal wisdom. Beliefs like these contribute to an assumption that ABs in any form are divine, rather than just beings different only in degrees from humans. The notion of a divine/nondivine dichotomy persists despite the absence of proof that one dimension of consciousness is not naturally available to another.

When people hear a story of humans exhibiting extraordinary powers (like religious men such as Sai Baba who exude the ash of *vibutti*, believers who ooze perfume from their hands, or others who manifest stigmata), they too readily assume there is special access to divine consciousness. Religious institutions take great pains to perpetuate the idea that only a few selected by their particular god are given access to such powers. A few years ago the *Washington Post* prominently reported the case of a local priest—observed by independent witnesses—who caused statues to weep in his presence. But the Catholic Church uses a bureaucratic process for assessing such incidents and classifying those that meet certain criteria as "divine" miracles. It has a vested interest in *not* acknowledging that such powers are intrinsic to very many common folks.

This religious effort to maintain classes of "divine consciousness," and thereby exert control by those higher on the ladder over those on allegedly lower rungs, has separated humans from humans for several thousand years. European kings, and many other political and economic elites, until recently continued to proclaim they ruled through "divine right." Another example is the misapplication of Hindu cosmology to justify a caste system that puts humans into separate and distinct spiritual categories. Such notions of "divine" hierarchies have permitted divisions based on prejudgments about race, culture, religion, education, and economic and technical development.

The emerging new view of humans and other conscious beings shatters the notion of hierarchies of access to universal consciousness. Metascience reveals the undivided nature of the subtle-energy and noumenal realms, and the potential for each individual to perform *all* the so-called divine miracles. The evidence indicates that all humans possess the inner powers—though still latent in many—to consciously transcend fragmentation of their physical, emotional, and intellectual senses to achieve wholeness. They can express and perceive noumenal information in the far corners of the universe, view the reality of the past and the potential of the future, mobilize unseen energies, and cause matter to move and coalesce in tangible form.

Yet these powers are not harnessed in today's human society. The obvious question is, why do beings deny the power within themselves? Is it fear or ignorance, or both? It does not matter which; both can be overcome through understanding of our Solarian legacy. Recognition of the egalitarian nature of inner reality will affect the future of human development at two levels: how social institutions evolve on Earth, and how humans as a species relate to other conscious races as we become involved with them.

Positioning ourselves as somehow subservient to the "gods" or their "representatives" narrows the scope of human vision and intellectual inquiry. Seeing ourselves as fallen souls or struggling animal-like creatures who seek deliverance by divine beings, we fail to exploit the cosmic reservoir of knowledge and wisdom all conscious beings possess. Having inadvertently convinced ourselves that we are incapable of self-redemption, individuals leave social havoc in our wake.

Our twenty-first-century challenge will be to cease underestimating ourselves and achieve congruence between human self-images and our true nature. The process will be a self-initiation into galactic citizenship.

Illusions and Delusions. Why do humans generally have such an inferiority complex? As illustrated below, supernatural religious traditions the world over have perpetuated the expectation of a return of a god who will usher in a new age of enlightenment or regeneration, thereby taking the responsibility from humans. Internationally known artist and philosopher Nicholas Roerich wrote:

> Kalmucks in Karashar are awaiting the coming manifestation of the chalice of Buddha. . . . On Altai, the Oyrots renounce Shamanism and are singing

> new chants to the Awaited White Burkhan. . . . The
> Mongols await the appearance of the Ruler of the
> World and prepare the Dukang of Shambhala. . . .
> The Jews await the Messiah at the Bridge. . . . The
> Moslems await the Muntazar. . . . The Christians of
> Saint Thomas await the Great Advent. . . . The
> Hindus know the Kalki Avatar and the Chinese at
> New Year light the fires before the images of Gessar
> Khan, ruler of the world.[21]

The historical analyses of Zecharia Sitchin and William
Bramley[22] suggest that this sense of expectation may have
evolved from the promises to return made by ABs as they left
behind our human ancestors. Supporting this notion is the
fact that the sixteenth-century Spanish conquistadors were
welcomed by the natives of Central and South America whose
legends predicted the return of powerful light beings. That
behavior expressed the same yearning motivating the Jewish
prophecy of a Messiah and the Christian belief in the Second
Coming. If core tenets of religions, like that of a "divine" messiah or savior, were actually based in historical experiences
with ABs and promises of their to return to Earth, do humans
have a natural need for religion?

Given a twenty-first-century, metascientific perception of
the nature of universal consciousness and individual access to it,
are traditional religions necessary? Our natural desire to understand the interaction of unseen energies and consciousness with
physical life no longer has to turn to religious institutions for
satisfaction. In fact, to do so limits the search. Even though religious institutions meet needs for a sense of community and personal support, that purpose can be served without the theology
that reinforces social exclusivity and power over others.

In other words, our psychological needs can be met without resort to unseen and argued-over gods. By falsely attributing divinity to their respectively chosen ABs or imagining
divine beings, religions have diminished humans by failing to
appreciate the power that derives from each individual's direct
membership in the universe's family of self-directing beings.

While people can be diverted by self-serving leaders of religion and other institutions, in the final analysis people demean themselves. When we turn to such authorities for spiritual answers, we give up personal responsibility. Some leaders may initially seek to inspire humanity to new heights, yet the limited expectations of the masses hold them back. A self-deprecating public forces the status quo on the would-be avatar who might otherwise manifest a more evolved state.

Millions of people, for example, believe that Sai Baba, a man from the village of Puttaparthy, India, is God-incarnate. For more than half a century, his miracles and teachings have attracted thousands of people for daily *darshan* (bestowing of a guru's blessing). Spending their time in acts of adulation, metaphorically grabbing for his feet, they prevent their own self-realization. Although Sai Baba, like Jesus 2,000 years ago, says, "Look within yourself. We are all the same," his followers tenaciously deny the divine consciousness within themselves. He preaches a vision of equality among all beings, a code of community service, and values that support enlightened human behavior. But the thousands awaiting his *darshan* expect him to provide the answers, from a magical cure for diabetes to a cost-free way to clean up the environment. They hope Sai Baba will accomplish these ends without any effort on their part.

Thinking of beings like Jesus and Sai Baba as gods-incarnate, people ascribe to them the characteristics of all-knowing, all-seeing, all-powerful paragons, thus making it psychologically possible to accept a lower standard of behavior for themselves. When such chosen beings are set apart by the misguided view that they must be crucified (Jesus), urged into battle (Mohammed), or adored but not emulated (Sai Baba), they serve as scapegoats for human failings. The Piscean Age presumption of an unbridgeable chasm between such "divine beings" and human consciousness resulted in a delusional escape from self-responsibility, in the expectation of an external savior.

The twenty-first century needs metascience-based myths that transcend politicized historical interpretations, for example, the fourth-century Nicean Council censorship of the founding principles of Christianity, and reveal the commonality joining humans and other species. Such a Solarian legacy will reflect our understanding that the universe and all its beings are consciously, energetically, and materially undivided and indivisible. The true "masters" of the twenty-first century will not be specialists who devote all their attention to mutually exclusive religious tenets or the self-limiting restrictions of conventional disciplines. Mastery will be self-mastery, but of a self responsible for one's impact on the whole.

Self-Responsibility. Ironically, communications with ABs will help humans realize more fully the scope of their own powers. When humans psychologically accept as siblings other conscious beings with powers that have traditionally been labeled "divine," they will in effect be accepting humanity's cosmic nature. Part of the process of assuming the mantle of cosmic self-governance must be a deliberate search for unknown family members. Humans must deliberately try to communicate with cosmic siblings through the subtle senses, as well as through the physical senses. All senses and instruments need to be tuned and aimed in the right directions.

On October 12, 1992 (500 years after Columbus "rediscovered" America), NASA launched the 100-million-dollar SETI (Search for Extraterrestrial Intelligence) Project to listen for possible radio signals from intelligent extraterrestrial beings. This program was justified on the statistical assumption that humans might not be alone in the universe.[23] If there are intelligent beings, so the argument went, they might be trying to communicate with us, and therefore we ought to electronically scan the skies for messages.

The project involved astronomers using telescopes in Puerto Rico, West Virginia, California, and Australia, and computer centers around the world. Designed to scan the quietest sector of the radio spectrum (1,000 to 10,000 megahertz), SETI sought—among billions of frequencies—signals that stand out from natural noises and emissions from Earth. The logic went like this: Intelligent beings would use one wavelength, keep it on for a period of time, call attention to it by transmitting in pulses, and compensate for the Doppler effect of their moving planet.

Fortunately, that expensive project was defunded by Congress.[24] Public resources should not be devoted to such a low-priority task when so much concrete evidence of nonhuman consciousness exists here on Earth. To ignore the evidence is analogous to staring at the sky for a single source of music while ignoring the songbirds in the trees. Society can no longer afford to ignore evidence in its front yard out of either intellectual conceit or fear of public reaction to the truth.

Carl Sagan, considered by many to be the government's "unofficial debunker" of alien research, writing in the mass-appeal medium of *Parade Magazine,* appeared in an unintended way to be preparing the public for the inevitable AB encounter. In September 1993, he wrote of SETI, "Conceivably, this might be the last generation before contact is made—and the last moment before we discover that someone in the darkness is calling out to us."

Sagan attempted to be reassuring when pointing out that SETI was passive and not likely to be detected by malevolent aliens. He reminded readers that since current science and knowledge would soon be outmoded by human progress, more advanced civilizations should not be feared. Recognizing the likely widespread impact of the denouement of ill-founded societal assumptions, before his death, he implicitly cautioned that acceptance of proof that humans are not the universe's only conscious beings will dramatically reshape politics, ethics, economics, and religions.

Individuals who have the most vested in the political and economic status quo may consider this inevitable revolution to be reason enough for the continued government denial of the growing evidence of UFO/AB activity. In 1960, the Brookings Institution in Washington, D.C., prepared a report for the U.S. government which warned that public knowledge of the existence of other intelligent life in the universe might lead to societal disintegration. Many believe fear of such an outcome has motivated almost fifty years of government cover-up.

Such fears are ill-founded: ordinary citizens, as is so often the case, are way out in front of their formal leaders. Many already recognize that opening to cosmic consciousness is essential for planetary progress; they understand that true participation in cosmic life is a collective experience, shared not only with fellow humans, but with all conscious beings.

To consciously claim a species' role in a singular or integral universe requires recognition that beings from *all* levels—angels, devas, spirit guides, and aliens—need one another. None exists just to give instruction or issue commands; their communications represent only their own experiences, from which others can learn. Through such egalitarian and symbiotic exchanges, the various species can nourish each other. Even those with hostile agendas must be dealt with in the same manner.

Currently on Earth, crime and violence anywhere constrain freedom of movement in the neighborhood or around the globe. Pollutants in the atmosphere deplete everyone's ozone. Poor ecological practices deprive all of wholesome food, air, and water. Emotional and mental alienation in some weakens the fabric of a whole species. Children are discarded, and even murdered, as adults fight over ephemeral issues and cringe with inner fear of honest and constructive engagement with other beings.

The result is species-wide alienation from its true nature in which each member is held in a lower, more unstable path by suppressing our connections to other realms and other beings. If creative energy is spent in avoiding responsibility for oneself, the web of defensiveness does not change and perpetual fears remain in place. But when individual energy is spent helping the whole community progress, and in giving more physical, social, and psychological freedom to other beings, all are individually freer to realize their cosmic potential.[25]

Why do humans attempt to avoid responsibility for discovering the truth about themselves? The highly educated, affluent devotees of a channeled entity displayed an easy acceptance of channeled platitudes while revealing a deep need for reassurance that they were his special charges. Perhaps this need to remain dependent in a "lower status" is a function of the anxiety felt when sensing one's own latent powers. Humans may be frightened by their own potential for greatness.

People can avoid the myopia of devoteeism by remembering that they equally share the weaknesses and strengths of the inappropriately elevated person (or being). Sai Baba, for example, admits to acquiescing to the Hindu tradition of dividing men from women in public, even though it contradicts his teachings. Just over five feet tall, he compensates for his short stature with wildly blown hair, exaggerating his claim to omniscience perhaps to bolster the confidence of the village child he once was. Everyone shares such psychological defenses of charismatics—in material or energetic form—as we forget, or are not allowed to exhibit, our natural limitations and potential.

If human society is to learn to perform at its peak, with everyone moving higher on the natural spiral of development, the false distinctions that set leaders and followers apart must be abandoned. All conscious beings are inherently equals. That privilege and responsibility characterize humanity's Solarian legacy as we begin the twenty-first century.

Notes

1. Brian O'Leary, *Second Coming of Science* (Berkeley, CA: North Atlantic Books, 1992).

2. Rudolf Steiner, *Cosmic Memory* (New York: Harper & Row, 1959).

3. Prior to Rupert Sheldrake, the idea of a morphogenetic field was advanced by Paul Weiss in the 1930s and more fully developed by J. V. Bronsted in the 1950s.

4. Richard Wilhelm and Cary F. Baynes, *The I Ching* or *Book of Changes* (Princeton, NJ: Princeton University Press, 1975).

5. It provides for the selection of relevant advice on personal issues from a book that describes general force fields and vectors. Individual selections from the various descriptions come through subconscious attraction to the symbol appropriate to one's question. From the Celtic tradition, a similar process used objects known as "runes" to relate personal questions to general information.

6. Robert J. Hannon, Letter to the Editor, *Mensa Bulletin* (January-February 1994).

7. Zecharia Sitchin, *Earth Chronicles and Genesis Revisited* (New

York: Avon Books, 1990).

8. Copies of papers may be obtained from IANS, P.O. Box 8127, Ft. Collins, CO 80526.

9. Linda Keen, *John Lennon in Heaven* (Ashland, OR: Pan Publishing, 1994).

10. The Monroe Institute is about twenty-five miles south of Charlottesville, at Route 1, Box 175, Faber, VA 22938; (804) 361-1252.

11. Alexander Borbely, *Secrets of Sleep* (New York: Basic Books, 1986).

12. Ian Stevenson, "Reincarnation: Field Studies and Theoretical Issues" in *Handbook of Parapsychology*, edited by B. B. Wolman (New York: Van Nostrand and Reinhold Co., 1977) and Keynote Speech, Conference of the International Association for New Science, Ft. Collins, Colorado, September 17, 1992.

13. Raymond A. Moody, *Life After Life* (New York: Bantam Books, 1988).

14. Kenneth Ring, *Omega Project* (New York: William Morrow, 1992).

15. Marcia Schafer, *Confessions of an Intergalactic Anthropologist* (Phoenix, AZ: Cosmic Destiny Press, 1999).

16. Budd Hopkins, *Intruders* (New York: Ballantine Books, 1988); John E. Mack, *Abduction* (New York: Crown Publishers, 1999).

17. Jacques Vallee, *Revelation: Alien Contact and Human Deception* (New York: Ballantine, 1992).

18. Vera Stanley Alder, *The Fifth Dimension: The Future of Mankind* (New York: Samuel Weiser, 1970).

19. Raymond E. Fowler, *The Watchers: The Secret Design Behind UFO Abduction* (New York: Bantam Books, 1990).

20. Willis Harman, *Global Mind Change* (Indianapolis, IN: Knowledge Systems, 1988).

21. Nicolas Roerich, *Archer* (New York: Society of Friends of Roerich Museum, 1929).

22. William Bramley, *Gods of Eden* (New York: Avon Books, 1993).

23. Assume there are about 100 billion galaxies, each with billions of stars. If only 10 percent of those stars have the life-giving capability of our Sun, and only 10 percent of those life-giving suns

have planets similar to Earth, statistically there could still be thousands of other advanced civilizations.

24. An indication of the citizen interest in learning if there are other beings out there is the fact that over 1.5 million computer users in more 100 countries have linked to a university-based SETI program to replace the government one.

25. This perspective was promoted in the late 1800s and early twentieth century by writers such as Ralph Waldo Emerson, Oliver Wendell Holmes, Walt Whitman, Mark Twain, Edwin Markham, and Walter Russell. They initiated several social movements through the Twilight Club, a modern version of which has recently been reorganized by the University of Science and Philosophy.

6

Mind as Local Incarnation

The stars and planets of our grand universe are massive, but modern technology has probed microcosmic depths to discover that their essence is fundamentally ephemeral. Somewhere between the near zero of subatomic particles and the unmapped galaxies light-years in width, suspended in space, we find Earth, home base for many conscious beings. These include everything from one-celled entities to humans, and perhaps more advanced beings, accompanied by untold numbers of species of plants and animals. Many of the experiments mentioned in this book demonstrate that all these levels experience the three-faceted reality of the noumena, energeia, and phenomena. Each physical being encompasses some degree of conscious awareness (mind) and some form of emotional energy.

Our present information suggests that all organic forms, all incarnated entities anywhere, derive life from and thrive in the interactions of all three facets. They perceive their relations with external reality through multilevel sensory systems. This input shapes their conscious reactions to the local environment, which in turn reshapes the environment, in a circular process of co-creation. In this self-directing universe, each entity with even the smallest degree of what Cleve Backster calls "primary perception" mirrors the nature of universal consciousness. Thus, any local entity is, by definition, an *incar-*

nation of that universal consciousness. This means that even beings of subtle energy or only consciousness are informed by, incarnated with, something of the whole consciousness. In this context, the state of awareness of that living connection is conscious beingness.

What is the source of this concept of beingness, wherein through some expression of desire, a consciousness in a state of full self-awareness concentrates and binds part of itself with subtle energy and matenergy of its own making? Who designed the process by which this breath of life results in beings who can become aware of their own origins? We do not know the answers to who, what, or why. But we seem to be learning something of the how.

I first heard the word "beingness" while listening to a taped psychic reading done by Ron Scolastico[1] in 1979. He was in Iowa, I was in Washington, D.C. A mutual friend had asked Ron to go into a trance and seek his spirit guides' responses to questions I had written.

The spirit guides, speaking through the channel that Ron allows himself to become, used a very stilted syntax, not unlike some of my early efforts to translate English thoughts into French or Spanish. One of the first things to strike me in that recording was the reference to my current life as "this beingness." As their comments unfolded, it became clear that this was a good use of English for the guides' meaning.

By "beingness" they implied my specific incarnation in space-time. The implication was that this beingness was me, but not all of me; the beingness was bounded in ways that I was not. I much later came to understand that a beingness is any organism that results when patterns of consciousness are focused in subtle energy and matenergy. In traditional terms, beingness is equivalent to incarnation, where consciousness that already exists takes on a different form. Therefore, all entities with conscious awareness, regardless of species, are incarnated beings. Some believe the Earth itself in this context is a conscious beingness, known as Gaia.

Individual Incarnations

Where does the concept of beingness or incarnation fit in the context of the three-faceted model? How does modern physics handle it? The late physicist David Bohm would have seen an incarnated being, at its primal level, arising from what he called the "implicate order" (and what theologian Paul Tillich called the "ground of being"). Combining the perspective of superstring theory (introduced in chapter 1) with the three-faceted model, an incarnation starts as a tiny, but perceptible ripple in the continuous field of consciousness, that is, a pattern within the noumena. Over time it results in a small concentration of consciousness, emerging in relation to similar amorphous entities composed of subtle energy activated by other patterns of intent. Although each is clothed in this subtle field and embodied in matenergy, no solid membrane fully divides one beingness from all others.

In quantum mechanics, the individual body is but a delicate pattern of cosmic position-holding, analogous to the invisible but well-defined space around airplanes circling in their various landing approaches. (Possible versions of such holding patterns are at www.pattern.org or www.rwgrayprojects.com/Lynn/newCH/.) These holding patterns of beingness (a local mind) are maintained by clusters of intentions not unlike the inner vision held by a performer on a tightrope, imaging the maintenance of place and form without permanent structures. In a metascientific context, a being-incarnate, in sum, is a set of bits of matter (itself only quanta of gross energy) focused by invisible conscious intent in a virtual field of subtle energy.

While the above paragraphs paint reasonable images of consciousness-incarnate, or the mind, we have very little understanding of that tenuous link between local consciousness (that of the whole contained in each individual entity) and general consciousness. If one assumes that the human experience of beingness is not unlike that of all species and dimensions of beingness (Principle of Correspondence), it can be inferred that the following descriptions apply to all conscious beings.

During a physical life or incarnation, the individual concentration of consciousness never totally breaks off from cosmic consciousness. As a being defocuses (in death) from material bonds, its mind/memories may meld back into cosmic consciousness, yet retain some degree of the integrity experienced during incarnation. Given the evidence we have that some departed personalities are able to continue to interact with the living, it appears that an individual identity can persist for an indefinite period beyond death. This tangible evidence is the strongest case that can be made for a form of immortality, believed by some to exist in the "noosphere," perhaps a combination of the energeia and noumena. This assumption is reinforced by reported NDE and OBE contacts with noumenal/luminal beings who communicate through the inner senses and also have subtle energy-type forms.

The force of intentions that hold a personality together derive from a combination of universal mind, group mind, and individual mind. In other words, we seem to be individually self-empowered, but not totally, to shape the scope and focus of the developing pool of consciousness known as our personality. The extent to which we are capable of self-managing the cohesion of the patterns that hold us together is not clear. We express this in such terms as "Mary has a strong personality," in contrast to "Bob who can't hold himself together very well."

When, within a human incarnation, there seems to be little or no volitional control of the boundaries of consciousness, psychologists label the individual "psychotic." If the boundaries are intentionally permeable, the being is called a "mystic," meriting respect and emulation. Both so-called psychotics and mystics generally define their respective states in relative isolation from others. When there is the need to engage socially, the psychotics are usually coerced by institutions to give up their "insane" communications. If psychotics resist, they are frequently drugged to insensitivity. A more humane approach would use subtly sensitive support from others, involving the reestablishment of joint parameters to define self. (For a fuller discussion, see chapter 8.)

Both the mystic and the psychotic teach us that maintaining the integrity (mentally, emotionally, and physically) of any being requires developing a certain degree of congruence with the expectations of the larger community. The term "joint parameters" is appropriate: a being must manage the creation of self, but must work together with others at the same time, taking into account their acts and thoughts. To this extent, ongoing personality development is a collective function, involving the embeddedness of the individual in the whole through our energeial and noumenal connections.

One can deliberately connect with other beings and objects, including collective and species memories (see the work of Stanislav Grof[2]) through the porous fields of local consciousness. Without falling into a mystical or psychotic state, one can give oneself permission to range far and wide, in the manner of a shaman[3] who walks daily with one foot in each world. One can choose to expand the scope of conscious experience far beyond ordinary definitions of personality.[4]

Moving with ease in the sea of consciousness, surfing the noumenal cosmic waves, one can engage in the play of "synchronicity." The phenomenon, so labeled by Carl Jung, manifests where physical events seem to conspire to meet one's needs for information and interaction with others. The frequency of synchronous events in a life relates to the degree of conscious openness exhibited.[5] The implicate order's self-learning impulse supports and accommodates such connection seeking. People get what they express a need for through prayer, holding a vision, or positive affirmations. Understanding the workings of synchronicity at the level of individual being provides insight into the functioning of the universe as a whole. Thoughts communicated from any point can elicit a response from anywhere else.

As discussed earlier, the Principles of Mentalism and Correspondence insure that thoughts affect all realms. When a thought is "consciously" expressed, it reverberates in the subtle-energy field. Like the proverbial stone dropped into a pond, it moves out in ever widening circles, but in all directions (not just the two-dimensional water surface). The vibrations of a thought pattern gather to it relevant subtle energies, giving rise to powerful forms in the energeia.

The resulting thought-form, in its energized state, interacts with organic and inorganic systems, affecting people, plants, animals, and machines. Radiating and becoming mingled with other forms and beings on the same frequency, it creates new energy flows and events in the never-ending process of creation. While intentions may be absorbed by more powerful forces of a similar nature, or may be largely neutralized by the opposite polarity, an impact discernible by the physical and subtle senses is always inevitable. The admonition, "Don't wish for it unless you really want it," is sound advice.

The quality of life for any beingness is therefore a function of the quality of consciousness it manifests in space-time. When thoughts remain negative too long, cells are thrown out of balance and become diseased. Animals and plants are agitated, and materials in machines and tools exhibit stress. Positive thought-forms have the opposite influence. (It is important to remember that each being is a combination of positive and negative thoughts and energies. We can't have one without the other, so the key is to find a constructive balance that contributes to progress or growth.) But neither radiates unimpeded throughout the universe. Each intention can only fit into a complementary receiver—an open being, an unprotected system, or neutral matter—that will reciprocate accordingly. In other words, intentions cannot create new reality unless they find a willing response somewhere in the whole.

Whether and how a thought's vibrations penetrate the thinking of another depends on its strength and precision, and also on the state of the potential recipient. Both parties must be "in tune." The intended receiver can be either open or self-defended. When beings are relatively unprotected they are susceptible to vibrations consciously focused in their direction. Experience shows that thoughts of hatred and alienation from a few can infect a society, and vice versa. (There are reports of humans being so unprotected that they are taken over by other beings called "walk-ins."[6]) Being open is not the same as being unprotected: the difference is in degree of conscious management of one's boundaries. Works by Richard Gerber and Barbara Hand Clow offer insight into the human ability to play openly with the flow of energeial and noumenal forces while protecting one's own development for more effective interactions with others.[7]

Experiments with address-based telepathic communications are so successful—both in sending and receiving—that it does not seem farfetched to conclude that each being possesses a unique subtle-energy signature. Though the process by which such communications work has not been discovered, people can focus on a "target," using a personal identifier or abstract location, and send and receive images or thought-forms. (Perhaps the Internet is a mechanized metaphor for this phenomenon.) These transmissions can be a combination of an abstract idea (word, concept, or form) and an emotional charge (fear, awe, anger, love, reverence, etc.). The ideas derive from the noumenal realm while the emotions are a function of the energeial. (Remember the discussion in chapter 4 on inner senses.)

Just because the noumena is ubiquitous does not mean every communication is loud and clear. We do not know why some are clear as a bell and others are like radio static. When telepathically receiving the vibration of thought-forms, most people are hazy about the ideational content. They project interpretations onto the other much in the same manner that dreamers apply their own content to externally generated stimuli. The emotional loads in the messages—because they are generic in humans—are generally more easily understood, even across cultural lines. The research of Manfred Clynes[8] demonstrates similar, measurable, internally generated patterns of physical tension that arise when different individuals experience the same emotions.

In the nonhuman context, certain thought-forms are believed to exist as separate "elementals," concentrations of consciousness, but without physical bodies. They have a limited life of their own, capable of influencing natural processes, as in gardens or human bodies. Other thought-forms may be used to intervene in natural phenomena such as weather patterns and behaviors of ecosystems of plants and animals, and even larger systems. Because human minds can perceive and manipulate them, these "elementals" clearly fit into a category of consciousness-incarnate.

Self-Defining Beingness

If universal consciousness is indivisible, as manifested in the split-particle physics, cell-to-cell communication, and ESP experiments mentioned in part 1, what metaphor appropriately represents the individually incarnated, locally concentrated part of the whole? Only a cell in a larger organism? A fragment of a cosmic hologram? A dream image of ultimate consciousness itself? A lower level of consciousness? All of these answers seem to imply no role for self-definition; they suggest the incarnated being has no influence on its incarnation.

To settle on one of the above or any particular hypothesis would require too much hubris; we simply do not know. At most, we can make some educated extrapolations—by synthesizing the evidence from various fields of inquiry and experience—and create a tentative view on the degrees of freedom an individual beingness has for self-control and definition.

Many see individual beings as having little or no power over the design of an incarnation and its ongoing development. The biological determinist would stipulate that it is the physical DNA that programs development from zygote to adult. The priest would argue that it is a function of the predetermined soul incarnated at conception. The behaviorist would assert that a being is conceived as a tabula rasa, with its character shaped entirely by the natural and social environments.

Recent evidence (discussed in chapter 2) from research in biology and consciousness indicates that development (mental, psychological, and physical) is always a reciprocal process. Even though mind is at the center, controlling the process, it also takes into account feedback from the biological organism and the reactions of other beings. The emerging view of a consciously unfolding universe seems to be on the side of those who believe some patterns (forms of consciousness) pre-exist human conception, and may be required to inform the act of conception itself. Therefore, the ongoing integrity of an act of conscious incarnation depends on the continued integrity of the whole package.

If the local concentration of consciousness precedes the cohesion of the subtle-energy body and the formation of the physical body, the termination of a fetus is no different than killing a twelve-year old or a person a half-century in age. In all cases, a particular conscious incarnation is irrevocably destroyed. If the essence of the being is fused with its physical host from the moment of conception until the breath of life leaves the body, the age of the physical carcass in no way diminishes the inherent integrity of the "personality." (If we believe we have the moral right to kill another incarnate being under a particular circumstance, how do we draw that line in the context of this paragraph?)

Current human genome research relating to homosexuality and schizophrenia leads some to believe that genes inevitably shape a being's behavioral pattern, as they appear to determine physical attributes. This adds complexity to the long-standing heredity-versus-environment argument. The determinists seek a particular gene or cluster of genes relating to a personality trait (schizophrenia) or behavioral predisposition (homosexuality). When they find a certain degree of correlation, they speculate that identified gene sequences interact with the rest of the body to shape behavior. Some go so far as to believe there is direct causation.

I believe as a broader understanding emerges, more people will theorize that inherited genes provide a predisposition toward certain outcomes, with the ultimate outcome a function of environmental influences and human choices. But that position still begs the question of whether or what role consciousness plays in the individual's initial and subsequent gene profiles. To stipulate that a biologically fixed gene pattern must precede a particular expression of consciousness (as a strict biological determinist would do) denies the possibility of nonlocal[9] consciousness, incarnation, and reincarnation.

214

On the other hand, evidence that patterns of energy (individual emotions) and forms of matter (gene sequences) follow—within certain cosmic parameters—conscious intent supports the concept of conscious incarnation. In this case, the inherited genetic patterns would reflect pre-incarnation and parental expressions of intent. The result is a unique brain/body, like a keyboard, with which the incarnated consciousness can "play" its own "tune." If this concept of incarnation is valid, it is logical to suppose the focus of consciousness expressed in conception holds the being together through its physical cycle. That means a significant degree of self-redefinition can take place during an incarnation, depending on the being's strength of will.

Beings with a strong sense of their conscious development may be able to maintain the integrity of a self through successive incarnations. The more energized the mental patterns during one or more lives of growth and self-direction, the more likely the perpetuation of an individual integrity through the rigors of death, birth, and childhood in the process of successive reincarnations.

It will be an interesting challenge to use cloning (creating duplicate plants and animals, and eventually humans, from the DNA of an existing being) to help decipher the effects of preexisting consciousness on the development of the new personality. Research by Ian Stevenson (referenced earlier in this book) has identified a number of cases that strongly suggest no direct DNA linkages between the current incarnation and the past life believed to be the person's former incarnation. Given separations in race and locations between the two lives, no direct gene connections are feasible. This contradicts the view of some that so-called past-life memories are really gene memories.

Regardless of the validity of any particular transpersonal hypothesis, each being is faced with the daily challenge of defining oneself in relation to other beings and the material world. Given at least three facets—physical body, subtle-energy field, and mind—maintaining the integrity of self is a multilevel process, ranging from largely instinctive physical acts of self-nourishment to highly structured regimens of exercise, diet, and conscious engagement. Although self-determination is inherent in human life, it is easier for people to go along with generally accepted physical and social norms. Traditionally defined jobs, professions, and other roles help an individual shortcut the process of self-definition. More consciously aware people realize the need for individualized and progressive control of their energy patterns and physical behaviors. The most aware realize the need for self-discipline over even their thoughts.

Just as some beings' bodies are more resistant to viral or bacterial invasions, so some minds are more resistant to penetration. Resistance on the physical level, including the maintenance of a healthy immune system, has its analog in the permeable membrane of consciousness. Susceptibility to spirit attachment, possession, multiple personality, or delusions is a function of weakness in one's psychological immune system (the personal subtle-energy field).

Because of the less obvious nature of subtle energy, conscious attention is required to maintain personal integrity at that level. Most humans are conscious of the need to monitor their feeling states and take appropriate actions to keep on a positive track. They realize that some degree of self-direction is not only possible but desirable. They know enlarging the sphere of self-direction frequently requires extending one's personal reach and encouraging change to group patterns.

Thus, beingness, as the local manifestation of consciousness, never stops changing. The Principles of Vibration and Rhythm result in the pushing force of accumulated experience and the simultaneous drawing forward by a vision of what might be. As in composing a symphony, the being has an almost infinite variety of motifs from which to choose, but the final "score" results from the note-by-note decisions of the self-composer. Such is the nature of self-definition for incarnate beings. However, as the animation of a musical score depends on musicians, so does the performance of one self-defined life. Several parameters inherent in the universe establish limits on one's freedom to self-create. The following ways limit the individual's range of freedom.

Reciprocity of Influence. Complementing its process of self-definition, a being requires the collective input of its primary community to maintain the internal integrity of self. (See chapter 8 for further discussion of these interactions between self and other.) The reactions of the larger community and nature to individual intentions constrain the evolving character of a beingness. For example, the more other members of a community permit the acting out of individuals' constructive or benign intents, the freer they become to explore their own potentials. Freeing others frees one's own creative energies. The more supportive beings are of others, the more support they receive.

In a reciprocal universe the negative actions (as well as positive ones) of all beings come back to haunt them. When a course of events is set in motion, even though one can never predict the final outcome, its effect will return to the initiator. The Hermetic Principle of Cause and Effect—reflected in the Hindu concept of karma and in the Biblical injunction, "As we sow, so shall we reap"—works on currently unimagined levels through the interconnectedness and indivisibility of universal consciousness.

As intent is the most important element of any action in determining the effects of individual behavior, so it is for the collective. Why is that so? As beings physically communicate, their inner message speaks telepathically more strongly than either voice or actions. Through their subtle senses, other cosmic beings perceive it through common access to the energeia and noumena. It is therefore not surprising that hidden hostile intent still evokes a defensive response from the core of the other person.

One may realize short-term gains by trying to conceal true intent, but the dynamic of action/reaction sets into motion a cycle of reciprocity on the inner level. Beings who have been originally deceived will not continue to be, and ultimately their lack of support through later connections, direct or indirect, will derail the progress of one's plans. Repetition of negative patterns can also debilitate the actor's own psychological well-being. (The case of someone like Lee Atwater—the former Republican "dirty tricks" strategist who died of a brain tumor—is illustrative. Before his death, he acknowledged a connection between his earlier behavior and his physical demise.) This cosmic principle is reflected in the Native American warning that the Sun should never set before a hostile arrow is recovered and wounds are healed.

Natural Limitations. Notwithstanding the power of intention, there are constraints beyond the social on the scope of a being's freedom: they result from the interdependence of physicality and consciousness. How much does the nature of a physical incarnation in this dimension limit the scope of conscious play? Inborn influences on human capacities have a role in this context. Current IQ and behavioral research on twins enables us to make inferences about the interactive process and to formulate new hypotheses.

Some social scientists have concluded that genes determine as much as 70 percent of an individual's behavior, setting the "nature/nurture-influence" ratio at 70/30. However, their assumptions have the effect of "proving" that genes, either the individual's or those in others who influence the individual, determine 100 percent of behavior. If everyone living today is genetically controlled to the same extent, then retrogression of the ratios would reach an earlier point in which essentially all behavior was genetically controlled.[10] However, that conclusion is not compatible with human experience. The evidence that non-time-bound consciousness influences both the physical and emotional conditions necessitates a rethinking of such biological determinism.

Let's think about this nature/nurture ratio in terms of twin research. About 70 percent of all fetuses appear to start out as twins, but in most cases one atrophies early in pregnancy. Of actual twin births, about one-third are identical (created out of split halves of a single fertilized egg). Empirical data on the experience of identical twins, and to a lesser degree, fraternal twins, offer some intriguing possibilities for insight into the power of conscious self-defining of physical characteristics and behavior.

Identical twins report uncanny similarities in lifestyle and even in the making of specific decisions. Likes and dislikes are frequently parallel. They say they feel each other's physical pain and often telepathically receive each other's thoughts. They sense a strong emotional bond and suffer profoundly when it is disturbed. At the same time, they experience a strong impulse to individuality that frequently tests the limits of interpersonal tolerance and understanding.

Twins are acutely aware of the subtle-energy ties that bind all beings, and more easily recognize the effect of disturbances in such ties. They intuitively perceive that their individuality is a function of both interdependence and independence. In other words, in demonstrating the reality of the interconnectedness of all beings, twins are just like the rest of us, only more so. The chaos perceived by twins separated at birth or during childhood is simply an exacerbation of the disorientation everyone feels in a society characterized by alienation.

What if we assume that the local concentration of consciousness in the two-being conception[11] in one egg is less differentiated than in a single-being egg. At the inception of fetal growth, each twin is therefore as physically and consciously identical as can be, given the minute differences created by dividing matter. Consequently, twins experience sharper ESP than the rest of us because they are literally more in tune with each other (Principle of Vibration). Having come from the same preincarnation field of consciousness and being endowed with almost identical physical sense receptors, they start out with almost perfect subtle-sense attunement. Obversely, the impact of a single preconception imprint of consciousness (single-egg birth of one being only) results in greater individuation.

Fraternal twins experience a lesser degree of synchronicity than identical twins because they are "informed" by less closely related conscious fields and by only half as much identical material imprinting. Therefore, their degree of physical commonality would exercise less influence than in identical twins, and their mental and emotional attunement would also be less. The degrees of consciousness and emotional separation increase the farther apart the places and times of conception. (But the influence of separate places and times are apparently overridden when a group of conscious beings intend to find common ground after incarnation regardless of birth families.)

In conclusion, current research on the development of siblings (twin and otherwise), rather than proving that matter unilaterally impacts thought and behavior, may indicate the opposite: that consciousness influences physical and behavioral traits. A new developmental paradigm is necessary to test this perspective. One place to start is with twins and self-identified conscious communities that will reveal their developmental influences to researchers.

Quantum Flaws. Another characteristic all beings inhabiting the universe share is being subject to its built-in "software" operating systems. One attribute of the software appears to be the statistical probability of flaws being introduced at the subparticle level (a phenomenon known to all computer operators). An accidental flaw can appear in the physical manifestation of consciousness when DNA strands slip into an incorrect sequence; the delicate chemical balance of certain molecules is jostled; a neural link is severed; or an accident occurs in the melding of energy forces. It is as though the clay through which the cosmic artist works has an imperfection in the mixture: the work of art has a minor flaw, although the conscious design was true.

In all incarnations, such accidental deviations from the intended pattern may result in epileptic seizures, Down's syndrome, misshapen limbs, defective organs, and so on, but they do not detract from the beauty and perfection of the conscious being. The affected may have sent well-formed ideas into the energeia, but the message got distorted in the physical transmission. Through help in understanding subtle communications and providing artificial aid (even implants or stimulation of neuron regeneration), the full scope of consciousness can shine through. The life of Stephen Hawking, whose long battle with a motor neuron disease did not reduce the clarity of his acumen as a physicist, is a magnificent model of how such a quantum flaw can be bypassed.

Such flaws play two roles in a self-learning universe. One provides gaps in the process for the exercise of free will. The other adds the opportunity to learn from chance.

Gender and Sex. Another key attribute of "beingness" is gender. The Principle of Polarity, operative at the subatomic levels of positive and negative charges, also manifests itself in the sexual nature of the universe's creative process. Every being, energy, and particle has both masculine and feminine characteristics (Principle of Gender). Femininity is the state of receptiveness, involving openness and the nurturing of seeds from masculine expressiveness. Following the Principle of Rhythm, these two characteristics, extending beyond one's physical sex, tend to balance out in each organic entity over time.

In our English language, we arbitrarily define "gender" as the broader term to imply the masculine/feminine polarity in all aspects of life. "Sex," as in male and female, deals more narrowly with the function of physical reproduction. Therefore, all sexual terms refer to gender, but not all uses of gender imply physical sexual differences.

For the female, the act of giving birth is masculine, requiring great force and concentration, following the feminine period of incubating the new being. Motherhood and fatherhood for the newborn are not naturally distinguished along sexual lines: both parent roles involve masculine and feminine aspects. Gender patterns are grounded in cosmic (Hermetic) principles, but the specifics of social sexual roles are largely a function of local traditions.[12]

The balancing of gender over a lifetime has interesting external manifestations. It is not uncommon for a man or woman who has been rigidly heterosexual to have homosexual experiences or relationships later in life. People who have been the most domineering in early life appear to need to become more dependent in later years. Partners who enjoy gender and sex role reversal throughout their lives seem to enjoy greater inner balance in their old age. Androgyny is the balancing of masculine and feminine poles; but as with all energetic charges, the positive, negative, and neutral are always present to varying degrees.

Research into the causes of human homosexual behavior has resulted in speculations about social and biological influences that are mutually contradictory. The range of actual homosexual and bisexual experiences, particularly those of transsexuals, indicates that sexual self-identification is not exclusively rooted in the biology of birth, but neither can it always be correlated to social factors. These disconcerting findings call into question assumptions about the primacy of either biology or environment. The primary factor in both sexual and gender behavior may more likely be the phase of transcendent consciousness present in the individual being at a given moment.

One of the tragedies of Western civilization's misunderstanding of the distinction between gender and physical sexuality is the romantic myth that each person must locate and forever bond with his or her mystical, opposite-sex other half. The myth causes an individual to believe the gap can be filled only by a single person; but sexual union alone, as in the convention of marriage, proves to be insufficient. Lifetime equilibrium in gender balancing occurs in the inner being, not as a result of the acts of another. A friend, colleague, or lover can provide only the raw material feeding into the internal rhythm of gender within the individual. Therefore, the choice of sexual and any other expressive/receptive behaviors in this seeking of balance can be understood only in terms of where individual's consciousness is in his or her own internal cycle.

Permeable Membranes. Neuroscientists who believe thinking arises from neurons say individuals are literally alone with their thoughts. Nothing could be further from the truth. The undifferentiated and interrelated nature of the universal phenomena, energeia, and noumena that intersect in an individual "beingness" means that each entity's boundaries[13] are highly permeable. We now know that our physical bodies continually exchange particles with all other bodies. The same ongoing interchange occurs with our subtle energies and mental activities.

The reciprocal flow through these membranes between a being and its cosmic setting alternates between positive and negative (Principle of Polarity) and expressing and receiving (Gender), both following the inherent Principle of Rhythm that requires rotation from one aspect to the other.

Fortunately, not all details of the interactions between a being and its environment have to be monitored in a focused way. Eyelids, sensing an impending invasion of sand, close automatically. Drivers develop a "feel" for the fenders of their cars while parking. Learning to drive, as in learning a sport, involves the heightened state of alertness that comes from incorporation of the noumenal and subtle senses. Their unbidden signals daily protect us from error, accident, missed appointments, and losses, big and small.

Most people experience gaps in their current knowledge being filled on occasion from a different level of consciousness.[14] Taking full advantage of the process involves the maintenance of a flexible focus that is permeable enough to receive this subliminal input. Blocked or congested five-sense information flows are covered by phrases like "fear rose in my throat" or "his jealousy blinds him to . . ." Significant distortions of perception and judgment quickly follow if similar blockages occur in the normally subconscious mental senses.

Clearing the impediments of distressed or callused mental patterns must be a conscious process. Just as we can consciously erect a mental shield around ourselves for protection against the bad intentions of others, we can ordain a healthy level of openness. With no self-defined boundaries to our consciousness we literally lose our identity. When intentions, emotions, and practices are harmonized, we can manage the input of subtle-level communications. Continual feedback from the environment and the community at large can keep us better integrated. This is why social constraints that cause people to arbitrarily close down their conscious boundaries result in later destructive behavior. Parents, teachers, and religious and political leaders have not yet learned this lesson.

Societies dominated by fear-based religion, reductionist science, and deadening economic exigencies foster the reduction of healthy permeable boundaries of consciousness. The current collective fear of death (ironically, demonstrated by the brutality with which people, directly or through surrogates, mete it out) signifies fear of anything that would move today's constricted human consciousness toward a more boundless realm of mind. When humans fearfully avoid any form of mind games, sex, drugs, physical play, or rituals that threaten to break through the barriers to the unknown, they cannot experience the expansion of consciousness that offers a higher level of development. However, the two poles require balance: openness must be countered with an appropriate degree of self-defense (Principle of Polarity).

Balanced Self-Protection. An understanding of the need (discussed earlier) for balancing openness with self-defense comes from the world of voodoo. Social scientists tell of people being bewitched by others, falling prey to the hexes of witch doctors, or succumbing to the spell of another's incantations. The way to avoid becoming the victim of another's bad intent is to ward it off with one's own magic. Finding the power to protect oneself from the evil designs of another may require assistance from a friendly sorcerer or from a particular ritual that girds one's psychic defenses. But ultimately, regardless of the procedure used, the self-expression of intent is the source of defensive power. Only the being can deploy his or her power into mental space. For example, the Hawaiian traditional teachers (Kahunas) show people how to use their own inner focus, either explicitly or implicitly, to cast a perimeter of safety around their "beingness."

Scientific evidence for the existence of the ability to cast some sort of protective shield around oneself may come from an unlikely source: a commercial piece of hardware that reads electronic signals. A Japanese company, Fujitsu, Ltd., is developing a computer that distinguishes "yes" and "no" thoughts by reading brain waves. As mentioned earlier, the U.S. military is developing the same process to direct equipment or weapons. If people can send messages that register electronically, they can also transmit energetic or noumenal messages that reach other beings.

The process of individuation, establishing the degree of interaction one has with each of the three facets (universal consciousness, the subtle energies, and the physical environment), has implications throughout the incarnation. In managing its own boundary, the being is erecting a protective membrane of conscious intent that will retain its integrity as long as it is mentally attended. The operation of this dynamic, for example, explains why no one can be hypnotized without giving concurrence. To be hypnotized, people must willingly allow another to penetrate their "beingness" and extract material from their pool of consciousness.

Honoring the multilevel flow of communications between self and others, yet avoiding being overwhelmed, is a delicate task. It is easier to ward off unwanted intrusions in the physical realm than at the mental and subtle-energy levels. However, all restrictions placed at these levels, as in the physical, have a cost.

In the physical plane, humans can wear surgical masks, sterilize their hands, or wear condoms to avoid exchange of harmful matter. On the plane of subtle energy, they can keep distant from those who want to stifle or harm them. They can suppress their own emotional outbursts, and decline to invite people into their homes who remind them of their own pain. On the mental plane, humans can deaden their awareness through excessive consumption or through drugs. They can deny messages that come through the subtle senses. But the price is a closing of the mind to new thoughts and ideas. Nonparticipation weakens emerging fields of consensus being developed by others. Thus, progress of the individual and the community is retarded.

Ironically, more concentration of consciousness and energy is required to isolate the self one seeks to protect than to deal with and transform the interactions one tries to avoid. Such head-in-the-sand reactions in business, politics, and intimate relationships are commonplace. They are based on the ill-founded assumption that out-of-sight tactics keep one from being tainted; but the inner linkages cannot be escaped. Paradoxically, the more that people accept the reciprocal connections among beings and ride their ebb and flow, the more they can ultimately shape themselves in their own fashion.

Boundary maintenance is necessary to health and wholeness and involves interactions from routine social contacts to encounters with alien beings. Kenneth Ring believes that "boundary problem people" appear to be more susceptible to negative UFO abduction experiences and to suffer from overt physical or sexual abuse. Some therapists have concluded that getting people to "shore up their boundaries"[15] helps stop such experiences or gain some control over them. The literature on abduction by alien beings indicates some people regard their experience as fear-filled while others see such experiences as growth-producing. The difference lies not in the experience but in the abductee's definition of self, which, as we have seen in the final analysis, results primarily from an act of consciousness.

Always on Duty. "Beingness" requires a continual process of incorporating sustenance from one's habitat—in the forms of food, emotional energy, and ideas. The choices for ingestion in all three categories mirror the degree of conscious awareness in the being: the more conditioned and automatic the being's behavior, the less varied and innovative the input.

Within the universe's built-in software, the impulse to self-realization seems to be innate. (The Greeks called this built-in drive toward self-development "entelechy.") The exploration of infinite possibilities and the selection of one's unique profile is, in Jungian terms, an ongoing process of individuation. In each person's orchestration of activities, he or she must balance a tendency to retire to the inner realms with an equally powerful inclination to engage with others and the external environment. Tilting too much in either direction results in distorted development, which in the social realm was labeled by Jung as extremes of introversion or extroversion.

The process of interaction never ceases. As we have seen, some level of awareness exists whether one is awake or asleep. Full individual development requires active engagement with one's entire spectrum of consciousness, including dream states and all so-called psychic phenomena. There are no periods during which the being's local consciousness totally goes off duty. Therefore the individual must define his or her integrity in each situation. Such conscious tending can be accomplished even in dreams (with lucid dreaming). Everyone is *always* responsible at some level for his or her actions: pleas of nonculpability by reason of insanity, stress, emotional trauma, and so on, are basically pretexts, not acceptable justifications for a mature being's behaviors.

If a group or society teaches its members that there are acceptable excuses for any type of abusive behavior toward others, it takes on responsibility for all such actions and is therefore culpable. Laws and regulations (such as easy bankruptcy options, corporate protections, and welfare loopholes) that permit some people to escape responsibility for their behavior encourage lack of integrity in all, and thereby weaken the moral fiber of the whole society. A healthy society keeps the assignment of responsibility for negative actions congruent with the amount of effort society places on positive input in the development of its members. In other words, the more a conscious society requires individual accountability to society, the more it nurtures the individual's inclusion in society. (American society does not meet this standard at the beginning of the twenty-first century.)

An Inner Monitor. Given the permeable nature of personal membranes, every being requires a focusing mechanism that maintains its cohesive core. It requires that DNA instructions keep the physical body intact and self-renewing. Can we describe the inertial guidance system or "gyroscope" that provides a conscious being with mental and emotional stability in the midst of an ever changing life?

Hardly anything short of actual destruction of the biological envelope permanently severs the functioning of a being's consciousness from the phenomenal realm. A being can experience severe emotional losses, comatose states, physical trauma, heights of ecstasy, loneliness, public acclaim, and all forms of social slight and injury, and through it all, remain self-contained and capable of remembering who and where one is in space-time. A being can also leave its material body, travel to other dimensions, and then recover it, resuming physical life.

Some kind of personal monitor must file into memory any patterns relevant to its preset search program, making it possible for beings to chart their course through the continually fluctuating state of ordinary existence. Various concepts about the dynamics of memory have been posited, but none has been generally accepted. Freud's concept of repression as the process by which data are placed in memory banks and "sealed" from full consciousness is not very useful. We have not been able to validate his realms of the unconscious and subconscious because validation requires their subject matter becoming conscious; once in the field of consciousness there is no confirmable trail to prove where the thoughts have been.

Physical scientists hypothesize that memory is rooted in neural circuits in the brain. According to this perspective, memories are stored in varying electrical patterns, based on the "charge" of the event, in specific sections of the brain. When these sections are stimulated by similar electrical charges, some memories are released. But such relationships do not prove the memories are biologically determined. The theory is at best only descriptive of the physiological effects of consciousness. It offers neither a rationale for discrepancies between different people's memory of the same facts nor one person's distorted memory of externally confirmable data. (If physically stored memories were entirely based on palpable material events, such discrepancies should not exist.)

Given these unverifiable theories, it is intriguing to shift the frame of reference to one that entails a different concept of memory: a multidimensional concentration of conscious awareness. A useful concept must explain not only personal memories, but also how beings contribute to the collective memory and receive from it with ease. It should also account for the existence of differences in personal perceptions of the same event, and cryptomnesia, the process of incorporating another's experience or ideas into one's own memory. The concept of noumena introduced here, within the three-faceted model of reality, points in a constructive direction. It equates memory with a being's idiosyncratic repository (local concentration) of relevant energetic and mental patterns from general consciousness.

If personal memory is both local and linked to the noumenal whole—a variation on the holographic concept—then it could explain the phenomenon of shared knowledge. In the individual's interaction with the noumena, information can be received from it and contributed to it. Therefore, retrieving memories (personal or cosmic) is not unlike dreaming or psychic knowing: it involves tuning into the selected frequencies. The self-determined interpretative screens, based on a being's personal learning, would account for distortions of memory among different individuals about the same event.

The observed ability to consciously direct and enhance various channels of access to local and universal memories indicates that modern science has been studying the brain backwards. The continually remanifesting brain does not create conscious activity: it is a tool to help filter subtle signals and control the level of five-sense awareness. Given the capability of conscious beings to access all past and current events, the brain is needed to maintain order among the data coming through the permeable membrane that envelopes a "beingness."

An incarnated being, in defining its personality, selects the sector or wave band of information that it wishes to attend and uses its brain to screen input and protect the self. This self-selected monitor works automatically until it is changed by choice or trauma from the outside.

Multifaceted Personalities

Stabilized by the inner gyroscope of local memory, each being has the capacity to take on different roles and to temporarily differentiate self along any behavioral spectrum. Such range of performance is applauded in actors, but it is often labeled a disease when it does not seem to be under obvious control.

Cases of what was long labeled a "multiple personality disorder or syndrome" (MPD or MPS) are now widely known. Productions such as *The Three Faces of Eve*, *Sybil*, and *The Minds of Billy Milligan* began to expose the general public to this syndrome, where one physical being serves as the "house" for a number of personalities that individually dominate overt behavior at different times. The American Psychological Association now labels the extreme form of this "Dissociative Identity Syndrome." While that is a more accurate description of the process involved, I prefer a more positive term:

229

Multifaceted Personality, or MFP. It implies the multifaceted gradient on which all humans exist and on which some have difficulty maintaining self-integration.

The differences among an MFP's subpersonalities can be striking: they can be male or female, adult or child, linguistically different, varied in philosophies, and diverse in value systems.[16] Practically any characteristic that a personality can exhibit to distinguish itself from others has shown up in these apparently unintegrated beings. Psychologists and other health care professionals have concluded that an extreme MFP results from early childhood trauma, involving emotional, physical, or sexual abuse that results in "dissociation." Dissociation means a reaction that separates one area of mental and behavioral activity from another, that is, a breaking up of awareness. Perceived as a defense mechanism, it is thought that abused children use dissociation to protect certain parts of their selfhood by denying the existence of other parts of their reality.

For one with an extreme MFP, it may be helpful to replace the construct "dissociation" with the concept of "underdeveloped skills in integration and orchestration." Dissociation implies the result of some external force over which the individual can exercise no conscious influence. A more self-defining concept, recognizing that conscious beings assign meaning to all external events, would reflect the inherent impulse they have to expand awareness and integrate ever increasing degrees of complexity. Only stifled opportunity, physical bondage, or self-maintained psychological constraints can inhibit this process. When young children who have been abused do not receive assistance in managing their own integration an MFP disorder can result.

The "cause" in this instance is not solely the abuse, as perceptions of it vary from one abused child to another, but also the lack of integrative skill development and/or support from others in the adult community. Although abusive behavior must be proscribed, the main focus of community reactions should be on assisting both the abused and the abuser in the formation of self that constructively integrates the full spectrum of potential thoughts and behaviors.

MFPs point the way to greater understanding of the incarnation of consciousness in a human form. Research data demonstrate that aspects of the MFP's physical body actually change when the personality changes. There may be variations in voice, posture, color sensitivity, left- or right-handedness, as well as changes in brain-wave patterns, immune system responses, and dermal electrical responses. Documented cases include changes in warts, scars, and rashes. A relatively simple but dramatic example is the turning on and off of allergic reactions as the personality shifts. Medical science claims a person cannot turn off allergic responses at will, but MFPs do. If they can, nothing prevents others from developing the same powers. (Drug companies would lose much income if people knew this.)

If a temporary and partial shift in consciousness can have such visible physiological impacts, imagine the influence deliberate shifts in a well-integrated personality could have on a person's physical condition. MFPs seem to have a very high self-healing capacity; they demonstrate more clearly than others the interaction of mind, energy, and matter discussed in chapter 4. All people influence their physical health every day, but for the most part as a function of habit. Conscious manipulation of one's repertory of personality traits demonstrates the power consciousness has over its own incarnation. Acting as if something is true makes it so.

Any extreme state experienced by an MFP can be found in the mental repertory of anyone who practices mind control, biofeedback, hypnosis, meditative trances, or other techniques that evoke altered states of consciousness. Therefore, the path to wholeness, or progressive integration, for any being—whether labeled MFP or not—brings into awareness all fragments of his or her consciousness and accepts them as facets of this personality. A responsible human family or other support group responds to dysfunctional fragmentation in young beings by providing a social environment that is conducive to acknowledging wholeness and integration.

Mature beings, using the skill of MFP development, show how all facets of behavior can be selectively used in relevant settings. Young beings could learn in the process of socialization to use discretion in their public personality, exhibiting only behaviors appropriate to the role being played. But they would also learn not to dismiss any of their emotional and behavioral repertory as unreal or not themselves. Consciously developing beings recognize that suppressing parts of self absorbs a detrimental share of available subtle energy, inhibiting the realization of their full potential.

Expanding Self

Paradoxically, the antidote to multiple personality fragmentation is greater openness of a conscious kind (or voluntary dissociation). Creation of an expanded self-awareness makes it easier to encompass parts that would otherwise appear threatening. Individuals determine, either on an instance-by-instance basis or through established patterns, their priorities on how many and what kind of physical stimuli to take in by the physical senses. The more alive and alert one is, the more (to a reasonable degree) one can take in. The same principle works on the emotional and noumenal levels. To be fully conscious means being fully engaged with mental and subtle stimuli in a manner consistent with self-selected priorities.

If beings deaden the capacity to experience pain (physical, emotional, or mental), they correspondingly reduce the ability to sense pleasure. The same principle applies to the polarities that characterize all emotional gradients: love/hate, attachment/detachment, fear/confidence, and so on. The range of behaviors available to any being is a function of one's ability to experience both ends of each spectrum, which, as shown below, is more like a circle than two segments of a straight line.

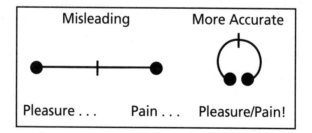

Both extremes are energetically close together. The circle model shows why it is so easy to transmute one pole of energy to another, as in flipping to sobs from laughter or vice versa. All emotions and ideas exist on a circular spectrum, so the stronger one aspect becomes, the closer it is to its polar opposite.

The key to self-management is learning how to appropriately attach emotion to each experience. For each event, we must label it (decide whether it is on a fear/confidence polarity or another kind of polarity) and place it on the positive or negative side of the spectrum. This process of conscious placement shapes our physical and emotional bodies' responses to the experience. Feeling follows thought. For example, a conscious being considers a physical or emotional experience painful (on the negative end of the pain/pleasure side of the spectrum) and feels hurt. When the event is relabeled as invigorating (positive side), an entirely different reaction occurs.

In addition to labeling and grading an experience on the polarity spectrum, an individual designates how close it falls to the core self. Choosing to label it as one of the following affects the intensity of the experience: (1) an externally stimulated dream, (2) a dissociated part of oneself, (3) a normal experience, or (4) a part of the core self. The greater the gap between the label (dream, dissociation, or normal) and one's immutable core self, the easier the pain is to bear. These forms of voluntary dissociation are used to advantage by people undergoing torture, accidents, or painful operations.

To lessen the ongoing impact of a painful event, one can redesignate it as a dream (an approach used in hypnosis with UFO abductees recalling invasive operations and with veterans reliving battle wounding). While placing the event on the dream shelf enables one to function temporarily in the world of physical senses, to totally heal the experience must be fully integrated into the being's sense of self (just as in working with MFPs). Thus, these definitions either expand or contract one's sense of self. Conscious beings with a high degree of control over those definitions can literally shape the reality of each experience.

As discussed earlier, a local incarnation of consciousness has a set of senses serving each of the three bodies (physical, emotional, and mental). Dreams and daydreams, ritual behaviors (verbal or otherwise), deep meditation, and trance are all ways to expand the receptivity of the subtle senses. To the extent that one synthesizes them with the five-sense mode of awareness, mastery of the incarnation's potential is expanded. For example, meditation (a process for transcending the physical senses) does not deny the reality of incarnation, but enhances it.

Even though meditative concepts and techniques are most frequently associated with Eastern religions, they have been known in most cultures for millennia. Until about 200 years ago, meditation was an active component of Judaism.[17] In the Kabbalistic tradition, meditation was viewed as the process by which one isolates self from uncontrolled mental stimuli and taps into generic consciousness. This act of filtering out local activity and awareness gives one conscious access to the noumenal logos. Spontaneous trances, as reported by many inventors and scientists, can expand access to the richness of the noumenal realm, but the deliberate practice of meditation can have the same result.

Deliberate inner searching is not the only way to expand the membrane of local consciousness; techniques such as hypnosis and guided imagery are available. They help bring material from the noumena, or collective consciousness, into awareness. They assist a person in recovering thoughts or experiences that have been temporarily pushed from the field of awareness, due either to the passage of time or their painful nature. Under hypnosis, the individual gives the hypnotist permission to probe the noumena through the subject's brain-mind channel of local memory. In guided imagery, the individual has more control over the probing, but otherwise the result is the same.

The ease of memory recall, in any state of consciousness, seems to be related to the magnitude of the subtle-energy charge attached to the idea or experience. The higher the energy load, the easier and clearer the recall. However, a blocking memory or belief can inhibit recall. Such blocking memories apparently can be artificially insinuated by other beings (human or AB) through the power of suggestion when the subject is sufficiently intimidated.

When a dominant or blocking memory exists, its energy polarity must be transformed before a shift to the hidden memory is possible. A good hypnotist or shaman knows how to do this, but any conscious being can develop self-guiding techniques for transmutation of energy polarities from one half of the circle (see previous graphic) to the other. These techniques involve controlled bursts of energy, deliberate redirection of flow, or personal commands to oneself. When such energy blockages are converted into open channels, more and more related data from the restricted area flow through. It is similar to a situation when one's sense of despair is converted to hope and all the reasons for hope rush into the awakened mind.

Consciousness Awareness Quotient

The concept of an Intelligence Quotient, or IQ, was developed early in the twentieth century to give some measure of a person's relative ability to learn and retain new information and problem solve. In the late 1990s, Daniel Goleman proposed the idea that humans also have emotional intelligence (EQ), in a book by that title. It implies people are distributed along a gradient of emotional skills that can be learned. EQ deals with the ability to appropriately express and relate to a wide range of emotional states. Goleman's evidence suggests one's EQ is correlated with success in society.

Even though there are theoretical and methodological problems with such taxonomies, I believe a new taxonomy analogous to but not covered by either IQ or EQ, is appropriate for a discussion of expanding self. I have called it "Consciousness Quotient," or CQ. It is a measure of a being's scope of awareness of its species' access to knowledge, of the degree to which reality is seen in its many dimensions. The CQ's range from low to high indicates how many of the species' various learning modalities are used by the individual. In other words, it signifies the extent to which one uses the senses in all three facets discussed in this book: physical, subtle, and noumenal. It also indicates the range of one's time perspective, as well as how broadly one casts the net searching for information.

CQ does not necessarily correlate with IQ and EQ. One may have a high IQ that is focused on a very narrow area of human knowledge. Another may have a good EQ that functions in a given cultural context but not in others. Neither would have a very high CQ. CQ does not mean having the same depth of awareness in all fields, but it does require being aware of the existence of all fields of knowledge and all ways of knowing. Neither a scientist who knows only his own specialty nor a psychic who remains in the noumenal realm would have a high CQ. High CQ beings attempt to identify and synthesize knowledge from all sources. Their desire to expand overall knowledge and understand its implications for the whole system motivates their engagement in the universal process of self-learning.

Selfhood can decide to undertake any number of steps to expand its CQ. The opening may start with the physical or emotional or mental realm. One will lead to another if not blocked by conscious avoidance.

Openness Does Not Insure Truth

The spontaneous or deliberate opening of self gives a being access to more noumenal and energeial information, but that does not mean it is all valid. Truth cannot always be distinguished from fiction through use of ordinary awareness; the same is true for subtle senses. Since the noumenal borders between personal experience and that of others are so porous, care is needed in interpreting all such communications. The universe's self-learning impulse mandates that the input from any one or combination of senses should be confirmed through other channels before a final meaning is accepted.

To take one area in hypnosis to illustrate, care must be taken to insure only personal memories get tapped by the hypnotist. Memories recovered in hypnosis will be misleading if they are influenced by the hypnotist's suggestion or by information bleeding through from the impersonal noumena. In the former, one may be led to create an event that did not happen; and in the latter, the experience of another may be read as one's own. Externally verifiable data should be sought to confirm at least partially the hypnotically reported experience. For example, in the case of the UFO abductee, obtaining field evidence (physical traces, scars, or other body markings) or confirmation of part of the experience by third parties is crucial for credibility and subsequent research. It's useful to note that people who consciously recall the same events that others have repressed can be used for cross-validation of hypnotically retrieved material.

The same caution should be applied to all subtle-sense ways of knowing. Receiving information through a disembodied channel does not guarantee its validity or relevance to the issue under consideration. When beings have access to anything in the noumena, they must be as careful using it as using gossip conveyed over the garden fence. Information in the noumenal realm can be just as deceiving or misleading as various aspects of the phenomenal realm. Unfortunately, many naive people have placed too much faith in the idiosyncratic perspective of a being from another plane.

The following incident exemplifies the way an apparently real memory or bit of knowledge can be based on something unreal. As a tool in therapy with a patient, psychologist Milton Erickson[18] once created a fictional man. After regressing the patient back to childhood, he suggested the memory of a person she might have known and created a character for her. In a subsequent therapy session, he regressed her to childhood, using the fictional being as a participant in the resolution of the disorder. Upon waking in her adult consciousness, the patient could not be talked out of her belief in the reality of that imaginal person.

As more and more beings become aware of the potential for multiple paths to knowledge, there is a need to encourage self-discipline in interpretation. Individuals wishing to be responsible can join in establishing a process of intersubjective validation. To gain a higher degree of confidence in one's subtle knowing, an individual can arrange to test interpretations by setting up predictive situations where a third party knows in advance the expected outcomes. In one example, the individual commits to writing a precognitive knowing, or informs another of it, and asks the third party to compare the subtle-sense message with the subsequent event. This way, one avoids misleading oneself about the accuracy of the precognitive perception. There is a strong temptation to retroactively shape one's memory to fit the circumstances that come to pass. By asking others to verify or duplicate one's own experience, it is possible to gain a degree of correlation, if not absolute validation, of the communication.

Since the subtle senses are largely invisible to third-party, five-sense observation, and often subject to ambiguity, it is important to realize that frequently so-called objective validation is not possible. Given the now broadly understood observer effect, where the manner of observation shapes the event, even matenergy events cannot be objectively verified. Therefore, intersubjective validation is the only recourse we have, that is, two or more beings separately test their perceptions and compare the extent to which they are in agreement. This approach makes it possible to be scientific about things not normally considered to be in the realm of science, facilitating the expansion of scientific knowledge to include much that has been considered paranormal. An excellent way to test this approach is through subtle-energy healing that involves observable physical results.

Self-Healing

Once incarnated, each being has an inherent self-correcting capacity that works at all levels, physical, mental, and emotional. In other words, a living system has an innate impulse to wholeness. When one of its elements is weakened by external circumstances or by inadequate inner nourishment, the system reacts automatically to protect its integrity. Only unabated aggressive invasion or perpetual lack of inner stability will be able to overwhelm the natural defense systems.[19] Unfortunately, many cultural patterns (aggressive legal and business norms, toxic pollutants, and incessant images of violence) undermine these natural cycles and rhythms and result in human dis-ease.

Treatments that run counter to the system's natural principles or induce deleterious side effects may serve as short-term palliatives, but they do not heal the being. Only interventions that arise from and support the natural processes will eliminate the causes of symptoms. This is true whether the problem is a headache, sleeplessness, cancer, heart disease, AIDS, neurosis, psychosis, moral turpitude, inner city riots, ethnic warfare, or spiritual malaise. The Principle of Correspondence insures that illness at any level will be manifested in all three facets or bodies. Conversely, the commencement of an appropriate cure in any one system will have positive ramifications for the whole organism.

At the simplest level, the physical body's response to microbial invasion is to defend its health. Some of those defenses appear as symptoms that modern drugs are designed to "cure." But each defense has its purpose. The fever humans hasten to suppress is stimulating the growth of white blood cells to inhibit the growth of bacteria. Nausea in pregnant women protects the embryo from getting trace poisons through the mother's diet. A headache is a signal of too much stress.[20] If such defenses are not properly allowed to run their course, other parts of the organism may suffer. Anxiety attacks treated with tranquilizers will recur as long as perceptions of dangers continue. When a person—failing to listen to the body and appreciate the Principle of Cause and Effect—acts inappropriately or without full awareness, he or she impedes the self-healing process.[21]

The most recent understanding of addictions (to alcohol, drugs, nicotine, sex, gambling, etc.) is that some have developed into cellular and organic dependencies (neuroadaptation) that can be satisfied only by infusions of a particular substance, or its artificial substitute. But all are first and foremost seen as rooted in behavioral patterns. Scientists don't know if it is the drugs or behavior that changes the brain chemistry. However, if consciousness is the predominant plane, physical dependencies reflect patterns either initiated or accepted by the individual noumenal being. An aspect of evolving "beingness" is the gaining of an understanding of the power local consciousness can bring to bear on the so-called addictions of the physical body.

If thought can create and modify basic configurations of matter, it can enable a strong being to determine its degree of dependency on any particular substance. Smoking, drug use, and other addictive behaviors can be broken by a change in mind-set: anyone who desires strongly enough should be able over time to change the underlying thought pattern, with the appropriate support of other beings.

Having been deluded into thinking that health and well-being are attainable through expensive prescriptions and over-the-counter drugs, humans have lost awareness of their significant capacity for self-healing. They no longer remember that cycles of activity must be balanced with rest and recuperation. They do not perceive symptoms as messages bodies send to minds, and vice versa. With the channels of communication between realms silenced, individual humans experience fragmentation among their constituent parts. (The same dynamic works at the societal level. Citizens suppressing inner-sense connections with others results in further fragmentation.)

A profound understanding of the nature of "beingness" or consciousness-incarnate requires recognition of its inner capacity for self-learning, self-maintenance, and self-healing. The principle works at the species level as it does at the single animal level. Humans who are inattentive to being an organic part of a conscious, three-faceted universe suffer the consequences.

Having explored the domain of universal consciousness in chapter 5, in this chapter we have focused on how it manifests itself in local incarnations (individual beings who compose groups that we call species). A species arises with a set of characteristics that limits the scope of consciousness any member can have. However, within the species, each conscious being has the freedom to experiment with itself and learn its capacity for growth. While there is an inherent design conducive to full self-realization of potential and self-healing, each incarnated being must consciously choose to follow such a path.

Notes

1. Ron Scholastico, *Doorway to the Soul* (New York: Charles Scribner, 1995).

2. Stanislav Grof, *The Adventure of Self-Discovery* (New York: State University of New York Press, 1988) and *The Holotropic Mind* (With Hal Zina Bennett, San Francisco: HarperSanFrancisco, 1992).

3. Michael Harner, *The Way of the Shaman* (San Francisco: Harper & Row, 1980).

4. Robert A. Monroe, *Far Journeys* (New York: Doubleday, 1985).

5. James Redfield, *The Celestine Prophecy* (New York: Warner Books, 1993).

6. Ruth Montgomery, *Strangers Among Us* (New York: Ballantine Books, 1982).

7. Richard Gerber, *Vibrational Medicine: New Choices for Healing Ourselves* (Santa Fe, NM: Bear & Co., 1988); Barbara Hand Clow, *Liquid Light of Sex* (Santa Fe, NM: Bear & Co., 1991).

8. Measured by sentographs, these recorded patterns of pressure exerted in a finger are "sentic forms" that correlate with basic and distinct emotions. Manfred Clynes, *Sentics: The Touch of Emotion* (Garden City, NY: Anchor Press/Doubleday, 1978).

9. The use of the terms "nonlocal" and "local" by physicists, and in this book, is itself not fully free of dualistic-thinking. We need a term that encompasses both.

10. If the "30 percent nurture" in my life comes from others who are 70 percent genetically influenced, it means my 30 percent is really 70/30 genetically controlled. In each preceding generation the 30 percent was more and more a function of genetic influence. This regression works for any ratio that attributes more than 50 percent influence to genetics.

11. The sensation many parents have of being joined by another conscious being at conception and during pregnancy coincides with

the studies of the influences of drugs and sound on postpartum behavior that conscious incarnation occurs at conception.

12. In the 1950s in the United States, nineteenth-century assumptions about gender roles were still accepted as divinely ordained. The next decades shattered such bland notions; the pendulum swung in extremes for both sexes. Thoughtful people have now realized that a healthy community of cosmic beings requires gender balance and harmony both within and between individual beings.

13. Boundary issues are a topic of discussion in the current popular literature of psychology, but this chapter focuses on dimensions not covered in conventional psychology—subtle energies and fields of consciousness.

14. A good example happened to me just as I was drafting this chapter. My neighbor and I were in conflict over our property line. I had composed a nasty complaint to city hall, but something told me I had overlooked a pertinent regulation. A quick phone call saved face for me and strengthened my case. Did my extended and open personal field of consciousness do a bit of clairvoyant scouting that protected my integrity?

15. Vicki Cooper, "Interview of William Cone," *UFO Journal* 7, no. 2 (1993).

16. Some reports of channeled entities indicate that while humans may see them as one being, ABs see themselves as various aspects of a group personality. The ABs reportedly come together in one presentation of self, and divide into different facets of consciousness for another. In an interesting variation of this, a researcher in the Harvard-based Program for Extraordinary Experience Research (PEER) works with abductees to access a subpersonality (altered state) to communicate with nonphysical entities.

17. Aryeh Kaplan, *Meditation and the Bible* (York Beach, ME: Samuel Weiser, 1992).

18. Milton Erickson, *The February Man: Evolving Consciousness and Identity in Hypnotherapy* (New York: Brunner/Mazel, 1989).

19. Lack of appreciation of this principle may lead to unnecessary suffering. Modern medical diagnostic techniques give a single-moment snapshot of a symptom. Without waiting for or helping

the being to heal itself, counterproductive treatments may be precipitously administered.

20. George C. Williams and Randolph M. Nesse, "The Dawn of Darwinian Medicine," *Quarterly Review of Biology* (December 1991).

21. The pharmaceutical industry in the U.S., along with narrowly focused physicians, has used the power of the media advertising to promulgate the notion that the body is a machine that can be kept in tune by the ingestion and application of chemicals. Every drip of the nose must be artificially dried up. Pains that signal something is wrong and needs conscious attention are anesthetized. Blocked bowels that cry out for nutritious food are treated with lubricants. Indigestion caused by stress is masked with chemical foam. Skin cells that need water from within are salved by external lotions.

PART 3

Humans as Solarians

Parts 1 and 2 reviewed selections from the mounds of evidence that support the ten hypotheses introduced in the preface. I hope you will test them further for yourself to help correct our history and science to make them more compatible with the realities of our legacy and potential. Part 3 assumes that the universe is a conscious organism, with purpose and direction, and that humans are Solarian manifestations of the consciousness that initiated it. It also assumes that we as Solarians belong to a larger family of conscious beings who recognize our potential contribution to the universe's grand experiment: to call on all its parts to learn how to survive and evolve as a cosmic organism.

I believe humanity stands on the threshold of understanding its true identity. Growing numbers of us now perceive the need for assuming a stewardship role vis-à-vis our home planet. We recognize that we are like provincials in the business of self-awareness, planetary maintenance, and stellar exploration. We will soon recognize our capacity and primary responsibility for nurturing all organic life under the Sun. Just this step alone will revolutionize human interactions with other species and our natural environment. Many of us are ready to meet and engage with more advanced beings. Some have already made the leap to adopt a nonhomocentric view of conscious evolution in the universe.

Fellow cosmologist Duane Elgin and I, with different reasoning, share the assessment that *Homo sapiens sapiens* now fall in the adolescent stage of development. Like youths approaching adulthood, we are just beginning to sense our power and potential. We don't know what lies ahead, but we are certain of our capability to "take the universe by storm." We have only a dim awareness of how the history of our family shaped us. As we contemplate adulthood, we know we must address some difficult questions: How will our legacy (physical, mental, and social) affect our potential for stardom? Are we up to the task of managing a process of self-evaluation and practice? What are the necessary steps to succeed in the independence of adulthood?

Part 1 gave a new perspective on our legacy in a multidimensional universe and suggested that humans are essential to its conscious development. Part 2 attempted to make the case that as local incarnations of a self-learning consciousness, humans, individually and collectively, have all the faculties necessary for the task. Part 3 identifies the next steps we must take to successfully achieve stellar adulthood.

If through fear we hang on to our childish concepts of reality, we will be overwhelmed in the face of the universe's awesome complexity and unanticipated potential. The more desirable alternative to blindly following our childhood habits (which may lead to the extinction of the species in the next thousand years, as Stephen Hawking and others have suggested) would be to identify and exploit the full range of our Solarian capacities.

Part 3 is, thus, designed to help us move beyond an adolescent stage of self-awareness to an age of self-learning, where we assume active responsibility for our own development. I believe the process of achieving adulthood in a community of stellar beings is a self-selecting one. We will get there on our own merits; no one else makes the application or helps us with the test. Deciding we are ready to apply for the status of cosmic beings (quite an expanded sense of citizenship) opens us to a whole new range of experiences. It involves us in a profound confrontation with our definition of self and new communications with other species and the universe itself.

Chapter 7 deals with the question of our potential for Solarian participation at a galactic level of responsibility. It reviews what we think we know of relevant human capacities. Chapter 8 considers the attitudes necessary for undertaking a fully conscious path of multidimensional development. It offers new concepts of self and ways human incarnations can interact successfully with other beings. Chapter 9 defines more clearly the concepts of self-selection and self-initiation for species that desire to assume a fully responsible role in what I have termed a self-learning universe. It suggests the possibilities for individual satisfaction and species-wide progress that come from accepting the mantle of cosmic adulthood.

7

Our Stellar Potential

I trust that the discussion so far (between my thoughts and yours) has given you some new insights into why humans often wear blinders that limit knowledge of our own historical legacy. Perhaps you now agree that we are neither special creations of a personalized god nor the unique result of a haphazard process of earthly evolution. Perhaps you share with me a desire to shed the limiting myths of scientific materialism and religious supernaturalism. Although we may have widely differing interpretations of the details, I hope we perceive ourselves as the progeny of mixed physical ancestry, but as direct incarnations of ultimate conscious-ness. I trust we are open to benefit from interactions with beings who may be far in advance of our twenty-first-century society.

In other words, I hope you by now are ready to think of yourself as a Solarian, a potential actor in a multifaceted drama of ongoing creation through conscious evolution. While recognizing the existence of many species of incarnated beings, this chapter focuses on the potential of humans. We cannot shape our role in the cosmic drama unless we have a good idea of our full potential. We've got to know who we really are before we step on a larger stage. For that reason this chapter reviews some of the reasons we need a more complete and accurate view of human history.

The chapter looks at the cast of beings, the different actors with whom we will be involved. It addresses the issue of how we can be both "actor" and "director" if we are just local fragments of the ultimate "playwright." It reviews the tools of consciousness that we bring to the role and how we fit into a multispecies universe.

Honesty with Ourselves

The most important factor constraining humanity from realizing our potential is our failure to be honest with ourselves about our past and our true nature. That is why the material in this book is so important. It reminds us of how much of our history has been forgotten or suppressed, and how much of our so-called modern knowledge are the assumptions held by elites.

The question remains, why do we hold so firmly to a history that leaves out so much of the evidence? We are afraid to publicly pose the questions in this book because we think they may threaten our established relationships with one another and other species. We fear that raising such questions about our central institutions would result in chaos.

I believe the facts would mitigate this fear. Being honest with ourselves would free all of us to make conscious choices about life and human relationships in a way that would serve our deepest individual needs, and thus, those of the larger society. I am convinced that recognition of our Solarian legacy would have an immediate, positive impact on education, religion, politics, economics, and society in general. Our failure to take the risk of fully opening our eyes lets us avoid responsibility for developing a more advanced moral and ethical society. In effect, settling for a sense of psychological comfort impedes the development of a greater civilization.

How can I justify labeling our very technical and materially comfortable society provincial? (Modern society seems to have forgotten that the level of maturation of a civilization does not necessarily coincide with its forms of technology.) Being provincial means having a narrow, local perspective, ignorant of the larger universe and one's own possibilities for development.

My childhood experiences in a very provincial setting may

shed some insight into the majority's reticence to question its own assumptions about its background and the status quo. Compared to my classmates who were children of the (relatively) more economically and socially advantaged families, I was not in a position to be complacent. Seeing themselves as paragons of the society, my more privileged classmates saw no reason to question their legacy. From one of the poorest families, with no incentive to maintain the status quo, I questioned assumptions and tried to expand my horizons. But for most of my friends, the society in which they were securely established appeared to be the most they could hope for. So the "best and brightest" eagerly sought positions as captains of local teams, leaders of the band and other clubs, homecoming queens, and class officers. And they remain in comparable community roles over forty years later.

These provincial "elites" believed in the "superior" vision of their WASP specialness, the primacy of their class values, the local disdain for cosmopolitan experience, and so on. By settling for such a narrow view of reality, they failed to see the potential for personal and community development. How different the stay-at-home, small-town personalities would now be if they had been able to see how their early assumptions were limited by time, place, and history. (In fairness, some of them did, and they have gone on to make great contributions to the larger society.)

The leading institutions in today's industrial societies are like my provincial classmates. They have limited themselves to partial visions of reality. Government and political parties, while thinking of themselves as the best on the planet, are not unlike my village town hall in its false hubris. Ivy League and great research universities, the elite of the elites, are like the local school board of my youth in its pedestrian vision of education. The global councils of churches and worldwide religions are no more expansive in their search for truth on a universal scale than were the poorly educated fundamentalists in my small hometown.

In other words, our most powerful institutions of today remain in the horse-and-buggy stage of stellar-scale development, due to a self-satisfied, hang-on-to-your-laurels perspective. Businesses are no better; even high-tech firms are pedestrian compared to what they could be if they dropped their blinders of materialistic and short-term interests. Only when our most advanced humans acknowledge our underdeveloped provincialism can we begin to grow up. When our adolescent pretensions (to mix metaphors) of sophistication are dropped, we will be free to blaze new paths.

The first step is to look at questions (introduced in chapter 3) about our family tree. We are currently no different than adopted or stepchildren who do not know the whole truth of their parentage. It appears we have been blinded by the illusions of a false paternity. We could grow older without probing our true genetic and conscious legacy, but that will leave some part of our potential never realized. Remember the fairy tales of urchins learning they were really princes or princesses? Assumption of their true roles benefited everyone. It is time to consider the possibility that we have an "urchin" perspective on humanity's family tree, one that perpetuates a narrow, false sense of who we really are.

Table 13 postulates a much more expansive view of our possible history. It is not presented as the truth of past civilizations, but as a broader framework in which we should conduct all feasible historical research. In his book *Exploring Inner and Outer Space,* Brian O'Leary demonstrates how the "official box" of science excludes so much of the evidence of our history.[1] As I do, he suggests that this parochialism diminishes the vision we hold of our potential. In an individual's life, a smaller vision of one's potential insures a smaller achievement. Similarly, anything less than the Solarian legacy leads to less self-actualization of our species.

Just how provincial are we? Suppressing evidence of the prehistory referred to in this book affects us in two ways. The obvious first is that it blinds us to earlier influences on current beliefs about power, violence, social hierarchy, sexual roles, and so on. Second, by ignoring the evidence of previous advanced civilizations, we overestimate our current intellectual prowess. Like the scions of my hometown families, current establishment elites do not recognize how provincial they are.

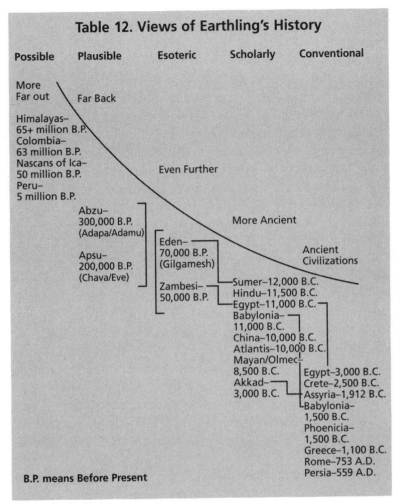

Table 12. Views of Earthling's History

Possible	Plausible	Esoteric	Scholarly	Conventional
More Far out	Far Back			
Himalayas–65+ million B.P.				
Colombia–63 million B.P.				
Nascans of Ica–50 million B.P.		Even Further		
Peru–5 million B.P.				
	Abzu–300,000 B.P. (Adapa/Adamu)		More Ancient	
		Eden–70,000 B.P. (Gilgamesh)		Ancient Civilizations
	Apsu–200,000 B.P. (Chava/Eve)			
		Zambesi–50,000 B.P.	Sumer–12,000 B.C.	
			Hindu–11,500 B.C.	
			Egypt–11,000 B.C.	
			Babylonia–11,000 B.C.	
			China–10,000 B.C.	
			Atlantis–10,000 B.C.	
			Mayan/Olmec–8,500 B.C.	Egypt–3,000 B.C.
			Akkad–3,000 B.C.	Crete–2,500 B.C.
				Assyria–1,912 B.C.
				Babylonia–1,500 B.C.
				Phoenicia–1,500 B.C.
				Greece–1,100 B.C.
				Rome–753 A.D.
				Persia–559 A.D.

B.P. means Before Present

Since the seventeenth century of Francis Bacon and Isaac Newton, mechanistic science has become the dominant perspective of human thought. (Remember, in a multidimensional universe, it represents only a partial picture.) With its logical process of observation, inference of explanation, construction of hypothesis, experimentation, and assessment, the so-called scientific method became the criterion by which new ideas and traditional wisdom are measured before they are classified as valid. While an appropriate process for a self-learning universe, its application has been limited to the physical realm.

If we developed a study purported to characterize all of humanity, we would not limit it to one culture. Why have we limited a science purported to characterize all reality to one facet? The more subtle aspects of human experience have been ignored in our collective decision to remain on the rural path of five-sense empiricism. It is now up to the current generation of new scientists to make us honest, fully integrating the experience of subtle energies and consciousness into our model of reality. We must connect the narrow pathways of materialism to the broader roads of human knowing.

Unfortunately, scientific provincialism is not the only limited approach to learning that restrains human civilization. The polarities of religious "orthodoxy" and religious "new thought" form another. While appearing to be opposites, both are still prisoners of the same spectrum: belief in an anthropomorphic divinity, albeit with different modes of operation, involved in human affairs in a miraculous universe that still absolves individuals of their responsibility for the ultimate outcome. This divine realm is variously seen as God, a higher dimension, or even Mother Nature standing by to bail us out (maybe after a little punishment to make sure we learn our lesson). These attitudes, almost completely pervasive in all religions, are even less conducive to new learning and intellectual growth than those of institutional science.

Some initiatives have been taken to expand the vision of science and remove human projected deities from our thinking about the fundamental relationship of humans to their universe. (Remember my reasoning at the beginning of the book that the solution to our current self-imposed limits to development lies not in the synthesis of science and religion, but the creation of a new perspective that transcends conventional science and religion.) The kinds of metascientific initiatives we need would deny neither the value of the scientific method nor the importance of reflecting on metaphysical questions. They would, however, insure that all evidence is appropriately taken into account and that no untestable assumptions are held up as truth.

The International Association for New Science exemplifies an attempt to define the parameters of a more inclusive science. (See its Web site at http://www.ians.org.) Founded in 1990, it builds on the "new science" of the 1920s and 1930s that included the emerging theosophical and "new thought" trends of the late nineteenth century. The organization's program includes scientific research that deals with all three facets. It has been particularly successful in providing a venue for projects dealing with the subtle energies, including so-called free energy demonstrations. Many more such organizations would significantly increase the honesty quotient among scientists.

The University of Science and Philosophy, a nonprofit educational organization founded in 1957, from the Walter Russell Foundation, promotes the millennia-old philosophical perspective that places humans and all other conscious species clearly in a natural universe. Its program of research, publishing, and various educational activities reflects the concept of "metascience." (See its Web site at http://www.philosophy.org.) This organization seeks authentic human behavior guided by an internally generated code of personal ethics. While not explicit in its literature, the university clearly treats humans and their consciousness as manifestations of a self-learning universe.

The university's Twilight Club, philosophically rooted in a group of the leading progressive thinkers of the late nineteenth and early twentieth centuries, links wholistic thinking to social action. (See the club's Web site at http://www.twilightclub.org.) Its program is based on the assumption that consciousness leads emotions and behavior, and works to enhance the social awareness of people without resorting to institutional dogma and followers who accept it unquestioningly.

One characteristic common to these two organizations and others like them is the respect they show for perennial wisdom from our past. They recognize that we progress only by building on the shoulders of our predecessors. Examples like the following suggest we need to reexamine many areas of early thinking (as I have done with the Hermetic Principles) to mine insights relevant to current scientific issues.

Interestingly, the earlier discussed work by Cleve Backster involving intercellular communication between species stands on broad shoulders. J. Chandra Bose of India was knighted by the British royal family in 1917. He invented the crescograph: it demonstrated that plants have nervous systems and respond to emotional stimuli from humans. And he was drawing on the ancient Hindu appreciation of the inner connections among all living organisms.

Before the turn of the century, several people were laying the groundwork for Einstein and twentieth-century physics. In 1908, Minkowsky conceptually united local space and local time into an absolute four-dimensional space-time. But he, too, was building on earlier work, that of Edward Morley, George Fitzgerald, and Hendrik Lorentz, all of whom had been working with the concepts of ether, contraction, and "local time." Some roots of Einstein's theory of relativity can even be seen in Jainism and Buddhism more than 4,000 years ago. The Jain story of several blind men feeling different parts of an elephant illustrates that perception of any whole is relative to one's location (physically or philosophically).

Given such examples, telling evidence of our true legacy and potential that has been pushed aside by our provincial science and equally narrow religions should be reexamined. In addition to reassessing our history, taking a more mature perspective requires an expanded model of reality, one that includes at least the three facets discussed in this book: noumena, energeia, and phenomena. This expansion in our vertical (scientific) and horizonal (historical) thinking leads to some vision of a multidimensional universe that is internally coherent and operationally congruent. I believe all apparent theoretical and experienced contradictions in our history and our current search for understanding must be satisfactorily resolved in the context of a purposeful universe.

Since no one else out there has been identified to play the role of cosmic coach or director for our species, we must take on ourselves the process of initiation. Channeled material, alleged AB communications, and noumenal insights often appear to be from other beings who would at least be armchair quarterbacks or drama critics; but the responsibility for how we grow up is really up to us. We must put ourselves through the testing of our adolescent myth of "already knowing it all" against the unknown frontiers of cosmic adulthood.

Family of Cosmic Beings

What does it mean to be a mature, self-learning species in the cosmos? Our provincial and parochial views about the possibilities for conscious life have restricted our thinking about the nature of beings in the universe. Homocentric assumptions have censored our thinking about how we relate to and are related to nonhuman forms of consciousness. The long record of reported interactions with other beings and channeled communications from some of them suggests it is time to think of humans as members of a multidimensional family of cosmic beings.

Our language has many terms that refer to other categories of beings: spiritual, divine, astral, godly, angelic, souls, higher beings, aliens, ETs, and so on. They mean different things to many people. With so many connotations, such terms do not help us distinguish different levels and categories of beingness. We cannot collect information about beings under one rubric and be sure other people use it the same way. Such confusion increases the difficulty of reaching a general consensus as to how much of this is real.

Ultimately, I believe the essential nature of all beings will be inherently simple and intellectually easy to grasp. If all experiences of a human being can be reduced to three areas (phenomenal, energeial, and noumenal), then I suggest these three categories may cover all other beings as well. As relatively distinct, but still interdependent, these three facets could provide explanations for our perceptions of and the activities of all other life-forms. Each likely has some combination of these three facets:

• Phenomenal: Consisting of either waves or particles (energy or mass), these beings function primarily in the material realm, using senses similar to those depended on by humans. Historical accounts as well as current ones indicate many levels of human contact with such beings.

- Energeial: Existing in the realm of subtle energies, beings who are primarily in this group would constitute what physicists might call "virtual beings." Once again much human experience with such beings, including humans who have transitioned to that realm, indicates the reality of this category. Any time we can sense an emotional bond with such an entity, it means that we are relating to the energeial realm.

- Noumenal: The realm of pure consciousness, reaching beyond ordinary physical and emotional awareness is accessible by all forms. But the beings who inhabit only this dimension are not constrained by the denser concentrations of energy and mass in which the other two function. These beings communicate directly with the human mind without the intervention of subtle or physical senses.

As shown earlier in this book, all aspects of human experience can be seen as a dynamic interaction involving two or three of the above. In humans the three facets are always interdependent, but mind or local consciousness is *primo inter pares,* the charioteer who directs the horses that pull the chariot. But other beings obviously operate with only one or two of these facets. As discussed earlier, mental patterns are the forms most susceptible to direct manipulation by conscious beings. Natural law appears to set fewer limits in this realm, where the degrees of freedom are much wider than for either energetic or physical activity. It then follows that the less-encumbered beings will be able to exercise greater creative power from the top down.

Let's review how the process works up from the human perspective, and then we can extrapolate in the other direction how more ephemeral beings function. The way the use of visualization in modern sports has expanded the boundaries of physical behavior exemplifies this principle.[2] What started with "inner tennis"—the imaging of perfect form serving to focus the athlete's emotional energy—has now led to performances that each year set new heights of achievement in most sports. The ancient practice of Tantric Yoga is another example, wherein physical practices help expand emotional and mental limits.

Coming from the reverse direction, noumenal-level beings would be able to harness subtle energies to cause the materialization of new objects. And energeial-level beings would be able to exercise psychokinesis in reverse and cause physical objects to move (as in poltergeist events). This illustrates how humans fit in the same three-faceted schema with all "flesh-and-blood" ABs that humans report to have experienced. Now let's look at the two nonphysical categories of beings and how we relate to them.

Energeial Beings

The concepts of phenomenal and noumenal beings are currently more easily grasped than energeial ones. The popular terms for these first two would be "physical" and "spiritual" beings. The problem with the term "subtle energy" or "energeial being" (called "astral being" by some) is that the common use of the word "energy" implies the counterpart of matter, the wave instead of the particle. But the energeial being does not involve electromagnetism and gravity. This is why reports of such beings have them passing through walls and floating in the air. (Remember from chapter 4 that the energeial realm is not constrained by the four forces of physics.)

We can better understand these beings if we review some history. Over the ages, subtle energy has been given various labels: *prana* (Hindu), Holy Spirit (Christian), *chi* (Chinese), and *ki* (Japanese). In the history of Western science, it has been conceived of as magnetism (Franz Mesmer), orgone energy (Wilhelm Reich), or an electric current (Robert Becker). Now physicists postulate psi forces, tachyons, Bell correlations, or collapsing wave functions. Physicist David Peat sees it as a force in the process of forming (clinging to form) in the material realm.

In the framework presented in this book, all the above labels refer to the energeial realm, and not the energy of the phenomenal realm. However, the subtle energies, like matenergy, do not act on their own. They require direction from a charioteer. That is why all energeial beings would involve the incarnation of consciousness. The subtle-energy category includes all luminal beings, including those we commonly term as ghostly beings. They are seen by humans through their subtle senses, which is why psychics experienced in using subtle senses see them more easily. (As three-faceted beings, humans, too, have this energeial reality. In that context our own aura is like an energeial being.)

Beings in this realm are more focused on their emotional existence. Some may still be suffering from experiences in physical form, while others may be sharing the angelic joy of noumenal creativity. Since feeling and emotions follow thought, energeial beings are manifestations of a state of mind, just as our physical condition reflects our mental state. (Proof of this power and direction of consciousness, oddly enough, comes from military research with so-called silent sound projects. When EEG patterns [E/M spectrum] are transmitted as inaudible sound to affect emotions, humans can override this artificial intervention by conscious effort.)

The emotional power of energeial beings may help explain a conundrum of science. Although scientists have learned a lot about how nerve cells, called "neurons," send signals, and how the signals in chemical form, called "neurotransmitters," pass from one cell to another, they still cannot explain how such chemical signals give rise to thoughts and feelings.[3] Can love and hate, ecstasy and despair, really be the result of nerve cells passing random molecules back and forth? Energeial beings help us understand that emotions reflect the conscious thoughts of cosmic beings, whether they have neurotransmitters or not.

Noumenal Beings

The other category of nonphysical beings includes those who inhabit only the noumena. Before looking at noumenal beings, let's briefly review our understanding of the noumena. Frontier science, as articulated at the center known by that name and founded by Beverly Rubik at Temple University,[4] has accepted the possibility that humans possess "an acausal mind-matter interrelationship that is fundamental." In other words, in human beings mind and matter coexist interdependently. In my three-faceted model, they are bonded by the field of subtle energy, or energeia. This means that you can't have a phenomenal being without mind and emotions, and you can't have an energeial being without consciousness. But theoretically you can have a local concentration of the universal consciousness without its devolution into emotions or matter.

The direction of influence that flows from consciousness to matter can be tested in human experience. Examples include the influence of consciousness on the onset of illness, enhanced athletic performance, addictions, remissions of disease, and so on. Human experience in these and other areas indicate the power of local mind to influence matter.

I believe one can reasonably assume that noumenal beings derive from the unlimited well of cosmic consciousness that permeates and animates all beings. It is the human mind that perceives noumenal beings; none of our other senses can do so. The ability to interact with noumenal beings in altered states of consciousness and when out-of-body, indicates humans are part of the same consciousness that incarnates all beings. Even though the consciousness-incarnate in humans is focused and has permeable boundaries, it is undivided and indivisible from the whole.

All this means that noumenal beings can relate to others of their kind, to energeial beings, and to phenomenal ones like humans. We perceive them through our inner senses as pure spirit, pure thought, or pure essence, depending on one's cosmology. In order to do this we must escape our fusion with the energeia and matenergy. That is why an altered state that bypasses emotional and physical constraints is necessary.

Local consciousness, when manifesting its essence in material form, incorporates multiple senses (see chapter 4) to enable itself to monitor its own participation in a space-time existence. This characteristic makes humans an integral part of the self-learning and self-directing universe. It seems reasonable to believe that all conscious beings, ABs or otherwise, would have one or more channels to sense the living universe. Since the noumenal senses directly link all conscious beings (even the energeial and phenomenal ones), it would follow that solely noumenal beings could also learn of the space-time universe indirectly through human emotional and physical experiences. This may be why some abductees report that some ABs want to draw on human emotions and learn from the physical sensations of humans.

Why some beings exist in noumenal or energeial form is unknown to us, although some cosmologies purport to have explanations. Some believe that noumenal beings can apparently determine in advance which forms to incarnate. Regardless of the mechanism and whether we chose it, awareness of our connections with cosmic consciousness never seems to totally dissipate. At one time or the other, every being seems to glimpse its transcendence. This results from the permeable membrane between local consciousness and universal consciousness (as discussed in chapter 4). We can pierce it by accident (being hit by a bolt of lightning) or design (through meditation).

The point to remember here is that humans share the same essence as noumenal beings (they are not to be feared or worshiped) and we can establish meaningful communication links with them (through a form of telepathy or channeling). This ability to communicate supports the notion of the indivisibility of the three realms. It means humans can directly relate to any category of conscious beings through one or more of our three sets of senses.

For millennia, people—interpreting it in their own ways—took information from these other beings. The Egyptians and the Hebrews considered some of their dreams to be divine messages, and on other occasions heard the voices of invisible beings like Yahweh, Thoth, and other ABs. Eskimos and Native Americans, as do most traditional people, saw their dreams and unbidden visions as natural communications from other beings.[5] Although visions or ideas perceived from noumenal beings may appear to be nonsensical, they sometimes are straightforward communications, a source of valuable knowledge and wisdom when seriously used.

All cosmic beings (ABs, humans, and others) swim in the noumenal sea of words, images, and visions. We can use it to create and express new concepts, interpret data from our multileveled universe, and engage in nuanced communications with other beings. I believe this noumenal activity contributes to the universe experiencing and learning from itself. When we recognize our cosmic role, the effects become intentional and we experience, with all noumenal beings, a sense of being participants in the ongoing development of the universe.

Consciousness as a force seems to follow the same laws as energy; for example, the law of conservation which ordains that energy cannot be created or destroyed. As a mental force, local consciousness can assume different states (see later in this chapter). The expansiveness of consciousness is inversely proportional to the inhibitions or prejudices that would limit its flow, as in Ohm's law of electricity in which the flow of current is inversely proportional to resistance. The isomorphic nature of the mental and physical realms shows itself in another manner: the way one focuses on an electron determines whether it will be a wave or particle, and the way one focuses on an idea shapes its polarity, that is, its positive or negative charge.[6] If this theory is correct, then we can grasp something of why thought and patterns are so powerful.

If incarnate beings at any level are conductors or transducers of the cosmic force of universal consciousness, then we are the means through which the universe works its way through space-time. In other words, we are connected to the ultimate powerhouse of the universe.

Connected to the Source

All types of beings described above, including humans, according to the Principle of Correspondence, would be imbued with consciousness arising from the ground of being that was discussed in chapter 1. The research dealing with consciousness referred to in this book gives credence to this view. But before it will be generally accepted, we have to overcome the legacy of a century of misleading concepts about human consciousness.

In the twentieth century, swayed by the pervasive sweep of dualism and the biological basis of human sciences, two people recast Western thinking about the nature of consciousness. Sigmund Freud and Carl Jung took largely uncharted intellectual territory and applied their particular homocentric constructs to the human experience of consciousness.

Freud started with the assumption that two basically separate components, the conscious and the unconscious, developed from the physical being. Jung was more exclusive in his approach, but like Freud essentially accepted the largely biological yet still dualistic model of the human being. Both attributed various fragments of consciousness to the human being—id, personal unconscious, ego, self, superego, and collective unconscious—and ascribed to each of them largely autonomous powers. Stated another way, they said the biological organism creates a consciousness, which then divides itself into separate and independent parts. Nowhere in nature do we find such disunity.

Freud asserted that the fundamentally independent personal unconscious developed desires so unacceptable to the other two (ego and superego) that it disguised them through hidden meanings and symbols in dreams, "Freudian slips," or compulsive behaviors. In fact, his idea of parts of an individual beyond one's conscious control has become so rooted in modern psychology that people now escape personal responsibility for murder and other serious crimes by claiming they were unconsciously (insanely) driven by the autonomous forces.

Jung's model, with its concept of the collective unconscious, expanded the range of interpretations for both the source and purposes of dream images and other cultural symbols. In recognizing a personal reality much larger than that perceived by the five physical senses, he opened the door to exploration of group consciousness (morphic fields and archetypes in the energeia). His early focus on the human dream world as the primary route into the collective unconscious, however, deemphasized the many paths of deliberate access, including meditation, remote viewing, trance, day dreaming, and the use of hallucinogens or ritual movement.

Jung did use his vast intellectual capacity, focused on the role of symbols[7] in consciousness, to show how dreams may contain material from other channels, like flashes of precognition and clairvoyance. He believed insights subliminally received from the environment or biologically inherited could be stored and spontaneously accessed from the individual's memory bank. But they were more like instincts than the conscious charioteer. He considered consciousness as a "recent acquisition of nature . . . still in an experimental state," and viewed civilization as necessary to establish a high level of continuity and avoid fragmentation of mind. For him dissociation was a problem related to "primitivism" that would be overcome by civilization. (Quite the opposite of my views on the constructive potential of multiple personalities in chapter 6.)

To account for the fact that material from the seeming fringes of consciousness frequently provided wise counsel or innovative insights to people, Jung posited the idea that dreams were from an independent unconscious that was somehow an autonomous "healer." Reverting to dualistic tradition, he attributed to this dream world an almost divine purposefulness, saying, "God speaks chiefly through dreams and visions." In his view, this realm of unconsciousness had a will of its own and could guide beings in a more balanced way through waking life, if only they heeded its supernatural message.

Now in order to recover a sense of an all-pervasive consciousness of which humans are only local manifestations, we must overcome the fragmentation in concept, and in practice, wrought by psychoanalysis. To do so we must reassert a traditional, nonhomocentric and nondualistic perspective. Interdisciplinary consciousness studies will be required to create a new theoretical perspective (what would be known as a Fifth Force) in psychology.

The narrow perspective of behaviorism and biological determinism also must be overcome. The former views the development of human consciousness as a function of influences from the environment, social and physical. The latter sees consciousness and its development in individuals as an epiphenomenon of biological evolution. Notable exceptions have been members of two professional communities that have fostered interdisciplinary research: the Association for Humanistic Psychology and the Institute for Transpersonal Psychology. (See their respective Web sites at http://www.ahp.org and http://www.ITP.edu.) They are potential leaders for the required reconceptualization of consciousness.

Some scientists among us who were not persuaded by the psychoanalytic school of thought and its modern variants turned to chemistry and biology to uncover the nature of consciousness. Equating consciousness to ordinary energy, the materialistic approach assumes that consciousness derives from a being's physical organs. For example, they imagine brain cells consolidate memories of the day's events, getting rid of some of the clutter, and then recharge themselves. Disparate cells are assumed to independently discern an order to events, make value judgments on what is relevant, and discard the rest. This set of assumptions is counter to the continuous and orderly nature of human experience, and likely counter to the experience of sentient beings elsewhere in the universe.

Surprisingly, physicists have helped bridge the gaps left by psychoanalytic and materialistic theorists. As physicists' experiments (discussed earlier) revealed the effects of consciousness on matenergy, it became possible to test psychology's assumptions in the laboratory and in ordinary life. Now we know individuals can access the universal field of consciousness directly, without resorting to some intermediary. Understanding of our direct connections with the source can come through rational review of dream content, interspecies communications, or similar images gained through meditation and other subtle channels.

Insights from brain/mind research reveal that consciousness, like the emotional and physical facets, operates on frequencies within a spectrum. This spectrum seems to be pervasive throughout the universe. But noumenal information is not always clear or ambiguous. Analogous to the background noise or static on a poorly tuned radio, conscious beings can pick up garbled bits and pieces (in dreams, meditations, etc.). The provision for accident or randomness in the quantum energy level (discussed in chapter 2) seems to apply in the realm of consciousness as well.

All this section is considered to apply to other beings with whom humans have come in contact, and those yet to be discovered. In a universe of seamless consciousness, there can be no beings separate from the rest of us and no independent parts within a local mind that heal or guide other parts. There may be aspects of the whole that receive less attention from the individual's focused awareness, but they are not outside the consciousness of which we are holograms. In a singular consciousness, dreams, visions, or other noumenal material cannot divine or come from another realm. They represent the degree of our focus on aspects of the whole that resonate with the energetic frequencies we chose to emit. We and all our sibling conscious beings are linked to the whole and relate to each other in this manner.

Attributes of Human Incarnation

In assessing the human potential for a stellar role in the universe, we concluded we are not alone. We are members of a cosmic family of beings who may compete with us, but who are also likely to be of assistance to us after we get our planet in order. Even more important, it appears that all conscious beings are indivisibly connected to each other and the ultimate source. Now let's review some of the attributes of the human incarnation that are likely to set limits on what we can achieve.

The Question of Reincarnation

Many believe individual humans arise from a more or less permanent individual consciousness—one that may comprise many incarnations—that operates outside of our space-time. (It should be noted that the reality of some reincarnations would not necessarily mean all individual incarnations are reincarnated beings.) Some speculate that different physical incarnations of a single conscious entity (one local concentration of universal mind) may exist simultaneously in parallel universes, but that is incompatible with the model used in this book. To be honest, we must state we do not know for sure if we are reincarnated beings. So, for the moment, let's describe what we seem to know of the process of reincarnation from new science research.

A useful metaphor for incarnation is a large undifferentiated plastic sheet representing the field of consciousness, where small concentrations of force push the sheet out of its plane at various points without puncturing it. Each three-dimensional point represents the incarnation of one localized field of consciousness. Each exists as long as the unseen force is thrust; but when it withdraws, the plastic sheet resumes its taut expanse with only slightly visible (ghostly) impressions of the former protrusions. (This same image illustrates how a planet's gravity field distorts the fabric of space-time.)

Another helpful analogy is a crystal wine glass (incarnation), formed from amorphous grains of sand (universal consciousness) to serve until melted down (death) to be recast (reincarnated) as a figurine. It captures three hypothesized aspects of incarnation: origin common to other beings, a transitory unique existence, and a return to the source for another incarnation.

Both these two metaphors illustrate a process, but they do not explain the factor of conscious intent behind incarnation. What is the force that produces the plastic sheet in the first place, or who conceives of the wine glass and figurine?

Descartes said, "I think, therefore I am," thereby at least proving to himself, and those who agree with him, the existence of a thinker. So if we think of ourselves as incarnated rather than created, we are part of both the thinking force that thrust us from the plastic sheet and the manifestation of that thrust. Does our Solarian existence indicate something of the nature of its source?

Even if the above description of the process of local consciousness arising through matter is correct, that still does not make the source's purpose clear. Hinduism and some Western psychics, such as Edgar Cayce, have portrayed the incarnation of souls in a particular body as the result of karma (the Principle of Cause and Effect) at play beyond local space-time. In this theory the newly incarnated being must face experiential challenges to overcome, along with opportunities for growth. Successive rebirths are required for the individual soul to balance its positive and negative reactions to the universe's imperative to evolve toward its potential. Past-life memories are seen by some as confirmation of reincarnation, but given the human ability to access the noumena, including shared memories, recollection of events and people from earlier times does not necessarily prove a purposeful reincarnation.

In a corollary to the idea of a karmic purpose, other religious cosmologies include a belief that human beings on Earth must pass some test before moving on to the next stage. The Judaic tradition indicates Yahweh expects humans to follow "the light" to be ready for an ultimate day of judgment. Christians must ritually accept spiritual salvation from a "divine" being to have access to the realm of the gods. Buddhists see each incarnation as another spiritual challenge to achieve nirvana. The Sumerians believed they had been left on Earth by the Anunnaki to develop themselves as they awaited the return of the twelfth planet. These belief systems all have the explicit or implicit assumption that humans can "move up the ladder" only with the approval of higher beings.

A corollary of the belief that humans must do something in particular to achieve a higher realm is the notion that incarnation reflects a "fall" from a more elevated state. Theologians have posited interpretations of the fall as a change in relationship to "God." Philosophers[8] have tried to explain such myths in metaphysical terms. One Earth-bound theory is much more straightforward: At some point there was a precipitous rupture in contact between humans and more advanced colonizers. Zecharia Sitchin, for example, describes the "fall" as the Anunnaki's expulsion of humans from their private domain (the Garden of Eden) into the wilds of nature.

From the perspective of this chapter, the local mind's sense of a "fall" may derive from its memory of the process of physical incarnation. That process would involve consciousness giving up degrees of its freedom as it bonds with the less malleable matenergy. In this way, personal growth in the incarnated being would be energized by a desire to regain those lost degrees of freedom. This would mean that humans have a natural impulse to work toward a higher level of conscious awareness, using all their senses to reach the maximum possible level of self-realization. (See the later discussion of a conscious awareness quotient as a measure of the strength of this impulse.)

If the Principle of Correspondence is valid, human life must give some indication of the purposefulness of its originator. If one's impulse in human life is to learn from our experimenting with the capacities of our transcendental self, then we can assume the transcendent desires to learn new things about itself. The logical, but awesome, extension of this reasoning is that humanity's galactic potential is to be a self-learning organism adding perceptions of its own learning into the conscious development of the universe.

Mind and Brain

What role does the brain play in this self-learning process undertaken by universal and local consciousness? As the key, but not exclusive, locus of mind-matter interaction, the human brain has neurons and neurotransmitters numbering in the billions. (Research mentioned earlier by Candace Pert and others documents some level of consciousness in all cells.) A materialist, believing that this combination of nerve cells creates the mind, would maintain that if we put enough neurons on a microchip to simulate the cerebral cortex, we would get a computer analog to the human brain that could produce the same thoughts. But this assertion does not recognize that the mind that fabricates the chip always precedes the product.

Physical scientists, such as Robert Ornstein and Richard F. Thompson, writing in *The Amazing Brain*,[9] make a special point of the brain's physical characteristics and assumed role:

It is about the size of a grapefruit. It weighs about as much as a head of cabbage. It is the one organ we cannot transplant and be ourselves. The brain regulates all bodily functions; it controls our most primitive behavior—eating, sleeping, and keeping warm; it is responsible for our most sophisticated activities—the creation of civilization, of music, art, science, and language. Our hopes, thoughts, emotions, and personality are all lodged somewhere inside there.

The materialist's speculative hypothesis that consciousness arose by the chance clustering of brain cells remains just that. But the opposite hypothesis is not easily proven either. The mentalist (mind-shapes-matter) point of view asserts it is the mind that orders the neurons in the first place. In response, the materialist asks why chemicals can affect the moods and other functions of the mind if it is independent of the material brain? The mentalist responds that the chemicals are only cluttering up the physical channels through which the mind must operate in the five-sense world. Materialists and mentalists, from two different perspectives, see the same reality: the interdependency of the mind and its material counterpart—the brain.

Incarnation is thus not a simple matter of a freewheeling mind lodging itself in just any physical host; there is obviously a complementary and interactive relationship. The fact that individuals receiving organ transplants have reported memories and tastes that could be traced only to the organ donors suggests that a partial transfer of mind occurs with transfer of matter. Cases of "walk-ins" suppressing an incarnated personality and so-called spirit attachments could be explained in this context if one assumes a partial ceding of position by the original mind.

Humans clearly exist at some stage between mind having total control over matter (including the brain) and being totally subject to it. We can exercise the power of psychokinesis, and perhaps teleportation in limited ways. The thoughts expressed by the mind ordering up neuropeptides to handle pain is an example of its ability to manipulate matenergy, but its power is limited. The following section attempts to identify the limitations physical incarnation imposes on consciousness.

Local Mind Powers

Human consciousness can neither convert energy from outside ourselves to sustain our own lives, nor convert inorganic matter to organic matter in a process of direct manifestation. We have to depend on plants (or animals that survive on plants) to transform inorganic elements (liquids, gases, and solids) to usable fats, proteins, sugars, and carbohydrates for us. We are dependent on other beings to conceptualize and breathe life into us. The creator of our limitations obviously has more power over the interaction of matter and consciousness than we do.

Will humans ever be able to independently manifest themselves or inanimate objects through the conscious concentration of charges from the vacuum? We already have the power to teleport certain objects from one place to another. (I know of several independently corroborated cases of spontaneous or deliberate teleportation of small personal objects.) Will the strengthening of human subtle senses make direct manifestations feasible? We cannot answer these questions yet, but we have made progress in understanding the powers of local consciousness (mind).

Two important areas of research are mind-body healing and subtle communications. The Institute of Noetic Sciences, founded in 1973 by *Apollo 14* astronaut Edgar Mitchell, has been a leader in these areas over three decades. (See its Web site at http://www.noetic.org.) The Institute, the nonprofit foundation Fetzer Institute, and Bill Moyers of PBS collaborated on television programs in the 1990s to expose more people to evidence of the mind's healing powers. Their series, other programs, and popular books have documented many different approaches to the harnessing of conscious intent in the interest of healing oneself and others. There are untold accounts of people who have cured themselves of cancer and other diseases after medical professionals have given up hope.

Despite such accumulating evidence, many doctors still dismiss these healings, which can only be explained by the power of the mind, as spontaneous remissions or anomalies. Even the many people taking placebos in drug tests who get well are not taken as serious evidence of the effects of intention. But growing numbers of professionals, as well as laypeople, are participating in research to identify techniques to improve the use of mind in one's own healing and in the distant healing of others. This high level of public interest resulted in the U.S. Congress and National Institutes of Health funding the complementary medicine research projects mentioned earlier. The final results are not in, but clearly consciousness-incarnate retains much of its undiluted power to influence the material facet of its own organism.

Practicing biofeedback to shift brain waves by visualising effects, in order to create changes at the cellular or organ level, is another demonstration of the power of mind over emotional energy and matter. These examples and the subtle communications research covered earlier give us a glimpse of the strength of consciousness, even when encumbered by dense energy and matter.

A Question of Hierarchy

At this point, humans seem to possess more "mind power" than other Earth species—although we cannot be sure; some students of dolphins would suggest otherwise. We currently have no way to know where the average human level of consciousness fits into the hierarchy of cosmic beings. Some channeled material, like the *Urantia Book* produced by a group in Chicago in the early twentieth century, purports to describe a complex hierarchy of beings. Religious cosmologies have claimed various levels of angels, archangels, demons, and any number of conscious entities between humanity and God. Some of them also include elementals like devas and nature spirits below humans on the hierarchy. In fact, we have no reliable indication as to what the universal hierarchy might be.

Why are humans the most consciously aware of Earth species, if we are? Several answers are possible. Humans progressed unaided to our current level of mind development. This could be the result of our inherent level of consciousness, or we could have developed ahead of others by chance, simply reacting to external factors beyond our control. Humans could have immigrated here, already having achieved a high status elsewhere. One option favored by some is that we were catapulted from a lower state by the intervention of more advanced beings. Two scientists whose work was discussed earlier have an intriguing perspective on this possible scenario.

Javier Cabrera believes colonizing beings implanted cognitive codes in humans through insertion of sets of nucleic acids and proteins into the cerebral cortex, and perhaps then reinforced the coding through electromagnetic effects. He postulates that such biochemical interventions or manipulations of the genetic code enhanced the capability of primitive humans to process knowledge. Sitchin, working independently of Cabrera with data from the other side of the world (in E-DIN in what is now Iraq) also describes evidence of AB gene splicing that moved prehistoric humans to a level of greater mental capability.

As mentioned earlier, such gene splicing by ABs could help explain Earth's confusing archaeological record (such as the coexistence of *Homo erectus* with *Homo sapiens* when the theory of evolution says the latter came from the former). However, the evidence is not clear that genetic engineering like that suggested by Cabrera and Sitchin would result in great increases in conscious awareness.

For example, humans and chimpanzees have more equivalent DNA sequences in common (only 1.6 percent difference) than either does with gorillas, orangutans, or the great apes.[10] If, from a physiological point of view, humans and chimps are so closely related, what accounts for such significant intellectual and psychological differences? While such slight genetic variations can account for differences in bone and muscle structures, hair patterns and skin pigmentation, can they account for such wide differences in brain function symbol manipulation skills? Should we try gene splicing with chimpanzees, in an attempt to have them approach our level of consciousness, to test the theory of AB manipulation?

We still cannot prove whether physically arranged DNA patterns, artificially ordered or not, can preempt preexisting conscious intent. An externally imposed gene manipulation route to increasing levels of consciousness does not appear, on the surface, to be compatible with the notion of a preincarnation intent that defines the consciousness level of a species. The answer awaits evidence showing that if we genetically engineer a new type of body, a recognizably different conscious being will inhabit it. (The mastery of cloning will also provide the opportunity, if we dare it with humans, to test the concept that individualized local minds are independent of their genetic heritage. Will a consciousness obviously different from that of the cell donor inhabit the physical body derived from the donor's gene patterns?)

States of Consciousness

One of the limitations pure consciousness incurs with incarnation is being subject to various states of awareness brought about by different conditions in physical existence. The consciousness that was unidimensional now experiences fluctuations (the Principles of Vibration and Rhythm, respectively). Labeled in various ways by different people, the states are called "waking," "altered," and "sleeping" by Rosemary McMullen (writer, artist, and philosopher). She relates the three to creativity in the "objective systems" of language, art, and formal images. The normal rhythms may fluctuate as a result of chemical intervention and deliberate self-manipulation.

Electrical waves in the brain associated with some of the different states of consciousness are: (1) wide awake, beta waves at 13+ hertz (waves per second); (2) relaxed, alpha at 8 to 12 hertz: (3) dreamlike, theta at 4 to 8 hertz; and (4) sleep, delta at less than 4 hertz. Many machines now assist people in moving up and down these frequencies, although the yogi or sufi does so without technology.

Regardless of the labels used—"alert," "dreaming," "meditative," "drugged," "inspired," "dazed," "sleeping," "focused," and so on—each one represents a position on a singular spectrum of consciousness. (The Principle of Correspondence predicts that a comparable range of states would occur in other cosmic beings. If such is the case, they are likely to experience distortion of perceptions as humans do.) The labels chosen for such a spectrum depend on what a society considers useful. For example, Sanskrit has hundreds of words to describe different states of consciousness. The table below shows one way of expressing various states in terms familiar to Americans.

Table 13. States of Human Consciousness

- Sleep (preconscious)
- Drugged (semiconscious)
- Dream (subconscious)
- Awake (conscious)
- High (superconscious)
- Hallucination (unstable consciousness)
- Meditation (supraconsciousness)
- Channel (cosmic consciousness)

One of the most obvious differentiations in the above continuum involves what many see as two poles, those of sleeping and waking (Principle of Polarity). As revealed earlier, science has not yet figured out the purpose of sleep and how it is precipitated. Most humans need to spend about one-third of life in it, with the individual amount dependent on idiosyncratic variables. Some scientists argue that a chemical shift causes the change in a conscious state, but it is also possible that the chemical change only reflects shifts in consciousness, that is, the physical body responds to the requirements of consciousness. For an extreme example, in many documented NDEs a person's indestructible consciousness is the most logical explanation of why a clinically dead body returns to life.[11]

Ordinary human experience would indicate that a being cannot combine both poles (asleep and awake) at the same time. The closest one can get to both would be a near-balance or equilibrium. (Recall the earlier discussion of polarities being very easy to shift from one state to the other.) An example of such a balance of the two states is the case of a meditating monk in the Himalayas who reportedly did not fall asleep for more than seventy years. This case and others involving people needing little sleep may suggest that the amount needed is in direct proportion to how much one's consciousness is required to keep the five physical senses on full alert. This would mean the more we inhibit access (use of subtle and inner senses) to universal consciousness while awake, the more we may require sleep. Parallel with the need for balance in consciousness may be a similar physiological need for balance in cell recuperation time.

An artificially induced state very close to sleep is drugged semiconsciousness, when chemical substances neutralize all the physical sensory input channels and their synthesizing nervous system. But access to the noumena in this state does not have the same quality of communication as in sleep. (Richard Alpert/Ram Dass reportedly gave up using LSD when he found that a meditating monk had clearer access to the noumena than his drug-induced states produced.) Several substances can induce this state, which, like all other states, ranges on a gradient from light to heavy. Its lighter phases also permit a slipping into the dream state.

With regard to the next popularly conceived state of consciousness—dreams that transcend periods of sleeping and waking—it may not be a separate state, but another channel of sensing that demonstrates the seamless nature of consciousness. Dreams seem to use some of the same data we access through the energeial and phenomenal senses, making it possible to experience in the dream seeing, talking, and feeling, and also tasting and smelling.

The assumption of one field of awareness, whether one is asleep or awake, is supported by the phenomenon of lucid dreaming. Stephen Laberge demonstrated that humans can be simultaneously awake (aware of the fact of their dreaming) and participating in their dreams.[12] The inner connections of multilevel senses make data from dream and other states available to the waking state, and vice versa. These subtle senses explain why the body's reactions, for example, sexual or fearful, are the same whether the stimuli come in dream or awake states.

The materialist's view that dreams arise from the random firing of overloaded neurons is undermined by human experience. Only dream use of the subtle senses would make it possible to receive information about distant events—problems experienced by a loved one, auspicious or catastrophic occurrences, and even unrelated incidents. Some persons experience precognitive dreams (of events to come) that could not possibly be stored in the brain's neurons. Any plausible theory of dreaming must account for all these characteristics of dreams.

The awake state is assumed to be so well-known that it hardly gets discussed. Yet it, as all other states, is not uniform; there are shades of awakeness. Dreams called "daydreams" find their way into it, as do reveries and other forms of musing. Local consciousness is sometimes focused by external stimuli like loud noises or other focusing action, but the maintenance of a particular desired state requires deliberate focus, even if the intent is to remain unfocused, as in meditation. Some integrating level of consciousness appears to establish and maintain the necessary level of wakefulness, permitting deviations when the organism's basic survival needs are met.

(A classic example of a spontaneous shift from one waking dimension to another was reportedly experienced by Nikola Tesla in 1882. One evening while walking with a companion in Prague, Tesla received an instantaneous vision of an unknown machine—an alternating-current motor. After a brief trance-like pause, he reported that a vision had come to him in such detail that he could later, with his eidetic memory, draw a complete blueprint of a workable invention.)

A high state of awareness, in which all the senses (physical and subtle) are alert, allows one to subsume and benefit from all the lesser states. Natural highs can come from certain physical exercises or postures, rhythmic music or dance, or group rituals. This is one of the natural benefits of certain religious ceremonies or large group events. The use of appropriate drugs can precipitate a high (superconscious) or a hallucinatory (unstable consciousness) state, depending on the amount used and the general mental condition of the recipient.

In a high state of awareness, an individual can direct the content of noumenal input by choosing a target or an area of focus (Principle of Mentalism). Through association, other topics with similar vibrational profiles then come into the person's field of awareness. (Freud described this principle with his concept of "free association.") In this way, related knowledge is brought to bear on the target regardless of the state in which it was originally registered.

People can learn to benefit from both the daydream and night-dream states, and also deliberately use the more subtle states. With access to the more subtle planes, they can integrate in the waking state the most comprehensive range of information for an enhanced perspective on any experience. The value of all these states lies in their usefulness to the highly aware, incarnated being, using all its ways of knowing, to understand and contribute to the self-learning universe.

For example, developing the ability to conduct a lucid dream enables one to bring more information from noumenal consciousness into ordinary awareness. Through the use of lucid dreams and other high volitional states (stimulated through meditation, ritual, or biofeedback), one gains access to the inner realm without the use of drugs.[13] Such access requires only the alignment of our conscious frequencies with the desired ideational field, which can be done by self-direction, as in self-guided remote viewing or shifts into a trance state.

Some of the higher states are not always considered creative or benign. The label "schizophrenic" is used for some people who report "hallucinating" a reality radically different from that of their associates. But others who have similar experiences and are not behaviorally impaired by them—shamans, religious leaders, and artists—are considered to be spiritual, prophetic, or visionary.

Perhaps the degree of social alienation in each instance is a function of how the behavior is initially defined by those making the judgment. Teachers and counselors may label one person's behavior "hallucinatory" while initiates may label similar behavior in their spiritual guide "inspirational." Instead of naturally encouraging shifts from a less integrated state to another (as group chants and musical patterns in many Hindu temples and Muslim mosques in India do), Western health professionals use a pharmacological fix for periods of unstable consciousness. The latter do not take advantage of the healing power of group intent and deprive the individual of learning how to manage self-integration.

When schizophrenics are overwhelmed by the deluge of uncontrolled stimuli from the energeia and noumena, antipsychotic drugs (such as clozapine, Haldol, or Thorazine) reduce the "aberrational" behavior through sedation (reducing the effectiveness of vision, memory, and movement). The patient's mentally dulled and physically diminished faculties limit the range for conscious self-management.[14] Instead of engaging in a natural process, one's state of consciousness is artificially shifted from the higher level of hallucination to the lower, drugged one. Another approach would be more appropriate, developing the human capacity to benefit from the full range of states, even when they are painful or frightening. Training in managing all states of consciousness and support for their integration into education practices are needed for social progress in the twenty-first century.

Consciousness beyond Intelligence

Among various minds, there are different levels of mental development, emotional maturity, or physical power. We see these differences in humans and in information we have about ABs. When faced with significant differences in other beings, we may project our own biases on them. With ABs, some people see angels, while others see devils.[15] For people focused on technology, other species of beings with advanced technology are perceived to be of superior intelligence, because intelligence is one indicator humans use to compare themselves to others. This raises the question, what is intelligence?

Are ABs more intelligent, or have they just had more time to develop? Before leaping to conclusions, we should clarify a misconception about the meaning of intelligence. (Recall the discussion of IQ and CQ in chapter 6.) For humans, IQ is a measure of a person's performance on a culturally based instrument that reflects how well certain skills relevant to a particular society have been developed and how well a selected portion of the culture's knowledge base has been memorized.

Other cultures or species are likely to have developed their own such measures. So, is there some way we will be able to compare ourselves to other beings? I believe the characteristic I have called CQ (Consciousness Quotient) may be useful here. Human experience suggests that varying levels of such a developmental gradient do exist. But we have no idea of the respective contributions of the being's state of original consciousness (at incarnation) versus what it learns from experience. In a self-learning universe, the scope for growth from experience would seem to be inherent. Therefore, a being born with a low CQ could learn to increase it over time.

If CQ reflects the overall scope of awareness a being has about all the facets of its universe, for both the individual and the species as a whole, a higher CQ would appear to be the developmental result of self-learning through interaction with and testing of oneself against the experience of living. (These concepts are more fully developed in chapter 8.) Therefore, within a species, changes to an individual's original CQ level are largely self-determined by the degree of openness one has to different ways of knowing and one's willingness to test assumptions against results.

While theorizing about the CQ levels of extraplanetary beings remains in a phase of interesting speculation, the issue of what causes different levels among human beings and between humans and other local species is subject to some data-based interpretation.

Apparently all human babies have the capability to recognize the differences among all the sounds of any language. In other words, they are born fully conscious in this aspect of local intelligence and CQ. By the age of seven months they begin to lose that capability for languages not used by others around them. So begins a socialization process that eliminates possibilities for experiencing the whole of consciousness through one important tool, language skills. Learning other languages later on, to some degree, reverses the process. The same narrowing and concentrating begins to take place in other CQ components as cultural patterns of emotional expression, thought, and action are adopted and inculcated.

Just as socialization, a necessary function of incarnation, causes the loss of ability to hear certain sounds, it may diminish use of the inner senses, the capacity to perceive much of the noumena and the energeia. While intrinsic capacities to feel and think with all senses begin as universal endowments, use of them is slowly shaped, limiting subsequent understanding. From early childhood experiences often comes a "self-limiting prophecy," and incarnated beings become less consciously aware than they are capable of being.

Can one minimize this self-limiting process? Can one deliberately develop and fine-tune the subtle senses? If local human consciousness is a scaled-down model (as "created in the image") of ultimate cosmic consciousness, can it consciously progress toward its full potential? The experience of some would indicate that we all can at least maintain and enhance to some degree our natural birthright of conscious awareness (CQ). For example, using clairvoyance, Edgar Cayce could diagnose a patient with only a name and address. Many people deliberately access a potential scene from the future using only an hour and a date as reference points. Everyone owns and can enhance these and all the other so-called paranormal capacities described in this book. Can we as a species collectively move ourselves to a new plateau of CQ? That is the question of the millennium.

Spectrum of Conscious Life

In the so-called chain of being, humans have traditionally placed themselves in a divine niche somewhere above animals but below angels. How our actual placement came to pass remains a great puzzle. But the assertion of such a special niche is becoming increasingly untenable. Able to extensively manipulate their physical environment, human beings undoubtedly have the most highly developed symbol and communication skills among current Earth animals. How we fit into the overall kingdom of conscious beings is another matter.

In a self-learning universe, a separate category of consciousness would exist for each level of complexity in which experience can occur. This means that the ability to produce similar offspring implies an exclusive level of self-learning, and therefore, a unique role in the total organism. All levels of beingness, including all the plant and animal kingdoms, would meet this criterion. Applying the perspective of earlier chapters, solar systems and larger elements of the universe may also have this reproductive potential. The criterion may also be met by microscopic particles that have been considered inert. Gaston Nassen, with a new type of microscope, observed heretofore unseen somatids[16] reproducing themselves. This leaves us with no indisputable dead/live or unconscious/conscious dividing lines. Every aspect of nature seems to have a role in the purposefulness of the universe.

Let's look at how the truth of this assumption is dawning on our species. The conventional wisdom was that plants could not move, feel, or see. But Cleve Backster and others have now disproved that hypothesis with research showing there is biocommunication within and between species.[17] Conversely, for several thousand years it was thought animals did not have the inherent patterns and energies to regenerate parts as plants do. But in the eighteenth century, Abraham Trembley started a line of scientific inquiry that proved they could. Now Robert Becker believes it is an inherent function in humans that may be expanded.[18]

Most people, except the biological determinists, still believe the fundamental distinction between the human species and the animal kingdom is human possession of a soul or unique form of consciousness. Is this, too, only anthropomorphic arrogance? The evidence is mounting that we have oversold ourselves on this final indicator of our special status. News articles now regularly report on research projects that demonstrate other species not only enjoy conscious awareness (CQ), but can understand human efforts to communicate with them.

According to various studies, dolphins receive instructions, coordinate their own behavior, and give a response showing they understand the human request. Upon seeing a hand signal, for example, they swim together, and then burst to the surface in concert with behavior that relates to the signal. A parrot identifies colors, counts, and expresses feeling with words. Chimpanzees have mastered a limited human-created symbolic language. (They do not have vocal cords to form words.) With these symbols they express preferences and indicate grammatical comprehension equal to a thirty-month-old child. What pet owners have known experientially is now being confirmed in the scientific research laboratory: understanding between species is clearly a two-way street. Even insects are known to respond quickly and appropriately to a thought request.

Some studies have revealed even deeper levels of communication among animals. Certain animals give other beings, including humans, warning of impending danger. Different species pass the emotions of depression and exhilaration among themselves. According to the experience of Native Americans, wild animals offer themselves as food to people dependent on them. These examples demonstrate that varying degrees of consciousness (CQ) among species is another one of the gradients that characterize every aspect of the universe, and we are no longer sure where human beings fall on that gradient. Interspecies communication appears to refute the idea that a separate "soul" is unique to humans.

In addition to the blurring of Earth interspecies distinctions, all the old views of human limitations are rapidly fading. Workshops teach how to have out-of-body experiences. Untold numbers tell of near-death experiences. Thousands have reported encounters with humanoid, ephemeral beings.

In this context, it is reasonable to conclude that humans are no more mortal and no less divine than any other species. We are simply and gloriously part of a conscious epic of self-learning life developing among the stars, called to expand our reach toward inner and outer space while grounded in this Earth. A Pueblo creation myth places us in this cosmic web of consciousness.

> In the beginning was Spider or Thought Mother who created the phenomenal world by spinning threads that became the universe. Then, from her own spider being, she spun threads to form the beings of people. For each being, she spun a delicate thread that connected it to her own web. So, as the Spider Woman spins a web of destiny, each being is somehow woven into the pattern (of consciousness).

In such a cosmos, to know something of an individual is to know something of the Thought Mother, or Logos, from which we all come. Since consciousness has no finite boundaries that we can discern, logic would indicate that it flows in all directions from the powerful center—the womb from which we were all extruded. Thus, limited ideas about our nature limit every aspect of our emotional and physical reality. By ignoring our broader selves and our connections with all life, we consign ourselves to limited versions of the potential beings we are.

Dualistic thinking is part of the problem: the idea that five senses are paramount separates us from the power in the nonmaterial realm. We can bring the power of our subtle selves into play and change our physical selves. Using our subtle senses, we can communicate more effectively with all beings. We can give and receive healing. We can understand the self-creation of our emotional reactions and use them constructively rather than allowing ourselves to be abused by them.

Realizing that no aspect of life is completely independent, we know that our volition is never completely blocked. We must only learn the inherent constraints on us in order to freely use our conscious intent effectively. That includes learning to nurture instead of destroying our habitat.

With a desire to assume our rightful place among the stars, we must master the long-term skills for creating a self-sustaining lifestyle on our home planet before we will be invited into the galactic neighborhood. No high-CQ species would welcome or provide assistance to beings who foul their own nest and export destructive attitudes, behaviors, and technologies. Understanding the power of subtle energies, they will not wish to open themselves to unwarranted invasions by neophytes who have not learned to harness their thoughts and emotions.

Humans, through development of our meditative capacities and our material sciences, are now capable of traversing the quantum gap between mind and matter. While avoiding for the moment the abyss of nuclear self-destruction, we have peered through the lens of subatomic matter and perceived our own consciousness at play. Although still in a state of relative naivete, we are equipped to probe for knowledge in all realms. Thus, humans are ready for the self-initiation rites into cosmic young adulthood. With the advent of a planetary renaissance, we will be able to engage with other conscious beings on common ground.

Notes

1. Brian O'Leary, *Exploring Inner and Outer Space* (Berkeley, CA: North Atlantic Books, 1989).

2. Michael Murphy, *Future of the Body* (Los Angeles: J.P. Tarcher, 1992).

3. John De Cuevas, "Mind, Brain and Behavior," *Harvard Magazine* (November 1994).

4. Beverly Rubik, *Frontier Perspectives* (Philadelphia: The Center for Frontier Sciences, Temple University, Fall/Winter 1991). Rubik now heads the Institute for Frontier Science in Oakland, California.

5. Dan Moonhawk Alford, Private e-mail communications, December 1999.

6. Danah Zohar, *Quantum Self* (New York: Quill/William Morrow, 1990).

7. Carl Jung, *Man and His Symbols* (New York: Dell Publishing, 1964).

8. William I. Thompson, *The Time Falling Bodies Take to Light* (New York: St. Martin's Press, 1981).

9. Robert Ornstein and Richard F. Thompson, *The Amazing Brain* (Boston: Houghton Mifflin, 1991).

10. Christopher Wills, *The Runaway Brain* (New York: Basic Books, 1993).

11. Dannion Brinkley, *Saved by the Light* (New York: HarperCollins, 1995).

12. Stephen Laberge, *Lucid Dreaming* (New York: Ballantine, 1986).

13. Cathleen J. Lapkoff, "Adventures in Consciousness," *Fate Magazine* (January 1994).

14. Sandra G. Boodman, "New Hope for Schizophrenia," *Washington Post* (February 16, 1993).

15. Nelson Pacheco and Tommy Blann, *Unmasking the Enemy* (Arlington, VA: Bendan Press, 1994).

16. Christopher Bird, *Persecution and Trial of Gaston Nassens* (Tiburon, CA: H.J. Kramer, Inc., 1991).

17. Peter Tompkins and Christopher Bird, *The Secret Life of Plants* (New York: Harper & Row, 1973).

18. Robert O. Becker and Gary Selden, *Body Electric* (New York: William Morrow, 1985).

8

Conscious Self-Realization

Conventional science sees individual beings and their behavior as products of the universe's physical forces that shape all its parts. Western religions give humans little more leeway: we are products of their distant god, subject to His divine machinations. In either view there is relatively little scope for personal power and responsibility, and conscious growth is incidental. In the late twentieth century, new views of the universe emerged: it is alive and conscious, filled with memory; it is holographic and reflexive; it is a living energy that evolves. However, when one takes a metascientific view of all that we know and what we can reasonably infer, a more purposeful feature becomes apparent. The universe seems self-learning, autodidactic for a purpose: self-realization. The universe appears to be a manifestation of its own conscious intent to fully actualize its inherent potential through conscious beings.

If humans, as local consciousnesses-incarnate, reflect the image of the self-learning yin/yang force from which the universe manifests itself, then we too are self-learning and self-realizing beings. Abraham Maslow's concept of self-actualizing humans and the Greek idea of entelechy capture this essence at a human level, but the truth appears to be much more awesome. We are simultaneously responsible for both our learning and the teaching. This is what self-learning means. Our role in the family of all beings is to become as fully self-aware as possible and to consciously shape our contributions to the universe in a manner that enhances the whole. In doing so we eventually—we're not there yet—become co-designers with all other conscious organisms of not only the outcome, but the process.

This chapter deals with the dynamics whereby human beings are both nourished and constrained by that which is external, but must inwardly design their own development and its impact on a portion of the cosmos. Conscious self-development involves all the Hermetic Principles: a mental grasp of all the parts and how one's intention operates through cause and effect; the harnessing of vibrational frequencies through the gender polarities of feminine receptivity and masculine expressiveness, internally and externally; the shifting of three-dimensional polarities in sync with the universe's rhythm of cycles and epicycles. In all of this, we act in the microcosm as we perceive the macrocosm to be. All conscious human beings engage in a tightrope act, requiring discovery of their freedom and making the most of their powers, balancing between self and other.

For the newly born infant, there is little sense of difference between self and other, with distinctions learned only as others fail to respond to its desires. As it experiences some delay in need satisfaction—perhaps the mother's breast is not available when hunger arises—the baby begins to comprehend the distinction between its beingness and that of others. Experiences of early childhood establish the patterns of physical and emotional separation. The profile varies from culture to culture, but by early adolescence the social boundaries are quite clear in all societies; in many, explicit rites of passage take place to mark the transitions to greater autonomy.

Adult life involves constant management of the boundaries between self and other. Extremes of isolation and codependence are usually meant to be momentary: sometimes we need to pull our "shell" about us, and at other times we reach out like a multiarmed octopus. The process is a continuous balancing act. In Western and particularly American society, people are lulled into a false sense of autonomy by the myth of individualism. They have come to underappreciate the benefits and limitations of human interdependence. Paradoxically, individualism defines itself in relation to the others it shuns, and too much autonomy results in growth-depriving alienation.

Chapter 7 dealt with individual beingness as an incarnation of consciousness within local space-time from the perspective of how the individual derives from the multidimensional cosmos. This present chapter looks at the three-level process from the other polarity: the self-defining nature of the individual's developmental interaction with other multilevel beings (who also have their own unique destinies). Danah Zohar, in *Quantum Self,* implicitly observing the Principle of Correspondence, compared the "thingness" of the particle to the self (personality) and its "wave nature" to the person's relationship to others. Using this quantum analogy, she notes that humans are therefore "waves" or "particles," depending on who is doing the observing. Employing the term "selfhood" combines these two aspects, indicating self is more than a static entity; selfhood implies the dynamic of relating to otherness. (Otherness, as used here, includes other beings and our habitat.)

Continuing with Zohar's analogy from the subatomic microcosm, from one observation point the being is a selfhood (particle) and from another it is otherness (wave). Thus, others are also selfhoods from their own perspectives. Consequently, social reality is always a function of "relatingness," that is, the outcome of reciprocal definitions along the selfhood-otherness continuum by equally powerful beings. This book recognizes that each being has at least three sources of senses and power (phenomena, energeia, and noumena) for use in this process of reciprocal definition of selves. Conceiving of the individual being in an integral, three-faceted universe recalls a lost sense of wholeness,[1] providing profound insights into broader human psychology missed by current homocentric theory.

Selfhood

To understand how beings participate in the self-learning, self-directing nature of the universe, the previous chapter started with the three-faceted model where beingness derives from dynamic interplay between ideas and material forms. The ability of "living forms" to consciously ingest ideas, as they do energy and matter, and transform them for their own use (through the cohesive forces of the energeia) makes self-development possible. Entities below the threshold of organic cells also engage in a constant interchange of matter and energy, but they lack sufficient mobility and flexibility to make the many quantum choices that are intrinsic to self-renewing life or selfhood.

My evolving model suggests the possibility that at some level of species-consciousness, humans literally hold their body cells together with a vision of who they are. On a larger scale, it is conceivable that conscious beings collectively maintain the integrity of parts of the material universe through group mind. (Some ABs have implied to contactees that they have more ability to use group mind than humans do.) Although the power of creation is subject to certain constraints at the human level, a single person can largely determine how well his or her body will perform as an athlete or dancer, or whether it will be ill or well. And the evidence is mounting that we also have a significant impact on other organic entities and our material surroundings. (Many anecdotes describe the ways computers, automobiles, and machines respond to changes in the user's moods. Deliberate psychokinesis and teleportation are other examples of the power of self on other.)

The ability of a being to self-monitor and self-renew does not arise accidentally. It derives from the universal intention expressed at conception that joins together the three realms through the natural principles[2] that support life. Not yet understanding the primal origin of this initiating consciousness, we can only accept and marvel at ourselves and other beings as the offspring of the yin/yang force I sometimes call the Grand Couple.

Does only one force in the universe have a powerful enough intent to initiate new life-forms? We simply do not know how many species, if any, have the power to take a primal idea and focus subtle energy enough to synthesize new life-forms, without depending on biogenesis (the development of living organisms from other living organisms) or mechanistic genetic manipulation. If the universe is truly self-learning, it could have produced different levels of the Grand Couple, each with its own scope of operation.

According to Raimon Panikkar, "The ancient Greeks . . . had already defined life (zoe) as *chronostou einai*, the time of being. The very temporality of the universe manifests that it is alive; it has youth, maturity, old age, infirmities and even death. Zoe is set against thanatos, death. . . . Time is the very flow of being itself . . . the peculiar way in which each thing lasts."[3]

For humans, beingness is in the here and now, in local space-time. Yet our beingness precludes neither the simultaneous existence of different beings in other dimensions nor our connections to them. In fact, the interconnectedness we experience through the subtle senses, OBE/NDE excursions, and other interdimensional communications reveals that local beingness cannot be severed from its internal, infinite source and context. In some manner, the cosmic umbilical cord is apparently never cut, even for a seemingly independent human incarnation for an Earthly lifetime.

Using Paul Tillich's concept, our local beingness derives from a preexisting ground of being. But since time is an integral part of this existence, the fourth dimension of the space-time, our sense of this self must be only temporary, limited to this incarnation. This logic notwithstanding, there is a long tradition of belief that the human self, or some part of it, is more than time and circumstance, and appears to have some degree of immortality.[4] This would mean that selfhood should have the ability to be aware of both local time and universal time. Many reported transcendental experiences indicate it apparently does.

More concretely, scientific evidence indicates that at birth humans bring preexisting "knowingness" into this beingness.

Recent research has shown that newborns less than an hour old can recognize a human face. Within twelve hours of birth they can distinguish their mother's voice. A father holds his daughter within seconds of her birth, establishing deep, mutual eye contact. But that which the father might label a moment of bonding, may in fact be a moment of mutual recognition. However, as the new being begins to focus more on the phenomenal realm, certain pathways to knowing appear to become constricted.

Noam Chomsky, noted Massachusetts Institute of Technology linguist, believes we are biologically prewired to learn language. Humans are born with the ability to distinguish among all the speech sounds in all languages, even artificial ones, but within a year the recognition skill narrows to those of the native language. Infants can even appreciate the emotional implication of words in a language they have never heard before. While most of the content of early learning appears to come from the environment, the process of comprehension and consolidation is innate. As infants, humans even appear to intuitively grasp physics, the difference between solid and holographic objects. Consciousness-incarnate apparently learns about the externals of this incarnation with skills brought from elsewhere.

Such early demonstrations of knowledge could come only from a holistic, multisense understanding of reality intrinsic to human nature. Much of this multilevel knowledge becomes suppressed by the focus of consciousness required for life in the phenomenal world and by self-limiting cultural patterns. This brief survey of what we seem to understand leaves us with questions that require further study by frontier researchers: What do newborns know? How is taking on human form self-limiting, and must it always carry the price of diminishing awareness? How can we maintain and enhance this broader awareness?

Many children report memories of specific earlier lifetimes, while others frequently have a sense of having already experienced a place or social situation. Much of the so-called fantasy life of children is surprisingly like material from other lives or times. However, society discourages such interpretations, and growing individuals soon forget their memories. Enough research has been done to convince many that the self does bring earlier experiences to bear on its interpretation of and reactions to this life. It is a hypothesis worth wide-scale testing. If all of us in this incarnation could consciously bring to the table previous individual histories, it would add richness to the communing that occurs with our fellow travelers in this space-time.

Otherness

Why is otherness so crucial to selfhood? To a large extent, intraspecies relationships determine how we evolve in a lifetime. The universe has unknown numbers of species and many forms of beingness, but all of them, like humans, live in communities of similar beings who mutually shape one another. These relationships with other form the basis for much, if not most of our self-learning. To live more consciously and take fuller advantage of their capacities requires that humans better understand how we are differentiated from myriad levels of otherness and, at the same time, what we have in common.

The individual's DNA "fingerprint" has only one chance in one trillion of having five matching sites on the estimated 30,000-plus genes in the 23 human chromosomes, yet every material particle in one's body has recently been in someone else or in the common resource base. (Although genes use only four letters, AGCT, the four are used in various sequences about 3.2 billion times in the human genome.) At the same time, nothing we think or feel is totally hidden from others. Until humans recognize and consciously sense these connections, we will not succeed in reducing alienation and its accompanying violence at all levels of society. Terrorism, ethnic violence, domestic abuse, and generalized anger and hostility are the results of failure to appreciate how all beings are part of one another. We must realize that such "relatingness" is more than just physical; it includes memories, energies, and things. The aspects of otherness in the three-faceted model are illustrated in the following graphic.

Otherness		
Subtle Energies	Other Beings	Collective Consciousness
&	Plants/Animals	
		&
Emotions	Matenergy	Information

In the reciprocating nature of self and other, we can choose to set the inner limits of selfhood, but we cannot impose its outer definitions on another. Therefore, the outer boundaries of selfhood have to be negotiated with otherness. The following graphic, used in psychology texts to demonstrate how one's mind-set affects whether one sees a vase or two faces, also helps illustrate this aspect of negotiating self-definition. The selfhood-otherness boundary space, while setting us apart from each other, also binds us together. The binding subtle energy fills the gap between the profile we have drawn for self and the configuration jointly drawn with others around us.

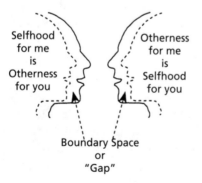

Selfhood for me is Otherness for you

Otherness for me is Selfhood for you

Boundary Space or "Gap"

If we want to change the inner boundary, we can unilaterally pull in toward the core (dotted line), but if we want to change the joint boundary, both of us (and many others) have to agree. One reason we have so many explicit roles (housewife, lawyer, teacher, parent, etc.) is that their conventions simplify the process of joint personality definition, removing a large degree of ambiguity and negotiation. That the fundamental definition of a personality is jointly defined can be illustrated by the fact that even the most individualistic artist's enduring sense of being talented depends on the receptivity of others (posthumously if not contemporaneously).

Consequently, although human development involves self-learning, selfhood is essentially a shared experience—as in the reciprocity between colleagues, lovers, parents and children, and teachers and students. To progress consciously is to grow with others, with each conscious being responsible for deciding where she or he fits on the spectrum of self-definition/other-directedness.

At one pole of that spectrum, we define self almost exclusively in opposition to the behavior and boundaries of others. At the opposite pole, we become essentially what others expect. Carl Jung labeled this polarity "introversion-extroversion." All life continually attempts to balance between these two poles. Persons tending to counter-formation, in contrast to con-formation, are considered to have "hard edges," a term descriptive of boundaries that counter the expectations of one's neighbors. Given the variety of human personalities, to be effective in intimate relationships or successful in social organizations requires learning how to flexibly range along the spectrum of self- versus other-directedness. But ultimately, we have to recognize that we cannot be all things to all people at all times, and that is where self-definition is crucial to personal integrity.

Otherness can be seen in terms of concentric circles, with the distance from self an indication of the other person or situation's degree of relevance and level of importance. Superimposed over such circles can be archetypal patterns of relationship that, like roles, define conventional ideas of similarities and differences. Terms like "family," "kinship," "community," and "neighbors" usually indicate similarity, while attributes like sex, race, and social classes highlight differences. Living consciously requires that we look at both categories more deeply, giving up the stereotypes for authentic being-to-being connection and communication.

Reality in the twenty-first century has increased by orders of magnitude the complexity of the otherness that must be consciously attended. In addition to the natural environment of Earth and all its species, we must now add ABs and all the inner dimensions. Further, we now recognize that the reach of our interactions literally touches the edges of the universe.

The importance of healthy joint boundaries and supportive circles becomes clear when a group's internal bonds are externally challenged. Similarly, when an individual's relations with others are under stress, and that person has insufficient inner focus to maintain equilibrium, destructive behavior results. School shootings and other forms of retaliatory violence result from just this deficiency in definition of the self-other boundary. The three-faceted model explains why such physical acting out can occur without apparent external provocation, as follows:

Alienating, destructive psychic (energeial) and attitudinal (noumenal) forces released covertly by individuals or groups damage the society's field of consciousness just as a bomb explosion injures the physical (phenomenal) world. Constructive reciprocity must be maintained in all three domains for a healthy community. To understand the current wave of "lashing-out" ripping apart community and nation, we need only to look for psychic holes in the conscious connections among the members of these social units. Large-scale engagement in emotional and intellectual activities that reinforce the inner connections of human beings could avoid such overt violence. Simply put, if we collectively heal our inner life, the public one will change.

Peter Breggin, a psychiatrist who has studied human emotional problems by looking beyond the blinders of his profession, believes the psychology of an individual is a function of the psychology of the whole community.[5] Clearly grasping the reciprocating dynamic between selfhood and otherness, Breggin concludes that traditional psychiatry too frequently perpetuates a severance of the bonds of effective group consciousness. The use of drugs, electroshock, and surgery, in his view, damages the connecting web of consciousness rather than heals it. He is correct.

Alienation from the whole social organism contributes to the creation of individual violence (evident in internecine warfare of gang members and violent acts of "loners"), and only the whole can heal it. Healing of communities starts with a conscious choice by its members to expand their inner sense of relatedness. Hillary Rodham Clinton's book *It Takes a Village* is intuitively based on the understanding that true self-awareness involves full awareness of community, and self-actualization requires other-actualization.

Personal Choice

Otherness begins at the point along the selfhood-otherness spectrum where an individual's obvious control ends. The human ability to maneuver up to that point is in many respects analogous to the capabilities of a cellular telephone: our movements are practically unimpeded; we send signals simultaneously with others; any one of us can contact any other on the planet if both parties desire; but each has the choice to answer the call or not.

Communication employing the subtle senses works in the same way: at least two beings must open the channel. We send out a call and receive responses from those with whom it resonates. We receive the busy signal of those who choose not to tune in. The scope of eventual communication depends on the intent and skill of the initiator (caller) and the willingness of other beings to engage (pick up the phone). The human's ability to exercise these choices provides the potential for reciprocal access through the subtle senses to any part and, ultimately, to the whole universe, through (to change metaphors) the "cosmic Internet."

The more we want to increase our conscious awareness quotient (the CQ discussed in chapter 7), the more we must engage in such multilevel interaction with others. Conscious, positive understanding seems infinite when we open ourselves in constructive engagement with other beings. Respect, like love, is infinite: the more one gives away, the more one gets. There is evidence that psi abilities like remote viewing increase as we open ourselves to different levels of otherness.

(This may be why some intuitives and remote viewers frequently become more active in social issues.)

The key to self-learning and individual growth is finding an appropriate level of openness between selfhood and otherness. Defining and realizing that balance is a daily goal of conscious beings. To be truly harmonious, we do not give up individuality, but enhance it with the help of others. Living according to our core needs and allowing others to do the same recognizes that the individual's desires are only one factor in the algebra of cosmic consciousness; as any student knows, both sides have to balance for the equation to work. The following four sections discuss contributions to healthy inter-being relationships.

Support Others

We have seen how otherness is essential for developing selfhood. But the best assistance others can offer the developing self is the opportunity for self-learning. The newborn may be mentally awakened by the more conscious beings around it. We adults can draw its attention with playfulness and soothe it with nurturing, but ultimately we help the new being learn how to balance between reception and expression, between venturing out and drawing into itself. Wise elders offer both stimulation and repose, but allow the infant to learn how to select between them at will. The child's early experiences either reinforce innate tendencies to experimentation or negate them, shaping a being's lifelong approach to self-learning. (As with IQ and EQ, early experiences influence one's CQ score.)

Insights derived from the three-faceted model have implications for our current theories about social behavior, particularly so-called antisocial behavior. Humans literally do not think or do anything alone: no thought or action occurs in isolation from other beings and our planetary habitat.[6] Consequently, our fate is to function like members of an improvisational jazz ensemble, playing the instruments we have in concert with other members, agreeing in advance to a set of chord changes, then making up parts in relation to each other in progression through the set. When the rhythms and harmonies "work," the outcome is music; when any element is off, the result is discordant sound. Therefore, any accurate analysis of one's discordant behavior involves both the self, as one "musician," and its multifaceted relationship with the whole group.

Any interaction between beings involves some form of energy. Even mental or verbal exchanges focus subtle energy (energeia) that in turn affects another's performance. If we unthinkingly project our shadows (the negative parts of ourselves that we ignore) on others, we project an energetic burden onto their role-playing. Public leaders are, to a large degree, either weighed down or uplifted by the subtle energies focused upon them by others. We can support more positive behavior in leaders by projecting constructive energy fields in their direction. The place to start political reform lies in the subtle force fields of our most intimate relations, whence it will ripple out in larger circles.

Individuals tend to perceive reality through their own constructs of selfhood, interpreting otherness through projecting them on it. To make our sense of reality more than a subjective attribution, there has to be confirmation from another being. Since the reality of otherness is a collaborative projection of respective selfhoods, so-called objective reality can only be a function of intersubjective agreement between selfhoods. Recognizing such a subjective and changing interpretation of external reality, useful science and effective politics involve continuous testing, modifications of assumptions, and repeated validations of what we think we know. The same principle of continual mutual validation supports self-learning interpersonal relationships.

Ignore Surface Differences

All species have their unique energy patterns in each of the three facets. Qualities of beingness include differing profiles of frequencies, amplitudes, and wavelengths on any spectrum. Such differing combinations would account for the existence of beings quite unlike us in outward appearance. For example, when people use the term "beings of light" to describe contacts in NDE or subtle-sense perceptions, they are obviously referring to more amorphous forms of beingness. The range of feasible combinations may be almost infinite, including familiar ones like ghosts, aliens, and angels. Humanity should not be surprised at the varieties of form (costumes) exhibited by the cosmic siblings to be encountered by coming generations.

Before we as a species can be ready to engage with advanced species from elsewhere in the universe, we must learn the lessons of commonality on one planet. If we cannot be mature at home, there is little reason to believe we will behave better elsewhere. Following are the implications of some "real" differences among humans and some "real" implications of differences that are only a matter of social convention.

Problems arise when individuals and groups alienate themselves from others by mentally and emotionally interpreting different "costumes" as the polarity of "outsiders/insiders." These judgments may involve polarizing distinctions in race, language, religion, sex, politics, economic status, dialect, life style, eating habits, or any one of scores of other categories. Every one of these costumes has, at some time and place, led to hostile behavior against the group perceived as "outsiders."

A poignant example is the brutality of the "ethnic cleansing" perpetrated by Serbs against Slavic Muslims and by Serbs and Croats against each other in the former Yugoslavia, where centuries of mutual hostilities-in-consciousness underlie the abuses of the 1990s. In that region, where there are few discernible physical and behavioral differences between neighbors, the religious costume alone is used as a pretext to commit atrocities of pillage, rape, and murder. This behavior, and examples like it in all parts of the world, can be explained in terms of energetics among conscious beings.

Violence against "outsiders" is the result of a two-step process. The first step labels others as sufficiently different to cause mental alienation. This deliberate act of conscious classification results in distortions of both the matenergy and subtle energy flows in the direction of the "outsiders." Within those doing the judging, the experience bottles up constructive energy that needs to be expressed to balance the output of negative energy. (Remember that the Principle of Rhythm requires periods of near equilibrium.) The recipients experience the distortions in subtle-energy flows as invasive, subliminal turbulence. This two-way stress occurs on the energeial and noumenal levels, even if the physical manifestations are not immediately obvious.

In the second step, the "insider" decides to take action against the "outsider" in order to relieve the internal energetic stress and return to equilibrium. In reaching this conclusion, one gives oneself "permission" to rampage. Attacks, looting, rape, murder, and other forms of mayhem, whether verbal or economic, result in a temporary dissipation of the clogged energy flows. There is an orgiastic release at one or more levels, returning the violators temporarily to a sense of ease and harmony.

But since the fundamental problem—the conscious denial of mutually beneficial interconnectedness—keeps the subtle-energy channels dysfunctional, the pressure soon rebuilds and the same illusory remedy is tried again. Ironically, this kind of "senseless" violence occurs only among conscious beings with minds capable of assigning labels or calling names. (The *Course in Miracles* very appropriately teaches that "only a stranger can evoke fear; call him brother and he comes into your heart.")

This model of the origins of violent behavior does not support the thesis that such negative outbursts are caused by genetic and chemical imbalances, or environmental pressures and social disadvantage or misfortune, although these factors can influence the degree of dysfunction. Thus, violence from within the homes of the "best in society" should not surprise us. This is the reason it happens every day in modern society.

Only by honoring the common bonds of consciousness, through an open acceptance of the reciprocal mental, energetic, and physical exchanges, can conscious beings avoid the explosion of internecine violence. Effective solutions may include conscious reopenings of the flows between beings by removal of the divisive label or by involvement in friendly games (some as simple as midnight basketball) and rituals that dislodge the thwarted energetic exchanges. Increasing external pressure or controls will only exaggerate the imbalance. So-called wars on behaviors that deviate from group norms have an opposite effect from that desired. Why have social and political leaders not recognized this? Could it be due the their vested interests in perpetuation of discord?

Overtly destructive behaviors differ from more subtle conflicts of ideas and emotions only in degree. Society pays too little attention to the milder end of the behavior-emotion-idea spectrum because of the lack of understanding of the physical impact of conflicts in the subtle realm. Since the dynamics of the subtle soon become manifest in the physical, we need to get as concerned about how people relate on the inner realms as we do about the way we engage on a physical level. Given the similarly patterned nature of the two, we can begin to cope with the overt problems of conflict by experimenting with how we relate to others on a verbal and feeling basis. The way to "civilize" undesirable behaviors is not to ban or suppress them, but to help channel the negative subtle energy involved into constructive forms. A simple exercise can prove the point.

The next time you encounter a minor frustration with anyone, try perceiving that person as a cosmic being like yourself. Recognize, through your inner eye, that she or he has the same essential attributes and powers you have. Think of his or her glowing selfhood, shaped by consciousness and infused with the same cosmic energy that courses through your chakras. Sense the pulsations of that energy channeled by his or her unique costume of incarnation, derived from the same reservoir of potentialities whence your differing qualities, skills, and aspirations. Express the rising pulse of energy as a compliment or encouragement for some specific trait in the other. Then sense the shift taking place in your internal energy balance and overt behaviors. As you see the other's behavior shift, reflect on the reasons for it. (Apply the same principle to stressed cells in your body and see what happens to the pain.)

To heal the divisions caused by the costumes listed earlier, we need only to review each one and observe that the differences so immediately important to us are of little significance on the cosmic scale of our existence. Below is an analysis of the phenomenon of race that reveals the lack of justification for its use in fomenting social divisiveness. Its use for psychic alienation is no more appropriate than gender, linguistic, religious, or any other such differences.

Currently we have not been able to explain satisfactorily why the human species has different races—another huge gap in scientific knowledge we choose to ignore. Theology, with its ad hominem assertions, attributes racial differences to an intentional act of God, one that justifies prejudice. Evolutionists offer two equally unsatisfactory theories. One is that the three basic races evolved from different subspecies in separate locations. Such speculation is undermined by the DNA evidence that traces all humankind back to a common gene pool.

The other evolutionist view holds that mutations in the genes shaping skin color were a response to different climates. The time frame of the DNA tree is too short for so much gene mutation (microevolution) to result from environmental factors. There is no evidence to preclude the presence of light-skinned peoples in hot, humid, or desert regions during the time scale presumed necessary. Racial differences also include varying facial features and body types that could not be accounted for by geographical variations in sunlight.

DNA studies now reveal that a wider range of genetic differences occurs among members of any local group than occurs between races. Thus, no species-related basis exists for the racial categories we use; they are based on human value judgments.

Although no definitive evidence of the origins of human races has emerged, at least one explanation—no less well documented than other theories—has the merits of being consistent with what humans are now capable of doing. Sitchin and Javier Cabrera offer a possible explanation as to why all human beings share the same basic gene pool with only recently developed racial differences. AB gene-splicers may have performed operations on slightly different families of hominids, resulting in the physical differences we now label as racial. Or if various ABs performed such genetic experiments somewhat independently, they could have, by chance or design, altered a few gene sequences that resulted in racial differences. In either case, racial differences make no contribution to IQ, EQ, or CQ and behavior, and remain substantively irrelevant among cosmic beings. They are analogous to differences in the colors of automobiles—immaterial to performance and worth.

Plants and animals have significant differences in relation to humans and more advanced beings, but they too are part of the indivisible web of cosmic consciousness. The way we choose to relate to them, just as the way in which we relate to advanced beings, joins the never-ending circle of cause and effect. Cruelty expressed toward any species by individuals or collectives will come back to haunt the whole and all of its constituents, while nurturing redounds to everyone's benefit. Although the costumes of consciousness may vary considerably, all beings are equal players in the drama of our universe.

Enlarge the Family Circle

Between 1950 and 2000, many people reported dramatic experiences with nonhuman beings. As we have seen, stories from most cultures indicate there have been such contacts with other realms throughout history. Examples of this aspect of otherness have been given in several sections of this book, but a selective review here reminds us that others from outside our mundane realm have historically shaped the lives of Earth beings and are likely to continue to do so, even if indirectly. Self-realization requires that we extend our concept of family to include them.

Many details about AB activity in the Near East have interesting parallels in Somerset, a county in southern England. The name Somerset itself may have been derived from Sumeria (land of summer and perpetual youth) around 5,000 to 6,000 B.P. The Druids apparently knew of the extraterrestrial Annunaki twelve-part zodiac and Sumerian astronomy. The name for King Arthur may have derived from Arcturus, the Great Bear of the Big Dipper and the brightest northern star.

Uncannily similar to the twelve tribes of Israel and the twelve tribes of Delphi, Glastonbury was divided into twelve Hides (1,440 acres each), which recall the twelve houses of the zodiac. Ancient Delphi and Glastonbury, both sited on springs with magic waters, were considered communications links to advanced beings. Some interpret the Glastonbury myths in spiritual or etheric energy terms, but they are equally plausible as accounts of AB-type activity.[7]

In the original Celtic language, *Iniswitrin* (now Glastonbury) meant "the isle of crystal." It was known as the location of a crystal palace (possibly a spaceship) in a fairy fort. In fact, all the area was known as the land of the fairies (nonhuman beings). Glastonbury was reportedly ruled by Gwynn ap Nudd, a being who came from deep underground. As the story goes, Saint Collen confronted Gwynn in the fairy fort and then later disappeared for a time in his palace cum space vehicle. In a parallel English legend, Guinevere, like Persephone of Greek legend, was abducted to another world. These stories are not unlike some told by modern-era abductees, but we have no easy way to confirm differing interpretations.

Whoever the ABs were, humans, co-existing with them in many locales, saw these beings as natural members of their cosmic family. In a period of suppression of such views, popular movie classics like *Star Trek* and *ET*, television programs on angels, and modern science fiction help keep alive these ideas of an expanded cosmic family. Until a new public consensus develops, we are left with isolated and disparate individual and small-group reports of communications with other members of our cosmic family. Without a generally accepted theory to explain these experiences, society is subjected to much misinformation and distortion of meaning in these interdimensional contacts. Some of the books on AB contacts and communications referenced here help to place such individual experiences into a larger family context.[8] Humans currently engaged in various forms of communication with other realms should keep in mind that such beings are shaped by the intellectual and cultural histories of whatever galaxy or dimension in which they exist. Therefore, the reception of a message from one of those beings via channeling, direct contact, or other media does not mean the human recipient has been given the cosmic truth; it is only talk within the family.

Communications with other realms should be taken for what they are: expressions of individual beings or groups sharing their idiosyncratic views with their human cousins. Reading, hearing, or being a channel for such communications sets no one apart: we are all channels, exchanging data continuously with beings and dimensions with whom we share a fundamental reality. The cosmic ordinariness of all this (the multidimensionality of conscious beingness, the multiplicity of messages and channels, and the inescapable links of any being with all others) should make it easy to avoid overly dramatizing any particular message or interpretation.

Polls in the new century reveal that over 50 percent (an increase of several percentage points over five years ago) of Americans believe UFOs are real, and about one-third think official contact has already been made with aliens. Although increasing numbers of humans now acknowledge their membership in a cosmic family, for many to take such a step would be a threatening experience. Even so, many members of our Earth family may have already made it.

In the early 1990s, the Roper Organization published a report entitled *Unusual Personal Experiences*.[9] It came to the incredible conclusion that, based on its sampling techniques, perhaps 2 percent of the American population—more than 5 million people—have had experiences consistent with a UFO abduction history. (Note that the term "abductees" excludes contactees—those who have had an encounter but have not been taken aboard a craft for physical and mental examinations.) Roper used as criteria for assuming abduction the subjective impressions given in response to survey questions.[10]

Extrapolating from the U.S. sample's responses to the world at large would indicate more than 100 million living abductees. Numbers of this magnitude dwarf even the most speculative estimates of UFO activity. Could the polling instruments be faulty, or could the phenomenon of shared memories discussed earlier explain such large numbers? Regardless of the ultimate explanation, humans are more and more counting themselves as members of a cosmic family.

Though the memories of many alleged abductees may be attributed to the current widespread media coverage or to shared memories, the impact is the same. Humans are choosing to redefine their concept of the universal family of beings.

Reconnect with Nature

As recognition of a larger conscious reality causes us to redefine ourselves in relation to other species, it also modifies the manner in which we relate to everything else that we have called "nature." Beyond our contact with specific beings, we are in constant communication with expressions of consciousness apparently emanating from both organic and inanimate sources. These communications with otherness involve something as complex as crop circles in the grain fields of England and as simple as flashes of intuition about IRS regulations.[11] Both examples represent different ends of the spectrum, from complex bilateral communication between species to unilateral forays of a local mind into a specific database. Both appear to illustrate interactions of human consciousness with the external environment for our benefit. Straightforward examples, like the dowser finding water or the shaman identifying an appropriate healing herb, provide instant help.

There is much evidence of the capacities of individuals to access information through the subtle senses that brings to their attention dangers or the need for constructive change. Common examples include previews of possible disasters or accidents. Some believe that communications involving complex formations in crops may point toward salvation for our species, somewhat analogous to the dreams Moses had that led to the survival of a nation. Could it be that crop circles involve human interaction with the plants?

I did some field research on this theme in the early 1990s. In August 1991, a crop formation resembling a human brain was found in a field of ripe grain near Froxfield, England.[12] Some speculated that this pattern was a warning from our collective inner selves to reform our selfish interaction with nature. Along the same vein, the repetitive snail formations in the crop of 1992 were seen as warnings that we were reacting too slowly—a snail's pace is not quick enough. Such interpretations are not susceptible to validation without talking to the creator of the circle. (Even where hoaxers are involved, they may unconsciously channel messages from the collective consciousness.) And what if the creator is only the consciousness of the crops themselves?

Could a more general self-learning process be at work here? Assume at some level a critical mass of people sense the impact of our behavior on the material world and know corrective action is required. Could their anxiety signals alert collective thinking in the noumena and the energeia, with the effect being a subtle-energy reaction in the crops, manifested as crop formations?

During the last twenty years, most of these patterns have appeared in fields in England, but there have been specimens on every continent, including my home state of Tennessee before and during 2000. One possibility is the crops themselves may be able to interact with more finesse than we give them credit for. (Remember the earlier-mentioned work with plants by Backster and the German Institute for Resonance Therapy.) If plants react at a cellular level in experiments, consideration should be given to conscious species reactions.

A crop formation, appearing in a field near Cambridge, England, in August 1991, clearly replicated the form of the Mandelbrot Set (shown below) generated in the 1960s by IBM's Benoit Mandelbrot. Through mathematics and computer graphics, Mandelbrot was able to depict the relationship of chaos to form. The fall into matter (a field of wheat) by a form (the Mandelbrot pattern) may demonstrate to us the potential that focused human consciousness has for creative interventions in nature. Both the process (human concern possibly manifested through plants) and the content (the inherent order in apparent chaos) deserve further research.

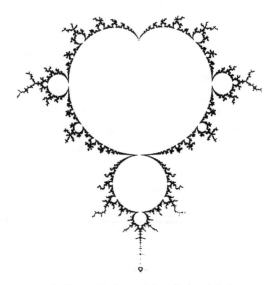

A Crop Circle as Mandlebrot Set

As of this writing, crop circle researchers have not been able to develop foolproof criteria to distinguish an authentic crop formation from a hoaxed one. But ignoring all of them due to some known hoaxes loses a precious opportunity for insight into our living planet. Many formations are associated with lights and shapes in the sky usually identified with ABs, but the UFOs may simply have been attracted to the phenomenon and not been creators of it.

In the summer of 1992, in an attempt to test the hypothesis that we can interact with the crops through the medium of consciousness, I designed an experiment to determine if we could influence the formation of particular shapes in the grain fields of a selected area in England.[13] Around midnight, a group of colleagues and I meditated at length on the same image (a bow tie, known only to us) on top of Silbury Hill. Some days later, a formation appeared in the field where we had focused our vision, with a bow tie included among the several designs composing the formation. Even though hoaxers made unproven claims to the formation, our experience was not unlike the sequence involving a letter Martyn Hughes sent to the *New Scientist* in August 1991. In it Hughes asked, "How long before we see a Mandelbrot Set (in a crop formation)?"—and a design like that shown above appeared a few days later.

A connection between human consciousness and the so-called crop circles may be only illustrative of the many possible interactions between individuals or groups and the vibrant nature of our cosmic habitat. Industrial society has forgotten the tradition of such human interaction as manifested in Native American rain dances, spring fertility rites, harvest festivals, hunting prayers, and so on. If the human mind can influence the pattern of falls by plastic balls in a cold mechanical cabinet—such are Robert Jahn and Brenda Dunne's findings in the Princeton Engineering Anomalies Research (PEAR) Laboratory at Princeton University[14]—what is the potential for a powerful exchange of influence between us and other living systems? If we can engage particles in a dance into and out of form, is it possible to consciously obtain responses from weather patterns and other aspects of our habitat? Wilhelm Reich reported success at producing rainfall with his deliberate focus of orgone (energeia). Ted Owens's psychic intent was reportedly associated with several dramatic weather events.[15]

Self-Learning Requires Testing

In the discussion of selfhood in relation to otherness in a self-learning universe composed of multiple conscious beings, two assumptions are implicit: (1) No single source of all knowledge can be controlled by any one being, and no beings have totally exclusive knowledge. (2) Any being has potential access to all knowledge through one's individual or group experience. But each being has the responsibility to distinguish between uniquely personal interpretations of that experience and what others would consider a valid interpretation. The following paragraphs illustrate my thinking about these two assumptions.

With regard to the first one, our self-initiation as Solarians requires us to recognize that one myth has kept us like passive children—the belief in a separate being as a magical source of all knowledge and control. Divine Father Gods, Holy Spirits, and Atmans/Brahmans, or Grand Couples for that matter, have not been revealed to be directly involved in human life in any confirmable way. In all the world's belief systems, attributions of such involvement are only unvalidated assumptions. The AB-intervention and multidimensional-being communication hypotheses reasonably explain how such ungrounded ideas of supernaturalism developed. Nevertheless, supernaturalism has served humanity as a crutch to evade responsibility for conscious self-management.

Self-learning and self-management place squarely on our own shoulders the responsibility for validating assumptions before we call them facts. Abraham, Buddha, Moses, Mohammed, Jesus, Edgar Cayce, Sai Baba, Rudolf Steiner, Albert Einstein, and Nikola Tesla may have benefited from insightful communications with other realms, but so have millions of others. If the universe is an integral organism and we are true microcosms of the whole, then any of us can receive messages from other realms and their validity can be tested in this realm.

The messages or reputed revelations of individuals like the above are inherently no more true than those received by many others. The value of each insight depends on the source (how wise was the nonhuman originator?) and its validation in Earth reality (can we test its implication in the space-time?). No longer can we evade responsibility for testing alleged universal principles by labeling them "truth" attributed to an invisible "god." Received "wisdom" cannot be considered definitive just because it appears to be from another realm. That a message is believed to be from an "angel" does not relieve humans of the responsibility to validate it on this plane. Knowledge from the noumena merits our consideration only when it may be based on broader experience than humans have and perhaps has stood the test of time in other realms. If it meets these criteria, I have no doubt it can stand the test of human scrutiny and efforts at confirmation.

The earlier discussion of the Roper poll on alleged abductions by nonhuman beings in our cosmic family is also relevant to the second assumption mentioned above. Since the end of World War II, the numbers of reported cases of abductions have increased at an almost geometric rate. Why should this be the case when there has not been an equal rate of increase in the discovery of actual physical evidence of AB visits? Perhaps there is another explanation: many people may be sharing the memories of one individual's experience (cryptomnesia). (Recall that shared memories are not the same as false memories.) If all memories exist in the noumena, it could account for the possibility that memories get shared, confusing people about whether or not they actually had a particular experience.

Many of us engage in a process of circular reasoning that could account for such an increase in unconfirmable abduction/contact reports. In the absence of validating physical evidence, it is plausible to conclude people are reporting experiences other than their own. Avoiding faulty, circular reasoning is central to a valid self-learning process. To see how it works, I use the case of abduction reports as an illustration, but the conclusions apply to all ways of knowing in a three-faceted universe.

Abduction reports come in three categories: (1) recall bolstered by clear physical evidence; (2) memory without loss of consciousness; and (3) lost memories recovered from the "unconscious." Abduction researchers have identified a reasonable number of self-contained cases with corroborating physical experience. They have described a larger number of cases where people report conscious awareness of abduction, but exhibit no physical symptoms and have no other objective evidence. But the largest number of cases come from "recovered memories." (Some of the memories are recalled spontaneously while awake or after dreams, but most recall is stimulated by hypnosis or therapy.) The problem arises when all in the third category are considered equal to the first two.

Many researchers seem to treat reports of unconscious memories elicited by hypnosis or other guided techniques as confirmations of ordinary reality. Some concerned about process withhold certain details from public reports for validation purposes, but given the porous noumenal field, that does not guarantee the absence of contamination. Since data can be exchanged through the subtle senses, the correlation with "unpublicized memories" should not be considered a validation of the reported experience.

The circular reasoning process (shown below) has no provision for external validation. When there is internal consistency between one confirmable report and many other noumenal-based memories, the latter are automatically assumed to represent an actual event. Even some psychosomatic and psychological symptoms could have third-party-memory explanations, but with this circular reasoning they could be interpreted as confirmation of a "recalled," even past-life, memory. Thus, the misleading loop feeds itself: repetition by more and more people of similar reports is taken as confirmation of actual events.

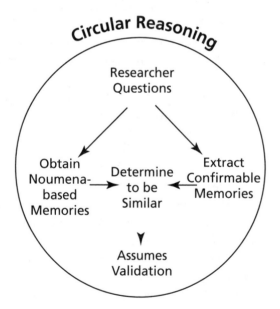

Self-conscious care must be taken to discern the difference between what is our own confirmable experience and what is not. Since such explicit filtering is not possible in a hypnotic state, the researcher must build in external controls. If the researcher takes the material literally and tells the subject's waking mind that jointly they have accessed reality, a susceptible person will accept it as truth without subjecting it to thoughtful external validation.

To be convincing, analysis of abduction reports must overcome the problem of generally available, noumenal memory. The existence of a common pool of AB-encounter images, accessible to anyone who is attuned to the same vibration as the participants in the originating event, cannot be dismissed. As we have seen earlier, individuals can tap into this common pool through dreams, fantasies, meditation, telepathic efforts, and hypnosis. This lesson applies to all information gained through the subtle senses. It must ultimately be confirmed with phenomenal evidence or shared testing by people outside the above process.

With the above-described flawed process, the self can obtain from the noumena information originally attached to the ordinary or artificially created experience of another, and act as if the information were its own. This process leads to erroneous conclusions in all fields of science as well as religion.

It is important to remember that the process of sharing ideas in the noumenal field also has advantages. Mutual awareness of values and shared intentions to accomplish a desirable goal can be seen as positive. But the unfiltered sharing of false information and destructive ideas is another matter.

My interpretations of my inner self are my affair, but it is crucial for self-regulation to externally validate my experiences with otherness. It requires seeking the help of disinterested others to confirm my own perceptions. Without such self-discipline, false and misleading beliefs held by us as individuals lead to distortions in the effectiveness of the overall universe's self-learning process.

Self-Aware Interdependence

Conscious living requires awareness, not only of the invisible web that binds all beings to each other, but of the different levels at which it connects us. Every "event" between an individual selfhood and otherness is no more than a defining point on a continual flow simultaneously involving all three facets of all beings. The material (phenomena), emotional (energeia), and informational (noumena) bodies of all beings engage without ceasing in the three-level vibrations that change according to their natural rhythms. Therefore, when we examine or discuss a specific event, its isolation from the ongoing flow is artificial; it is embedded in a larger context of change, because reality never stops.

For example, in the case of a "shared-memory," where another's reality is made part of one's own reality by appropriating the other's memories, the borrower subconsciously incorporates (take into one's own corpus) not only the other's ideas, but also their emotions and physical reactions. When self-responsibility for personal validation is abdicated, we deceive ourselves and in turn mislead others.

The successful dance between selfhood and otherness always demands personal responsibility. We have a choice, whether to be a leader or follower in the testing of knowledge. One either primarily creates and tests original experiences or shares in those created by others. Every situation requires a combination of both, but choice focuses on the degree to which one is dominant over the other. With the Principles of Polarity and Rhythm in play, we alternate between them. Given continual self-other interactions, successful living depends on self-aware balancing of these polarities in an inescapable field of interdependence.

Our state of interdependence with others involves a rhythmic dynamic that manifests in gender cycles of giving and taking, passing through a neutral phase in between, like the reversing of electrical charges or the phase changes of a magnet. In the romantic's vocabulary, we easily become both the lover and the beloved, shifting roles at will. The polar impulses to merge and to separate have equal force, with the latter totally dominant at birth and the former at death. How we play the yin and yang aspects of many different roles in the changing rhythms of life will determine the nature of the being we become.

As science moves beyond a biological theory of psychology and a psychoanalytic model that invented unconfirmable sub-components of personalities to account for anomalous behaviors, we will approach psychological theory building and research from the perspective of interdependence with at least three aspects. The psychology of the future will start with the study of indivisible, nonhomocentric consciousness, then move on to local minds (incarnate beings) and how they depend on and integrate with the whole. Practical psychology will focus on self-directed management of personal awareness and its interdependence with otherness.

All the details of our interdependence with any one facet of otherness currently elude us. Resorting to metaphor, we see interdependence like the force of love between beings. Never completely without its presence, we become fully aware of it only when we are in physical proximity or deliberately focusing on each other. Although moments of awareness of the unbroken web of life-shaping connections may appear in a serendipitous manner, these two-way flows do not occur by chance. They are always operative and available for self-conscious use.

With the Principle of Cause and Effect, we can feed ideas into the noumena and observe their effects coming back to us. Conversely, as we express the need for information or assistance, it comes to us. The surprise should be not that it comes, but that the source (otherness over which we think we have no control) actually cooperates with us. As we "feed" others ideas and subtle energies, they in turn "feed" us. There is no better evidence of the human power of co-creation in a self-learning universe.

After I became interested in noting such "coincidences," my ideas on Third World economic development, still in draft for future columns I was writing for the newspaper *Washington International*, also surfaced in other organizations or publications with no direct access to my work. As I was following a path of psychic development at the time, I became impressed by my powers of remote influence. Then it dawned on me, it was a two-way street: these ideas were equally "in the air," "floated" by some unknown being. Given the interdependence between realms, we can find subtle energies or emotional fields in the air to serve us as easily as we can find ideas.

What an empowering insight, to realize that all the ideas and energy we need for a twenty-first-century renaissance exist already in the noumena and energeia, awaiting our attunement with them. However, their realization requires our self-involvement in the process. Some in the New Age movement erroneously tout the idea that mind, exercised through visualization and positive thinking, can unilaterally influence, cause, induce, or persuade matter and other beings to behave differently than they would if left to their own processes.

This hypothesis is based on the implicit, and false, assumption that our mind and matter, and other minds, are separate, where the others respond to our more powerful unilateral communications in some mechanical way. This concept represents an advance over the conventional scientific paradigm in that it presupposes that the local mind can influence matter and other beings. But in all other respects, it is a variation on Cartesian dualism. In an interdependent universe there can be no unilateral flow of influence.

The Hermetic Principles provide for no dualisms, either at the microcosmic or social levels. As we have seen, the proof of such unity can be found in modern physics, where quantum theory suggests an undivided context surrounding any event or phenomenon. Even a scientific experiment cannot be divided into separate components; the experimenter as observer helps shape the outcomes at the same time she or he is constrained by its boundaries. One personality cannot exist independently of other persons. Our vocabulary makes it difficult to describe the process because we define as distinct such states as brutality, love, hunger, heat, solitude, maturity, and so on, when they are really points on many continua, facets on the same cosmic diamond. We need new metaphors for these interdependent processes if we wish keep them in the forefront of our consciousness.

The image of the dowser provides a useful metaphor for grasping how one can obtain and use noumenal information in the material realm. Dowsing generally implies the process of locating water or material objects through an inner sensing reflected in the movement of rods held in the dowser's hands. But dowsing can mean extending the field of a person's conscious awareness to access any data that already exist; the metascientific dowser opens herself to the multilayered vibrations from the desired object, person, event, or energy field. Dowsers of ideas can tune in to others' thoughts with their divining mental antennae. Reciprocity occurs when such dowsers—which we all are—have their own ideas picked up by others.

Another useful metaphor is the gardener who plants seeds, nurtures, and protects, yet depends on elements outside of self to determine if the right temperature, light, and moisture are provided for growth and maturation. Cosmic gardeners can take the initiative, respecting relevant principles like the Hermetic ones and others we discover, but must be in congruence with the vast otherness to ultimately enjoy the fruits of their labors.

To illustrate just how difficult it is to convey the essence of interdependence, even the Hermetic idea of cause and effect may seem to imply separateness and an independent flow of force. However, a cause and effect relationship in a totally unified field is different from one in a system of segmented parts. In an integral universe it is impossible to isolate a single, independent, causal relationship. While we do not have an understanding of how the interrelationships work, the subtle-sense mechanisms earlier hypothesized merit further study. They are a starting point for understanding what is likely to be multiple flows of interactions at work.

At this point, even if we do not understand how the subtle senses work, humans take advantage of them just as people enjoy television without knowledge of the electromagnetic spectrum. Humans can enhance their subtle abilities in the dark, so to speak, but great leaps are likely when we better grasp the principles involved. Two basic assumptions for research are (1) faster-than-light, but physically measurable links parallel to the electromagnetic spectrum (suggested in chapter 4), and (2) intangible connections involving no physically measurable force or interaction. John S. Bell is among the theorists who believe this inner reality must be vibrating faster than light. F. David Peat is among those who infer no activity as such is involved.

From the perspective of the Principle of Correspondence, one would expect subtle channels to be varied but comparable to those we know. Though radio waves were always present, now that they have been "discovered," we can use them to transmit sound. Gaining broader vision will likely "reveal" forces linking all beings and species and realms that we now mistakenly label "inert" (like the 90 percent of the brain we allegedly do not use, like the 90-plus percent of DNA we consider to be "junk," like the 95 percent of hypothesized matter in the universe that we can't locate).

Balance in the universe is sometimes obvious and sometimes subtle. Playing the ever changing boundary between selfhood and otherness is a part of that subtlety. Each being plays a dual "teacher/student" role in the dance between chaos and harmony. In our mutual relationship with the cosmos, we are acted upon as we act. As Raimon Panikkar says, "We leave our traces on things, and the things on us." This principle of reciprocal impact becomes increasingly more applicable the higher the level of consciousness (CQ) involved.

The insight of interdependent self-learning requires careful reflection during its application to daily events. If our focus is solely on the indivisible aspect of reality, ignoring the polarity of gender and its creative rhythm, we may find ourselves believing that all is preordained from the moment of chapter 1's Grand Rebirth. However, to remember that one is always a self-directing actor in a cosmic play reveals choices about finite (quantum) acts, each with its own short- and long-term cosmic implications. In the selection of one course of action over another to close a quantum gap, we exercise our bit of free will in the cosmic play of co-creation. Our individual selves thus co-design a reality that outlives our personal moment in space-time.

Notes

1. Anna F. Lemkow, *The Wholeness Principle* (Wheaton, IL: Quest Books, The Theosophical Publishing House, 1990).

2. Though these principles seem almost totally beyond an individual's influence, speculation grows that conscious beings acting in concert might have the power to influence the direction and degree of some of the universe's most constant constraints, such as the speed of light and gravity. Rupert Sheldrake, *Seven Experiments That Could Change the World* (New York: Riverhead Books, 1995).

3. Raimon Panikkar, *The Cosmotheandric Experience: Emerging Religious Consciousness* (Maryknoll, NY: Orbis Books, 1993).

4. Noel Langley, *Edgar Cayce on Reincarnation* (New York: Warner Books, 1967); Jane Roberts, *Adventures in Consciousness* (New York: Prentice-Hall, 1975).

5. Peter R. Breggin, *Toxic Psychiatry: Assault on the Brain with Drugs and Electroshock* (New York: St. Martin's, 1991).

6. James Lovelock, *Gaia* (New York: W.W. Norton, 1988).

7. John Michell, *New Light on the Ancient Mystery of Glastonbury* (Glastonbury, UK: Gothic Image Publications, 1990). Richard Leviton, *Searching for Arthur* (Charlottesville, VA: Hampton Roads Publishing, 1997). Barbara Marciniak, *Bringers of the Dawn: Teachings from the Pleiadians* (Santa Fe, NM: Bear & Co., 1992) and *Earth: Pleiadian Keys to the Living Library* (Santa Fe, NM: Bear & Co., 1995).

8. Katharina Wilson, *The Alien Jigsaw* (Portland, OR: Puzzle Publishing, 1995); Marcia Schafer, *Confessions of an Intergalactic Anthropologist* (Phoenix, AZ: Cosmic Destiny Press, 1999).

9. The Roper Organization, *Unusual Personal Experiences: An Analysis of the Data from Three National Surveys* (Las Vegas: Bigelow Holding Corporation, 1991).

10. The "right" responses were from case studies of two researchers (Budd Hopkins and David Jacobs, widely known counselors and authors of abduction-based books). Five types of unusual experiences revealed by their hypnotized subjects were codified into yes/no questions. Using them, Roper asked a random sample of respondents if they had: (1) awakened, paralyzed with a sense of a presence in the room, (2) believed they could not account for an hour or more of lost time, (3) felt as if they were flying through the air, (4) seen unusual lights in a room, or (5) discovered scars on the

body without a memory of how they got there. Hopkins and Jacobs concluded that persons who answered yes to at least four of these questions were probably abductees.

11. While working on both this text and my income tax return one day, I let my awareness wander as I contemplated how to pay an amount I had not anticipated. Suddenly I felt the urge to check a particular section of the regulations. Sure enough, a deduction of which I had not been aware was available for the problem area.

12. Alick Bartholomew (ed.), *Crop Circles—Harbingers of Change* (Bath, UK: Gateway Books, 1991); Beth Dew (ed.), *Gophers in the Crops* (Bath, UK: Gateway Books, 1992).

13. Paul Von Ward, "Consciousness Input in Crop Circle Formation," Proceedings, International Forum on New Science, Ft. Collins, Colorado, September 1992.

14. R. G. Jahn and B. J. Dunne, *Margins of Reality: The Role of Consciousness in the Physical World* (New York: Harcourt Brace Jovanovich, 1987).

15. Jeffrey Mishlove, *The PK Man* (Charlottesville, VA: Hampton Roads Publishing, 2000).

9

Opting for
Galactic Citizenship

Imagining your perspective as a reader sustained me in writing this book. I believe you are open to the burgeoning expansion of knowledge about the complex, yet inherently purposeful, character of the universe. I think you have an inner sense of being an integral part of the grand reality of nature. By the time you read this, you may have had some information or experience that has persuaded you that humans are not the sole conscious beings in the universe. Whether it came from a NASA Mars study, other scientific research, news stories, or personal experience, it may have been the "last straw" that challenged you to redefine your role in the cosmic drama. I hope you find my work supportive of this challenge. If you have not had such an experience, I hope you are now willing to consider the possibility.

If, as I believe is clear, we are not alone on the stage, humans do not have a particularly unique role. Yet, what a powerful role we appear to have! With access to all realms of consciousness, we are no less than co-creators of space-time in our corner of the universe and perhaps beyond. The quality of our conscious self-awareness empowers humans to consider independently, with no help from the gods or ABs, how to improvise our own destiny. We are ready to assume our dual role as both student and teacher in an inherently self-learning universe.

This final chapter considers the implications of commencing the next phase of self-initiation into the status of cosmic beings. It suggests some species-established standards for achieving galactic citizenship. I believe meeting them will result in a planetary renaissance and the launching of humanity toward the farthest reaches of inner and outer space.

In the twenty-first century, the human species faces a fundamental challenge to the old order that can energize a new renaissance with global reach. The old order is being shaken by a shift toward a Solarian consciousness more liberating of the human spirit and more sweeping in its social implications than the European Renaissance of the fifteenth and sixteenth centuries. The emergence of the nonhomocentric view expounded in this book is a greater revolution in human perspectives than the Copernican heliocentrism of the middle decades of the sixteenth century.

In the preceding chapters, I have described the elements of the new metascience replacing the Newtonian and Cartesian assumptions undergirding Western science, technology, and social systems. These elements offer humans a more creative role in renewing the planetary society and fulfilling their destiny as a cosmic species. This final chapter explores specific ways a metascientific perspective can transform how humans think and live and the ways we organize our lives.

As we know, institutions and societies can be built on theories or assertions for which there is no evidence of validity. People ignore their own intelligence and inner wisdom when they acquiesce to those who claim divine or official authority. With rediscovery of the full human story, humanity must rethink the personal and institutional implications of the biased history that has been written by those with vested interests.

We all have been faced with pretexts of such interests: It is God's will, plan, or commandment! The origins of this holy book, and therefore my interpretations of it, are divine! Our family has owned this land from the beginning, or we were given it by the crown, who had it from God! This is the government ordained by God and we are the anointed representatives! Since we are officials, we understand the problems and issues better than anyone; our perspective must prevail! This is the truth according to science, or it has been interpreted by people authorized by the university or government laboratory (chartered by those with "divine" or "official" authority) to speak for science! So the list of authoritarian assertions goes on.

When anyone works up the nerve to raise challenges, they are belittled by those who benefit from the conventional wisdom; and others who fear loss of their own status often join the censure. Examples of this are put-downs in the mass media and professional journals of people who dare to propose or try out new ideas. Others have funding withdrawn for research that results in unpopular findings. Individuals who continue to stand up are belittled, with some suffering more sanctions. In modern America, people are still put in jail for using alternative medical and energy technologies. Patents are confiscated in the name of national security. These routine censures and many more serious sanctions mean the established past chokes out alternative futures.

One important purpose of this book is to give an expanded foundation for thinking about the individual's access to truth and power. While humans are dependent on the whole, each individual has not only the natural right but the power to help shape the whole. With independent access and capacity to validate the knowledge claimed by any other being, each Solarian is equal to all others as a co-creator of life in this galactic neighborhood and as a powerful interpreter and validator of meta-scientific knowledge. This truth is the foundation of the Solarian legacy for all who have entered and for those yet to come in the twenty-first century.

Dangers of Stellar Space

The review in chapter 3 of the natural, and apparently consciousness-influenced, history of our solar system and the Earth makes concern about the integrity of our home base the first standard for galactic citizenship. We live in a volatile vehicle spinning through the heavens filled with dangerous debris. Two areas call for attention: Earth changes (polar shift, geologic activity, or climatic transformation) and the potential impact on Earth of an off-planet event (comet passage, meteor collision, solar flares, radiation bursts, etc.).

First, when we consider the impact of human activities on places like parts of Central Asia, the Middle East, North Africa, and sections of the Americas (where deserts have replaced verdant forests) and the atmosphere (with the greenhouse effect from our fossil fuel energy emissions), we see clearly our contributions to the demise of our own habitat. Given the indications that previous civilizations, on Earth and possibly Mars, may have also wreaked widespread destruction, there is sufficient cause to be very careful when introducing new technologies. Major governments appear to have sufficiently frightened themselves with the potential for a nuclear Armageddon, but societies have not yet adequately focused on the damage that overuse of industrial technology causes to the planet's resource base and ecosystems. The damage that rogue states or terrorist groups could do with small nuclear weapons is dwarfed by the worldwide destruction that modern materialism and population growth have already wrought.

Since Plato, Western scholars have been intrigued by reports of the violent end to the continent and civilization known as Atlantis. Some legends imply that human mistakes with energy generation destroyed the continent. Cabrera believes technology developed by highly intelligent beings could have contributed to such physical turbulence in prehistory. Common sense says conscious management of our current civilization could benefit from understanding why so many civilizations ended abruptly: Machu Picchu and related Andean cities, Easter Island, pyramidal Egypt, Mayan centers, Atlantis, and others.

Some endings may have had natural causes, like the cataclysm that almost wiped out humanity in 11,500 B.P. Study of the demise of antediluvian cultures in various parts of the world could help ascertain whether natural forces or the activities of intelligent beings precipitated their destruction. We need a concerted review of all information from prehistory to focus on just this point. Our future may depend on it.

For example, American and Russian experiments with weather modification through electromagnetic devices, and more recently the military use of very low and extremely low frequencies (VLF and ELF) for "Star Wars" programs (communications, radar, and electronic countermeasures), have raised serious concerns about the state of the Earth's oceans and ionosphere as it affects human health and our natural environment. Before proceeding with such technologically enhanced projects, scientists should investigate the causes of the destruction of ancient cities in what is now Iraq, Turkey, Jordan, Lebanon, and Israel. The possibility that atomic or comparable warfare over parts of the Middle East and India (suggested in Jewish, Greek, and Hindu legends) resulted in areas barren of and inhospitable to life is one that should be studied for the lessons it could teach today's policy makers.

A primary objective of future Mars missions should be to test the hypothesis of destructive consciousness, deliberate as well as unintentional, having contributed to current conditions on that planet. Mars may give insights into the mistakes of earlier civilizations and ways to practice better stewardship of Earth. If, by terraforming, humans can reverse some of the processes that made Mars so desolate, we can learn how to avoid similar disasters on this planet. I suspect that much of the desertification of Earth can be traced to human mistakes, and I don't mean just letting too many sheep overgraze the vegetation.

The possibility of unintended planetary disaster should become part of the long-range planning of every government and corporate entity. Our present concept of EIS, or Environmental Impact Statements, needs to be expanded to encompass the indirect effects of a given project on planetary viability. EIS should be changed to GIS, or Global Impact Statements. (In this context "Earth Day" would take on a whole new meaning.) The same requirement should apply to the introduction of all new technologies. In the biological arena, particularly genetic engineering, concern for unleashing destructive or unmanageable chain reactions ought to serve as yes/no decision points for all inventions and interventions in the web of life.

This does not mean we should not constructively use such technologies; but we should do so with full awareness of their possible implications, and we should act responsibly. Legend is filled with stories of creatures half-human or hybrids of two or more animals. We may be on the threshold of another such era unless we publicly manage the field of biotechnology and gene engineering.

With regards to the second threat, we must also maintain a watch on the heavens and prepare for the possibility of having to cope with a direct hit or near miss from a heavenly body. This also involves a better understanding of the effects of energy bursts from the Sun (like those that knock out our communications satellites) and the effects of galactic activities on our own energetic fields, from the human to the planetary. The first step is simply to recognize possible vulnerabilities and accept responsibility for avoiding the extremes of social chaos that would result from an unanticipated calamity.

On the average of almost one per week, fireballs come screaming through Earth's atmosphere, but most go largely unnoticed. Nevertheless, within the last century there have been many cases of local and regional damage, the most noted being the Tunguska event described earlier. Space satellites now detect frequent kilo-ton detonations in the Earth's atmosphere.

The second step is the sharing of resources and knowledge among institutions and countries to prepare all of humanity as much as possible. Up to this point, the highest quality information on potential threats has been classified secret by the U.S. military. Their information should be included in the new Global Disaster Information Network set up by President Clinton in 2000. The European Community sky watch program, an international group of scientists known as Spaceguard U.K., and growing U.S. efforts to monitor the movement of bodies that pose a potential danger for Earth are good ideas. The reality of the overall threat needs to be incorporated into public education programs and political debates.

For threats from self-inflicted damage and stellar catastrophes, we need contingency planning, in order to maximize the possibility of an effective response. This stage requires active involvement from all sectors of society. I do not mean humans should live in constant dread, but all should be aware of the realities of living in a stellar neighborhood where risk exists. This public facing of reality is an important element in the process of self-initiation into galactic citizenship.

Honoring Our Legacy

Before we officially meet other beings, who may already know us well, we must be prepared to be honest about who we are. An accurate-as-possible accounting for our origins and development up to this point must be completed before we can in good conscience declare ourselves to be candidates for galactic citizenship. Thus, the second standard to be met is a full and honest rendering of our genealogy. Correcting our genealogy is important because it will make us reshape the society we want to present to interstellar visitors.

For decades now, the evidence has been mounting that human beings are not the sole conscious inhabitants of the universe. But the widely publicized hypothesis that one-celled life has existed on Mars, as simple and as tentative as it is, was the long-awaited signal of legitimacy for the idea of exobiology. Coverage by the mainstream media of the Mars rock[1] gives the impression that if life existed on Mars, it must have been very primitive. But people will soon begin to realize that enough time lapsed on Mars to permit the development of life-forms not unlike those the Earth has experienced. Once those assumptions begin to circulate in the noumena, the possibility of even more radical concepts, like some described in this book, will no longer be considered so farfetched.

In less than a decade, we could have concrete evidence of past intelligent life on Mars, if not contact with extant beings. The United States launched two probes in late 1996 to reach the red planet in the second half of 1997. The first to arrive, *Pathfinder*, sent back to Earth the first photos from that planet since the *Viking* missions of 1976. Other 1990s launches have not been very successful, with only one of the six, with its famous little ground rover, meeting its objective. This has delayed the U.S. schedule for 2001 to 2005, and called into question the hoped-for human expedition as early as 2012. But the human impulse to explore Mars directly will not be long denied.

The "Rudolf Steiner scenario," that Mars was a living habitat destroyed in the Solarian odyssey of humanity's ancestors, may be validated as human astronauts discover evidence relevant to their own history. Such Martian discoveries will turn the focus back on this planet and the manner in which people are destructive of themselves and the planet's ecosystems. The history of our ancestors there, perhaps calling for atonement, may show us the need to nurture Earth more carefully.

Confirmation of ancient cities and monuments on Mars, or artifacts on the Moon, would also stimulate serious study of similar sites and legends about them on Earth. (Many people believe evidence of such sites already exists.) As described in earlier chapters, ruins of ancient cities, oral and written legends, technologically advanced prehistoric artifacts, geologic records, information received from the Akashic and other noumenal records, and subtle communications with other species of conscious beings all point to ancestors of the human race who lived and were active on Earth millions of years ago. The evidence, while significant, is not yet available in any coherent form; it is therefore impossible to be certain whether humans are natives or the offspring of colonizers. Nevertheless, given the discoveries at our fingertips, all too briefly summarized in this book, it is imperative that we revise humanity's genealogy to provide for the likelihood of prehistoric, intelligent planetary, stellar, and galactic parentage.

Zecharia Sitchin, Cabrera, and others have started the research, but there is so much more to be learned. Sitchin has revealed a past center of joint AB/human activity in the Middle East that answers many questions about the stream of advanced life that eventually led to so-called Western civilization, but his work does not adequately account for other centers in Asia and South America. Cabrera has tantalized us with evidence of even more ancient joint cultures, but his research has not yet garnered the widespread interest and assessment it deserves. Researchers into the mists of human history need a large, multidisciplined, multisense effort to fill the gaps in their analyses and to incorporate evidence from all parts of the globe. Their findings will eventually require reassessment of how we think our current institutions came into being.

One of the most crucial reexaminations will be that of the current doctrines of governance. Sitchin makes a strong case in his series of books that the visiting "gods" instructed humans in concepts for social institutions, in addition to hard science and technologies for practical living. These institutions included the concept of allegiance by groups of humans to aliens, or royal beings, who commanded their support in internecine alien conflicts. (According to Cabrera, adoptions of similar alien tactics may have led to tribal divisions among the pre-Incas of Peru.) In this context, the subsequent appointments of local human leaders by the "royal" beings gave rise to the idea of kingship by divine anointment. This belief in divine rights has provided the excuse for wars and untold accounts of domination of the unanointed by the anointed. It is evident that such a single divisive concept has caused the human race untold suffering over the last 8,000 years.

Even our modern concepts of a democratic republic have been distorted by this historical bias in their implementation. The eighteenth-century democratic innovations were grafted onto old structures derived from a notion of "holy or anointed officials." Thus, the residual concept of "official power" justifies a legal distance between those on the inside and those on the outside (as in pharaonic Egypt), facilitating the keeping of secrets and resources from public knowledge. Judges seem analogous to the putative priesthoods of supernaturalism, even down to the robes of religion. These official practices were not invented by egalitarian humans.

How many human psychological and behaviorial defects result from such exogenous interventions? Were patronizing

AB-colonizers responsible for giving humans a sense of being flawed, of being abandoned orphans, inclined to intrafamily squabbling, and addicted to dysfunctional rituals of adulation for absent parents, sometimes called gods?

For example, if our ancestors were abused by aliens, modern humans need to come to grips with the physical and psychological imprint of having been treated like inferior beings. What scars have such experiences left on our collective psyche? Can humans assuage the guilt of selling their sisters to higher species and groveling as their servants? Perhaps the impact of such practices has been more destructive to humans than intraspecies enslavement. Perhaps interspecies (AB-over-human) concepts of ownership of humans led to such enslavement among ourselves.

Conversely, are there positive human attributes that can be found to have their origins in our prehistoric experience? May we be the repository of advanced values and insights that can enrich life in the solar neighborhood and among our galactic cousins beyond? Some of the most advanced human thinking reflects an appreciation of principles like the prime directives of noninterference and self-sustainability. They appear to be lessons from experience over long and complex periods.

If our AB-forebears manufactured the sophisticated artifacts recently discovered from antiquity, why does much of the technology differ from our current levels and forms? It must have been based on entirely different principles, outside modern science's current understanding of natural laws. The capability to move structural and monumental stones weighing many tons (found on numerous prehistoric sites) without apparent mechanical power is one example of the application of unknown principles. Knowledge about the impact of the Earth's magnetic field and its extraterrestrial gravitational forces on the lives of humans is another. Ancient flying machines reportedly using the natural forces of gravity and electromagnetic fields are outside current technological capabilities and need to be publicly researched. (Allegedly, current government research and development in this area is being secretly carried out.) In instances like these, a mother lode of promising knowledge in extant texts and artifacts from earlier civilizations may be waiting to be mined.

Ancient wisdom can prove helpful beyond the development of machines and energy sources for transport and mechanical power. Society can even learn from the Sumerian tablets' focus on justice, instead of the later ones of Hammurabi which focused on crime and punishment. With serious concerns about many aspects of the American system of criminal justice, society could benefit from a second look at such ancient wisdom. What would a system not influenced by the supernatural view of divine judgment and punishment for individuals look like? In an egalitarian society in which everyone is aware of the interdependence of all beings and the reciprocal influences that shape them, the focus in a criminal matter would be to identify all the people who contributed to the act of violence and assess responsibility for ameloriation among them.

Medicine is another rich area for such a process of rediscovery. Much has been preserved through the folk traditions of many societies. Instead of simply dismissing out of hand the claims of traditional medicine men and women, or totally accepting their views, the healers of the future will use modern concepts and technology to evaluate folk medicine and incorporate into their practice whatever therapies work. Combining new science insights with the perennial wisdom that predates the current Nicene-Newtonian era could revolutionize our understanding of human psychology, including our ability to conceive and manifest changes in mental, emotional, and physical diseases.

Having recognized and incorporated our Solarian legacy into twenty-first-century institutions, humans could offer advanced contributions to the ongoing spiral of cosmic life. We could demonstrate to other beings our capacity to become the sentient and sapient race that maintains this planet, reseeds Mars, and exports sparks of organic life and cosmic consciousness to barren planets afar. Accomplishing such an honest adult review and making the mature decisions to accept responsibility for our future will meet the second standard for galactic citizenship.

Adopting a Metascientific Perspective

The third standard for galactic citizenship is the adoption of a more advanced approach to seeking knowledge and relating to the multidimensional universe. The concept of isomorphism can help us to understand the multidimensional, yet integral, nature of our universe.

Applying the term "isomorphic" to two systems implies that, except for one variable, both behave according to the same principles. For example, in hydraulics and aerodynamics, all the laws that apply to one apply to the other, though the former deals with fluids and the latter with air. A similar isomorphism applies in the fields of ecology and consciousness research. What we have learned about the interrelated and indivisible nature of ecological systems applies equally to the study of cosmic consciousness. While developing an understanding of how our physical pollutants affect the whole system, we have yet to grasp that our mental and psychological pollutants contaminate the global society and the cosmos beyond. In a three-faceted universe, just as physical pollution causes global warming that distorts our planetary weather patterns, hostile or destructive personal thoughts and emotions engender distress for all consciousness, and return to darken our own souls.

Metascience using all human senses (physical and subtle) and all sources of wisdom can help us gain a deeper understanding of our universe. It assumes a priori that exclusion of any source of knowledge, or failure to take advantage of any sense, dooms humanity to a diminished life—less than the full birthright of our Solarian legacy. Thus, adoption of metascience will help us meet the third standard.

Three examples can illustrate the value of metascience combining ancient wisdom with frontier science: (1) Using the early human notions of a singular consciousness to teach people how best to relate to the natural environment. Early American rituals and prayers reinforce the values of modern ecological insights. (2) Enhancing practical applications of telepathy and intuition through experimental development of the subtle senses. We now have mechanical devices that provide feedback to the individual on his or her success rates. (3) Explaining the uses of traditional divinatory texts like *I Ching* and other forms of divination in terms of biocommunications and synchronicity. Recognition of the mechanism through which such practices work will enhance their reliability.

It is clear to most people that undisciplined advances in technology can disturb the finely tuned balance that now exists among natural systems. As discussed earlier, genetic engineering may pose more danger to conscious life than nuclear power and other heavy technologies. Even in these new areas, I believe the use of ancient concepts such as the Hermetic Principles can be helpful in framing theoretical issues and research design. The following examples illustrate their relevance to some questions facing modern science.

Will thinking of aging as a problem of "quality control" for certain genes (as does the Scripps Research Institute and other centers) that can be easily remedied by insertions of new DNA strings, lead to problems? The Principle of Rhythm suggests that each element in an organism has its own inherent cycle. If this is so, intervention at one point (on one element) without being able to predict its effect on the other elements can serve to destroy the larger system. Use of subtle sensing could help map the connections that require consideration. And conscious intent may be harnessed to have the same effect more efficiently, if such life expansion is compatible with the demands of consciousness.

In the macrocosm, the Principle of Cause and Effect controls the play between the Moon and the tides, between the stars and our solar system. In the microcosm, it helps explain the creative dance between mind and matter, including distortions in physical and subtle energies. Physical and emotional diseases must be traced to their roots in consciousness if deep healing is desired. Observing the physical universe's cycles of birth, growth, decline, death, and rebirth, synchronized by the Principle of Correspondence, we can better understand the behavior and life cycles of individuals, societies, and interspecies systems. Just as the Principle of Polarity balances matter and antimatter or positive and negative charges in cell nuclei, it governs the dynamics of constructive and destructive predispositions and forces in human behavior.

Greater understanding of such dynamics will enhance our freedom from and our use of the material systems at the same time it increases respect for our interdependence with them. Going further with the Principle of Polarity, it is seen in the contrasts of centripetal and centrifugal spins (cyclones and hurricanes) and in the rise and fall of acid/base ratios. On an emotional level, love and anger and good and evil are polarities, not unlike the inseparable twins of particles and antiparticles. We may avoid misinterpreting the dynamics of emotions and misleading ourselves by recognizing that emotions, too, act like polarities—aspects on different parts of the gradient of the same behavioral force. This has profound implications for interpersonal relationships, psychological therapy, and social interventions.

The new science of biotechnology—like the phenomena-based field of physics—brings us back to the nonphysical underpinnings of matter. Little more than a decade ago, the young industry used genetic engineering to create new drugs to invade or reinforce the body's organs. Now biotechnicians, working cooperatively with large drug manufacturers, use computers to design compounds, molecule by molecule, that hook into isolated diseased cells and modify their behavior. Soon these scientists will begin to see evidence of their own conscious interaction with the cells under their scrutiny. When they do, the circle will be complete. Systematic delving into the material realm will have led them back to the intuitive power of our own minds. The ancient Ayruvedic concept—that the expression of intent can create physical changes—will be validated in gleaming metallic research laboratories.

Where will such metascientific breakthroughs lead us? Legend has it that ancient Hawaiian goddesses were shapeshifters—able to change form at will—as were aboriginal shamans. Their expressions of intent from the realm of consciousness (noumena) gave rise to patterns of force (energeia) that worked their will on matenergy (phenomena). These and other "miracles" by humans and ABs[2] will be routinely studied to understand the anomalous aspects of the manifestation and disappearance of matter and the bilocation of people. Searching for information along the arrow of time will become plausible as precognition and recall of past events are studied on presently unknown spectra parallel to the travel of subparticles and the flow of ordinary energy. Using all of our senses in multilevel learning may enable future Solarians to live out the legends of old.

Using All Senses

The most important contribution of metascience to human development is its requirement for the deliberate use of the subtle senses. Some groups, like members of the Intuition Network who are practicing intuitives, already take their use as almost routine, but most people do not see them as central to life. In our integral but three-faceted universe, humans have the capacity to see the heavens through electronic telescopes or from spaceships and also confirm their reality through the subtle senses, without the aid of technology or leaving home. Success in subtle-sense exploration of currently invisible aspects of the universe will reverse the modern human tendency to let these senses atrophy through excessive focus on the rational and physical. As more scientists access the noumena for concepts that can be tested in the laboratory, they will be convinced of their inner senses.

As all Solarians become receptive to more cues, we will open ourselves to the gifts of synchronicity. We will learn how to recognize its power as the multifaceted and biocommunication-based "grantor-of-wishes" or "manifester-of-intentions." For example, I now use it to meet the right people at conferences and to discover the materials I need for my work. With conscious use of these additional facets of beingness at our disposal, humans will more readily master new levels of creativity. Enough examples of reinforcement will make us conscious self-learners.

In a cosmos that integrates matenergy, subtle energy, and mind, precipitous leaps to action or reaction in attempts to achieve a desired end will be recognized for their futility. We will learn that behavior incongruent with inner-sense communications precipitates reverberations with unforeseen consequences, in effect undermining the desired outcome. For example, the legal killing of people who kill ignores the inner implications of the death penalty for the whole society. This violent form of dealing with destructive behavior reinforces its causal energies—psychological or energetic alienation and severance of conscious connections. Regardless of how many killers are physically killed, unless society eliminates its support for violations of subtle and mental bodies (by anyone in a position of economic or personal authority over others), high murder rates and other expressions of violence will remain.

In the "unitary or integral" system that characterizes our universe, there are no strictly local effects; perturbations in any person or group reverberate throughout the whole. As ecoethics evoke a sense of our personal responsibility for the health of the whole planet, we need a Solarian ethical code for conscious living that holds our focus on the long-range implications for others, and for ourselves, of our thoughts, words, and deeds. Because the physical, emotional, and intellectual development of any one being is dependent on the progress made by all, no individual punishment or unique reward is appropriate. Paradoxically, self-realization must occur collectively as well as individually.

Recognizing that any situation results from a set of consequences accumulated from myriad prior events (and their indirect, inner connections) leads to the conclusion that only a comparable confluence of complex and synchronistic forces can bring about a desired change. Making good social policy is like riding the rapids of a swollen stream to reach a rock on the opposite shore: mastery of society's river is accomplished by making integrated sets of small adjustments suggested by all senses in a given instant. All postmodern institutions could benefit from the leadership experience of metascientific white-water rafting guides. Any new law, policy, or program should be based on a three-faceted assessment of its reverberations throughout the species and beyond. Its impact on human emotions (subtle energies) and mental vibrations must be taken into account.

Multilevel Learning

Solarian learning will always include attention to the dynamics of a three-faceted universe. For example, there is even a subtle-energy aspect to the need for new learning (as any good teacher intuitively knows). A vacuum of knowledge or a perceived deficit of understanding (one pole) charges an energetic impulse, or emotional desire, to acquire new information or answers (the opposite pole). During the phase of actively seeking the new answer, one attempts to reach a new energeial threshold, a point of emotional conviction, where the kinetic energy dissipates into an "I see" experience.

When this process operates at low CQ levels (introduced in chapter 7), energetic satisfaction may be achieved with little qualitative judgment. Most any answers from sources deemed acceptable will do. (This is why propaganda works with unthinking people and converts are the most energetic proponents of the new dogma they have accepted.) Since answers are the energetic polarity to the quest, a being strongly holds them until it feels an internal incongruence. Only then will a new round of seeking begin. Human emphasis on the cross-discipline testing of answers or assumptions facilitates escape from closed-loop thinking. In other words, only the more advanced beings will continually monitor the congruency of their conclusions with other areas of knowledge.[3]

The role of subtle energy in learning explains why most sentient beings have an energized resistance to external pressure to shift a mind-set. Just as there are ingrained matenergy patterns (as in genes, muscular memories, and planetary orbits), embedded emotional or subtle-energy patterns, regardless of their validity or current relevance, stay in place until reconfigured by deliberate acts or trauma that transmute their polarities.

Successful societies develop individual and group practices that facilitate transmutation of dysfunctional energy blocks to new learning. In traditional societies, activities that led to new answers included group festivals, ritual dance, or other physical disciplines. In some societies, to underscore the importance of self-learning, individuals were sent alone into the wilderness or on a quest to discover new answers for themselves. The more dramatic the instability, the more motivated people are in the search for a new personal order. Therefore, consciousness-state-shifting rituals and emotion-laden initiations have similar results. (Limited applications of this concept have been incorporated in some modern consulting and personal growth techniques.)

Institutional Change

We must apply the energetic and consciousness insights of self-learning on individual issues to their possible use on institutional questions. To think that organizations can simply order the transformation of pent-up energy charges or smother their expression to elicit new behavior is no longer credible. Exclusive reliance on the external use of force to bring about a learning shift must be eliminated; whether laws, police regulation, or religious prescriptions, they all harden the resistance or divert it into a different channel of expression.

Only when individuals freely participate in their own transformation will constructive transmutation of the undesired polarity (fear, anger, etc.) occur. As forest experts are beginning to grasp the wisdom of permitting small fires that are necessary to the forest's health, thereby avoiding the infrequent but huge conflagrations that destroy the entire forest, society's future leaders will learn how to facilitate the transformation of destructive energy polarities before they get out of hand. Management of subtle energies in the process of self-learning and growth will characterize Solarians.

Mastery of the subtle senses will revolutionize human understanding and behaviors on every level. Such mastery will dramatically change the character of human intercourse, eliminating much of the intentional use of hypocrisy and deceit prevalent in business and politics, as well as personal relationships. In a turn to fully conscious leadership practices, societal, political, and organizational processes will be very different from our current legalistic, confrontational, and top-down approaches. Until the subtle senses are publicly incorporated into the deliberations of the U.S. Congress and other governmental councils, these bodies cannot effectively serve the humans touched by their actions.

How would such governance feel? What would it be like to begin official deliberations by focusing on everyone's inner communications, and responding to them in a cooperative way?

With widespread use of the power conveyed by the subtle senses, officials would find themselves subject to the will of their equally powerful Solarian followers, whose potency resides in their ability to give or withhold their subtle-energy support. The inner power of the individual rests in the control one has over the opening of personal energeial and noumenal membranes. Without that mental and subtle-energy support from the group, no leader can maintain authority very long.

How different the court system would be if the subtle senses were used to reorient the current criminal justice approach of legalistic confrontation about physical evidence. Imagine how the behavior of defendants and plaintiffs alike would change if the purposes of the investigation and trial processes were to ascertain the truth of the inner and outer realms, in addition to what can be proved by the narrow rules of evidence. What if the jury's responsibility was to assign appropriate responsibility for corrective action and compensation to all in the society who had contributed to the "crime." If the focus were on personal intent and impact, not on bureaucratic procedures, everyone would become more concerned about the effect of their actions on the whole.

Depersonalization and the monstrous scale of current financial, business, government, and even nonprofit organizations have undermined the self-disciplining forces of community ethos and personal accountability. The energy available for self-learning is consumed by efforts at self-protection. Formal social control mechanisms such as elections, audits, financial reports, and so on, cannot keep up with this erosion of social integrity. We need social inventions that incorporate knowledge of the three facets and intervene in the processes of multilevel co-creation. One such social invention would be the systematic introduction of the use of the subtle senses into the leadership and management of organizations.

Nonintrusive soundings of an organization by skilled and responsible use of subtle communication channels could tap into negative, confused, or blocked energies that presage problematic performance. Intuitive professionals could diagnose the noumenal origins of the energy patterns and relate them to behavioral trends. (A number of corporations now turn to emerging intuition consultants for help.) Trusting in the full range of senses, they could use multiple insights to develop interventions that lead to greater organizational clarity and interpersonal harmony. With the professions of management consulting and organizational development radically reformed, people would have nothing to fear but their own intentions.

The realization of this three-level model of effective behavior requires an approach that is the opposite of the Western system of education, in which the objective is to create people who are alike and who can serve the status quo. Instead of the right answers being given to the students by the teachers, teaching the process of self-learning would assist children in realizing the power of their inner senses. The roles of shaman and apprentice provide useful models for the process of Solarian education. In this process, the teacher encourages confidence in the inner wisdom of each being and its innate impulse to wholeness. The teacher helps the student learn how to become the teacher.

Conscious role-playing helps to learn this new way of being. As in improvisational theater, the players make up the script in concert with each other. In other words, they play the dual role of actor/director. All that is required is a commitment to pay attention to every possible cue, regardless of the sense through which it comes. The technique can be used in every field.

By knowing that positive energy flows easily through the autonomous nerve/muscle system while negative energy sets up resistance, one can easily shift polarities using a conscious reinterpretation of the idea or event. The need for catharsis, the recognition or expression of repressed fears or other negative feelings, on the battlefield and in political or bureaucratic warfare, can be satisfied by improvised games or encounters created explicitly for the temporary assumption of different modes of expression. This allows for simulated self-learning that can then be transferred to the actual arena. Currently, certain energy-shifting training techniques used by body workers, therapists, and drill sergeants unwittingly involve such subtle pattern reprogramming.

The Solarian challenge is to create collective experiences of consciously designed catalytic events that transform society's inertial energy into a force for openness and experimentation. In other words, people must consciously stimulate and involve the energeia and the noumena, as well as the phenomena, in efforts to develop their full potential. When most people learn these transformative methods, humans will have met the third standard. A quality of social cohesion will evolve that makes possible planetary transformation, the flowering of humanity's Solarian potential.

The Human as Self-Learner/Teacher

The implications of the Solarian legacy have much broader scope than we have imagined. We, as a mature civilization, will have an open-ended dual role in the universe, to both design and participate in its evolution. Attempts to describe with certainty particular limits to these roles, to logically and empirically prove that any such finite boundaries exist, founder for lack of proof. The physical boundaries of cells disappear under the microscope, atoms change their nature, subatomic particles flash in and out of existence, and energy is easily transmuted from one form to another. There are no ideas or memories that one can call exclusively one's own. The boundaries between life and death vanish in the face of other dimensions. Even gravity and time prove flexible in the experiments of frontier scientists.

343

How in a universe of such flexible nature can we define natural boundaries to our own existence? Only by testing each limit to selfhood that we manage to bump against, in a continual flow of experimentation and learning from the results. This means we must design the lesson we wish to learn and then try it out on ourselves. We instinctively do this to some extent in every arena of life, but as we have seen from the experiments described in earlier chapters, we are farther along the path of self-knowledge in some areas than we are in others. Some frontier scientists suggest that breakthroughs in understanding more profound than those of twentieth-century physics and chemistry are imminent. The first step to becoming a self-learning species is to master self-healing.

Conscious Healing

The power of conscious healing has become one of the first breaches in the self-defined limits in our traditional paradigm. Using ourselves as subjects (true self-learning), we have tapped into ways to access our subtle and noumenal powers. Many scientists who have felt the power of meditation and friends' prayers, or the energy of psychic healers, are leading the way. Some physicians now systematically combine their inner-sense knowing with modern tools of diagnosis and treatment. For a good example, see Judith Orloff's *Guide to Intuitive Healing*.[4] Taking advantage of our invisible thoughts and energy patterns to heal diseased cells without physical contact will transform the field of medicine. In the year 2000, Blue Cross of California exemplified progress in this area when they incorporated patient use of guided imagery as a part of their authorized presurgical preparations.

While not yet widely accepted, healers can use computers to focus and transmit patterns of energy through light waves that potentize (or patternize) clear water. Recognition of this by the scientific establishment will help many to accept the same focusing of healing patterns (intent) by a conscious healer. Individuals in turn will be encouraged to assume such power in their heads and hearts, issuing guidance to their own cells. Those who would be facilitators of healing will soon learn that their most useful role is that of reinforcing thoughts of health and the flow of subtle energies that a person permits into his or her body.

Gone will be the days of antibiotics, vaccinations, super drugs, and massive doses of radiation and chemicals that in the long run destroy more than they heal. The physician of tomorrow will return to the realm of metascience to incorporate thoughts and emotions into treatments of the body. She (all true healers, regardless of their sex, practice the "feminine" art of receptive channeling of subtle energies) will encourage the individual to tune into the thought-forms and the emotional state relevant to the area of dis-ease.

Environmental Healing

Extrapolating from self-healing, Solarians learn that their conscious interaction with the environment is an integral part of the self-learning cycle. People then master the channels of communication with plants and animals, and establish cooperative relationships with ecological systems. Food scarcity will be a thing of the past as humans consciously cooperate with other species who share their nurturing life forces with them. People will no longer want to eat matter that has had the life frightened, squeezed, or burned out of it.

With multirealm ecological thinking, we will envision the interactions of our thoughts, feelings, and actions with all beings. Individuals will take into account the perspective of the rivers, the birds and the bees, the earthworms and the viruses, the rocks and the trees, and on and on, when we intervene in their lives. Using subtle senses to augment physical ones, humans will "listen" to the desires of other life-forms as well as our own.

Human self-learning with natural systems will expand understanding of our interrelationships with the mechanical realm. Sometime in the future there will be general access to the power of psychokinesis and even manifestation. Consciously directed interaction of the subtle energies with matenergy could fuel power transformers and transport vehicles, and many other forms of consciousness-assisted technology. The result would be a fundamental shift in economic systems as subtle energy is ̣ ̇oven to be a limitless resource easily available to everyone.

Reintegrating with Nature

Direct participation in the healing of self and ecosystems will lead humans to rediscover their niche in the natural system. The creation of "academies for remembering" could help facilitate rediscovery of our natural heritage. Using multi-sense processes, we can deepen our appreciation of the alive universe. We will perceive that everyone is inextricably and fundamentally connected to the universe, as did traditional hunters, who believed that in seeking their prey in the wilderness they were also being sought by it.

Modern society has delegated to impersonal systems the acquisition of food, the reading of the weather signs, and the provision of mechanical communication channels. While such systems will be difficult to dismantle in urban and suburban centers, control of them will become more community-based as people engage in the maximum use of subtle communications to access their inner power. By inserting themselves back into the natural flow of intraspecies and interspecies life, people will experience the ecological whole as conscious participants. Feeling less alienated from others, each will become more connected with the essential self.

Anyone can learn this natural approach from examples like that of the Arhuaco Indians who live in the Sierra Nevadas of Colombia, South America. They continue to hold a worldview that predates the arrival of Columbus: living correctly means being in harmony with the natural principles of the universe. They believe illness or other problems occur when the laws of nature are violated. Their earth is alive, filled with an inner spirit that transcends time and finite matter. Everything, including rocks and all beings, lives forever, with only shifts in form and place. The right motivation is crucial in starting any action or interaction: if one begins with the wrong intention, nothing goes well.

When we recognize that basic assumptions or intentions shape all elements of life, we must reexamine the concept of the artificial division we have created between the institutions of government and inner reality. This does not mean we should invite dogmatic religions, as they currently manifest themselves, into public positions of authority, for all the reasons previously discussed. However, the American relegation of the nonphysical realms to the church, restricting government to the five-sense, left-brain, mechanistic mode of thinking and problem solving, has deprived politics and other public discussions of constructive input from the energeial and noumenal realms. Citizens need to find a way to introduce browing, hearting, splaning, shading, and rooting (see chapter 4), as well as the senses of consciousness, into the process of public dialogue and political discourse.

Once again, a key example is the environmental arena, where there is apparently no a priori limit to our destructiveness. The only constraints on human behavior toward the planet depend on the exercise of personal judgment. Given that the current state of the Earth is the result of countless generations of intervention by conscious beings, perhaps even to the point of creating myriad species, there is no question of letting the planet go back to a natural state. As apparent stewards of the planet, we must devise satisfactory alternatives to the destructive trends and seek the support and concurrence of other species. Only with their cooperation are we likely to succeed.

Obtaining Galactic Citizenship

With the advent of a truly self-learning society, humans become qualified for membership in the galactic community. Membership will open new doors to greater participation in the vast, conscious, perhaps 20-billion-year-old universe into which we have incarnated. The price of admission is a simple declaration of independence from any would-be rulers (human or otherwise) who wish to deny, or are blind to, our Solarian legacy. For unknown reasons, perhaps our earlier immaturity, older races appear to have been partially responsible for keeping humans in the dark about their true nature. However, to the extent that myopia is self-imposed, there is no longer any excuse for failing to outgrow adolescent innocence and assume our galactic roles.

As adults, we cannot escape our cosmic responsibility by blaming governments that fail to share the knowledge they have and refuse to engage in frank conversations with citizens. Official secrecy does not prevent efforts to correct the human story. If covert human organizations are actively involved in sub rosa and perhaps cooperative projects involving ABs, the facts can be publicized and brought into open discussion. If technology transfer is under way in hidden facilities where military forces, using crafts recovered from UFO crashes or interspecies technology transfers, gain access to advanced material, design, and propulsion system concepts, there is no reason not to publish the news for all humanity.

The fact that government officials, from the U.S. president on down, refuse to engage in a dialogue with responsible and well-informed citizens on the UFO/AB issue only tosses the ball back to the private sector. Private individuals and groups from various areas of American society can take the initiative to bring about more honesty and openness. Several private groups have taken up this challenge, and they should be supported and encouraged by the rest of us.

Even if all the answers are not yet clear, the information now widely available to the public is enough to call into question official motivations and their attempts to suppress information. (See the book *Cosmic Test Tube* by Randall Fitzgerald for an important overview.) We are at a point where a new covenant, providing for joint validation of important truths, must be negotiated between the electorate and those who would assume positions of leadership. Citizens can forgive deceptions in the past and forge a new bond of cooperation with institutions that pledge to obey the new rules—universal access to all knowledge and respect for the integrity and interdependence of all beings. (The late 1990s U.S. Air Force release of a new Roswell crash-site study, claiming that people reporting alien bodies must have seen weather balloon crash dummies, fails to meet either of these criteria.)

Like African teenagers fearfully approaching traumatic Poro initiations into adulthood, some humans may be anxious about giving up the comfort of adolescence, but most are much more resilient than we have given ourselves credit for. Most people will welcome being part of an historic opportunity like the dawning of an unprecedented age of understanding and the advent of the universal family. The predictions of mass fear are no longer well founded: there will be no repeat of the widespread reactions to Orson Welles' 1938 provocative radio broadcast of H.G. Wells' *War of the Worlds*. There was no evidence during the last half-century of potential for social hysteria and chaos strong enough to justify further secrecy or hesitancy in unveiling the Solarian legacy.

Surveys show that many religious leaders believe they can incorporate knowledge of ABs into their theistic concepts. But their followers are way ahead of them in understanding and accepting the vision of an even larger conscious order. This is demonstrated by widespread interest in movies, TV shows, books, newspaper articles, and conferences portraying alien involvement in human affairs.

The AB perspective in entertainment offerings vary from hostile (*Independence Day*) to benign (*Michael* and *Touched by an Angel*) to satirical (*Men in Black*), and they all seem to be taken in stride. This deluge of images, combined with the extraordinary experiences from subtle senses and inner knowings that we all share, has made it easier for everyone to entertain new ideas about the nature of reality. Most people are now primed to progress quickly beyond the age of cosmic adolescence. They are ready for the excitement of working out new forms of interaction with partners from all planes of existence.

Isaac Asimov invented a multispecies universe to serve as the background for multiauthored science fiction stories. He posited the emergence of six sentient races, from among hundreds in the galaxy, with the capability of interstellar flight. Among them were the newcomers Erthumos (ourselves), "the warm-blooded bipeds from the third planet of an obscure, third rate sun." These six races represented widely different cultures and technologies, springing from beings whose physiologies were as distinct from each other as human imagination could make them. In stories set a thousand years in the future, these races managed to abide by an accord of galactic peace, and served as models or development specialists for less advanced, planet-bound peoples.

Humans possess the potential to fulfill that visionary role. It is time to begin consciously rehearsing for the ultimate family reunion. Scott Jones, through his Foundation on Human Potential, in 1995 presciently organized a conference in Washington, D.C., on the knowledge and skills needed for meeting alien cultures. As made clear by several presenters, humans have already demonstrated how quickly they can reorient their thinking about other beings, even former enemies (Americans vis-à-vis Germans, Japanese, Russians, and Vietnamese). Transmuting their subtle emotions, groups that previously found it easy to kill the others, were, in a very short time, able to embrace them as friends and new business partners. With a capacity for such transformations, humans may be good candidates for galactic leadership roles in a fraternity of many cosmic cultures.

As humans come to recognize their Solarian legacy and take cognizance of nonhuman cousins, what are the psychological and behavioral implications of this rite of passage? Self-consciously admitting themselves to the fellowship of a more mature cosmic community dramatically broadens perceptions of roles and responsibilities, and thereby enhances the joy and pleasure from daily life in this incarnation. The expansion of consciousness enhances not only the sense of doing, but the power of doing! Individual strength is multiplied by orders of magnitude when large numbers concentrate their energeial and noumenal forces for the same purpose.

Benefits of Self-Initiation

Moving from a state of Earth-bound somnambulism to one of appreciation for a fully living universe activates our underused inner powers. Knowing we possess such powers, humans cannot help but behave differently. The old approaches of seeking personal advantage, using any manipulation necessary, and attempting unilateral control over events are recognized for their pettiness in the multileveled universe. In such a reality, impulses to covertly manage processes and people in one's own interest, or even in service to family and community, are seen as intellectually and ethically immature.

Reaching this point means we now understand the interactive nature of membership in the larger community of consciousness. We have learned that the extreme desire to produce (the expressive pole) has an integral counterpart in selfhood (the receptive pole of greed). We know that if the expressive energy is too strong, the receptive one is equally so. If we do not pay attention, the latter may lead us to believe we deserve the benefits of our galactic role with no need to share with others. But in the galactic community, as between individuals, we cannot escape the balancing power of universal principles. That which is gained in one form must also be given in another. Karmic justice comes calling when we halt the open give-and-take and try to close an account in our personal favor.

This means we cannot play the role of conquering colonists if we aspire to acceptance as positive contributors to stellar progress. We must go into space, as we must learn to live on Earth, respectfully working with other beings as conscious co-creators of our sphere of influence in the universe.

Honoring the connections that bind all beings together, we learn to interpret the waves of subtle energy from other beings. Recognizing that they too wish to maintain their own integrity, we exhibit mutual respect for jointly designed outcomes, leaving behind our attempts to manipulate otherness for selfish purposes. Respect for physical, emotional, and mental boundaries results in the reactions of others becoming more positive and supportive, with everyone requiring less expenditure of physical and subtle energies.

We can test these principles in Earth circumstances, where decisions and actions based in the multileveled knowingness of the subtle senses are found to be more satisfying. Such positive and powerful interactions make an immediate difference in daily life: people accomplish more with less, and feel better doing it. Instead of lonely self-promotion as unique stars, cosmic actors glory in the camaraderie of joint success.

Becoming aware of one's co-creative power gives rise to a sense of responsibility for its use. Knowing that the capability to unleash subtle energies that wreak havoc on unprotected others also has the potential to destroy oneself, conscious beings learn to exercise judicious constraint. The functioning of the Principle of Cause and Effect makes it impossible to escape the ramifications of one's intentions: for beings with the inborn-power humans possess, the universe guarantees accountability by individuals, groups, and nations. Solarians have no choice but to cooperate in the interest of their own long-term well-being.

A leisurely pace for developing interplanetary cooperation may be fine in Asimov's fiction, but humans do not have another thousand years to prepare for membership in the cosmic fraternity. From within human society come the challenges of interracial, intercultural, and intragroup breakdowns that are straining social institutions on every continent. And at any moment, humans could be faced with learning to interact constructively with a variety of sentient beings: co-habitants of Earth, co-Solarians, or beings from without this solar system. Humans now have no choice but to accept a cosmic perspective: the internal and external pressures to expand our vision cannot be held back.

Humanity's twentieth century, an explosive period of emotion-charged creativity and violence, must certainly have been of interest to older, more advanced cultures. They may seek overt dialogue if we do not seek them, providing answers to questions we did not know to ask. Who knows, we may be seen by other civilizations as the "generation to come," with ideas and energy that will change the course of Solarian or galactic development. We could be offering them as much hope for the future of the larger community of cosmic beings as our children do for us. (Some channeled materials suggest this, but maybe the messages are only our hopeful projections.)

Self-Regulating Membership

Sustaining membership in a galactic fraternity of a self-learning universe must be a self-regulating process. Our Solarian legacy and our inner powers make it easy to envisage our participation in an intergalactic era of cosmic creativity. But whether we obtain and maintain the rights of cosmic citizenship remains our responsibility.

I suspect that even the tentative acceptance of the likelihood of the existence of other actors in the cosmic drama puts us on the tryout list. But as long as we are concerned about being upstaged, replaced in the homocentric role we have given ourselves in the universe, we are not likely to be called for tryouts. We are probably still a bit too anxious because we do not yet know the power and attitudes of our fellow cosmic players. Whether their intent will be hostile, cooperative, supportive, or disdainful of the human level of development remains to be seen. With no clear idea of what to expect in terms of languages and appearances, their personal habits, or their social norms, how can humans prepare for all the possible scenarios?

We can only work on ourselves, knowing that breakthroughs cannot come until we imagine another way of being. Many believe that humanity is already in some sort of transition. I believe the ultimate transition will be a planetary renaissance. With such an act of discovery and redefinition, we will emerge from the current phase of constricted consciousness and emerge into an expanded level of awareness of our legacy and potential. (See some of the eight books by Jacquelyn Small dealing with this kind of transformative process. She uses an integrative breathwork technique to help individuals clear the channels of the energeial and noumenal senses.) We must do the same thing on the species level.

I believe metascience can help prepare us for the shock of full awakening. Its model of a three-level universe provides a set of principles that give us the basis for reasonable assumptions. First, the Principle of Correspondence suggests that obvious differences between humans and ABs are in form, not substance. Thus, the term "alien" is inappropriate for beings who are fundamentally like us—in reality our cosmic siblings. All incarnated beings, regardless of planet of origin, are irrevocably linked to one another beyond space-time at the emotional and mental levels. And as we saw earlier, humans have no difficulty communicating with subtle-energy beings or beings of pure consciousness. We need only to open ourselves to these other dimensions.

One likely surprise for many people will be the discovery of the parallels between humans and other cosmic beings in the area of psychic capacities. One of the desirable, and probable, outcomes of recognition of our cosmic siblings, in spite of surface differences, will be a change for the better in attitudes and behaviors among members of the human family. We will recognize, like the early Mahayanist reform movement in Buddhism, that in the search for greater illumination and wisdom we must consciously improve the performances of the species before any individual can fully progress. Most likely, more advanced beings will have already learned this lesson, so we should begin to put it into practice among humans before we get on the larger stage.

The physical differences among cosmic siblings with which humans will have to cope will generally require only adjustments in the way we think of them in relation to ourselves. While this incarnation may have us in different species, humans may recognize beings they have known in other incarnations. This recognition is possible because the physical life spans of beings from other planets are likely to be a function of some factor such as the duration of their home's orbit around its sun, while the longevity of noumenal entities may be comparable across the galaxies.

One of the confusions that apparently arose in earlier human contacts with extraterrestrials was the impression that they were immortal. To ancient humans, the normal life spans of beings whose home-base years were so much longer than humanity seemed like eternity. Judging from the perceptions of human civilizations during the period from 6,000 to 3,000 B.P., the visiting beings chose not to share knowledge of differing life spans with humanity. Some humans came to believe that the offering of extended life to a few faithful human servants was the gift of immortality. Unfortunately, that understanding has been used to buttress belief in misleading religions by holding out the promise of eternal life to those who die in service of their causes. Loss of such a lure should return life's focus to the cosmic here-and-now.

Another benefit to society of initiating the process for full membership in the cosmic community will be the demise of myths about divine beings, created to gain obedience from millions of believers. All the debate about the appearances of various "gods" and their miraculous feats, explained by Zecharia Sitchin and historians like him, will become moot. When people understand that tales in religious texts of seemingly divine travel in and communications from the air, and other seemingly miraculous feats, were only the normal activities of advanced civilizations, there will be no support for belief in divine commandments and special dispensations from such ordinary cosmic beings. When the concept of Yahweh is seen as a composite representation of several senior officials among visiting interstellar travelers, his alleged rules, and those of Mohammed (perhaps another such traveler) and other religious leaders, will no longer be taken as holy writ. Only scriptures that have experiential relevance to our multidimensional lives in this space-time will be considered worthy of teaching our children.

This means that religions still viable at the end of the twenty-first century, those truly relinking humans to their inner realities, will have divested themselves of "divinely inspired" scriptures and holy books. They will have eliminated their historically rooted hierarchies, done away with "special revelations," ceased artificial ritual, and stopped professing supernatural power. Instead, they will form natural communities of seekers after truth, using the experiences of all members to allow for the broadest possible use of noumenal knowledge integrated with daily experience. They will invite other communities of seekers to share their own findings and test conclusions of any group in public forums.

Thus, our membership in the galactic neighborhood will come from our own efforts to participate with all beings as

consciously as possible in the natural reality of our multidimensional, self-learning universe.

Fully-Conscious Living

How will it feel to become fully Solarian? As one gains an
appreciation of the intricate and multidimensional nature of
cosmic consciousness, the vision of performing at a higher
level, in congruence with this new knowledge, becomes a
strong motivating force. Solarians will be like the Olympic
athletes who are spurred on by the awareness of their potential and the opportunity to demonstrate it before their peers.

To act routinely when there has been no opportunity for or
awareness of greater possibilities is excusable, but not to attempt
one's potential after the dawn of self-awareness leaves one feeling unsatisfied. For example, now that we know about multiple-
leveled senses, to live without taking full advantage of them is
analogous to engaging in a boxing match with one hand tied, or
trying to paint by numbers without the color code. We feel the
frustration of functioning with only half the resources available
to us, and that knowledge incongruency (as discussed earlier)
feeds the quest for new information and experience.

The quality that distinguishes the conscious performer
from the uninitiated one is a desire to continually expand the
circles of awareness of both the inner and outer worlds, using
all the senses or gateways between the realms to enhance the
richness of the incarnation. The ability to shift frequently,
maintaining an overall balanced state, lessens the need for
drugged sleep or artificial mood changers and converts the
pace of waking life to one of sustained alertness to subtle
information. This enhanced state of consciousness provides
more options for deliberate self-direction in the management
of one's own life, in collaboration with other conscious beings.

Solarians living in full awareness of their true legacy and
its potential are awakened to assume responsibility for the
quality of theirs and others' lives. People who know that their
thoughts make a difference can no longer remain indifferent
to their mental state. The idea of focusing constructive
thoughts through large group meditations (coordinated over

distance) has gained wide acceptance. Some groups have organized times for small groups to gather at UN headquarters to meditate on peace and other themes, backed up by simultaneous meditations around the globe.

In a fully conscious state, life is seen as a cosmic dance, in which certain capacities and patterns of behavior are intrinsic to the incarnation, but where the design of the specific steps is left to choices made in conjunction with one's partners. Mature selfhood uses all the senses, stretching to the fullness of all polarities: anguish and joy, satisfaction and guilt, initiating and reacting, holding steady and abruptly changing course, and receiving and expressing. A single incarnation has many stages with all these qualities, with plenty of time to learn and practice. In maturity, the being, positioned and energized by the experience, clearly portrays its totality for all to see.

Precognition or prophecies will be part of everyone's portfolio. But they will be seen as only a glance at the possibilities or probabilities of events extrapolated from present trends. With that insight, instead of perceiving them as certainties, we will see them as options that require conscious choice on our part: whether to change the stream of events or to let our earlier habits determine the future.

Living as Solarians takes only a few crucial assumptions that provide the basis for self-direction. They involve appreciation of all senses and the power of conscious thought in shaping all aspects of life.

- Any person has all the cosmic powers that are inherent in others.

- Each being can test the assertion of knowledge by any other.

- Many developmental paths lead to self-realization.

- Conscious choice is required to stay on a chosen path.

- Intentions manifest themselves through both subtle and physical energies.

One implication of these assumptions is that the knowledge one has about self deserves the respect of others. A corollary of this is that, when two or more beings decide to act in concert, they have equal access to wisdom and should equally share in the design of their chosen joint ventures. Individuals should be careful not to define joint ventures in a manner that infringes on their valued inner boundaries. The maintenance of that equality in all interactions leads to the next insight: Social progress comes from learning how to balance between the two, providing for both individuality and cooperation.

In the final analysis, conscious self-awareness of unrealized potential for our universe motivates humans to step on the cosmic stage for a significantly bigger role. In one of life's great paradoxes, the only way to calm our trepidations about shouldering such new responsibilities is to give up our long-held security crutches. Acceptance of our Solarian legacy (the emerging human story) provides the basic framework we need to assume the galactic mantle of citizenship.

Filling out the new remaining holes in the human story requires an animated, community effort. I have attempted to suggest general directions for different disciplines and institutions, but a planetary renaissance depends on widespread individual enthusiasm. I offer the following meditation on what assuming the Solarian mantle means to me, for whatever resonance it may find in you.

No longer wrapped in the anthropomorphic arms of a father-figure, protective god of my childhood, no longer inhabiting a predictable universe in which my brothers and I had dominion, I now feel more at home and secure in my roles as both actor and director. Gone is the fear of a vengeful wrath if I fail to maintain obeisance to an unseen judge. Gone is the sense of puppet-like, supernatural strings that I can depend on to hold me up or jerk me offstage if I make a mistake. Released from admonitions that I accept on blind faith the answers of a few who claim divine connections, my curiosity quickens as I realize partial answers to any question lead to a more profound, more illuminating plateau of untold possibilities. With the end of my dependence on traditional religion and conventional science, I opt for a metascience of broad scope. Accepting all of my senses as valid, the rush of knowing gives me an awesome sense of power flowing through me from throughout the universe.

My sense of being part of a seamless universe—where anything is connected to everything else and where each being is securely embedded in an eternal and vibrant pulsing of consciousness—feels even stronger now than in the cosmology of my childhood. While recognizing that my current thinking, with its unknown interweavings, has more uncertainty than the explanations of any religion or current intellectual school of thought, I nevertheless am more psychologically at ease than ever before.

I see a marvelous galactic field of luminous beings—flowering plants and gamboling animals and soaring humans and ABs—adorned by the stars and planets in a matrix of patterns and forces visible to the mind's eye and linking all elements to each other. I see all of us playing both onstage and in the wings, adding our own variations of form, movement, sound, and color. We change roles at will, moving from that of actor to that of director, from coach to player.

With my inner eye open, I can no longer avoid "seeing" the luminal and subluminal vibrations of all the organic and inorganic entities around me. The boulder beside the path is as vibrant as the tree; its patterns, more stable in a field of flitting forms, helps to ground me to our material planet, and at the same time releases my vision, inner and outer, to soar to the stars. I feel myself suspended among all facets of the cosmic diamond, like the astronaut in microgravity. The winds of subtle forces cause the bodies to waft back and forth throughout the rhythmic patterns of night and day, life and death.

I stand under the starlit sky and glory in the existence of innumerable conscious beings clustered throughout the universe. I am drawn to merge my partial story of creation and visions of the Grand Couple with my cosmic siblings' perceptions of our origins and our cosmic legacy. I no longer wish to hide in my human uniqueness, but yearn to reach out to the entire family of consciousness, across the galaxies and through the dimensions, to pool our human wisdom in a partnership of beings that vaults everyone to the next expansive plain of cosmic development.

I imagine swimming together in the ever flowing lake of the cosmic void filled with potentialities beyond imagination, aware that the manner in which we play the games of the day will determine a significant aspect of tomorrow's cosmic reality. Knowing that the pace of universal development overshadows the span of human lifetimes, I nevertheless sense each being's incarnation as an essential link in the unbroken spiral of progress. I know the reverberations of our efforts, creative and destructive, will live on in all realms until future generations transform them.

Why would admitting to the many gaps in our current knowledge, giving up the safe conventional theories, result in such a sense of release and ease? I believe dropping the childish pretense of scientific and religious dogma transmutes our suppressed energy of insecurity, caused by the unspoken fear that our certainties may be false after all. Admitting to our ignorance, ironically, gives us a full measure of self-confidence in the value of our own Solarian legacy, and in our collective ability to realize more fully its potential in the twenty-first century.

Notes

1. Labeled ALH 84001, it landed on Earth 11,000 years ago.

2. The work of the Program for Extraordinary Experience Research (PEER), established by Harvard psychiatrist John Mack at the Center for Psychology and Social Change, with humans who experience AB communications or abductions has helped to legitimize such efforts. See their Web site at www.peer-mack.org.

3. This is why we in academic and professional disciplines have not added to human wisdom as rapidly as needed. Attempting self-learning with mental blinders limits our recognition of incongruencies not directly in our path. The previously mentioned Intuition Network—see www.intution.org—helps to create a world in which all people are encouraged to cultivate and apply their inner senses.

4. Judith Orloff, *Guide to Intuitive Healing* (New York: Times Books, 2000)

Suggested Reading in Addition to Works Already Referenced

1. William Collinge, *Subtle Energy* (New York: Warner Books, 1998).

2. Paul Davies, *The Mind of God* (New York: Simon & Schuster, 1992).

3. John Eccles (ed.), *Mind and Brain: The Many-Faceted Problem* (New York: Paragon House, 1985).

4. Timothy Ferris, *The Mind's Sky: Human Intelligence in a Cosmic Context* (New York: Bantam Books, 1992).

5. Randall Fitzgerald, *Cosmic Test Tube* (Los Angeles: Moon Lake Media, 1998).

6. Michael Grosso, *Frontiers of the Soul* (Wheaton, IL: Quest Books, 1992).

7. Don Trent Jacobs, *Primal Awareness* (Rochester, VT: Inner Traditions, 1998).

8. Jaegwon Kim, *Mind in a Physical World* (Cambridge, MA: MIT Press, 2000).

9. Yasuhiko G. Kimura, *Think Kosmically, Act Globally* (Waynesboro, VA: University of Science and Philosophy Press, 2000).

10. David Loye, *An Arrow Through Chaos* (Rochester, VT: Park Street Press, 2000).

11. Marc S. Micozzi, (ed.), *Fundamentals of Complementary and*

Alternative Medicine (Philadelphia: Churchill Livingston, 1996).

12. Jayant Narlikar, *The Lighter Side of Gravity* (New York: Cambridge University Press, 1996).

13. Robert Ornstein and Paul Ehrlich, *New World/New Mind: Moving Toward Conscious Evolution* (New York: Doubeday, 1989).

14. Maurie D. Pressman, *Enter the Supermind* (Philadelphia: CeShore, 1999).

15. Dean Radin, *The Conscious Universe* (New York: HarperEdge, 1997).

16. Michael J. Reiss and Roger Straughan, *Improving Nature? The Science and Ethics of Genetic Engineering* (New York: Cambridge University Press, 1996).

17. Chao Kok Sui, *Advanced Pranic Healing* (York Beach, ME: Samuel Weiser, 1995).

18. John White, *The Meeting of Science and Spirit* (New York: Paragon House, 1990).

19. Ivar Zapp and George Erikson, *Atlantis in America* (Kempton, IL: Adventures Unlimited Press, 1998).

20. Robert Zubrin, *The Case for Mars: The Plan to Settle the Red Planet and Why We Must* (New York: Free Press, 1996).

Index

Paul Von Ward is a cosmologist who combines the disciplines of philosophy, the physical and natural sciences, psychology, and prehistory. He is the author of *Dismantling the Pyramid: Government by the People* (Delphi Press, 1981). He has graduate degrees in public administration and psychology from Harvard and Florida State University. Von Ward is a multilingual researcher who lectures in the U.S. and abroad. He lives near Chattanooga, Tennessee.

Hampton Roads Publishing Company

. . . for the evolving human spirit

Hampton Roads Publishing Company
publishes books on a variety of subjects,
including metaphysics, health, integrative medicine,
visionary fiction, and other related topics.

For a copy of our latest catalog, call toll-free
(800) 766-8009, or send your name and address to:

Hampton Roads Publishing Company, Inc.
1125 Stoney Ridge Road
Charlottesville, VA 22902

e-mail: hrpc@hrpub.com
www.hrpub.com